# Contents

doctrine – The form and procedure for a reference – The distinction between interpretation and application – The situation pending the reference – The legal effects of preliminary rulings – Reforming the preliminary reference procedure

## TEXTBOOK

# Law of The European Union

**FOURTH EDITION**

**JOANNE COLES**
LLB (Hons), LLM

**OLD BAILEY PRESS**

OLD BAILEY PRESS
at Holborn College, Woolwich Road,
Charlton, London SE7 8LN

First published 1997
Fourth edition 2003

ISBN 1 85836 501 5

*British Library Cataloguing-in-Publication.*
A CIP Catalogue record for this book is
available from the British Library.

*Acknowledgement*
The publishers and author would
like to thank the Incorporated
Council of Law Reporting for
England and Wales for kind
permission to reproduce extracts
from the Weekly Law Reports, and
Butterworths for their kind
permission to reproduce extracts
from the All England Law Reports.

Printed and bound in Great Britain

# Preface

Old Bailey Press textbooks are written specifically for students. Whatever their course they will find our books clear and concise, providing comprehensive and up-to-date coverage. Written by specialists in their fields, our textbooks are reviewed and updated on a regular basis. Companion 150 Leading Cases, Revision WorkBooks and Cracknell's Statutes are also published.

This *Law of the European Union* textbook is designed for use by undergraduates who have European law/European Community law within their syllabus. It will be equally useful for all CPE/LLDip students who must study European Union/European Community law as one of their 'core' subjects.

This third edition has required considerable updating in light of recent developments. For ease of reference, it has been divided into four parts. The first provides a detailed analysis of what may be termed the constitutional and administrative law of the European Community, and is followed by sections on the free movement of persons, the free movement of goods and competition law.

The Treaty of Amsterdam provided for the 'tidying-up' of what had become a complicated system through the range of Treaty amendments. This resulted in a number of provisions being deleted and the renumbering of the articles of both the EC Treaty and the TEU. Thus, this book will refer to the new Treaty article numbers, indicating the old in brackets only where relevant. For example, art 48 of the EC Treaty, providing for the free movement of workers, is now art 39 EC.

Equally, significant developments have taken place in other areas of EU/EC law, including monetary union (with the creation of the single currency), competition law and the internal market. Important developments have been reported where appropriate. Important cases before the ECJ and CFI have also been included.

This textbook takes into account the developments in the European Union as at 1 April 2003.

# Table of Cases

# Table of Treaties, Conventions, Statutes and Other Materials

# PART A

# From the European Economic Community to the European Union: The Development, Institutions, Sources, Enforcement and Fundamental Principles of Community Law

The study of European Community law may be a daunting prospect, since it is a large and complex legal system. Before proceeding, it must be clearly understood that EC law is not based on a common law system, such as that in the United Kingdom. Consequently, for any law student it is imperative that they examine the constitutional structure of the EC before proceeding to study any substantive provisions.

To this end, this Part will examine the birth and development of European integration, and the promotion of 'ever closer union' that has been at the heart of much of the political and federal debate. The institutions of the Community will be examined, with analysis of their respective roles and powers. In order to understand and appreciate the later substantive law of the Community, we will then proceed to examine the various sources of EC law, since they are considerably different from those of English law.

Further chapters will assess the means of enforcing Community law, in terms of controlling the actions of the Community institutions and the Member States, providing a Community remedy for breaches of Community law and the preliminary reference procedure. There will also be analysis of the fundamental principles of Community law in the shape of supremacy and direct effect and the controversial issue of State liability.

# 1

# The Birth, Development and Legal Status of the European Union

1.1 Creating the Communities

1.2 The 1960s to 1980s – a new approach

1.3 The Single European Act 1986 (SEA)

1.4 The Treaty on European Union 1992 (TEU)

1.5 Post 1992 – further developments

1.6 The Treaty of Amsterdam 1997 (ToA)

1.7 Continued expanding membership

1.8 The Treaty of Nice (ToN)

1.9 The legal nature of the European Union

## 1.1 Creating the Communities

The traditional origin of European integration is often cited as being the devastation created by the aftermath of the Second World War. The idea, though, of an integrated Europe, free from intense political fragmentation, is one that is indeed much older. However, the popular support needed for the success of such a concept did not fully emerge until the War ended, when federalists such as Spinelli and politicians such as Churchill canvassed the idea. The impetus behind the start of European co-operation, however, came from the United States of America.

In 1947 the Americans devised the Marshall Plan. This envisaged the creation of an organisation to administer the financial aid required by Europe to rebuild its damaged infrastructure. In 1960 this body became the Organisation for Economic Co-operation and Development (OECD).

The Marshall Plan was followed by proposals from Robert Schuman to bring together the production of coal and steel in France and Germany. The plan itself was devised by Jean Monnet, a strong supporter of European co-operation. Coal and steel production was not selected at random. The tension between France and

3

Germany had often been centred on the regions between the two countries that were rich in these essential products, and the plan was to promote co-operation in order to prevent further hostilities and to re-establish stable relations. The Schuman Plan led to the creation of the European Coal and Steel Community (ECSC) in 1951, a supranational body with independent institutions, set up under the Treaty of Paris. The Treaty was signed by six States, namely France, Germany, Italy, The Netherlands, Belgium and Luxembourg. The Preamble to the Treaty states that its aim was 'to substitute for age-old rivalries the merging of ... essential interests; to create ... the basis for a broader and deeper community among peoples long divided by bloody conflicts'. Article 97 ECSC stated that the Treaty was to run for a period of 50 years. Consequently, in 2002 the ECSC Treaty expired and its functions were taken over by the European Community.

Whilst the successful creation of the ECSC was followed by some setbacks, such as the collapse of a European Defence Community in 1953, the moves towards further economic integration and co-operation continued. In 1956 Paul-Henri Spaak published a report specifically focussed on economic integration, and the placing of the development of atomic energy under an independent authority. The Spaak Report led to the creation of two Treaties of Rome both signed on the same day in 1957. One treaty created the European Atomic Energy Community (Euratom), whilst the other created the more famous European Economic Community (EEC). The original six Member States of the ECSC signed both Treaties.

The EEC Treaty's main aim was to create an economic community – a single 'common' market. This was to be achieved through the integration of the Member States' economic and monetary policies; by abolishing barriers to trade; by promoting competition free from distortion; and by harmonising both fiscal and social policies. The structure created by the EEC Treaty had four main features:

1. the liberalisation of the factors of production inside the territory of the Community. Four key fundamental freedoms were introduced to facilitate this goal, namely the free movement of goods, labour, services and capital;
2. the progressive approximation of the key economic policies that underpin trade liberalisation by harmonising national legislation relating to certain economic activities and introducing common Community policies in sectors such as agriculture, transport and competition;
3. the erection of a Common Customs Tariff (CCT) to regulate and administer customs duties and related charges for goods imported into the Community from non-Member States; and
4. the formulation of a Common Commercial Policy (CCP) for the conduct of trading relationships between the Community and the rest of the international trading system.

The aims though were not solely economic. The Preamble to the EEC Treaty clearly stated that its Member States were '[d]etermined to lay the foundations of an ever closer union among the peoples of Europe' by 'pooling their resources to preserve and strengthen peace and liberty'. This ideal or purpose has always remained at the heart of European integration and it is, as we shall see, one that the European Court of Justice (ECJ) has constantly referred to when interpreting European Community law.

The three Communities shared two institutions, the Assembly (later to be renamed the Parliament) and the ECJ. However, in 1965, the Merger Treaty established one set of institutions to preside over the Communities, by merging the three Councils and the ECSC High Authority with the EEC and Euratom Commissions.

## 1.2 The 1960s to 1980s – a new approach

From the very beginning of European co-operation there were differences in opinion and ideology as to how the process should proceed, and its eventual aim. The federalists believed in the creation of a supranational entity that would take over the functions of the individual states. However, the predominant theory underpinning the integration process during the 1950s was probably that described as functionalism. The rationale of this approach was to begin by selecting individual and discrete economic sectors that were non-political, and which lent themselves to control by an individual body, in order to improve their efficiency and production levels. Such an idea was behind the creation of the ECSC.

The next step taken though was to move away from clearly defined economic sectors towards broader objectives, as witnessed in the creation of the EEC. This was described as neofunctionalism. This is a process which begins in a similar manner to functionalism but which identifies integration as a process that begins with non-controversial subjects. The process would then move on to more politically controversial areas that require reduction in the power of national governments, whilst at the same time increasing the power of a central body. However, in the 1960s the neofunctionalist approach faced problems, and a new phase of integration emerged.

The problems stemmed from conflict between French ideas of co-operation, based on President de Gaulle's ideas, and the Commission's vision. The latter adopted a very activist approach based largely on the granting of greater autonomous power for the Community's institutions. The French opposed this 'federalist' approach, and desired one based more on governmental co-operation. This conflict came to a head when the time came for the Council to move from unanimous voting to qualified-majority voting, and the Commission proposed changes to agricultural policy.

When consensus could not be reached, the French pulled out of Council meetings for seven months – this became known as the 'empty-chair policy'. In 1966 a compromise was reached with the creation of the Luxembourg Accords. The Accords permitted a Member State to plead 'very important interests' in which case a unanimous vote was required. In other words, the Accords provided a power of veto for each Member State, and qualified-majority voting became exceptional. This enhanced the power of the governments, who could effectively block measures even if supported by the majority. This new approach became known as intergovernmentalism.

This shift of emphasis and power enhanced the role of the Council and greatly influenced the decision-making process for many years. The supranational institutions lost some of their influence, and the predominant interests driving the process of co-operation became those of the Member States' governments who had their own interests to protect and promote. The influence of this new approach was perhaps best witnessed in the creation of a new institution, the European Council, in 1974. This institution (which was not recognised formally until 1986) is comprised of the heads of government of each Member State. These 'summits' were to provide direction, but they were influenced by governmental rather than supranational interests.

The years between the Luxembourg Accords and mid-1980s have often been described as those of political stagnation or decisional malaise. The process was not helped by a world-wide recession and oil crisis. The 1970s and 1980s witnessed particular problems in relation to the finances of the Community, which were compounded by the massive budget required for the Common Agricultural Policy (CAP).

However there were some positive steps towards progress, particularly in relation to institutional development and monetary union. There were developments in the control of the budgetary process, with the Parliament given an increased role in that it was permitted the final power of adoption of the budget, and the creation in 1975 of a Court of Auditors to oversee expenditure and to make an annual financial report. (The Court became a formally recognised institution in 1992.) In 1979 positive steps were made in relation to economic and monetary union, ideas first agreed upon in 1969, with the creation of the European Monetary System, the Exchange Rate Mechanism (ERM) and a European Currency Unit (ECU). In 1979 direct elections to the Parliament were held, thus providing the institution with a democratic mandate.

Importantly, in 1973, the first stage of enlargement took place. The UK had remained outside of the EEC for a number of reasons: it had concentrated on its links with the Commonwealth and its so-called 'special relationship' with the USA; and it had not suffered the devastation of infrastructure that occupied Europe had. The UK also had considerable concerns in relation to the perceived transfer of sovereignty that membership required and instead chose to join the European Free Trade Area (EFTA) in 1959, along with Norway, Sweden, Austria, Denmark, Switzerland and Portugal. However, the obvious economic success of the EEC could not be ignored, and a change in government policy led to the UK's first attempt to join in 1961. The application was rejected when it was vetoed by de Gaulle, a process which happened again in 1967. De Gaulle's reasoning behind the French veto of membership was largely based on his belief that the UK should have remained more closely tied with the Commonwealth rather than with the EEC, but he also believed that the British did not have the heart to participate in European integration.

However, de Gaulle was to resign, and in 1973, along with Ireland and Denmark, the UK acceded by passing the European Communities Act 1972. This first enlargement encountered problems. Norway had also applied and been successful, but a national referendum resulted in rejection of membership. However, the process of enlargement was to continue, with Greece joining in 1981 and Spain and Portugal in 1986, bringing membership to 12 Member States. That year was also to witness the first major revision of the original treaties, with the adoption of the Single European Act.

## 1.3 The Single European Act 1986 (SEA)

In 1985 the Commission produced a White Paper, which clearly revealed that the Community was facing problems, particularly in relation to removing barriers to the achievement of the Common Market. The date of completion was to be 31 December 1992, but in order to remove those barriers a new initiative was required. This new initiative came in the form of a treaty, the Single European Act 1986 (SEA), which had at its core the aim of completing the single market, making it attractive to the majority of Member States. The SEA is often cited as the force behind the revitalisation of the Community, or as providing a new dynamism to the whole process. It should perhaps, however, be noted that the SEA came about at a time of economic boom, when Member States' governments had perhaps less pressing national problems. Notwithstanding the economic prosperity of the time, the SEA did do much to promote those ideals that had withered after the Luxembourg Accords.

The SEA made a number of institutional reforms. The European Council was formally recognised, and a new Court of First Instance (CFI) was created to help the ECJ with an ever-expanding workload. There were also legislative reforms with the creation of a new process known as the 'co-operation procedure'. This procedure enhanced the power of the now directly elected Parliament, a reform required to reflect its status as the one democratically elected institution. The Parliament was also awarded the power of veto in relation to the accession of any new Member States. There were procedural changes, such as the introduction of qualified-majority voting in the Council on certain issues, designed to accelerate the decision-making process after the problems created by the Luxembourg Accords. In addition to these institutional and procedural reforms, the SEA revealed a shift towards less economic objectives, with the formal extension of Community competency to new areas such as social policy, research and technological development, and environmental policy.

Whilst the SEA certainly provided a new impetus to the Community, it was not without its critics. Perhaps the most vocal of these was Pescatore (a former ECJ judge), who claimed that all the SEA did was to re-start to whole process of integration again, and that it was badly drafted. The power of veto had also not been formally removed and Member States continued to threaten its use. However, in practice the SEA proved influential since it brought the Commission back into the heart of the integration process. It provided for the Council to vote by qualified majority, which to some extent removed the dominance of intergovernmentalism. It provided an increased role for the Parliament and it also began the process of extending the Community beyond purely economic objectives.

## 1.4  The Treaty on European Union 1992 (TEU)

The progress towards closer European union continued, and in 1989 two intergovernmental conferences (IGCs) were held. The first was based on the Commission President's (Jacques Delors) three-stage plan for attainment of European Monetary Union (EMU). The second was to deal with political union. The conferences took a year to complete and culminated in the signing of the Treaty on European Union at Maastricht on 7 February 1992. However, the Treaty was to take a year to come into force, since there were political and constitutional difficulties for the ratification process in the UK, Denmark and Germany. Much of the negative publicity appeared to hinge on the use of the controversial term 'union', with its 'federalist' connotations.

Article 1 of the TEU named the geographical area covered by the European Community Treaties and the TEU as the European Union (EU). One part of the TEU (art 8) introduced a substantial number of amendments to the original EEC Treaty. The Treaty was also renamed the European Communities Treaty (hence when reference is made to the law it should be to EC rather than EU law since the law does stem from the EC Treaty). The TEU was to also create what was to become known as the three pillars of the EU. The first pillar, called the European Communities, is comprised of the three original Communities (EC, ECSC and Euratom). Another part of the TEU (arts 1–6 and 9–53) provided for co-operation in the area of foreign and security policy with the aim of development in the field of defence. It also provided for co-operation and joint policies in justice and home affairs. These two areas became the second and third pillars.

### Title I of the TEU

This Title set out the common principles of the newly established European Union, such as taking decisions that were consistent and demonstrated solidarity, and to respect national identities and human rights. One objective was stable and balanced economic and social progress with emphasis on the creation of EMU and a single currency, but with respect for the principle of subsidiarity. The Union was also to implement a common foreign and security policy, and to develop co-operation in relation to justice and home affairs, although these matters were to be, for the time being, outside of the jurisdiction of the ECJ. The concept of European citizenship was also created under the TEU. Citizenship entails the right to free movement as well as the right to vote and stand for national and European parliamentary elections. However, it remains a rather vague concept, one which may be expanded in the future, perhaps towards some common European identity in place of a national one: see the introduction to Part B (below).

## Titles II–IV of th TEU

A number of institutional changes were made, including the creation of a Parliamentary Ombudsman and a Committee of the Regions, and the formal recognition of the Court of Auditors. The principal institutional reform was to create the co-decision procedure thereby granting the Parliament a strengthened legislative role. Parliament also gained the right to request the Commission to initiate legislation and to approve the appointment of the Commission.

The objectives of the Community were amended to include EMU, environmental objectives, social protection, economic and social cohesion, and sustainable development, along with a commitment to raise the standard of living and quality of life experienced by EU citizens. The Community's activities were to include research and technical development, trans-European networks, health, education, cultural protection, consumer protection, energy, civil protection and tourism. However, the most politically controversial competency was the inclusion of a detailed and specific plan for full economic and monetary union by 1999.

Stage One (the completion of the internal market and the removal of controls on the movement of capital) had already been completed. Stage Two was to begin on 1 January 1994 with the creation of convergence criteria designed to ensure that the economies of the Member States were ready for joining the single currency. Stage Three was to be the locking of the Member States' exchange rates and introduction of the 'euro' on the 1 January 1999. Detailed provisions also provided for the powers and operation of the necessary institutions, namely the European System of Central Banks (ESCB), the European Central Bank (ECB) and the Council of Economic and Finance Investment (ECOFIN).

## Pillars 2 and 3 of the European Union

These two pillars were to be outside of the Communities' institutional and legislative competence. However, whilst they may have been based on intergovernmental co-operation, they still involved the limited participation of the Communities' institutions. Decision-making was to be primarily by the Council, with decisions generally requiring unanimity (apart from procedural matters); this necessity was to contribute to the slow progress initially made in these areas.

Common foreign and security policy (CFSP) did permit the Council to conclude that an area was that of 'joint action', but only after the European Council had identified the principles and guidelines. The Council could then identify subjects that were to be decided by qualified majority voting. The Parliament was to be fully informed with the ability to make recommendations to the Council and to hold an annual debate, and the Commission to be 'fully associated' with any works undertaken.

The justice and home affairs (JHA) pillar dealt with matters such as immigration and asylum (very sensitive issues for a number of Member States), and co-operation in the areas of international crime and policing. The Council again played the central role, but under this pillar there was no requirement for the European Council to first identify the general principles and guidelines before the Council could adopt a joint position. The Commission and Parliament also had a limited role, again under the same conditions as the CFSC pillar: to be informed and to be able to bring matters to the attention of the Council, and to hold an annual conference.

## 1.5 Post 1992 – further developments

After the TEU further enlargement took place. In May 1992 an agreement was reached between certain members of EFTA and the EC to provide for a new European Economic Area. The agreement, which came into force in 1994, provides for the free movement of goods, persons, capital and services in a similar way to those provisions existing under the EC Treaty. Between 1989 and 1991 Austria and Sweden applied for full membership of the EU. These applications were closely followed by applications from Finland and Norway in 1992. Whilst Acts of Accession were signed by all the applicants, Norway eventually failed to accede with the others in 1995, after a national referendum again produced a 'no' majority.

The overall success of the European Union, particularly in terms of its economic success, spawned a flood of applications from a variety of central and east European states anxious to join. Turkey applied as early as 1989, although there are continuing problems with its application due to its poor human rights record and the opposition to its membership from Greece. In 1990 Cyprus and Malta applied. This large number of applications from new states was to create numerous potential problems for the EU – many of these states had their own economic problems and the EU itself was entering a period of difficult monetary integration.

The potential expansion of membership of the EU beyond the current 15 Member States raises considerable concerns. The conflict rests in the problems of trying to 'deepen' the existing EU legal and political structure (seen in EMU, JHA and CFSP), whilst simultaneously expanding in territorial terms to include states which would have to join an already well established legal system incurring numerous obligations. Indeed, integration would perhaps have to slow down, or temporarily halt, for the new states to have sufficient time to bring their legal systems in line. The economic problems that some of these states face may also have implications on the stability and future success of the EU. This 'deepening versus widening' problem was at the heart of much of the debate surrounding the EU after the TEU.

At the same time however, the EU was already encountering problems within its existing membership, in that some states were unwilling (or unable) to proceed at the same pace as others. This is best seen in the various protocols signed and annexed to the TEU. The Social Protocol, with an Agreement on Social Policy, was originally not signed by the UK. Other protocols included the Irish 'abortion' protocol, and one relating to the purchase of second homes was included for Denmark. Such protocols provide 'opt-outs' for the relevant Member States. Perhaps the most controversial protocol is that in relation to EMU, which permits the UK and Denmark to opt-out of the single currency. The debate on this issue has been described in a number of ways, including the development of a 'multi-speed' Europe, or as a Europe of 'variable geometry'. The problems of 'widening' and 'deepening', along with issues in relation to institutional effectiveness, were to be at the centre of the IGC held in 1996 and which preceded the next treaty development.

## 1.6 The Treaty of Amsterdam 1997 (ToA)

Between 1996 and 1997 the IGC reviewed the policies and institutional structure of the EU in light of proposed increased membership, and with particular emphasis on the issues of democracy, efficiency and transparency. The resulting treaty was agreed at Amsterdam and signed in October 1997, although it did not come into force until 1 May 1999. The problems facing the EU were perhaps reflected in the rather unambitious content of the ToA, especially when compared to the TEU. The difficulties encountered in the ratification of the TEU perhaps influenced the content and scope of the ToA, which did little to deal with one of the most pressing problems – enlargement. However, the ToA does indicate a clear shift in emphasis away from the original economic aims to ones of a more social and/or political nature.

The ToA's recognition of these 'ideals' is perhaps a reflection of the direction long-taken by the ECJ. The EC Treaty prohibited discrimination based on nationality, but the ToA strengthens this by providing the Council with the power to 'take appropriate action to combat discrimination based on sex, racial or ethnic origin, religion or belief, disability, age or sexual orientation': art 13 EC (see Chapter 12). The fundamental principles of liberty, democracy, respect for human rights and fundamental freedoms, and the rule of law (provided under art 6 TEU), are also given greater protection under the ToA. Henceforth, any Member State that commits a 'persistent and serious breach' of these principles, may be suspended from voting in the Council (art 7 TEU) and have further Treaty rights suspended: art 309 EC. Article 46 TEU was also amended so that the ECJ has the jurisdiction to ensure that the Union respects the rights protected under the European Convention on Human Rights (ECHR).

As has been mentioned in the Preface, the ToA renumbered almost all the articles of the EC Treaty and adopted numbered articles for the TEU. This re-numbering is followed in the text.

## Changes to the EC pillar

### Expansion of scope

A substantial part of Pillar 3 (JHA) was moved by the ToA to the EC Pillar. This was achieved under the creation of a new Title IV in Part Three of the EC Treaty. This new Title deals with the free movement of persons and includes visas, asylum and immigration. A protocol to the ToA also incorporates the 1985 Schengen Agreement and Convention (the Schengen acquis) into the EC Treaty. The Schengen Agreement deals with the abolition of frontier checks and had been signed by 13 Member States – the UK and Ireland were originally not bound by the provisions and Denmark is considered as a 'special' case. However, the Member States are now permitted to undertake closer co-operation (see below) in this area. (For discussion of the Schengen acquis see the introduction to Part B.)

The ToA also introduces totally new provisions and objectives into the EC Treaty. The promotion of sexual equality and protection and improvement of the environment are now explicitly mentioned as tasks within their own rights, rather than as ancillary to economic objectives. Indeed, economic development itself must now also be 'sustainable'.

The Protocol on Social Policy (annexed to the EC Treaty by the TEU), which provided an opt-out for the UK, was no longer required when the newly elected Labour government supported the provisions of the Social Policy Agreement. Therefore, the Protocol was repealed and a new Agreement incorporated into the EC Treaty to replace the old provisions dealing with social policy.

A new Title dealing with the sensitive issue of unemployment was also introduced – an issue that had been central to much of the IGC discussions. The measures that may be used in this field are only those described as 'soft law' and the emphasis will remain with the policies and practices of the individual Member States which these new provisions must 'respect'. However, these new measures include a more 'centralised' response to the unemployment issue, and include the establishment of an advisory body, the Employment Committee, and power for the Council to issue guidelines, recommendations and incentive measures.

### Institutional changes and decision-making

The decision-making process was streamlined by the ToA, with the co-decision process now modified and extended to a wide range of subject matters. The extension of the use of this process means that co-operation is now only relevant in the context of EMU decision-making. This change reflects a continuing process in the life of the Parliament, which has been granted an increasingly important role, also witnessed in new rights to be consulted on matters such as citizenship, discrimination and 'closer co-operation' (see below).

In terms of institutional changes, the Parliament was set at a maximum number of 700 (in response to some of the concerns expressed about the impact of new membership on the size of the EU institutions). The Parliament may also consult with the Committee of the Regions and the Economic and Social Committee. The Commission's procedure for appointment was altered and the Court of Auditors now has locus standi (similar to that granted to the Parliament: see Chapter 2) before the Court.

The ToA also touched on issues in relation to the perceived lack of democracy in the EU and provided for: a right of access to documents in art 255 EC (formerly art 191a) in order to improve transparency; a right to information in relation to consumer protection; and a new provision in art 285 EC dealing with the sensitive issue of data protection.

### Closer co-operation

The introduction of this concept was perhaps one of the most important aspects of the ToA, although in reality it is merely the formal recognition of a practice that had been occurring for some time. Closer co-operation has also been described as 'flexibility' and provides for the formal occurrence of 'multi-speed' progress, as referred to above. Hence, Member States may now decide under a new art 11 EC, and art 40 EC in relation to JHA, to co-operate in certain matters within the general scope of the Treaties, but which are not yet subject to legislation. They must do so, however, in a way that does not conflict with EC law. The new Treaty article provides for certain controls on the use of closer co-operation; it cannot proceed unless a majority of Member States participate, and cannot affect the rights and obligations of those not involved.

Steiner, the academic, suggests that this new provision may relieve the EU of some of the tension within its membership. The minority have traditionally been able to block the aims of the majority, but this principle enables those states with integrationist aims to move forward, whilst others may remain outside if they so wish. The result is, of course, a process that will promote political compromise, but it does place on a more formal and legitimate footing a general practice that has been used on a number of previous occasions. There are now also controls about how it can be used, which will in turn be subject to review by the ECJ. However, Steiner also suggests that closer co-operation may have a number of disadvantages, such as problems in defining what exactly states may co-operate over. The principal problem though probably relates to the need for the closer co-operation not to affect the rights and obligations of other Member States. Steiner comments that this may be impossible in reality, particularly in terms of the internal market, and that Member States should, therefore, be permitted to participate in any discussions so that their concerns, problems and wishes are represented, even though they themselves will not be bound by any final decision. To do otherwise, it is suggested, may result in enormous tension between those Member States continuously proceeding with integrationist plans, and those States taking what perhaps may best be described as a 'cautious approach'. The potential for conflict to result from this approach is great, and it remains to be seen how or if it will affect the solidarity so necessary for a successful European Union.

## Changes to Pillar 2 – common foreign and security policy (CFSP)

The changes made by the ToA to this pillar were minimal in terms of institutional changes – the Parliament and ECJ's roles were not altered. However, the pillar had attracted criticisms post-TEU, and these were to some extent dealt with by the ToA. First, in order to give a more international identity to the CFSP, the Council Presidency, which represents the EU, has been supplemented with the Secretary-General of the Council to act as a 'High Representative'. They will assist in the formulation of policy and may enter into 'political dialogue' on behalf of the Council with third parties, if requested to do so by the Presidency. The Council may also appoint a special representative should they so wish, to deal with particular policy issues.

The Council may also conclude international agreements that are necessary to implement CFSP. Hence, instead of the Member States representing themselves at this level, they will be represented by the Council of Ministers. A Declaration was also adopted to allay the fears of some Member States, which concludes that this new power in the hands of the Council does not imply any 'transfer of competence', although in practice the Council will now represent those Member States.

The various instruments that may be adopted to implement CFSP were more clearly defined under the ToA. Joint actions are those that deal with specific situations, where action by the EU is required, whereas common positions are those that define the approach of the EU to a particular geographical or subject matter.

The decision-making process under this pillar was also amended and reflects the interests of both the EU and the individual Member States. Council decisions require unanimity, but a Member State may abstain and make a declaration so that it is not compelled to abide by the decision (although it will not be able to obstruct the achievement of the decision either). The decision will not be adopted if the total of abstentions equates to over one-third. However, Council decisions require only a qualified majority if they are to be on joint actions, common positions, or other issues where there is a common agreed policy. A qualified majority requires 62 votes cast by at least ten Member States. Again, though, there is recognition of governmental interests with the inclusion of an in-built veto, somewhat similar to the Luxembourg Accords referred to earlier in this chapter.

A Member State may declare that it will oppose a qualified majority decision in the interests of national policy. The Council is then required to hold a vote on whether to refer the matter to the European Council. Should this occur, the European Council is required to make the decision by unanimity. The authors Craig and de Burca suggest that this complex voting procedure is a compromise between conflicting interests within the European Union:

> 'The interests of the Union in being able to take effective action even if one State is opposed are protected by the "unanimity with declared abstention" provision, and the important national interests of individual Member States are protected by the "qualified majority with veto" provision.'

The ToA also provided for the reconsideration of the Common Defence Policy (CDP) as envisaged under the TEU. However, the CDP had become highly controversial and the language adopted by the ToA was far less assertive than that in the TEU. The CDP was only progressively framed, rather than eventually framed, and the decision on common defence is in the hands of the European Council. CFSP also includes combat forces in crisis management, peacekeeping, peacemaking, and humanitarian and rescue tasks. A protocol annexed to the ToA provided for increased co-operation between the EU and the Western European Union.

## Changes to Pillar 3 – police and judicial co-operation in criminal matters (PJCC)

As already noted, some provisions relating to JHA were moved to the EC Treaty. This was in part a response to criticisms that the subject matters under JHA lent themselves to the need for greater institutional control, such as judicial review by the ECJ. They were also issues closely linked with the free movement of persons provided for under the EC Treaty.

The third pillar under the ToA provides for the creation of an area of freedom, security and justice. The aim was to develop common action in the fields of police co-operation, judicial co-operation in criminal matters and the prevention and combating of racism and xenophobia. Specifically targeted issues include drug-trafficking, terrorism, arms-trafficking, offences against children and fraud/corruption. There are a number of methods that are available to deal with these issues, including co-operation between police and customs forces, and co-operation between judiciaries and other relevant Member States' authorities, and by standardising some criminal laws throughout the Union. Such co-operation is facilitated through use of Europol.

There is express provision (art 40 EC) for Member States to participate in closer co-operation under the third pillar, although in this instance the Parliament need only be informed of requests.

## 1.7 Continued expanding membership

The ToA was intended to deal with the issues arising out of increased membership, but in fact did little to achieve this. In 1998 Cyprus, Hungary, Poland, Estonia, Slovenia and the Czech Republic opened treaty negotiations for full membership of the EU. This was closely followed in 1999 by the Helsinki Council Meeting, which agreed to begin negotiations with the remaining states wishing to join. The countries that have applied for full EU membership have all signed association agreements and are all preparing themselves for membership. The EU itself, even after the 1996 IGC and the ToA, was not as well prepared – the potential problems were great and included the need for changes to an institutional structure that was created to manage only six Member States rather than the potential 27 or more. It was debatable whether the existing membership would be prepared to foot the bill in order to promote the European Union, or whether their own national interests would dominate the process.

The ToA only dealt with increased membership in any substantive manner by its inclusion of a protocol on enlargement that provided for a comprehensive review of the institutional infrastructure at least one year before membership exceeded 20 Member States.

The Commission however, spent some considerable time and effort examining the issue of enlargement. In 1997 it produced 'Agenda 2000' which considered and offered opinions on all the applications that had been received. The European Council studied the Agenda and entered into negotiations as to the proposed accession of new states. Agenda 2000 proposed that new states joined in two 'waves'. The first wave would probably include Poland, Hungary, the Czech Republic, Slovenia, Estonia and Cyprus, whereas the second would perhaps include Latvia, Lithuania, Bulgaria, Romania, Slovakia and Malta: see section 1.8. Any new Member States have to show that they have complied with art 6 TEU in that they respect the principles of 'liberty, democracy, respect for human rights and fundamental freedoms, and the rule of law'. They must also prove that they have the necessary political and economic structures.

Wider membership could, of course, make it more difficult for consensus to be reached, particularly given the fact that the above examples reveal problems in attaining the consensus of even the current membership. The UK believes that widening couldl slow down the integration process, to allow the new members the chance to bring their legal systems in line, and therefore generally supports enlargement. However, others recognised the problems that new Member States could bring to the process of integration, and argued that the institutions of the EU should have greater powers in order to avoid what could become a complicated and ineffective decision-making process. Such powers would include the greater use of qualified majority voting and increased powers for the Parliament. Such issues dominated the debate as the EU entered into the new millennium, and were at the heart of the most recent round of Treaty negotiations.

## 1.8 The Treaty of Nice (ToN)

Article 4 TEU charged the European Council with the obligation of providing the 'necessary impetus' for further development of the European Union. It was also obligated to define the 'general political guidelines' and to determine 'by common accord the amendments to be made': art 48 TEU. The IGC was formally convened in February 2000 to negotiate under an agenda provided by the December 1999 Helsinki European Council. The culmination of this was the convening of the European Council at the Nice Summit during December 2000. The primary objective was to reach consensus on the next Treaty amendments and developments needed in order to ensure that the Community could enter into a period of enlargement. This enlargement will result in the European Union expanding from the current 15 Member States to approximately 27. There are six States in advanced negotiations for accession, namely the Czech Republic, Poland, Hungary, Slovenia, Estonia and Cyprus. The Treaty of Nice was signed on 26 February 2001, although there were some difficulties in securing its ratification – in June 2001 the Irish referendum returned a 'no' vote, although this was reversed in a second referendum held in October 2002. The majority of the changes resulting from the Treaty of Nice are designed to secure institutional change and are contained in a Protocol on Enlargement. The initial problems identified prior to Nice and the changes proposed will be discussed in further detail in Chapter 2.

In brief, the main institutional reforms will be as follows:

1. The alteration of the voting weights in the Council of Ministers for qualified majority voting (to be put into operation in 2005) and the change of the formula required for minimum qualified majority voting success.
2. The increased use of qualified majority voting.
3. The allocation of seats in the Parliament for the new Member States.
4. Reform of the judicial system under a new art 220(2) EC which will attach chambers to the Court of First Instance (CFI). These chambers will have jurisdiction to decide on specified subject matters/issues. More importantly, the CFI will be able to hear preliminary references and will have its direct action jurisdiction enhanced. Further, the Treaty provides for the creation of new 'judicial panels'. These may be established and will exist under the current authority of the CFI, therefore providing for a three-tier legal system with the European Court of Justice (ECJ), in a more appellate role, at the apex.
5. The Nice Summit also voiced approval of the Charter of Fundamental Rights. This is discussed in detail in Chapter 3.

All of the above reforms are discussed in more detail in Chapter 2, which considers the Community institutions.

Changes to each of the Treaties can be briefly summarised as follows:

1. Amendment of the TEU common provisions in the context of suspending the

rights of a Member State in serious and persistent breach of democracy, human rights and/or the rule of law (art 7 TEU). This amendment was introduced after Austria found itself the victim of ad hoc political sanctions when a right-wing party was elected to government in 2000. Consequently, the ToN introduces detailed procedures, within the jurisdiction of the ECJ to review, before such suspension may occur; includes a right for the Member State to be heard; and permits the use of the procedure where there is a risk of serious and persistent breach.

2.  The CFSP pillar has been amended with the introduction of a provision permitting the use of enhanced co-operation (formerly closer co-operation – see below), but it should be noted that this does not extend to the controversial areas of military and defence matters. It also does extend to the implementation of joint actions or common positions, and in reflection of the sensitive and controversial nature of CFSP, the institutions retaining power and influence in this field remain the Member States and the Council, although there is some involvement of the Commission and Parliament in advisory capacities. An effective power of veto is included, whereby a State may request that the matter be referred to the European Council for a unanimous decision.

3.  The PJCC pillar has seen only minor amendments. If enhanced co-operation is to occur under this pillar, the Commission must now be informed first of a Member State's request, with the proviso that if the Commission refuses to deal with the request, the Member State may bring it before the Council. The Parliament, as in the CFSP pillar, has been granted a consultative role. There is no veto-style power; instead Member States may simply request that the matter be referred to the European Council.

4.  Those provisions in the ToA on 'closer co-operation' have been amended. Article 43 EC (Title VII) now reads 'enhanced co-operation'. This may only take place as a last resort, encourage as many States to participate as possible, and be open to all Member States to participate in at any point. A minimum number of eight States is now required to establish enhanced co-operation and the co-operation must now only 'respect' the Community acquis and the rights of non-participating States, although it does have to ensure that it does not affect the internal market or social and economic cohesion.

5.  The Community pillar changes are primarily focused on the institutional reforms (see above and Chapter 2). Additional amendments include the granting of full locus standi to the Parliament to bring actions under art 230 EC and the ability to request an opinion on the compatibility of international agreements with the Treaty. Article 11 EC is amended and provides now for enhanced, rather than closer, co-operation, in line with those changes made to the other pillars. The Commission and the Parliament are granted a more positive role and the veto has been removed, with a Member State instead having the right to refer the matter to the European Council. The need for unanimity under art 18 EC to adopt measures designed to ensure free movement and residency has been removed,

although the UK did secure exclusions to this in respect of matters such as passports, identity cards, residence permits, and social security provisions.

Immediately after the signing of the Nice Treaty, two developments occurred that were perhaps more significant. The Laeken Declaration of December 2001 and the Declaration on the Future of the Union (see Europe 2004 – Le Grand Débat: Setting the Agenda and Outlining the Options, European Commission www.europa.eu.int/comm/governance/whats_new/europe2004_en.pdf.) call for the European Union at the 2004 IGC to discuss what the latter calls the 'deeper and wider' debate about the future of the Union, with reference not just to what the Member States would like but to public opinion that is representative of 'civil society' as a whole. The former makes reference to the need for a European constitutional document, and this has now become an important, albeit controversial, political objective. The next IGC will, therefore, probably focus on delimiting power between the EU and the Member States in a more 'formalised' manner.

Tillotson, the academic, suggests that this may herald 'a definite step towards the establishment of an EU constitution within some form of federal system of government'. The federal debate has taken place within the Union since its very beginning, and it is one outlined below at section 1.9.

## 1.9 The legal nature of the European Union

There has, and continues to be, much debate and discussion about the legal nature of the Community/Union. The EU is not a state, but it possesses characteristics that distinguish it from an ordinary intergovernmental association. These characteristics include a sophisticated institutional structure, which is evidence of far more than simply an international agreement between sovereign states. It is suggested that the EU is even more than a confederation, which would be between sovereign states with unlimited veto power. However, it is also clear that the EU is not a federal state.

Within a federal system the basic institutional framework requires at least two tiers of government, with a clearly defined separation of powers laid down by a constitution. When one examines the EU these factors are only present in certain fields. For example, in terms of economic regulation there are federal characteristics: the EU institutions decide on the separation of powers; the ECJ delivers judgments; and the Member States have no control over future developments in those areas of majority voting. However, this is only one example of a specific area of legal regulation. If one considers the institutional structure as a whole, it does not display the characteristics of a federal state. The next chapter will consider each of the institutions and their roles in detail, but we can state here that the institutions do not operate under a separation of powers doctrine necessary for the existence of a democratic, federal state. For example, the 'central' legislative forces are the

Commission and the Council, neither of whom are directly elected; the legislation produced rests in the hands of the national governments of the Member States; the Commission has an exclusive right to initiate legislation, rather than a directly elected 'legislature'; and both the ECJ and the Commission are delegated by the national executives of the Member States. Such factors lead us to the conclusion that the EU lacks the essential requirements for the existence of a federal state. The author Hartley has suggested that there may be an 'embryonic federation', an entity with federal potential, but only time will tell whether this is indeed a future possibility.

We cannot describe the EU as a federation, whilst we also cannot label it as merely an international agreement. The question then remains as to how we do describe the legal nature of the EU. It could perhaps be best described as a 'supranational organisation', meaning that it has transcended the form of a mere international organisation, but has not yet attained the level of integration among its participants to achieve the quality of statehood. Alternatively, Hartley has described it as a 'hybrid'. The ECJ considered the original Community to be 'unique', or sui generis: *Van Gend en Loos* v *Netherlands* Case 26/62 [1963] ECR 1. Indeed, there is some merit in using this description since there has been no other similar entity; it recognises the unusual nature of the EU, without trying to manipulate its characteristics into something we can easily recognise.

The 'unique' characteristics of the EU may be witnessed both in its relationship with its Member States and in its external relations. If we consider the former, we can see that the Community was established with the creation of permanent institutions that have been vested with legislative, executive and judicial powers. These powers were transferred from the Member States so that the institutions were able to exercise authority in those areas in which they had competence. Whilst the ECJ in *Van Gend en Loos* stated that those fields were 'limited', those competencies have expanded considerably, through treaty developments and the production of a considerable body of secondary legislation. The legal existence of the EU is based therefore on the transfer of sovereign power, which correspondingly limits the sovereign rights of each Member State. A unilateral measure incompatible with EC law will not be given effect. Further, the Member States are under a positive obligation (art 10 EC) to ensure that they take all appropriate action to ensure compliance with their obligations under EC law, and must abstain from any measure that would jeopardise the attainment of Community objectives.

In terms of the EU's relations with non-Member States, the EU acts as a 'legal person' because it has legal personality in international law. Customary international law has ascribed certain international organisations with such status: see *ILO Convention Case* Opinion 2/91 [1993] 3 CMLR 800. This status is also provided for under the treaties themselves, for example, art 281 EC states that 'the Community shall have legal personality'. Hence, the EU has the capacity to enter into international agreements (or treaties) with third states and international organisations, in its own right in those fields of its competence. There are basically three forms of treaty that may be entered into:

1. Community agreements: these are treaties entered into by the Community/EU in its own right. The Member States are not involved in the negotiation or conclusion of this type of agreement except through the medium of the Council of Ministers. Community agreements are used when the subject matter of the agreement falls exclusively within the competence of the Community. The subjects covered by such agreements include: (a) mutlilateral trade agreements (usually concluded through the forum of the World Trade Organisation); (b) bilateral trade agreements (such as the European Economic Area Agreement, or free trade agreements such as those concluded between the EC and Poland, Hungary and Czechoslovakia in 1992); (c) association agreements (for example, those entered into with Poland, Spain and Greece prior to their full membership); (d) co-operation agreements (dealing with such matters as the provision of aid); and (e) development and assistance agreements (which regulate the relationship with developing countries, such as the Lomé agreements.)

2. Mixed agreements: these are treaties involving both the Community and the Member States in the negotiation and conclusion of their terms. Such agreements are required when the subject-matter of an agreement concerns matters within the competencies of both the Community and the Member States. One example of such an agreement is the Final Act of the UN Convention on the Law of the Sea 1982 which relates to issues within the jurisdiction of the Community, such as fishing rights, as well as those of the Member States, such as territorial sea delimitation, nationality of ships etc. Another example of a mixed agreement is the Montreal Protocol on Substances that Deplete the Ozone Layer 1989.

3. International agreements entered into by the Member States: these are treaties that the individual Member States have entered into either before or after the Community came into being. They concern matters outside the jurisdiction of the Community. Even though all the Member States participate in such agreements, the obligations are assumed by the Member States as individual countries. The Community may, however, succeed to treaties concluded before 1957 if they contain matters within its competence. This occurred in relation to the General Agreement on Tariffs and Trade (GATT) when the ECJ stated in *International Fruit Company* v *Produktschap voor Groenten en Fruit* Cases 51 and 54/71 [1972] ECR 1219 that:

> 'In so far as under the EEC Treaty the Community has assumed the powers previously exercised by the Member States in the area governed by the GATT, the provisions of that agreement have the effect of binding the Community.'

It should not be surprising that, because EC law is a 'unique' species of law, it also has a special general nature and special qualities. This special character is derived from the fact that the Community legal system is supranational, uniform and unitary. According to the ECJ in *Van Gend en Loos* (above) the Community belongs neither to the realm of public international law nor of municipal law. EC law and the national laws of the Member States constitute two distinct legal orders that are separate yet, at the same time, related. The former is based on the constitutional treaties of the organisation while the others are based on national constitutions.

Following from the logic of this separation, Community institutions have no jurisdiction to interpret, apply, enforce, repeal or annul legislative or administrative acts: *Schumacher* v *Hauptzollamt Frankfurt am Main-Ost* Case C–215/87 [1991] 2 CMLR 465. The Community institutions can only require Member States, within the framework of Community proceedings, to adjust any national provisions that have been found contrary to Community law.

Conversely, while national organs have to interpret, apply and enforce Community law, they have, in principle, no jurisdiction to test the validity of Community provisions or their compatibility with national law, even constitutional law, and so cannot declare invalid or annul Community measures or suspend their application or enforcement. The validity of Community measures can only be judged by the ECJ in light of Community law: *Firma Foto-Frost* v *Hauptzollamt Lubeck-Ost* Case 314/85 [1987] ECR 4199. To do otherwise would of course undermine the legal and constitutional basis on which the Community operates.

The ECJ has made a number of important pronouncements on the nature of Community law. In one of its early landmark cases, *Costa* v *ENEL* Case 6/64 [1964] ECR 585, it observed that:

> '[B]y creating a Community of unlimited duration, having its own institutions, its own personality and its own capacity in law, apart from having international standing and, more particularly, real powers resulting from a limitation of competence or a transfer of powers from the States to the Community, the Member States, albeit within limited fields, have restricted their sovereign rights and created a body of law applicable to both their nationals and to themselves. The integration into the laws of each Member State of provisions which derive from the Community, and more generally the terms and the spirit of the Treaty, make it impossible for the states ... to accord precedence to a unilateral and subsequent measure over a legal system accepted by them on a basis of reciprocity.'

This judgement identifies two of the most fundamental principles of Community law: the principle of the supremacy of Community law over national law and the concept of the direct effect of Community law. The principle of supremacy means that Community law, whatever its form, prevails over prior and subsequent inconsistent provisions of national law. This doctrine has had numerous and controversial implications on the constitutional laws of the Member States: Germany and the United Kingdom particularly have had legal and political difficulties 'accepting' the supremacy of EC law. The concept of direct effect, on the other hand, allows for private individuals to rely on certain Community rights and obligations. (Direct effect and supremacy will be expanded upon in Chapter 8.) Thus, individuals and other legal persons are entitled to rely on Community law to enforce rights and to defend themselves against illegally imposed restrictions or obligations. Further, these rights may be relied on in national courts and tribunals.

Community law also defines the substantive powers, rights and obligations of its subjects and has created a wide range of sanctions, remedies and procedures for the vindication of these rights and duties. Many of these rights are embodied in the EC Treaty itself, including the right of free movement of workers, the right to equal pay for equal work and the right not to be subjected to discrimination on the grounds of nationality. Other rights have been created by the ECJ through its role as the guardian of Community law, such as the direct effect of directives and State liability, both of which will be discussed in further detail later.

## *Conclusion*

Whilst it is perhaps difficult to ignore the continuing political debate on the policies and development of the European Union, and the 'anti-European' rhetoric that often envelopes such debate, it should not be forgotten that much has been achieved. The future may appear unclear, but there are certain achievements that the Member States should be proud of. The EU is the largest trading bloc in the world and is responsible for approximately 20 per cent of all world trade. One of the promises contained in the old ECSC Treaty was to remove 'age-old rivalries' in favour of a 'community of peoples', and certainly over the years the EU has placed great emphasis on democratic government and respect for human rights. Apart from events in the former Yugoslavia, the EU has managed to secure a considerable period of peace and prosperity, and this is unfortunately often forgotten in the heated political debate that surrounds issues such as monetary union.

However, recent events in the build-up to the British decision to join with the USA in pursuing war in Iraq reveal perhaps to many that the 'age-old rivalries' have not been forgotten. The obvious tension between many of the Member States and the ambitious expansion planned for 2004, but which may now be delayed, point towards an extremely interesting, if somewhat turbulent, time ahead for the European Union.

# 2

# The Institutions of the European Union

2.1 Introduction

2.2 The Commission – arts 211–219 EC

2.3 The Council of Ministers – arts 202–210 EC

2.4 The European Council

2.5 The European Parliament – arts 189–201 EC

2.6 The European Court of Justice – arts 220–248 EC

2.7 The Court of First Instance (CFI)

2.8 The Court of Auditors

2.9 Additional bodies

2.10 Institutional reform under the Treaty of Nice

## 2.1 Introduction

Despite the changes brought about by the Treaty on European Union and the Treaty of Amsterdam, the functions of the institutions remain largely defined by the terms of the EC Treaty. The Council and the Commission, however, have had their respective powers enlarged by the assumption of competencies in the fields of foreign and security policy and justice and home affairs. This chapter, though, will deal predominately with the operation of the institutions of the European Union under the EC Treaty. Unless otherwise stated, all references throughout this text to the constitution of the organisation will be to the EC Treaty, as amended, and the operation of the European Community as a component part of the European Union. This is due to the present prevailing influence of the EC Treaty in the operations of the EU.

Article 7 EC provides that the tasks entrusted to the Community will be carried out by the following institutions: a European Parliament, a Council, a Commission, a

Court of Justice and a Court of Auditors. The institutions are required to act within the powers conferred on them by the EC Treaty and subsequent Treaties and Acts. An Economic and Social Committee and a Committee of the Regions, acting in advisory capacities, assist the Council and the Commission.

The European Council is not specifically identified in art 7 as a Community institution, because it is more a mechanism for inter-governmental co-operation. Its existence and functions, originally recognised in the SEA 1986, are now dealt with by art 4 TEU. As we shall see, however, the European Council plays an important role in the Community. Similarly, the Court of First Instance is technically attached to the Court of Justice and is not a separate Community institution, yet its functions and role within the Community legal order require that it be treated in its own right. For the purposes of this chapter, the political institutions will be considered first, before moving on to discussion of the judicial bodies. Whilst considering the political institutions, reference will also be made to the various legislative processes used by the Community.

Before studying the institutional infrastructure of the Community, we must understand one important point; the Community does not adhere to any rigid separation of powers doctrine. Indeed, there is little about the institutions which can be characterised within the traditional terms used in constitutional law, such as the executive, legislature, administration and judiciary. Instead, the Community institutions operate a 'separation of interests', and each has powers overlapping traditional governmental functions. As we shall see, these interests and powers have evolved throughout the development of the Community and continue to be the basis of much discussion and debate.

The following describes the composition, roles and functions of the various political and judicial institutions as provided under EU law at the time of writing. The important institutional changes introduced under the Treaty of Nice can be found at the end of this chapter (see 2.10).

## 2.2 The Commission – arts 211–219 EC

The Commission represents the interests of the Community and currently consists of 20 members, selected on the grounds of their general competence and whose independence is beyond doubt. The numbers of the Commission may only be increased by the Council, acting unanimously. Only nationals of the 15 Member States may be members of the Commission. The Commission must include at least one but no more than two nationals of each of the Member States and each member must act in the general interest of the Community and be completely independent in the performance of their duties: art 213 EC. This means that the Commissioners must neither seek nor take instructions from any government or any other body. They should also refrain from any activities that are incompatible with their duties.

In return, each Member State undertakes to respect this principle and to avoid influencing the members of the Commission in the performance of their tasks.

The Commissioners may not, during their terms of office, engage in any other occupation, whether gainful or not. When entering upon their duties they are required to give a solemn undertaking that, both during and after their terms of office, they will respect the obligations arising therefrom. In particular, they have a duty to behave with integrity and discretion if accepting, after they have ceased office, certain appointments or benefits. In the event of any breach of these obligations, the ECJ may, on application by the Council or the Commission, rule that the member concerned be, according to the circumstances, either compulsorily retired (in accordance with art 216 EC) or deprived of their rights to a pension or benefits. The first time such action occurred was in July 1999, when proceedings were initiated against former Commissioner Bangemann for accepting a position in a Spanish telecommunications company previously regulated by his Commission department.

## Appointment

By virtue of art 214 EC, members of the Commission are appointed for a five-year period. Their term of office is renewable. The governments of the Member States nominate by common accord the person whom they intend to appoint as President of the Commission. This nomination has to then be approved by the European Parliament. The governments of the Member States then, by common accord with the nominee for President, nominate the other persons whom they intend to appoint as Commissioners. The President and the other members of the Commission are then subject to a vote of approval by the European Parliament. If approved, the members are then appointed by the common accord of the governments of the Member States. These rules were introduced by the Treaty of Amsterdam, and provide the Parliament with a greater say in the process. They were used for the first time in March 1999 when Mr Prodi was appointed President. The Commission may also appoint up to two Vice-Presidents from among its members: art 217 EC.

Vacancies in the Commission may occur through resignation, compulsory retirement, or death. Any such vacancy will be filled for the remainder of the duration of the member's term of office by a new member appointed by the common accord of the governments of the Member States. The Council may, unanimously, decide not to fill the vacancy. Unless compulsorily retired, a Commissioner will remain in office until they have been replaced.

## The Presidency

The influence of the Presidency should not be underestimated. The post was intended to be primes inter pares (first amongst equals) and art 219 EC states that the 'Commission shall work under the guidance of its President'. The President has an important role in shaping the overall policy of the Commission and is the negotiating face of the Commission when dealing with the Council and the Parliament. They may also have influence over the future direction and development of the Community. The impact of this last role will, to a certain extent, depend on the personality and ambition of the appointee. This is perhaps best witnessed in the presidency of Jacques Delors, who had a forceful personality and a strong vision, which included European Monetary Union. It should perhaps be obvious that such a 'personality' may create friction with some of the governments of the Member States and, indeed, with their leaders.

## Procedure

In accordance with art 218 EC, the Council and the Commission consult each other and settle by common accord their methods of co-operation. The Commission adopts its rules of procedure so as to ensure that both it and its departments operate in accordance with the provisions of the Treaty. The Commission acts by a majority of its members, and a meeting is only valid if the number of members laid down in its rules of procedure are present: art 219. The Commission is required to publish an annual general report on its activities no later than one month before the opening of the session of the European Parliament.

To assist in its work, each Commissioner will have a cabinet (of around six or seven people, although the President has about 12) and the Commission itself has a permanent administrative staff. This administration is organised into 24 Directorates General (DG), each dealing with a particular, defined subject matter. For example, there are DGs dealing with transport, fisheries, agriculture and energy. In 1993 the Commission employed 18,000 people, 8,000 of whom were employed as researchers, translators and interpreters – the latter two being required because of the numerous official languages used in the Community.

## Functions

The functions and powers of the Commission are set out in art 211 EC. They may be classified as the following:

1. to ensure respect for the rights and obligations imposed on Member States and Community institutions by both the Community Treaties and measures made under the authority of these agreements;
2. to formulate, participate in and initiate policy decisions authorised under the Community Treaties;
3. to promote the interests of the Community both internally and externally; and
4. to exercise the powers delegated to it by the Council for the implementation and administration of Community policy.

The Commission therefore represents the interests of the Community, and has the ultimate responsibility of ensuring that its interests are protected. It is at the heart of nearly all aspects of Community life and, as stated in the introduction, has a multitude of functions that include legislative, executive, administrative and judicial responsibilities. Whilst the Commission must work with, and reach consensus with, the other political institutions, it is the Commission that has constantly striven to maintain the momentum of development and has been described by the author Fitzmaurice as the 'player-manager' of the EC system. Craig and de Burca describe the central role of the Commission as follows:

> 'The Commission has always been the single most important political force for integration and federalism, ever seeking to press forward to attain the Community's initial objectives as expeditiously as possible, with the aim of moving on to a closer form of union.'

## Legislative functions

The most important legislative power of the Commission is a power of legislative initiation. Generally the Council will act on a proposal from the Commission, although it should be noted that approval will also have to come from the Council and usually the Parliament as well. The Commission is therefore often referred to as the initiator of policy and can propose any of the secondary forms of EC legislation provided for under art 249 EC, such as regulations and directives, or take decisions, make recommendations or deliver opinions. On occasion the Council may be the original source of legislative proposals, but even in this scenario the Commission will provide the proposal with more substance.

The Commission also plays a part in the development of Community-wide policies, for example the Commission White Paper that preceded the SEA 1986. It also has delegated legislative powers under the Treaty, for example under art 83 EC. The purpose of delegating such decision-making powers is to prevent the day-to-day administration of the Community from stifling the work of the Council of Ministers. The Council will delegate power to the Commission to produce regulations in fields such as agriculture and competition. The Commission has considerable competence in the area of anti-dumping, mostly obtained by delegation, although the Council will adopt any final measures.

## Executive functions

The Commission has two important executive functions, namely, dealing with financial aspects of the Community and external relations. The Commission has an important role to play in the budgetary process since it is responsible for preparing the Preliminary Draft Budget, which is then discussed by the Commission, Council and Parliament before being approved by the Commission itself.

The Commission also has responsibility over expenditure, particularly in relation to agricultural and structural policies. Under art 270 EC, the Commission must not make any proposal for a Community act, or alter its proposals, or adopt any implementing measure that is likely to have appreciable implications for the budget, without providing the assurance that the proposal or measure is capable of being financed within the limit of the Community's own resources.

In terms of external relations, the Commission, under art 133 EC, represents and acts on behalf of the EU in formal and informal negotiations. It also represents the EU within a number of important international organisations, such as the UN and the OECD. The Commission is often seen by non-Member States as a point of contact, and staffs the extensive range of diplomatic missions throughout the world that represent the EU. The Commission is also involved with non-Member States that have made applications for full membership; it will carry out a detailed investigation and deliver an opinion and will often be the public face of any negotiations. Finally, the Commission also has responsibility to be 'fully associated' with developments in the field of common foreign and security policy: art 18 TEU.

## Administrative functions

In brief, the function of the Commission is to ensure that the rules and principles of the Community are respected and that the rules are applied correctly. If a Member State desires a waiver or derogation from the rules, then the Commission will decide the matter.

The Commission is often described as the 'watchdog' or 'guardian' of the Treaties, and as such has powers of detection. Under arts 88(3) and 134 EC the Member States are under a duty to keep the Commission informed on certain matters. The Commission also has powers of investigation; under art 284 EC the Commission may gather information and carry out checks necessary for the performance of the tasks entrusted to it, subject to the provisions of the Treaty. Member States and individuals will sometimes bring matters to the attention of the Commission by way of a complaint, and the Parliament has the power to submit a written question under art 197 EC.

## Judicial functions

The Commission also has some judicial powers, the most important probably being the power to bring actions against Member States for breaches of EC law under art 226 EC. The process will begin with attempts to achieve a 'diplomatic' solution before resort is made to the European Court. However, the Court has dealt with numerous enforcement actions, and has developed a number of important EC legal principles (see Chapter 4 for detailed discussion of these principles).

The Commission also has the power to act as investigator and 'judge' in some areas of EC law – the two most important being competition law and State aid: see Part D. In the discharge of its duty under Community competition policy, the Commission has authority, in certain circumstances, to investigate complaints, to impose fines on companies considered to have infringed the competition rules and to require Member States to take appropriate action against unlawful State aid: see Chapters 17 and 18. Its powers under the anti-dumping basic regulations are similar; the Commission is empowered to impose duties on foreign companies found to have been dumping, to investigate allegations, to hold discussions and conferences and to conduct reviews. The decisions made by the Commission in this capacity are subject to review by the Community's judiciary, and usually proceed to the Court of First Instance.

## 2.3 The Council of Ministers – arts 202–210 EC

The Council consists of a representative of each Member State at ministerial level, authorised to commit the government of that Member State: art 203 EC. The Council of Ministers therefore represents national interests and there have been tensions between it and the Commission throughout the history of the European Union. In 1993 the Council decided that it would be known as the Council of the European Union.

Unlike that of the Commission, the membership of the Council may vary from time to time, depending on the nature and subject matter of the meeting. Therefore, if the meeting is to discuss general matters (known as the General Affairs Council), the foreign ministers will attend; if it is to consider a specialist matter, such as agriculture, the meeting will be attended by the appropriate minister of the Member State. The Council may convene at the request of its President, one of its members, or at the request of the Commission: art 204 EC.

### Conduct of meetings

The Presidency of the Council rotates among the Member States according to six-year cycles, each holding the office for six months: art 203 EC. The meetings may take place anywhere in the EU (there are around 100 of them per year), although they do usually take place in Brussels. Article 205(1) EC states that:

> 'Save as otherwise provided in this Treaty, the Council shall act by a majority of its members.'

In practice the Council will rarely act by a simple majority. Unanimity used to be the rule until it was established that Community business was hopelessly slow and cumbersome. The Council began to act more frequently by means of a qualified majority vote (QMV), defined by art 205(2). After the amendments made by the Treaty of Accession for Austria, Finland and Sweden, the total votes of 87 were weighted in the following manner:

Germany, France, Italy, and the United Kingdom – 10 votes each;
Spain – 8 votes;

Belgium, Greece, The Netherlands, and Portugal – 5 votes each;
Austria and Sweden – 4 votes each;
Denmark, Ireland and Finland – 3 votes each; and
Luxembourg – 2 votes.

For the adoption of measures by a qualified majority, there must be at least 62 votes in favour where the EC Treaty requires such acts to be adopted on a proposal from the Commission, and 62 votes in favour, cast by at least ten members, in all other cases. This formula was created in an attempt to prevent the larger states from coercing the smaller Member States. After the accession of new Member States in 1995, a blocking minority became 26 votes. This block allows a coalition of Member States to prevent the adoption of measures that require a qualified majority vote. (See section 2.10 for proposed changes to this system under the Treaty of Nice.)

After the passing of the SEA in 1986, the use of majority voting became more common place, since it was extended to a substantial range of subject matters. Similarly, the TEU and ToA continued this process, and enlarged the number of areas subject to majority voting.

Unanimity is usually required in matters of great importance, such as the admission of new Member States (art 49 TEU) and matters concerning the approximation of laws: art 94 EC. In addition, the appointment of the President of the Commission requires unanimity among the Member States. This requirement allowed the UK to veto the Franco-German sponsored nomination for President in June 1994. Abstentions by members present in person or represented do not prevent the adoption by the Council of acts that require unanimity: art 205(3) EC.

The Luxembourg Accords provide that if the vital interest of a Member State is threatened, it may effectively veto the measure. Hence, whenever important interests are at stake, discussion should be continued until a unanimous decision is reached.

## The Presidency

This position has become one of increasing significance, as the legislative process has become more complex, and the need for co-ordination even greater. The various interests represented in the Council creates a situation that requires strong leadership, particularly since it has developed a desire to become a stronger player in the development of the Community. The President performs functions such as: the arranging and setting of agendas for meetings; the development of policy initiatives; liasing with the Commission President and the Parliament; and representing the Council in discussion with external bodies. Holding the Presidency may permit a Member State to promote its own particular initiatives, although this may bring the incumbent into conflict with the remaining members of the Council.

## Functions

Under art 202 EC, to ensure that the objectives set out in the EC Treaty are attained, the Council is required, in accordance with the Treaty's provisions, to:

1. ensure the co-ordination of the general economic policies of the Member States;
2. take decisions; and
3. confer on the Commission powers for the implementation of the rules which the Council lays down.

The Council may impose certain requirements in respect of the exercise of those powers. The Council may also reserve the right to itself, in specific cases, to exercise directly implementing powers.

The Committee of the Permanent Representatives of the Member States (COREPER) under art 207 EC is responsible for preparing the work of the Council and for carrying out the tasks assigned to it by the Council. COREPER can play a central role in the decision-making process since it is responsible for helping set up the agenda of Council meetings and because it will review draft legislation from the Commission. The Council is also assisted by a General Secretariat, which operates under the direction of a Secretary-General appointed by a unanimous decision of the Council: art 207.

As with the Commission, the Council undertakes a number of functions.

## Legislative functions

Before legislative proposals from the Commission may become law, they will have to be approved by the Council. Therefore, it is the Member States, through their representatives on the Council, which pass European legislation and decide on its overall substantive content. The Council will have to approve legislation under the stipulated method, be it unanimity, qualified or simple majority voting. In order to enact a measure, the Council must ensure that the procedural requirements have been complied with, and that its authority to enact the measure is derived from the terms of the Community Treaties. Therefore, if the Council acts ultra vires it may find the ECJ striking down its measures on the basis of a complaint from either another Community institution or a Member State. Individuals also have standing to bring actions for judicial review of the Council's actions (see Chapter 5).

The most common ground for complaint from Member States against measures adopted in the Council is when a measure is approved on the basis of an article requiring a qualified majority, as opposed to another provision needing a stricter voting requirement, such as unanimity. If a Member State believes that a measure is being adopted on the incorrect legal basis, an application for annulment to the ECJ is the proper procedure. For example, in *United Kingdom* v *Council (Re Hormones)* Case 68/86 [1988] ECR 855 the UK government challenged the legal basis on which the Council adopted a directive prohibiting the use of certain types of hormones.

The critical point was that the measure was adopted under art 37 EC, which required a qualified majority. The UK claimed that the legitimate legal authority was art 94 EC, requiring unanimity. The Court held that the proper legal basis was art 37 EC, although the measure was eventually declared void due to technical, procedural grounds.

Similarly, in *United Kingdom* v *Council (Re Working Hours Directive)* Case C–84/94 [1996] ECR I–5755, the UK challenged the Working Hours Directive on the grounds that it should have been adopted under either art 94 EC or 308 EC, both of which required unanimity. The ECJ held that the Council had adopted the directive under art 138 EC, by a majority vote, and that it was the appropriate legal basis in the circumstances.

The Commission is also a frequent visitor to the ECJ to challenge measures adopted by the Council, which they have opted to alter from the contents or legal basis proposed by the Commission. In *Commission* v *Council (Re Generalised Tariff Preferences)* Case 45/86 [1987] ECR 1493 such a dispute arose in relation to two Council regulations concerning tariff preferences for developing countries. The Council had adopted the measures on the authority of art 308 EC, which specified unanimity, while the Commission believed that the Council had authority to adopt the measures under art 133 EC, a provision requiring merely a qualified majority. The ECJ supported the arguments of the Commission and declared the measures void on the ground that they had been adopted on the incorrect legal basis.

Private parties may also challenge the legal basis for the adoption of measures, under either art 230 EC or the preliminary reference procedure under art 234 EC (see Chapters 5 and 6 respectively). The latter procedure was used in *Eurotunnel SA and Others* v *SeaFrance* Case C–408/95 [1997] ECR I–6315. In the case, Eurotunnel brought proceedings in the French courts against SeaFrance, claiming that it was cross-subsidising its ferry fares with revenues from the sale of tax and excise free goods. SeaFrance had been authorised to provide duty free sales by the French government. Eurotunnel claimed that such authorisation gave SeaFrance an unfair competitive advantage. As part of its case, Eurotunnel claimed that two Council directives authorising exemptions from excise tax had been unlawfully adopted by the Council. This was because, when the Council adopted the measures, it had departed from the terms of the Commission's original proposal to such an extent that the final text could not be said to have been adopted on the basis of the Commission's proposal. The ECJ held that the Council had power to amend the proposal from the Commission, provided that the voting requirements on which the measure was based had been fulfilled. Hence, it concluded that the Council had not exceeded its powers to make amendments to the proposal and, consequently, the regulations in question could not be annulled on this ground.

The Commission also has power under art 208 EC to 'request the Commission to undertake any studies which the Council considers desirable for the attainment of the common objectives, and to submit to it any appropriate proposals'. The Council, in its desire to take a more proactive role in the Community legislative process, has used this provision to require the Commission to undertake investigations into specific areas and to produce legislation on these issues. It may also force the Commission into taking positive legislative action by producing opinions or resolutions on a particular topic.

Finally, the Council also has legislative powers in relation to CFSP, since it is responsible for taking decisions for defining and implementing the policy, under guidelines established by the European Council. The Council also has to adopt any joint actions: art 14 TEU.

## Powers to conclude international agreements

Article 300 EC stipulates that, where the Treaty provides for the conclusion of agreements between the Community and one or more States, or international organisations, the Commission makes recommendations to the Council, which, in turn, authorises the Commission to open the necessary negotiations. The Commission conducts these negotiations in consultation with special committees appointed by the Council to assist it in this task, and within the framework of any directives the Council may issue.

Subject to the powers vested in the Commission in this field, the agreements are concluded by the Council, acting by a qualified majority on a proposal from the Commission. However, the Council acts unanimously when the agreement covers a field for which unanimity is required for the adoption of internal rules, and for the agreements referred to in art 310 EC (agreements establishing an association involving reciprocal rights and obligations, common action and special procedures).

The Council normally concludes agreements after only consultation with the Parliament. However, agreements referred to in art 310, other agreements establishing a specific institutional framework by organising co-operation procedures, agreements having important budgetary implications for the Community, and agreements entailing amendment of an act adopted under the procedure referred to in art 251 EC, can only be concluded after obtaining the assent of the Parliament.

The Council, the Commission or a Member State may obtain the opinion of the European Court as to whether an envisaged agreement is compatible with the provisions of the Treaty. Where the opinion of the ECJ is adverse, the agreement may enter into force only in accordance with art 48 TEU.

## Public access to the Council's deliberations and documents

The TEU contained, as an appendix, a declaration on the rights of public access to information from the Community institutions. The objectives of this declaration were given effect by Council Decision 93/731 on public access to Council documents. Article 1 of that Decision states that the public shall have access to measures adopted by the Council unless the release of such documents would undermine the protection of the following:

1.  the public interest;
2.  individual privacy;
3.  commercial and industrial secrecy;
4.  the Community's financial interests; or
5.  confidentiality requested by natural or legal persons providing information on the contents of that document.

The right of interested private individuals to obtain access to the Council's deliberations and documents under this measure was tested in the Court of First Instance in *Carvel & Guardian Newspapers Ltd* v *Council* Case T–194/94 [1995] ECR II–2765. The European Affairs editor of *The Guardian* made a request for the documents, reports, minutes and the voting record of the Social Affairs and Justice Council meetings held in October and November 1993, and the Agricultural Council meeting in January 1994. The Council's Secretariat refused this request on the basis that the documents directly referred to the deliberations of the Council and could therefore not be disclosed. The ECJ held that the Council failed to properly balance the interests involved before refusing access to these documents. The correspondence between the parties indicated that the Council automatically refused to meet the applicant's request; such a response could not be considered a proper appraisal of the merits of a request as required by the terms of the Council's decision.

The issue of access to such documentation has remained an issue of importance within the Community system. The demands for increased access are based on the need for greater transparency in the decision-making process of the EU. Improved transparency also improves the quality of the democratic process – an issue that has been of concern within the Community system for some considerable time.

## 2.4 The European Council

Article 4 TEU states that:

> 'The European Council shall provide the Union with the necessary impetus for its development and shall define the general political guidelines thereof. The European Council shall bring together the Heads of State or Government of the Member States and the President of the Commission. They shall be assisted by the Ministers for Foreign Affairs of the Member States and by a Member of the Commission ... The European Council shall submit to the European Parliament a report after each of it meetings and a yearly written report on the progress achieved by the Union.'

There was no provision in the original EEC Treaty for such a periodic meeting, but the dictates of closer economic and political integration required the co-ordination and harmonisation of common positions in the fields of foreign and economic policy. After a meeting in Paris in 1974, a decision was made to arrange such meetings (known as summits) regularly, three times a year, to discuss issues generally affecting European and international concerns. During the 1970s and 1980s such summits were held without formal recognition of the body as a European institution. However, the SEA 1986 recognised its existence and its formal position was established under the TEU.

The European Council deals with important issues, including the development of the Community in a broad context. It will also discuss changes to the institutional structure; constitutional initiatives; the European economy; broad policy initiatives (such as the Social Charter 1989); external relations (for example the negotiating rounds of GATT/WTO); and will often be the forum in which conflicts (such as those over the budget and EU finances) are resolved. The influence of this institution should not be underestimated – it plays a central role in the shaping of Community policies and whilst its conclusions have no binding force in their own right they will provide the framework for further legislative initiatives.

The European Council is headed by the Head of State (or Government) of the Member State holding the Presidency of the Council of Ministers. This position is important because it gives an opportunity for individual Member States to influence the agenda for discussion and, indirectly, the direction of the Community. Thus, when the German, French or Dutch governments hold the Presidency, the agenda usually deals with matters of accelerating European integration, whereas the presidency of the British or Danish government often involves slowing down the process of integration.

The European Council may formulate policy at this high level, but the Commission and the Parliament are also closely involved. For example, the views of the Parliament are continuously sought, and the body is regularly informed about current political issues. Indeed, the President of the Parliament will address a plenary session of the Council, and has done so since 1988.

European Council discussions range across a whole host of matters of both European and international concern. For example, the final conference held during the UK Presidency in 1992, the Edinburgh Summit, proved to be particularly successful and agreement was reached on the expansion of the representatives of the European Parliament, the conclusion of the single European market and the promotion of the principle of subsidiarity. The Danish and Belgian Presidencies held in 1993 focused on encouraging greater transparency in EC affairs, enlargement of the membership of the Community and economic assistance for central and eastern Europe.

In recent years much of the efforts of the Presidencies has been focused on economic and monetary union. This was the case for the Italian Presidency which lasted for the first six months of 1996, and during which much of the preparatory work for the IGC was achieved. Simultaneously, though, Italian national interests were not forgotten. In particular, the Italian Presidency placed high on its agenda the pacification and reconstruction of the former Yugoslavia; the Middle East peace process; and strengthening co-operation and dialogue with Russia and other countries of the former USSR.

In the first half of 1999 the Federal Republic of Germany took over the Presidency. The start of this coincided with the launch of the European unit of currency – the euro. The principal political tasks taken up by the German Presidency were:

1. to improve the framework of conditions for higher levels of employment;
2. to adopt a policy of integration of energy markets;
3. the pursuit of a successful conclusion to the Agenda 2000 issue;
4. to improve the framework conditions for industry, particularly small and medium-sized enterprises;
5. the liberalisation in the telecommunications sector and further liberalisation of the postal sector;
6. to create an effective transport policy; and
7. the development and consolidation of existing relations with third countries and international organisations.

The respective agendas of these countries illustrate the ability of individual Member States to influence the internal and external policies of the EU during their tenure of the Presidencies and to pursue goals close to their national interests during such times.

## 2.5 The European Parliament – arts 189–201 EC

The European Parliament sits in plenary session in Strasbourg (although it holds some sessions and committee meetings in Brussels), for a five-year term, and currently consists of a total of 626 Members of the European Parliament (MEPs). The total number may not exceed 700: art 189 EC. The distribution of seats, as modified by the Treaty of Accession for Austria, Finland and Sweden, is as follows:

99 representatives  – Germany;
87 representatives  – France, Italy and the United Kingdom;
64 representatives  – Spain;
31 representatives  – The Netherlands;
25 representatives  – Belgium, Greece and Portugal;
22 representatives  – Sweden;
21 representatives  – Austria;
16 representatives  – Denmark and Finland;
15 representatives  – Ireland; and
6 representatives   – Luxembourg.

The number of representatives does not reflect the population size of the individual Member States and this has attracted some considerable criticism. However, amended art 190 EC now states that 'the number of representatives elected in each Member State must ensure appropriate representation of the peoples of the States brought together in the Community'.

The European Parliament in its original composition was not an elected body – the MEPs were delegates of the national governments of the Member States. However, in 1979 direct elections to the Parliament were introduced in accordance with Council Decision 76/787. The TEU provided for European 'citizenship' and citizens of the union are now permitted, if they are resident in a Member State, to vote and stand as candidates in European parliamentary elections.

There is, however, a criticism of the electoral system for the European Parliament in that there is still no uniform process, a fact that runs contrary to what was envisaged under the Treaty: see art 190 EC. In 1993, an action was bought for failure to act on this issue by the UK Liberal Democratic Party against the European Parliament: *Liberal Democrats* v *Parliament* Case C–41/92 [1993] ECR I–3153. However, whilst legal proceedings were being brought, the Parliament adopted a resolution on a uniform electoral procedure. The procedure was based on a form of proportional representation, but which permitted the use of a formula that allowed some Member States to continue to elect up to two-thirds of their representatives via single member seats. For this reason the ECJ struck out the action, although the Council did not agree the resolution. The ToA amended art 190 so that it provided for the possibility of a common electoral system based not on uniformity but on only 'common principles'. However, pre-empting the coming into force of the Treaty, the Parliament adopted another resolution (Resolution A4–0212/1998), which proposed that the electoral system be based on ten common principles. However, any new system must be unanimously accepted by the Council (art 190) and this seems unlikely in the current climate. Unsurprisingly, this issue is a contentious one throughout the Community, particularly given the diversity of electoral systems in operation and the link often held between elections and State sovereignty. Consequently it appears that progress on this issue will be incredibly slow. The Treaty provides under art 190 that the ultimate responsibility for the creation of a uniform electoral process will be in the hands of the Council, acting only on proposals from the Parliament.

The majority of parties in the Parliament are coalitions between national parties. The MEPs are seated according to their political affiliations and views, and not their nationalities. For example, in June 1999 the European Peoples Party (EPP) was the largest single party, followed by the Socialist Party (PES) and the Liberal Democratic and Reformist Group (ELDR). Article 191 EC specifically states that the Community supports the idea of European political parties, stating that:

'Political parties at European level are important as a factor for integration within the Union. They contribute to forming a European awareness and to expressing the political will of the citizens of the Union.'

The MEPs have three main tasks:

1. to advise the Council about the Commission's proposals for Community-wide laws;

2. to consider the Community budget; and

3. to exert some control over the Council and Commission by means of questions about aspects of the Community's business. A number of other tasks were added by the Treaty on European Union.

The Parliament elects a President and 14 vice-presidents for two-and-a-half year terms. When combined with the various political party leaders they are known collectively as the Conference of Presidents. The Parliament is assisted in its tasks by a secretariat (which is based in Luxembourg) and a range of specialist committees. According to r109 of the Rules of Procedure, the Parliament may set up both standing and ad hoc committees. The rules of the standing committees, are defined when they are established. There are over 20 standing committees covering matters such as foreign affairs and security, budgets, environment, public health and consumer protection, women's rights and institutional affairs. Occasionally the Parliament may also set up temporary committees to deal with matters that fall outside the ambit of the permanent committees.

The reports of the committees serve as the basis for most debates in the Parliament. Any MEP may table a motion for a resolution on a matter within the range of Community activities. That motion will then be referred to the appropriate committee. A similar procedure is followed when the Council asks for an opinion on a matter. A report will then be prepared and each committee will appoint one of its members to be responsible for a particular report. That person is known as the rapporteur, and they will lead the debate when the matter comes before the Parliament.

## Legislative functions

The legislative function and competence of the Parliament has progressed through three distinct phases, introduced through various Treaty amendments. The first phase may be described as the original legislative role of the Parliament, when it was primarily merely a consultative body. The second phase was introduced by amendments made by the SEA 1986 which introduced the so-called 'co-operation procedure'. The third phase is the revised legislative role introduced by the TEU.

The Parliament's traditional role was a rather weak one – it was to comment on proposals put forward by the Commission before the Council made its decision on the final text of the legislation. The Parliament had the right to be consulted on certain matters and failure to do so resulted in the adoption of a measure being declared null and void. However, in practice, the Commission regularly sought the opinion of the Parliament on proposed legislation even though technically it was not required to do so. Proposals were submitted to the Parliament and discussed in the relevant parliamentary committees. These committees prepared reports on the proposed measures, which were debated by the full Parliament prior to being returned to the Commission.

The second stage in the development of the Parliament's legislative competence was brought about by the SEA. The Act established the co-operation procedure which ensured that, on certain matters, both the Council and the Commission were required to consider the amendments to any legislation proposed by the Parliament. Whilst this new procedure certainly strengthened the legislative role of the Parliament, even in this process the Parliament's proposals were not binding and could be superseded by a unanimous vote of the Council.

The co-operation procedure was to effectively introduce a 'second parliamentary reading' for legislative proposals on measures requiring approval through the process. The first reading was required when the Commission submitted its draft proposals for consideration, and the second reading was required when the Council passed the measure to the Parliament, after it had arrived at a 'common position'.

The third stage in the evolution of the Parliament's legislative role was established by the amendments made by the TEU, which introduced the 'co-decision procedure'. This system is complicated, but essentially arts 250–252 EC introduced a new, comprehensive legislative process modelled on the co-operation procedure. The essential difference is that this procedure applies to a considerable range of legislative proposals, although not all. Its application is far more extensive than the co-operation procedure, which was the Parliament's main previous influence on the legislative process.

The Commission is required under the co-decision procedure to submit a significant amount of legislative proposals to both the Parliament and the Council. The Council, acting by qualified majority, after obtaining the opinion of the Parliament, adopts a common position on the proposal. This common position is then communicated to the Parliament. The Parliament may approve the common position, in which case the Council may adopt the measure. If no decision is taken by the Parliament, within three months of the transmission of a proposal, the Council may adopt the measure. However, if the Parliament suggests amendments to the common position then, depending on whether the relevant legislative process is that of art 251 or art 252, either the matter is referred to a Conciliation Committee where both organs explain their views, or the matter is returned to the Council for reconsideration. Ultimately, if no agreement is reached between the organs, the Council may only adopt a measure by a unanimous vote.

The most significant amendment made by the Treaty of Amsterdam to the existing legislative process was the extension of the co-decision procedure to a further 23 subject matters. The co-decision procedure itself was also refined with the abolition of the third reading in Parliament – in such cases, if the Council and Parliament do not reach a compromise in the Conciliation Committee there is simply no agreement and the proposed measure falls: art 251. This effectively amounts to a power of veto in the hands of the Parliament, which in turn is a reflection of its strengthened role in the legislative process of the Community.

In certain specific matters the process will be one known as assent. In such cases the Parliament has the power of veto since its agreement is essential to the success of the measure. In such cases the Parliament will be prepared to influence the content of measures by threatening a veto. For example, it has insisted on clauses on human rights and democracy being included within international agreements. This power has been somewhat reduced by the removal of the need for an absolute majority to a simple majority by the TEU. This means that it is easier for the other institutions to gain the support required for the measure.

However, there remain some areas where the Parliament has a limited legislative role. In the case of some international agreements, such as those on common commercial policy (see Chapter 13), the Parliament has no say at all. The Parliament also has a limited role under the CFSP pillar, with its views merely being 'taken into consideration'; asking questions; being informed of developments; and holding an annual debate. However, the ToA extended the role of the Parliament in relation to the third pillar (police and judicial co-operation in criminal matters).

The Council must now consult the Parliament before adopting any measure and the Council cannot act until it has received the Parliament's opinion, unless the Parliament acts outside of the set time limit. In addition, under the Treaty of Nice the Parliament gains a consultative role in authorising enhanced co-operation under the third pillar (see Chapter 1, section 1.8).

The Parliament also has additional, more informal, legislative functions. It will participate in inter-institutional conferences, where it will attempt to reach consensus via representation of the interests of the peoples of Europe with the interests of the national governments, as represented in the Council. Under art 192 EC the Parliament also has the power to request the Commission to submit a proposal on any matter on which the Parliament believes a Community act is necessary, although the Commission is not bound to act upon such a request.

## *The budgetary function*

Initially the EC was financed by contributions from the exchequers of the Member States. It was always intended that these contributions would be replaced by the Community's own resources. It was not until 1970 that a decision was taken to establish an 'own resource' system (now Council Decision of 31 October 1994 on the Communities' System of Own Resources). A Financial Provisions Treaty 1975 was agreed and came into force in 1977.

The Treaty originally gave the Parliament increased powers over the budget and created the Court of Auditors. The Parliament now has the final say on all 'non-compulsory' expenditure (administrative and operational expenditure such as the Social Fund and research) which amounts to around 30 per cent of the budget. As regards the rest of the budget, which is expenditure that is the inevitable consequence of Community legislation, such as agriculture, the Parliament can propose modifications. They are permitted to do this as long as they do not increase total expenditure. Such modifications are deemed accepted, unless the Council rejects them by a qualified majority. Finally, the Parliament has the power to reject the entire budget under art 272(8) EC which provides that:

'... the European Parliament acting by a majority of its members and two-thirds of the votes cast, may if there are important reasons reject the draft budget and ask for a new draft to be submitted to it.'

It is the Parliament's President who has the task of declaring that the budget has been adopted once all the procedures have been complied with.

The TEU made a number of important changes to the budgetary provisions. Article 268 EC now states that all items of revenue and expenditure of the Community, including those relating to the European Social Fund, are to be included in estimates to be drawn up for each financial year and shown in the budget. Administrative expenditure occasioned for the institutions by the provisions of the TEU relating to common foreign and security policy and co-operation in the fields of justice and home affairs must be charged to the budget. The operations expenditure occasioned by the implementation of these provisions may, under the conditions referred to therein, be charged to the budget. Finally, the revenue and expenditure shown in the budget must be in balance.

## Supervisory functions

Article 189 EC states that the Parliament shall exercise the advisory and supervisory powers conferred on it by the Treaty. To give substance to these powers, art 201 gives to the Parliament a powerful weapon in that Members may, by a two-thirds majority, compel the Commission to resign as a body. This motion of censure is circumscribed by certain procedural requirements. To date, it has only been effectively invoked on one occasion. In January 1999 the European Socialist Party in the Parliament tabled a motion to compel the Commission, under the Presidency of Jacques Santer, to resign. This motion was defeated since the necessary two-thirds majority was not obtained. However, a committee of inquiry was established to investigate allegations of maladministration by the Commission, which resulted in an adverse report criticising a number of individual Commissioners. As a result of the report, all the Commissioners resigned their positions since liability for maladministration involves the collective responsibility of all members.

The Parliament also has the right to participate in the appointment of the Commission; the TEU provides that the Parliament must be consulted on the nominations made by the Member States for both Commissioners and the Commission Presidency. The entire Commission, as a collective body, must be approved by the Parliament. In the case of the Presidency, the Parliament's powers were strengthened by the ToA. This amendment occurred after the difficulties encountered in appointing Jacques Santer; the UK vetoed the original candidate and the compromise candidate's selection was criticised by the Socialists as being contrary to the principles of democracy. The amendment now means that

Parliament's approval of the nomination for Commission President must be obtained.

The Parliament may also, at the request of a quarter of its members, set up a temporary committee of inquiry to investigate alleged contravention or maladministration in the implementation of EC law. This applies unless the matter is being examined by the Court of Justice or while the case is subject to legal proceedings. This was the procedure invoked that ultimately led to the resignation of the Santer Commission.

Under the terms of art 212 EC, as amended, the Commission must publish annually, no later than one month before the opening session of the Parliament, a general report on its activities. The Parliament must discuss this report in open session. Since 1970, the Commission's President has also presented to the Parliament an annual programme of the future activity of the Communities. The report is generally presented at the beginning of each year. This enables the Parliament to scrutinise and comment on the framing of Community policies at an early stage and, indeed, challenge the proposals.

Article 194 EC entitles any citizen of the EU, and any natural or legal person having their registered office in a Member State, to petition the Parliament on matters that fall within the Community's fields of activity and which affect them directly. Under the TEU, the Parliament has also appointed an Ombudsman (art 195 EC) who is empowered to receive complaints from any citizen of the EU or any natural or legal person residing or having their registered office in a Member State. The jurisdiction of the Ombudsman extends to maladministration on the part of all Community institutions or bodies except the European Court of Justice and the Court of First Instance. The post has been reasonably successful – the first two reports to the Parliament revealed that the Ombudsman had received 842 complaints in 1996. However, there is a limitation to the effectiveness of the Ombudsman in that their jurisdiction extends to only EU, and not national, institutions. Unfortunately, it appears that a considerable number of complaints addressed to the Ombudsman fall into this category and consequently there is a lack of redress in this context.

Once the Ombudsman has received a complaint, they will refer the matter to the institution concerned, which has three months to submit its views on the matter. The Ombudsman then forwards a report on the complaint to the institution concerned and the Parliament, and the person who lodged the complaint is informed of the outcome of the inquiries. The Ombudsman must submit an annual report to the Parliament on the outcome of their inquiries. The ToA now provides the Ombudsman with the power to inquire into matters falling within the third pillar. The Ombudsman may also undertake their own inquiries, such as that conducted by Jacob Söderman into the public accessibility of EC institutional documentation.

Finally, MEPs enjoy the right to be informed about the progress of the Commission's work. They may exercise this right by means of parliamentary questions. Article 197(3) EC and rr58–62 of Parliament's Rules of Procedure determine that the Commission must reply to questions put to it by the Parliament or its members. The questions must be replied to within a prescribed time period. Questions may be produced for a written answer, or for an oral one, with or without debate. The answers are published in the Official Journal. Written answers are the norm, because the pressure on the Parliament's time necessitates a limit to oral question time. The advantage of the oral question is that a related supplementary question may be asked. Questions may also be asked of the Council or of the foreign ministers meeting in European political co-operation.

## Power of the Parliament to compel judicial review of the acts of other institutions

The power of the European Parliament to challenge the validity of acts of other Community institutions, and Member States, was not explicitly stated in the EEC Treaty. However, the Parliament brought a series of such actions in repeated attempts to have its right to bring them recognised: see Chapter 5. In 1980, in *SA Roquette Frères* v *Council* Case 138/79 [1980] ECR 3333 and *Maizena* v *Council* Case 139/79 [1980] ECR 3393, the ECJ held that Parliament had the right, under art 37 of the Statute of the Court, to intervene in any case before it, without the need to show a special interest in the outcome of the case.

The Parliament's right to bring actions for failure to act under art 232 EC was eventually recognised in *European Parliament* v *Council (Re Common Transport Policy)* Case 13/83 [1985] ECR 1513 where the ECJ held that the term 'institutions of the Community' referred to in art 232 EC (formerly art 175) included the Parliament. These developments reflect those of the increasing importance of the Parliament within the legislative process, and together reveal a process of extending the powers of the Parliament from those it was originally intended to have.

As regards art 230 EC (formerly art 173), bringing an action for annulment, the ECJ concluded that the Parliament could be a defendant to such an action: *Partie Ecologiste Les Verts* v *European Parliament* Case 294/83 [1986] ECR 1339. However, the Parliament was not as successful in gaining acknowledgement of a right to bring such an action. In *European Parliament* v *Council (Re Comitology)* Case 302/87 [1988] ECR 5615, the ECJ held that only the Council and the Commission were capable of bringing such proceedings. However, in 1990 the ECJ's position changed. In *European Parliament* v *Council (Re Chernobyl)* Case C–70/88 [1990] ECR I–2041 the ECJ held that Parliament had the necessary locus standi to bring an action for annulment so long as it was based on the infringement of one of the Parliament's prerogatives. Therefore, if there was no other likely applicant, the Parliament could step in and bring proceedings to challenge the action to protect one of its prerogatives. (See Chapter 5 for a more detailed discussion of art 230.)

Articles 230 and 232 were both amended by the TEU. Article 230 now provides, inter alia, that the ECJ shall review the legality of acts adopted jointly by the Parliament and the Council, of acts of the Council, of the Commission and of the

European Central Bank, other than recommendations and opinions, and of acts of the European Parliament intended to produce legal effects vis-à-vis third parties. For this purpose, the European Court of Justice has jurisdiction in actions brought by Member States, the Council, or the Commission on grounds of lack of competence, infringement of an essential procedural requirement, infringement of the Treaty or of any rule of law relating to its application, or misuse of powers. The Court has jurisdiction, under the same conditions, in actions brought by the European Parliament and by the European Central Bank for the purpose of protecting their prerogatives.

Article 232 provides, inter alia, that should the Parliament, the Council or the Commission, in infringement of the Treaty, fail to act, the Member States and the other institutions of the Community may bring an action before the European Court of Justice to have the infringement established. The ECJ has jurisdiction, under the same conditions, in actions or proceedings brought by the European Central Bank in the areas falling within the latter's field of competence and in actions or proceedings brought against the latter.

## 2.6 The European Court of Justice – arts 220–248 EC

The European Court of Justice, which sits in Luxembourg, is comprised 15 judges who are assisted by eight Advocates-General, although as a transitional compromise an additional Advocate-General has been appointed. They are appointed for six years by the Member States and are eligible for re-appointment. As with Commissioners, their independence is assured by the provisions of the EC Treaty.

The appointment of judges and Advocates-General is by mutual agreement (art 222 EC) among the governments of the Member States. They are chosen from 'persons whose independence is beyond doubt and who possess the qualifications required for appointment to the highest judicial offices in their respective countries, or who are jurisconsults of recognised importance': art 223 EC. Provisions relating to the taking of the oath, privileges and immunities, incompatible secondary functions and deprivation of office are intended to ensure the continued independence of both judges and Advocates-General.

Every three years there will be a partial replacement of judges (eight and seven alternately) and Advocates-General (four on each occasion). The judges will elect a President from among their number, to serve for a term of three years, although they may be re-elected.

The ECJ sits in plenary session, although it may form chambers (art 221), each consisting of three, five or seven judges, either to undertake certain preparatory inquiries or to adjudicate on particular categories of cases in accordance with rules laid down for such purposes. Nevertheless, the ECJ sits in plenary session when a Member State or a Community institution that is party to the proceedings so requests.

The Advocates-General have a duty to act 'with complete impartiality and independence, to make, in open court, reasoned submissions on cases brought before the Court of Justice'. Their activities are of great importance, especially because their impartial submissions regarding facts as well as legal argument can form a valuable basis for the decision to be taken by the ECJ. Indeed, it is unusual to find a situation where the European Court's final decision has been contrary to that suggested in the Advocate-General's opinion.

Should the ECJ so request, the Council may, acting unanimously, increase the number of judges and make necessary adjustments to the second and third paragraphs of art 221 EC (sittings) and to the second paragraph of art 223 EC (partial replacement of judges).

## Duties, powers and jurisdiction

The ECJ ensures the observance of the law in the interpretation and application of the Treaties and their implementing rules: arts 220 EC and 136 Euratom. To this end, a number of powers have been conferred on the Court. These are mainly intended to enable the Court to judge the acts and omissions of the institutions and the Member States in accordance with Community law, and to ensure uniformity of interpretation of Community law in its application by national courts (art 234 EC, known as the preliminary reference procedure). The conditions and manner in which the ECJ exercises these powers will be discussed later.

The ECJ therefore has a duty to both control the legality of the conduct of the institutions and assess the conformity of the law of the Member States with that of the Community, and to safeguard the rights and legitimate interests of all those subject to Community jurisdiction – the Community itself, the Member States and private individuals.

The Treaty of Amsterdam extended the ECJ's jurisdiction to give rulings on the validity and interpretation of decisions, on the interpretation of conventions, and on the validity and interpretation of measures implementing conventions adopted in the field of co-operation in justice and home affairs.

In addition, the ECJ may be given jurisdiction under an arbitration clause in a contract concluded by the Community: art 238 EC. It also has jurisdiction in any dispute involving a Member State where the subject matter is dealt with under the Treaty and the parties have consented to submitting the dispute to the ECJ. Some international agreements confer jurisdiction on the ECJ, for example, under the EEA Agreement the national courts of the EFTA states may make references on interpretative matters to the ECJ.

Both the Council of Ministers and the Commission are authorised to submit legal questions to the ECJ for advisory opinions. This power has been used most often by the Commission to limit the competence of the Council to act, or alternatively to reinforce its own constitutional position: see *Commission* v *Council (Re ERTA)* Case 22/70 [1971] ECR 263.

One of the most significant advisory opinions was that given in *Re the Draft Treaty on a European Economic Area (No 1)* Opinion 1/91 [1991] ECR I–6079. This centred on the question of whether a treaty between the EC and the European Free Trade Association (EFTA) was legal. The agreement in question sought to create a territorial area consisting of the Member States of both organisations in which the four Community freedoms – free movement of goods, persons, capital and services – as well as Community competition law, would apply.

The Court ruled parts of the treaty as being contrary to the EC Treaty; the agreement undermined the rule of law in the Community and in particular the jurisdiction of the ECJ to settle disputes arising in connection with the interpretation of the EC Treaty. The concept of 'homogeneity' was developed by the ECJ to explain that the agreement would prevent the application of any subsequent European law to the whole territory covered by the intended treaty. The treaty establishing the European Economic Area was subsequently amended before being adopted in March 1992.

## Rules of Procedure of the European Court of Justice

The ordinary procedure before the ECJ consists of two parts, written and oral. Unlike the emphasis placed on oral proceedings in English courts, the ECJ places greater reliance on the written stage. Generally speaking, the written stage, which is not open to the public, is by far the most important part of the procedure. It consists of the communication by the Registrar to the parties, and to the institutions whose measures are in dispute, of the various pleadings, such as applications, defences and statements of case, as well as all papers and documents submitted to them.

Within a month of service by the Registrar of the application on the defendant, a defence must be lodged; failure to do so may lead to the Court giving judgment by default. The remaining part of the written procedure is also subject to strict time limits. The written procedure ends with the judge rapporteur's preliminary report as to whether a preliminary inquiry is necessary. When the ECJ orders such an inquiry, it may undertake it itself, or may assign it to a chamber which may then exercise the powers vested in the Court. Where the Court decides to open the oral proceedings without an inquiry, the President of the Court is required to fix the opening date.

The oral stage is much shorter, since the main arguments of the parties are already set out in the written pleadings. The judge rapporteur will present the case to the Court. The various legal representatives will make oral submissions, and these will be followed by the Advocate-General's report. There may be also be witnesses and experts called. The Court may ask the legal representatives oral questions, should they so wish.

Upon the conclusion of the oral stage the Court goes on to the deliberation of the case. The opinion reached by the majority of judges after final discussion determines the decision of the Court. A single judgment is always given, and no separate or dissenting opinions are published. The final judgment will consist of three parts: a summary of the facts and of the conclusions, submissions and arguments of the parties; the grounds for the decision; and the operative part including the decision as to costs.

In all contentious proceedings before it, the ECJ must adjudicate upon costs even if the parties have made no submissions in this respect. As a matter of practice, the judgment or order of the Court merely states who is to bear the costs without quantifying them. Generally speaking, there are three main rules as to how costs are to be disposed of between the parties:

1. The unsuccessful party is ordered to pay the costs, but only if they have been asked for in that party's submissions. Where a successful party has made no formal submissions on this matter, they must bear their own costs. Where neither party has made any submission on costs, each must be ordered to bear their own costs.
2. Where each party succeeds on some and fails on other heads, the ECJ may apportion the costs.
3. The ECJ may order even a successful party to pay costs, which it considers that party to have unreasonable or vexatiously caused the opposite party to incur.

In addition, under art 243 EC, the ECJ may in any cases before it prescribe interim measures. An application for interim measures may only be made by a party in a case before the Court. Such a measure will only be granted if a prima facie case is made out for it and it is necessary to avoid serious and irreparable damage: see *NTN Toyo* v *Council* Case 121/77R [1977] ECR 1721 and *Ford AG and Ford of Europe* v *Commission* Cases 225 and 229/82 [1982] ECR 3091.

There is no appeal available from the ECJ since it is the Supreme Court of the Community. Should a Member State fail to comply with a judgment against it, the Court may, under art 228 EC introduced under the TEU, impose a fine on that State. Article 39 of the Statute of the ECJ, however, does grant Member States, Community institutions and parties the right to contest a judgment in certain specified circumstances where it is prejudicial to their rights. Article 40 of the same Statute provides any party with the right to apply to the ECJ for guidance on the meaning or scope of a judgment that is in doubt. Finally, art 41 of the Statute provides that revision of a judgment may be made up to ten years after its delivery 'on discovery of a fact which is of such nature as to be a decisive factor' but that was not known at the time of the original judgment.

Finally, it should be noted that the ECJ does not consider itself bound by any formal doctrine of stare decisis or precedent. However, the ECJ has shown itself willing to follow its previous judgments to such an extent that it has created an informal doctrine of precedent, witnessed perhaps best in the acte clair doctrine on the preliminary reference procedure: art 234 EC. This will be considered in Chapter 6. In the unusual cases where the ECJ does alter its reasoning, it will clearly indicate the reason for doing so: see *Criminal Proceedings against Keck and Mithouard* Joined Cases C–267 and 268/91 [1993] ECR I–6097 (discussed in detail in Chapter 14).

## Role and methodology of the European Court of Justice

The ECJ has based much of its methodology on art 220 EC which provides that:

'... the Court of Justice shall ensure that in the interpretation and application of this Treaty, the law is observed.'

The ECJ has, therefore, justified extending its jurisdiction by referring to this Treaty provision. Examples of such action include granting the Parliament locus standi and extending its ability to review measures not listed in the Treaty. In other situations it has created general principles of EC law, such as proportionality and protection of human rights, and has then imposed such principles on the Community institutions and Member States. It has also provided the interpretation and definition of important aspects of EC law, such as that given to 'workers' entitled to free movement under art 39 EC: see Chapter 9.

It has been suggested that the ECJ has used art 220 to justify extending its competence beyond that envisaged and provided for under the Treaties, and has justified such action by claiming to protect the 'rule of law'. In other words, it claims to have an 'inherent' jurisdiction. The Court also uses a method of interpretation known as teleological or purposive interpretation. This means that they are not concerned with a literal, or even narrow historical purpose approach, but with one that examines the entire context of a particular measure. The result of such an approach may be one that is in fact entirely contrary to any literal interpretation, but one that meets the broader objectives of the Community, as identified by the Court. Lord Diplock described this method of interpretation in the following way:

'The European Court, in contrast to English courts, applies teleological rather than historical methods to the interpretation of the Treaties and other Community legislation. It seeks to give effect to what it conceives to be the spirit rather than the letter of the Treaties; sometimes, indeed, to an English judge, it may seem to the exclusion of the letter. It views the Communities as living and expanding organisms and the interpretation of the provisions of the Treaties as changing to match their growth:' *R v Henn and Darby* [1980] 2 WLR 597 (HL).

These two factors have combined over the years to place the European Court in what has been described as a strong and 'proactive' position. This is most evident when considering the jurisprudence of the ECJ in comparison to times when the political institutions were experiencing difficulties. Whilst the latter may have been struggling under the weight of disputes and cumbersome legislative processes, such as the Luxembourg Accords, the ECJ was attempting to enforce both the Treaties and secondary legislation in order to maximise the effectiveness of EC law. This is perhaps most controversially witnessed in the creation and extension of direct effect to various forms of secondary legislation, including directives, which will be dealt with in detail in Chapter 8.

The inherent jurisdiction claimed by the European Court, and its proactive approach to developing and enforcing EC law through purposive interpretation, have proved the basis of some considerable criticism. Rasmussen, the academic, argues that the proactive approach of the Court has gone too far and that it is pursuing its own vision rather than basing its argument in law. However, others have supported the activist approach of the European Court.

Another academic, Capelletti, argues that the ECJ should be considered as akin to a constitutional Supreme Court, which is therefore responsible for protecting the highest interests of the Community. He also argues that the Preamble and the first few articles of the EC Treaty provide the ECJ with the legitimacy to adopt such an approach. Former Advocate-General Jacobs follows a similar line when he argues that the ECJ is a 'Constitutional Court' that has merely developed constitutional principles. He argues that those who criticise the Court do so because they do not understand nor appreciate the nature of such a constitutional court. The most pragmatic support for the ECJ's approach, though, probably comes from Lord Howe (ex UK Foreign Secretary) who argues that since the ECJ was faced with an outline, or framework, Treaty it had no alternative but to operate in an activist manner.

There are some suggestions that this period has now come to a close: that the European Court has 'filled all the gaps' and that there is little need for any proactive approach. However, as we shall see throughout this text, there are still examples of the ECJ adopting an extremely activist approach in various aspects of EC law, such as sex discrimination, for example: see *Barber* v *Guardian Royal Exchange Assurance Group* Case C–262/88 [1990] ECR I–1889, discussed in Chapter 12.

## 2.7 The Court of First Instance (CFI)

The European Court of Justice has, to some extent, become a victim of its own success. During the 1980s it became clear that the ECJ had a tremendous workload which resulted in a large backlog of cases and a lengthy time delay for conclusions to be reached, or references to be sent back to the national courts. Such delays may, it was suggested, prevent the achievement of justice, ie that justice delayed is justice denied. The ECJ adopted the use of chambers to attempt to resolve the problems but this was not successful. One means of resolving the problem was authorisation for the creation of an additional court by the SEA 1986, which inserted art 225 into the EC Treaty. A Court of First Instance (CFI) was duly established by Council Decision 88/91 as an integral part of the ECJ, and its powers and jurisdiction are derived from those of the original Court. The creation of the new Court did not, therefore, alter the jurisdictional relationship between the European Court system and the individual national courts and tribunals of the Member States.

Article 225 was replaced when the TEU came into effect. Paragraph 1 provides that the CFI has jurisdiction to hear and determine, at first instance, certain classes of action or proceedings defined in accordance with the conditions specified in para 2.

The CFI is composed of 15 judges for terms of six years. The judges are not assisted by Advocates-General, although they can themselves be called upon to perform the task. The members of the Court are chosen from persons whose independence is beyond doubt and who possess the ability required for appointment to judicial office. The CFI elects its own President and appoints a Registrar. Generally, the CFI only sits in plenary session, with one of its members as Advocate-General, when the case is particularly complex. The majority of the time the CFI will hear cases in chambers of three or five.

The original jurisdiction of the CFI was strictly circumscribed by Council Decision 88/91. Three classes of action fell within the jurisdiction of the Court:

1. actions or proceedings brought by the staff of the Community against their employers (staff cases);
2. actions for annulment and actions for failure to act brought against the Commission by natural or legal persons and concerning the application of arts 50 and 57–66 ECSC. Such actions related to decisions issued by the Commission concerning levies, production controls, pricing practices, agreements and concentrations; and
3. actions for annulment or actions for failure to act brought by natural or legal persons against a Community institution and relating to the implementation and execution of Community competition policy.

In addition to these original grounds of jurisdiction, two additional grounds were added in 1993 to allow the CFI to review all actions brought by natural or legal persons under arts 230 and 232: see Council Decision 93/350 and Council Decision 94/149. Where these actions are accompanied by claims for damages, the CFI has no jurisdiction to hear the related claim. The CFI, at present, cannot hear cases brought by either Member States or Community institutions. Nor may the CFI answer questions submitted by way of preliminary references under art 234 EC – such questions are reserved for the ECJ, although this will change under the Treaty of Nice (see 2.10 below).

An unsuccessful plaintiff may appeal against a decision of the CFI to the ECJ on any one of three grounds:

1. lack of competence on the part of the CFI, such as the Court ruling on a matter that exceeded its jurisdiction;
2. a breach of an essential procedural requirement which has an adverse effect on the interests of the appellant; or
3. an infringement of Community law by the CFI, such as an error in the interpretation or application of the principles of Community law.

A substantial number of appeals have been heard by the ECJ, the majority of which concern decisions of the CFI on competition matters: for example, *Publishers Association* v *Commission* Case C–360/92 [1995] ECR I–23. The ECJ, as can be witnessed in *Hilti AG* v *Commission (No 2)* Case C–53/92P [1994] ECR I–667, has assiduously stood by the principle that it will refuse to consider appeals alleging errors of fact as opposed to errors of law.

Appeals must be brought within a period of two months from the publication of the decision of the CFI. Articles 49–54 of the Statute of the ECJ, together with arts 110–123 of the Rules of Procedure of the ECJ, have been inserted to regulate the matter of appeal between the two Courts.

An appeal does not suspend the decision of the CFI, unless an order to that effect is made by the ECJ. However, a decision by the CFI annulling a Community regulation does not take effect before the expiry of the two-month period permitted for the lodging of the appeal.

## Reform of the judicial system

Since the creation of the CFI, and increased transfer of jurisdiction to it, little has changed to the heavy workload of the ECJ. Cases may still take over two years to be heard. Article 221 EC permits an increase in the number of judges, which may be an obvious solution to the problem. However, it was realised that merely increasing the size of the Court, in a proportionate way to increased membership, would by no means resolve the on-going problems of delay.

Other suggestions for reform included the following:

1. The UK argued for the right to appeal to a court higher than the ECJ. This has not been accepted and it is difficult to see how it would have resolved any of the immediate problems; and

2. Lord Slynn, a former ECJ judge, suggested that the ECJ be transformed into a European High Court. This would in essence be a Supreme Court that would hear only very specific cases. He suggested that a second tier of four regional courts would then be established to deal with preliminary references. This would most certainly be a federal style legal system, but one to which the ECJ gave no support at the time.

The Treaty of Amsterdam made few changes to the judicial system. This may have been in part due to the comments of the European Court itself in a Reflection Group meeting set up before the IGC. In its report the ECJ strongly opposed the concept of reforming and transferring its jurisdiction. The ECJ considers itself as a strong maintainer of uniformity – an essential element in the success of EC law – and that to provide other courts with jurisdiction may eventually lead to the destruction of such uniformity. Indeed, the eventual result of the ToA was to expand the ECJ's jurisdiction even further, with provisions extending the ability of the Court to deal with matters under the third pillar, and to exercise a constrained preliminary reference jurisdiction on matters such as visas, asylum and immigration.

The need for reform was, however, recognised via the IGC preceding the Nice Summit, and the Treaty of Nice does provide for such reform: see section 2.10.

## 2.8 The Court of Auditors

The Court of Auditors was created by the Financial Provisions Treaty 1975 and attained institutional status under the TEU. It took over the responsibilities of the EC and Euratom Audit Board and the ECSC Auditor. It audits the accounts of the Community and of Community bodies, examines whether revenue and expenditure have been properly and lawfully received and incurred, checks that financial management has been sound and reports back to the Community institutions.

After Treaty of Nice amendments, the Court will be comprised one national from each Member State who is chosen from among persons who belong or have belonged in their respective countries to external audit bodies, or who is especially qualified for the office. Their independence must be beyond doubt. They are appointed for a term of six years by the Council. The members are eligible for reappointment. They elect a President from among their members for a term of three years, although they may be re-elected. The members must, in the general interests of the Community, be completely independent in the performance of their duties; they must neither seek nor take instructions from any government or from any other body. They must also refrain from any action incompatible with their duties.

A member of the Court of Auditors may be deprived of their office, or of their right to a pension or other benefits, only if the ECJ, at the request of the Court of Auditors, finds that they no longer fulfil the requisite conditions or meet the obligations arising from their office. The Council, acting by qualified majority, determines the conditions of employment of the President and the members of the Court of Auditors and, in particular, their salary, allowances and pensions. It also, by the same majority, determines any payment to be made instead of remuneration. The provisions of the Protocol on the Privileges and Immunities of the European Communities, applicable to the judges of the ECJ, also applies to the members of the Court of Auditors: art 247 EC.

The Court of Auditors examines the accounts of all revenue and expenditure of the Community; it also examines the accounts of all revenue and expenditure of all bodies set up by the Community in so far as the relevant constituent instrument does not preclude such examination. The Court of Auditors provides the Parliament and the Council with a statement of assurance as to the reliability of the accounts and the legality and regularity of the underlying transactions. It draws up an annual report after the end of each financial year, which is forwarded to the other institutions of the Community and published, together with replies of these institutions to the observations of the Court, in the Official Journal of the European Communities.

The Court of Auditors may also, at any time, submit observations, in the form of special reports, on specific questions and opinions at the request of one of the other institutions of the Community. It adopts its annual reports, special reports or opinions by a majority of its members. More generally, under art 248 EC, it assists the Parliament and the Council in exercising powers of control over implementation of the budget.

## 2.9 Additional bodies

The Economic and Social Committee (ECOSOC) plays a consultative role in the decision-making process: art 7(2) EC. The Council appoints its membership which, under art 257 EC, will be representative of a range of interests, such as trade unionists, workers, producers, farmers, carriers, dealers, craftsman, professionals and the general public. Article 258 provides that ECOSOC has a total membership of 224, with specified numbers representing each Member State. The Treaty does provide for consultation with ECOSOC, and should this not occur there will have been breach of an essential procedural requirement. ECOSOC may also be consulted by the Council, the Commission or the Parliament whenever they consider it appropriate. The members serve for a period of four years though this may be renewed. They must be independent and must act in the general interests of the Community.

The Committee of the Regions was established under the TEU to represent regional interests. The total membership and allocation between Member States is the same as for ECOSOC. The Council will appoint the members for a four-year, potentially renewable term. Members must, as with ECOSOC, be independent and represent the interests of the Community. Consultation of the Committee by the Council and the Commission is essential under certain provisions of the Treaty: for example, education under art 149(4); culture under art 151(5); and regional development under arts 161 and 162. Article 265 also provides the Parliament with the ability to consult the Committee.

Since the Treaty of Amsterdam, ECOSOC and the Committee of the Regions have separate organisational/administrative structures.

The European Central Bank (ECB) was created under a protocol attached to the TEU, which provided for a Central Bank for the European Union. The ECB had responsibility for EU monetary policy transferred to it on 1 January 1999. The ECB has the power to adopt regulations, take decisions, make recommendations and deliver opinions in relation to monetary policy, and issues European currency.

## 2.10 Institutional reform under the Treaty of Nice

The European Community's institutional structure was never designed to deal with even the current membership of 15 Member States; any problems currently experienced could only be made worse on further enlargement. For example, reaching consensus could become more difficult; a large geographical area would be included within the territory of the European Union, and a variety of additional languages and cultures need to be accommodated. Simultaneously the Community continues to expand its range of competencies into new fields. These two factors place a heavy burden on the existing institutional infrastructure of the Community. A Protocol was attached to the ToA providing for institutional reform, intending for the Community to deal with the problems in two stages (arts 1 and 2 of the Protocol). The first stage was to provide for a limited range of reforms prior to any further enlargement, whilst the second stage was to occur when membership exceeded 20 Member States. However, enlargement beyond the 20 was already being negotiated.

The process of enlargement itself occurs outside of the IGC framework and is achieved via individual negotiations with representatives of the applicant states. The eventual result of successful negotiations will be Treaties of Accession passed by a unanimous vote in the Council and with the assent of the European Parliament (see Chapter 1). Since this process was already underway, it was decided that the IGC following the ToA would deal primarily with institutional reform.

In June 1999 the meeting of the Cologne European Council reasserted the need for an IGC to deal with the institutional issues unresolved by the ToA. In December 1999 the Helsinki European Council, in its brief for the IGC, dropped the two-stage approach referred to above. Because of the proposed enlargement of the European Union, a one-stage process was adopted. Confirming the agenda for the IGC, the Helsinki European Council announced that efforts would concentrate on the following four aspects:

1. the weighting of votes in the Council;
2. the possible extension of qualified majority voting (QMV) in the Council;
3. the size and composition of the Commission; and
4. any other necessary amendments required to the institutions as a result of the ToA.

With this agenda, the IGC formally convened in February 2000 and completed its task on schedule for the December Nice Summit (see Chapter 1). To aid the process, a number of reports were produced. For example, opinions were provided by the Commission and the European Parliament in January 2000; a report on the impact of enlargement on the institutions was provided by a group of experts; and reports were given by the Member States themselves.

The main problems associated with each of the main institutions were identified as the following:

1. *The Commission* – the principle problem related to the size that the Commission would become on further enlargement, since each Member State must be represented. Suggestions for reform included strengthening the role of the President to aid organisation of the process. An additional issue, given the scandals in 1999, was to remove collective responsibility so that individual Commissioners could be made accountable. This was, however, not strongly supported. The Commission itself suggested the need for it to be comprised fewer members on a rotation basis or for it to be comprised of only one Commissioner from each Member State. There was also, in the opinion of the Commission, the need for reform of the organisational process.

2. *The Council* – the two main issues in relation to reform of the Council rested on the use of qualified majority voting and the allocation of votes between Member States. Both of these issues are highly contentious – in the case of the latter, no State wished to see the number of its votes reduced, since this in turn obviously reduced their influence within this important institution. In turn, there were concerns that the smaller Member States were over-represented, and could therefore wield disproportionate power within the infrastructure of the Community. The Commission suggested that the use of QMV should be extended so that it became the normal voting process used in decision-making within the EU. There would, however, be a range of exceptions to that rule, such as those decisions affecting institutions, taxation and social security, and derogations from the basic rules of the EC Treaty. In relation to the weighting of votes, the Commission suggested that a QMV decision would require only a simple majority of the Member States that represented a majority of the EU's population. This is also known as a 'double simple majority'. Although another suggestion was to merely re-weight the voting system.

3. *The Parliament* – the maximum size of the Parliament as provided for under art 189 EC is 700. This number would be exceeded if membership expanded.

4. *The European Court of Justice* – The Court already faces a huge workload and increased membership was recognised as liable to expand that workload even further. The suggested greater use of chambers would aid the Court, but was recognised as probably providing no long-term solution. It was suggested that there should be some ability to set up 'specialised courts' to deal with specific issues, before they were open to possible appeal to the CFI and/or the ECJ. Another suggestion was to provide the CFI with jurisdiction to hear preliminary references: art 234 EC.

The Nice Summit, held in December 2000 came to the following consensus on institutional reform. The Treaty of Nice was delayed in terms of coming into force as a result of the difficulties of securing ratification in, for example, Ireland.

## Voting weights in the Council

The complex question of reform of the voting system in the Council was to be the issue that preoccupied most of the discussions in the ICG prior to the drawing up of the Nice Treaty. With a rapidly expanding membership, the need for securing unanimity would become almost impossible, but many States were unwilling to agree to shift voting requirements to QMV since to do so removed an effective power of veto. The eventual agreement was codified in the Protocol on Enlargement of the European Union and Declaration 20 on Enlargement. The agreement is based on the premise that there will be 27 Member States and the changes will be introduced via an amended art 205 EC, which will become operative from 1 January 2005. The new formula is based on population size. The 12 candidate States (even though not all of them will accede at the same time) have been allocated votes. In descending order of the voting weights designated, the changes made to the existing Member States' voting weights, as summarised by Tillotson, are as follows:

| | *Population (million)* | *QMV weight* Old | *QMV weight* New |
|---|---|---|---|
| Germany | 82.0 | 10 | 29 |
| United Kingdom | 59.2 | 10 | 29 |
| France | 59.0 | 10 | 29 |
| Italy | 57.6 | 10 | 29 |
| Spain | 39.4 | 8 | 27 |
| The Netherlands | 15.8 | 5 | 13 |
| Greece | 10.5 | 5 | 12 |
| Belgium | 10.2 | 5 | 12 |
| Portugal | 10.0 | 5 | 12 |
| Sweden | 8.9 | 4 | 10 |
| Austria | 8.1 | 4 | 10 |
| Denmark | 5.3 | 3 | 7 |
| Finland | 5.2 | 3 | 7 |
| Ireland | 3.7 | 3 | 7 |
| Luxembourg | 0.4 | 2 | 4 |

The new Member States' weighting will be as follows:

| | | | |
|---|---|---|---|
| Poland | 38.7 | 0 | 27 |
| Romania | 22.5 | 0 | 14 |
| Czech Republic | 10.3 | 0 | 12 |
| Hungary | 10.1 | 0 | 12 |
| Bulgaria | 8.2 | 0 | 10 |
| Slovakia | 5.4 | 0 | 7 |
| Lithuania | 3.7 | 0 | 7 |
| Latvia | 2.4 | 0 | 4 |
| Slovenia | 2.0 | 0 | 4 |

|          | Population (million) | QMV weight Old | New |
|----------|----------------------|----------------|-----|
| Estonia  | 1.4                  | 0              | 4   |
| Cyprus   | 0.8                  | 0              | 4   |
| Malta    | 0.4                  | 0              | 3   |

For those areas of Community legislation requiring QMV by the Council of Ministers, the new situation will be as follows:

|                       | Current QMV 15 Member States | New QMV 27 Member States |
|-----------------------|------------------------------|--------------------------|
| Total numbers of votes | 87                          | 345                      |
| Qualified Majority    | 62                           | 258                      |
| Blocking Minority     | 26                           | 88                       |

Thus, the larger Member States have proportionately more of the votes. Under this new system, an affirmative majority vote will be reached when the positive votes cast represent 75.1 per cent of the total. Article 205(4) EC permits a Member State to request a check of the QMV result to ensure that it represents a minimum of 62 per cent of the population.

## The size of the Commission

The proposal to reduce the size of the Commission was unsuccessful. As an alternative, Germany, the UK, France, Italy and Spain will have only one Commissioner, instead of their current two, as from 1 January 2005 (art 213(1) EC will be amended). Once membership reaches a total of 27, art 213(1) will be amended again so that the total number of Commissioners is less than the number of Member States and the Council will approve both a system designed to secure rotational membership and the total membership of the Commission. The rationale for reducing the membership of the Commission below that of the Union itself is based on the notion that since the Commission does not in fact represent the interests of States at all, but the interests of the Community at large, there is, therefore, no need for each State to be permanently represented.

## The size of the Parliament

Current membership of the European Parliament is 626 MEPs. However, the ToA amended art 189 EC to increase the ceiling of membership to 700, and this was further increased by the Treaty of Nice to 732, all in preparation for expanding membership. There is, in addition, provision under art 2 of the Protocol on Enlargement to temporarily increase this ceiling during the years 2004–2009, providing for any further expansion that may take place in the next decade. Those seats allocated to new members will be as follows:

| | |
|---|---|
| Poland | 50 |
| Romania | 33 |
| Czech Republic | 20 |
| Hungary | 20 |
| Bulgaria | 17 |
| Slovakia | 13 |
| Lithuania | 12 |
| Latvia | 8 |
| Slovenia | 7 |
| Estonia | 6 |
| Cyprus | 6 |
| Malta | 5 |

The numbers of existing Member States seats will all be reduced, except in the cases of Germany and Luxembourg, and will be as follows (in alphabetical order):

| | *Current seats* | *Seats in 2004–2009* |
|---|---|---|
| Austria | 21 | 17 |
| Belgium | 25 | 22 |
| Denmark | 16 | 13 |
| Finland | 16 | 13 |
| France | 87 | 72 |
| Germany | 99 | 99 |
| Greece | 25 | 22 |
| Ireland | 15 | 12 |
| Italy | 87 | 72 |
| Luxembourg | 6 | 6 |
| Netherlands | 31 | 25 |
| Portugal | 25 | 22 |
| Spain | 64 | 50 |
| Sweden | 22 | 18 |
| United Kingdom | 87 | 72 |

## Increased use of QMV

The use of QMV has been expanded over the years, and it is to be extended further in the future as a practical solution to the problem of having to gain unanimity from 27 Member States. However, a number of existing Member States expressed their concern over the loss of unanimity in certain areas. As a result, the need for unanimity will probably be in harmonisation of internal taxation; social security provisions facilitating free movement; free movement of professionals; regulation of asylum seekers; and trade in services within the Common Commercial Policy.

## *Reform of the legal system*

The ever-expanding workload of the ECJ has been a controversial issue for a
considerable time, and was not to any great extent relieved by the creation of the
Court of First Instance under the SEA – the last significant reform to the
Community's judicial system. The Treaty of Nice, however, makes what may be a
number of very significant changes that can be summarised as follows:

1.  In general terms, rather than providing organisational and procedural rules under
    the Treaty, which is cumbersome to change, such rules will be contained in the
    Statute, providing the judicial system with a greater degree of flexibility to cope
    with the demands placed upon it.
2.  There will be the creation of a new 'layer' in the system, with the establishment
    of specialised judicial panels, which will exist below the CFI and the ECJ: art
    225a EC. These will be able to determine at first instance what the article
    describes as 'certain forms of action' and 'proceedings brought in certain cases'.
    Exactly what these are will be determined by the Council. Panel decisions will be
    subject to appeal to the CFI.
3.  The jurisdiction of the CFI will be extended so that it can hear the majority of
    direct actions, although enforcement action under arts 226–227 EC will remain in
    the hands of the ECJ. The CFI will also hear appeals from the new panels,
    which will in turn be subject to review by the ECJ, but only when there is
    'serious risk of the unity or consistency of Community law begin affected'. More
    significantly, the CFI will be granted the jurisdiction to hear preliminary
    references in areas to be laid down by the Statute: art 225(3) EC. Article 225
    does recognise that in certain circumstances a preliminary ruling may be taken
    over by the ECJ. These circumstances include where the CFI considers the case
    as one 'likely to affect the unity or consistency of Community law'. Alternatively,
    the ECJ may review a CFI reference where there is 'serious risk of the unity of
    consistency of Community law being affected'.
4.  A new Protocol on the Statute of the Court of Justice will provide for
    organisation and procedure.
5.  Amendment to art 221 EC will provide that the total number of ECJ judges will
    be the same as the number of Member States.
6.  Amended art 20 of the Statute of the Court provides that Advocates-General are
    no longer required to produce an opinion in a case where the Court believes
    there is no new point of law.
7.  The size of chambers will no longer be required to be of three, five or seven
    members, but will be left to the Court to determine for itself under the Statute
    of the Court. The Treaty of Nice also provides for the Court to sit as a 'Grand
    Chamber'.
8.  The CFI will be comprised at least one judge from each Member State, implying
    that there could be more if required, unlike the ECJ: art 224 EC.

Reform of the judicial system has long been mooted, and these reforms introduced by the Treaty of Nice may go some considerable way towards relieving the workload of the ECJ. The reforms also strengthen the federal characteristics of the Community's judicial system. However, there has been a mixed reaction to the changes. The academics Dashwood and Johnston state that the changes do not introduce anything radical but instead 'put in place a framework within which further progress can undoubtedly be made'. Weiler rather negatively comments that 'Europe continues to drive in its rusty and trusted 1950 model with the steering wheel firmly in the hands of the Court of Justice'. On a more positive note, Craig and de Burca describe the creation of the specialised panels (see above) as the 'most significant steps taken to reform the EU judicial system since the establishment of the CFI itself'.

# 3

# The Sources of Community Law

3.1 Introduction

3.2 The primary sources

3.3 Secondary legislation

3.4 Tertiary sources

## 3.1 Introduction

The Community Treaties themselves do not define what the sources of Community law are. The Treaties give instruction to the European Court of Justice in broad terms, calling on it only to ensure that in the interpretation and application of the Treaties 'the law' is observed: art 220 EC. The sources of Community law, though, may be classified into three categories, namely primary, secondary and tertiary sources.

There are two primary sources of Community law:

1. the Treaties creating the European Union; and
2. treaties entered into by the European Community with third states.

The Community Treaties, as amended from time to time, form the 'constitution' of the organisation and are the ultimate source of legal authority. International agreements entered into the European Community with third states, if directly enforceable, form a second category of rules that may be classified as a primary source mainly because such rules prevail over secondary and tertiary sources.

However, the Treaties provide only a framework, which requires further amplification. This task belongs to the Community institutions. Article 249 EC identifies the secondary sources of Community law, which consist of acts of the Community institutions. These are alternatively known as secondary legislation, and consist of the following:

1. regulations;
2. directives; and
3. decisions.

In addition, art 249 identifies two further secondary sources that are not legally binding:

4. recommendations; and
5. opinions.

As a residual category, there are a number of tertiary sources, the legal authority for which lies not in the Community Treaties, but mainly in the jurisprudence of the European Court. These sources may fill any legal vacuum created by omissions in the Treaties. The following are the most significant tertiary sources:

1. acts adopted by the representatives of the governments of the Member States meeting in the Council;
2. the case law of the ECJ;
3. national laws of the Member States;
4. general principles of law; and
5. principles of public international law.


## 3.2 The primary sources

### *The Treaties establishing the European Community*

These Treaties are those establishing the Community, as supplemented or amended by other treaties and acts, including the Treaties of Accession, the Treaty on European Union, the Treaty of Amsterdam and its protocols and the Treaty of Nice. In the United Kingdom these various agreements are included in the concept of 'European Community Treaties' under the European Communities Act 1972, and a special procedure is laid down for the participation of the UK therein. Within the framework of Community law, the Treaties are 'self-executing'. This means that they become law on ratification by the Member States. Generally, there is no derogation available from the obligations imposed by them, unless such grounds are provided.

The Treaties define the territorial scope of their application, but they have also been held in some circumstances to have extra-territorial effect. In *Ahlström and Others* v *Commission (Re Wood Pulp Cartel)* Cases 89, 104, 114, 116, 117 and 125–129/85 [1994] ECR I–99 the ECJ upheld fines imposed on suppliers of wood pulp whose registered offices were in Canada, Sweden, Finland and the USA. The basis of this decision was the so-called 'effects principle' of international law, which permits states to extend the jurisdiction of their courts to acts that have effects within their territory. In this case, the fixing of prices of the wood pulp on the world market was the anti-competitive practice being attacked: see Chapter 16.

## *The treaties entered into by the European Community with other States*

Each of the three principal European Community Treaties authorises the European Community to enter into international agreements with third States, or groups of States, as well as with certain types of international organisations. The nature and contents of the agreements must fall within the scope of the competence of the European Community and commonly take the form of free trade agreements and association agreements.

Since association agreements are a preliminary step towards membership of the European Communities, these treaties often contain detailed arrangements and rights, even for individuals. Similarly, a number of free trade agreements contain provisions concerning the customs treatment of goods flowing between parties. When the terms of such agreements are sufficiently precise, they may be capable of providing a source of effective principles of Community law: see *Demirel* v *Stadt Schwabisch GmbH* Case 12/86 [1987] ECR 3719.

In order to constitute a formal source of Community law, capable of being enforced, the provisions relied on must be capable of direct effect. This concept will be explained in further detail later (see Chapter 8), but for present purposes it should be noted that treaties entered into with third states by the European Community may be capable of having such effects. In the case of *Hauptzollamt Mainz* v *Kupferburg* Case 104/81 [1982] ECR 3641 a German importer was charged duties on imports of Portuguese port which were later reduced by the German Finance Court which applied art 21 of the trade agreement between Portugal and the European Community. This agreement prohibited, on a reciprocal basis, discriminatory internal taxation between imported and domestic producers. The German tax authorities appealed against the decision, and a preliminary reference was made to the European Court for a ruling.

The ECJ held that the terms of the agreement could be given direct effect if the following conditions were satisfied:

1. the provision being relied on was sufficiently precise and unconditional;
2. the provision was capable of conferring rights on individuals; and
3. national courts or tribunals could enforce the obligation created.

These requirements were also discussed in the case of *SZ Sevince* v *Staatssecretaris van Justitie* Case 192/89 [1990] ECR I–3461. This case concerned the legal effects of a series of decisions made by a Council of Association established under the Turkish-EC Association Agreement and Additional Protocol. The applicant relied on a number of provisions of these decisions to challenge an order of a Dutch court deporting him. This order, it was claimed, was contrary to the right of free movement of persons contained in the relevant provisions of the Council decisions.

The ECJ held that a provision in an agreement concluded by the European Community with a non-Member State must be regarded as being directly effective when, regard being had to its wording and to the purpose and nature of the agreement itself, the provision contains a clear and precise obligation. This obligation could not, however, be subject in its implementation or effect to the adoption of any subsequent measures. In other words, the same criteria that apply to the direct effect of treaties apply to a determination as to whether a decision of an organisation to which the European Community is a party has direct effect.

There have been suggestions that the Community should make an attempt to consolidate all of its fundamental treaty rules into just one document. Advocate-General Jacobs made the following comment in the mid-1990s on how this could be achieved:

> '... strip out from the Maastricht morass those basic Treaty provisions governing the competences of the Community, the competences of the institutions and the fundamental principles of the Community legal order, which could then be incorporated in a basic text as an incipient constitution, and one which could be amended only by a special procedure ...'

The response to this in the ToA was to renumber the EC Treaty articles in an effort to simplify what had become a complex system. Whether this solution will be successful in the long term remains to be seen.

## 3.3 Secondary legislation

The expression 'secondary legislation' is a collective term. It comprises all the acts of the two 'law-making' bodies, the Council and the Commission, which they can adopt under the terms of the Treaties in their capacity as European Community institutions, and which may create enforceable rights and obligations for Community subjects. Article 249 EC provides that:

> 'In order to carry out their task and in accordance with the provisions of this Treaty, the European Parliament acting jointly with the Council, the Council and the Commission, shall make regulations, issue directives, take decisions, make recommendations or deliver opinions.'

The secondary nature of this legislation implies that it is derived from, limited by, and hierarchically subordinate to, the primary sources. This means, in general, that a secondary Community law, whatever its title or nature, cannot legally have the aim and the effect of amending, repealing or altering the scope of a primary Treaty provision. It also means, in particular, that the law-making power of the two institutions is subject to two important limitations, non-observance of which entails the invalidity of illegality of the resulting act and renders it liable to annulment by the European Court. Hence, the institutions may only act in order to carry out their tasks in accordance with the provisions of the Treaties, and must do so within the limits of their respective powers.

## *Regulations*

According to art 249 a regulation 'shall have general application. It shall be binding in its entirety and directly applicable in all Member States.' In substance, regulations are of a truly legislative nature, creating rights and obligations directly and uniformly applicable throughout the whole European Community, both to the Member States and to individuals within the Member States. Regulations enter into force on the date specified within them. Under art 249 regulations have the following four characteristics:

### General applicability

It follows from the essentially legislative nature of a regulation that it is applicable not to an individual case or situation, nor to a limited number of defined or identifiable persons, but to objectively determined situations, and involves immediate legal consequences in all Member States for categories of persons defined in a general and abstract manner.

### Binding in their entirety

This distinguishes a regulation from a directive. A Member State must give effect to a regulation in its entirety, rather than merely being bound, as under a directive, to achieve the result by any chosen method.

### Direct applicability

Briefly, direct applicability has three aspects in relation to regulations:

1.  Regulations are incorporated automatically into the law of each Member State and the legal force of the regulation lies in the measure itself, independent of any attempt at implementing legislation: *Bussone* v *Ministry of Agriculture* Case 31/78 [1978] ECR 2429;
2.  Generally speaking, regulations are automatically implemented, and to try to implement one would in itself constitute a breach of Community law. The rationale for this is that implementation measures may destroy the uniformity provided for by use of a regulation. Occasionally, though, a regulation will require a Member State to enact supplementary national legislation, for example, to provide penalties or sanctions for failure to respect the terms of the regulation: *Anklagemyndigheden* v *Hansen and Son* Case C–326/88 [1990] ECR 2911.
3.  Regulations may create individual rights and obligations, enforceable in national courts.

### Applicability in all Member States

Community law requires the simultaneous and uniform application of regulations in all Member States. Consequently, Member States are prohibited from adopting any method of implementation that may jeopardise such application and which would result in different or discriminatory treatment of European Community citizens according to national criteria: see *Variola* v *Amministrazione delle Finanze* Case 34/73 [1973] ECR 981.

In addition to these four characteristics, it follows from the fundamental principle of the supremacy of the EC legal system as a whole that directly applicable provisions of regulations must enjoy the same priority over the national laws of the Member State as directly applicable provisions of the Treaty: see Chapter 8 for discussion of the supremacy of Community law. Article 253 EC indicates that regulations (along with directives and decisions) must be reasoned and refer to any proposals or opinions which were required to be obtained. Failure to comply with this requirement may lead to an annulment action under art 230: see Chapter 5.

## Directives

The EC Treaty places two different courses of action at the institutions' disposal to enable them to carry out the European Community's tasks. One is for them to lay down, in direct implementation of the Treaties, uniform common rules, directly applicable throughout the Community. For this the legislative means is a regulation.

The second is for them to call upon the Member States to exercise their own legislative powers, either for the purpose of adapting their laws to common standards laid down by the institutions (mainly in areas where the diversity of national laws could adversely affect the establishment or functioning of the Common Market) or for the purpose of carrying out the obligations arising from the Treaties. For this, the legislative form is the directive, which accordingly provides an indirect means for the implementation of Treaty objectives.

While a regulation is applicable to both Member States and individuals, a directive is primarily intended to create legal relationships between the European Community and the Member State to which it is addressed. It is binding upon those States, but only as to the result to be achieved. The national authorities retain the right to select the appropriate form and method to achieve the result. Directives must be notified to those to whom they are addressed, and take effect upon such notification: art 191(3) EC.

Directives, as we shall see, may also be capable of creating rights for individuals should they fail to be implemented or are done so incorrectly. This will be discussed in detail in Chapters 7 and 8.

## Decisions

These represent perhaps one of the most versatile forms of secondary legislation. The term may describe a legally binding measure taken in a specified form and having specific legal effects, as well as non-binding informal acts laying down a programme, a declaration of intention or guidelines which, in order to generate legal effects, must be implemented by further legislative measures. Its most striking feature is that it is binding only upon those to whom it is addressed. A decision therefore is characterised by the limited number of persons, identified or identifiable, to whom it is applicable.

## Recommendations and opinions

These differ from the other secondary forms of legislation in that they have no binding force. They may be issued by the Council and the Commission on any matter within the Community Treaties, at any time when the institutions consider it necessary, and not only upon an express authorisation granted in specific cases. Although not binding in law, recommendations and opinions may carry significant political and/or moral weight.

It is interesting to note that the European Court insists that the different acts under art 249 EC are distinguishable by reference to their nature, and not their form or title. In the case of *International Fruit Company* v *Commission* Cases 41–44/70 [1971] ECR 411 the measure in question had been labelled as a regulation. The applicant company, however, argued that in reality it was merely a set of decisions. The ECJ examined the measure and concluded that the so-called 'regulation' was

'… not a provision of general application within the meaning of … [art 249] of the Treaty, but must be regarded as a conglomeration of individual decisions taken by the Commission under the guise of a regulation …'

The consequences of such a conclusion may be serious, since the ability of the individual to rely on the provisions or to challenge its validity etc will depend on the nature of the measure. For example, it will be easier for an individual to persuade the European Court to challenge the validity of a decision than it would a regulation.

## Publication and notification

Originally, only regulations were required to be published in the Official Journal. Directives and decisions merely had to be notified to the persons to whom they were addressed, although in practice they were often also published in the Journal. The TEU introduced the need for Council and Commission directives to be published, if they are addressed to all Member States. Further, all regulations, directives and decisions jointly adopted by the Parliament and the Council must be published. All other directives, decisions, recommendations and opinions are published in the Journal, unless COREPER decides that this is not necessary.

If an instrument is published in the Official Journal, it will come into force on the date specified within it or, if there is no such date, 20 days following the date of publication. Those instruments that have to be notified to those to whom they are addressed will take effect upon that notification.

If there is a failure to publish, or indeed notify, the act will continue to exist, in other words it will not be declared invalid or annulled, but there may be some affect on its legal consequences: see, for examples, *Hauptzollamt Bielefeld* v *König* Case 185/73 [1974] ECR 607 and *ICI* v *Commission* Case 48/69 [1972] ECR 619.

## 3.4 Tertiary sources

### *Acts adopted by the representatives of the governments of the Member States meeting in Council*

The Council exercises two different types of function. Primarily, it is a Community institution set up under the Treaties and endowed with specific powers and competencies, as we have already seen. The Council, though, is also the setting in which the representatives of the governments of the Member States concentrate their activities and decide on principles and methods of joint action. When it is acting in its first function, as an organ of the Community, its measures fall within the concept of secondary legislation as defined under art 249 EC. However, the Council does not have the necessary authority under the basic Treaties to pass Community measures when it is acting as a meeting of the representatives of the governments of the Member States. Such acts that are adopted are alternatively known as 'decisions and agreements adopted by the representatives of the governments of the Member States meeting in Council'.

The legal nature of such acts is somewhat ambiguous, falling within both Community law – and forming a source of it– and international law. However, the European Court has considered such acts in its jurisprudence. In the case of *Commission* v *Council (Re ERTA)* Case 22/70 [1971] ECR 263 the ECJ dealt with a Resolution adopted by the Member States acting together in the Council. The Resolution, adopted in March 1970, provided for agreement to co-ordinate their approaches in negotiation for the conclusion of a European Road Transport Agreement. The Commission brought proceedings for judicial review of the measure and some debate arose as to its legal nature. The ECJ concluded that, whilst art 249 (formerly art 189) did not include such acts within its terms, it should not be considered an exhaustive list of the types of acts that were capable of legally binding effects. Consequently, the ECJ held that the Resolution was capable of having legal effects and therefore the Commission could challenge its validity.

In *Luxembourg* v *European Parliament* Case 230/81 [1983] ECR 255 Luxembourg challenged the Parliament's decision to establish its seat in Strasbourg and Brussels. The ECJ in this case attributed to decisions of the representatives of the Member States the same legislative effect as a decision of the Council.

The advantage of this form of decision-making is that it provides a quick and simple way for the Member States to take action in areas outside European Community competences. At the same time, it has the disadvantage of enabling the Council to take action in disregard of the conditions and procedures laid down by the Treaties, in situations where in reality it might have acted as a European Community institution. This has the potential to upset the institutional balance within the Community.

## The case law of the European Court of Justice

Technically, unlike the position in common law countries, in a Continental civil law system the doctrine of the binding force of precedent does not apply. Since the European Court is modelled upon the Continental courts, it is generally not bound by its own previous decisions. However, it may be expected that wherever the ECJ has given a leading judgment/preliminary ruling it will be unlikely to depart from it in subsequent cases without strong reasons, even though it retains the right to do so. Certainly the case law of the ECJ, as we shall see throughout the remaining chapters of this book, reveals a remarkable consistency of adjudication, on both substantive and procedural issues. In addition, the ECJ's 'manipulation' of the preliminary reference procedure (see Chapter 6) provides that the decisions of the ECJ have an effect going beyond the individual case at hand. Indeed, as we shall see, the ECJ has created an informal doctrine of precedent on which national courts may rely.

## The national laws of the Member States

The division between national and Community powers and competences inevitably prevents the national laws of the Member States from forming a formal source of Community law. Nevertheless, there are two specific situations where the Court does apply, or at least calls upon, rules and concepts of municipal law.

The first is where Community law, expressly or by implication, refers to the laws of the Member States. This is normally the case where the nationality, personal status or legal status of individuals, or the status, legal capacity or representation of legal persons or of entities without legal personality, is in question. The relevant municipal law will be applied to determine whether the condition is fulfilled. The second is where Community law has developed in the legal systems of the Member States, and here the ECJ turns for guidance to the laws of those states, particularly where there is any gap in Community law. It could be suggested that the Court has developed a technique whereby Community law is developed by using national law as a 'building block', and the national law, in turn, may also be further developed. In addition, as Koopmans, a former judge of the ECJ, suggests, general principles may be 'discovered by the Court of Justice, on the basis of the existing national legal systems, but they then "travel back" to these same systems with a kind of added force'.

Such a 'technique' can be seen in *Transocean Marine Paint* v *Commission* Case 17/74 [1974] ECR 1063, a case involving the competition law of the EC. The Advocate-General was of the opinion that there may have been a 'right to be heard' (audi alteram partem) and ordered an investigation into the national laws of the

Member States to identify whether they too accepted this principle of 'natural justice'. The investigation revealed that the rule was acknowledged and accepted in the English, Scots, French and Belgian legal systems, as well as that of Luxembourg. However, he also identified that Italy and The Netherlands had 'no general principle of law requiring an administrative authority to inform those concerned of its proposals so as to enable them to comment'. The Advocate-General's opinion concluded with the following statement:

> '... review ... of the laws of the Member States must, I think, on balance, lead to the conclusion that the right to be heard forms part of those rights which "the law" referred to in [art 220] of the Treaty upholds, and which ... it is the duty of this Court to ensure the observance of.'

## General principles of law

Except for the single case of non-contractual liability (art 288 EC), the ECJ is not directed by any explicit Treaty provision to apply the general principles of law in deciding disputes submitted to it. However, it is generally recognised that the law the Court is directed to apply includes the general principles of law of the legal systems of the Member States, which the Court will incorporate into the common law of the Community. A number of such general principles of law have been recognised.

### Protection of fundamental human rights

The original Treaty of Rome included no explicit reference to the protection of fundamental human rights, although there is reference, for example, to non-discrimination on the basis of nationality: art 12 EC. This was perhaps not an oversight as such, but perhaps more of a reflection of the times in which the Treaty was drafted, or indeed a result of the fact that it was primarily economic based. Since then Community law has expanded to include a large range of social aspects and most certainly touches the lives of every citizen of the European Union. The Community, though, was somewhat slow in recognising the need for protection of human rights.

In *Stauder* v *City of Ulm* Case 29/69 [1969] ECR 419 an art 234 EC preliminary reference was made by a German court, hearing a claim that a European Community measure involved an infringement of fundamental human rights. The ECJ gave an interpretation that was both consistent with Community law and, in an implicit manner, with the protection of fundamental human rights. Its response, though, was somewhat terse and brief – para 7 of the judgment states that 'the provision at issue contains nothing capable of prejudicing the fundamental human rights enshrined in the general principles of Community law and protected by the Court.'

In *Internationale Handelsgesellschaft GmbH* v *EVGF* Case 11/70 [1970] ECR 1125 the judgment included the explicit comment that:

'... respect for fundamental human rights forms an integral part of general principles of law protected by the Court of Justice. The protection of such rights, while inspired by the constitutional traditions common to the Member States, must be ensured within the framework of the structure and objectives of the [European Community].'

In the case of *Nold KG* v *Commission* Case 4/73 [1974] ECR 491 the European Court again explicitly stated that, in addition to the 'constitutional traditions' of the Member States, there were 'international treaties for the protection of human rights' as guidelines which should be followed (see also *Hauer* v *Land Rheinland-Pfaltz* Case 44/79 [1979] ECR 3727).

The most obvious international treaty relevant to the Member States of the Community is the European Convention for the Protection of Human Rights and Fundamental Freedoms (ECHR), to which all Member States of the Community are party.

The importance of respecting human rights may also be seen now in the Treaties. Article 6(1) EC, as amended by the ToA, states that:

'The Union is founded on the principles of liberty, democracy, respect for human rights and fundamental freedoms, and the rule of law, principles which are common to the Member States.'

Further, the Council now has the ability to suspend the voting rights of any Member State found to be in breach of these principles: art 7(2) TEU, 309 EC and 204 Euratom.

In relation to the ECHR, art 6(2) TEU provided that the ECJ may apply the principles of the Convention insofar as they may relate to matters that are within the competence of the Community. It states that the Community shall

'... respect fundamental rights, as guaranteed by the European Convention for the Protection of Fundamental Freedoms signed in Rome on 4 November 1950 and as they result from the constitutional traditions common to Member States, as general principles of Community law.'

However, the ECJ concluded in *Re the Accession of the Community to the ECHR* Opinion 2/94 [1996] ECR I–1759 that the Community lacked the necessary competence to actually accede to the Convention itself:

'Accession to the Convention would ... entail a subsequent change in the present Community system for the protection of human rights in that it would entail the entry of the Community into a distinct international system as well as the integration of all the provisions of the Convention into the Community legal order.

Such a modification of the system for the protection of human rights in the Community, with equally fundamental institutional implications for the Community and for the Member States, would be of constitutional significance ... It could be brought about only by way of Treaty amendment.'

In December 1999 the Helsinki European Council issued a 'millennium declaration'. This asserts that the European Union is based on democracy and the rule of law, and that all of its citizens have shared common values including freedom, tolerance, equality, solidarity and cultural diversity. On 3 and 4 June of the same year, the Cologne European Council decided that the Council, Parliament and Commission would draw up an EU Charter of Fundamental Rights. One purpose behind this decision was to provide a more 'visible' form of protection for citizens of the Union; 'the present system of protecting fundamental rights is not immediately visible to the European public, as it is rooted in Court decisions taken on the basis of the general principles of Community law.'

At an extraordinary European Council on Justice and Home Affairs, held in Tampere in October 1999, the composition and working methods of the body responsible for the drawing up of the Draft Charter were laid down. This Convention comprised the 15 representatives of the Heads of State or Government, a representative of the Commission President, 16 Members of the European Parliament and some 30 national Members of Parliament. The Convention elected Roman Herzog as its President.

The Convention met with numerous non-governmental organisations before publishing a draft Charter containing 52 articles on the 28 July 2000. The Draft Charter appears to have been inspired by a range of sources protecting human rights such as: the European Convention on Human Rights; the European Social Charter of the Council; the Community Charter of the Fundamental Social Rights of Workers 1989; European Court of Justice rulings; ECHR rulings; Community legislation; common constitutional traditions; and various international conventions.

There are six fundamental values expressed in the Charter: dignity, freedom, equality, solidarity, citizenship and justice. Certain rights that were originally envisaged as relevant or worthy of inclusion were not, such as the right to work and the right to an equitable wage. This was because it was concluded that they were inappropriate since they set policy objectives. Other rights, such as the right to a minimum wage, were not included since they were considered implicit in other provisions of the Charter. However, the Charter does include a range of rights not originally thought of by the Convention when it began work. These include the following: freedom of scientific research, freedom to conduct a business, protection of intellectual property, the right to good administration, children's rights, access to services of general economic interest, protection in the event of unfair dismissal, equality before the law and equality for men and women.

The majority of rights in the Charter are available to everyone, although there are some that are specifically granted to certain categories of people, such as children and workers. In addition, European Union citizens are specifically granted a range of rights, such as to settle, to have access to social security benefits and welfare assistance, and to have diplomatic and consular protection. Finally, citizens of the Union and non-Member States who reside within the EU are granted rights, such as the right of access to institution documents, the right to refer cases to the Ombudsman and the right to petition the European Parliament.

Interestingly, instead of including specific restrictions in relation to each or any right, the Charter includes a 'horizontal' article (art 52) providing the scope and limits of the guaranteed rights. Article 52(1) will apply to almost all of the rights and reads as follows:

> 'Any limitation on the exercise of the rights and freedoms recognised by this Charter must be provided for by law and respect the essence of those rights and freedoms. Subject to the principle of proportionality, limitations may be made only if they are necessary and genuinely meet objectives of general interest recognised by the Union or the need to protect the rights and freedoms of others.'

In September 2000, the Commission issued a communication offering its support, in principle, of the Draft Charter, stating that the European Union 'must henceforth seek its roots in the fundamental human values common to all European countries. This is a necessary precondition if the people of Europe are to place their trust in the continuing task of European integration.' The Commission believes that the Draft Charter provides 'genuine value' since it codifies rights previously contained within a wide range of national and international instruments. It also breaks with the traditional approach of separating political and civil rights from economic and social rights, a distinction that has traditionally prevailed in both European and international documents.

The Commission, however, also produced a communication in October 2000, which concluded that the Charter will 'sooner or later' have to be incorporated in the Treaties, either by the insertion of a new title headed 'Fundamental Rights', or in a protocol annexed to the Treaties. This statement has caused some political difficulties, for example the UK believes that the Charter should be merely a political declaration.

At the Nice Summit in December 2000 the European Council 'welcomed' the Charter. The question remaining is whether it will remain merely declaratory or whether it will be transformed into a legally binding Charter. This issue was not dealt with at the Summit. The legal status of the Charter will be a matter for future negotiations, although the European Court will probably make reference to it.

## Proportionality

This principle involves the notion that administrative measures must be proportionate to the aim to be achieved. It can be applied both in the case of legislation (for example, whether a regulation has gone beyond what was contained in the enabling provision) and in the review of the actions taken by the Community institutions.

The principle was first mooted in the *Internationale Handelsgesellschaft* case (above), where German law was cited as providing that 'the individual should not have his freedom of action limited beyond the degree necessary for the public interest'. It was expanded upon in *Balkan Imp-Exp GmbH v Hauptzollampt Berlin-Packhof* Case 5/73 [1973] ECR 1091. In *R v Intervention Board, ex parte Man (Sugar) Ltd* Case 181/84 [1985] ECR 2889 Man, a British sugar trader, submitted tenders to the Intervention Board, which regulated the export of sugar to non-

Community states. However, Man applied for the export licences late. The four-hour delay resulted in their losing all of the securities they had lodged with a bank. The bank, acting according to the provisions of Regulation 1880/83, declared the securities forfeit. Man argued that the loss, which came to £1,670,370, was disproportionate to the 'offence' committed, and applied for judicial review on the basis that the Regulation should be invalid because of its disproportionate effects. Under the preliminary reference procedure, the European Court stated that 'the automatic forfeiture of the entire security ... must be considered too drastic a penalty in relation to the export licence's function of ensuring the sound management of the market in question.' The Court also stated that the relevant measure of the Regulation was 'invalid inasmuch as it prescribes forfeiture of the entire security as the penalty for failure to comply with the time-limit.'

The principle has also been applied in non-economic matters and in cases concerning the actions taken by the Member States in derogating from the basic rules of the Treaty. In *Lynne Watson and Alessandro Belmann* Case 118/75 [1976] ECR 1185 it was found that the suggested deportation of Watson from Italy by the authorities was a measure disproportionate to the crime committed, which was failure to comply with administrative requirements. This conclusion can also be seen as an example of the jealous way in which the ECJ protects the basic rights provided in the Treaty, in this case free movement of workers under art 39 EC. (See also *R* v *Pieck* Case 157/79 [1980] ECR 2171, discussed in Chapter 11.)

The ECJ has explained its role in scrutinising the acts of Community institutions and Community legislation in terms of requiring them to be proportionate. It stated in *United Kingdom* v *Council* Case C–84/94 [1996] ECR I–5755 on Council Directive 93/104, the Working Time Directive, that:

'... in order to establish whether a provision of Community law complies with that principle, it must be ascertained whether the means which it employs are suitable for the purpose of achieving the desired objective and whether they do not go beyond what is necessary to achieve it.'

However, in relation to judicial review the Court stated:

'... the Council must be allowed a wide discretion in an area which ... involves the legislature in making social policy choices and requires it to carry out complex assessments. Judicial review of the exercise of that discretion must therefore be limited to examining whether it has been vitiated by manifest error or misuse of powers, or whether the institution concerned has manifestly exceeded the limits of its discretion.'

## Legal certainty

In *Da Costa en Schaake* v *Nederlandse Belastingadministratie* Cases 28–30/62 [1963] ECR 31 Advocate-General Lagrande stated:

'The rule that res judicata binds only the particular case is the weapon which permits the Court to do this [alter its view of the law]. Of course they should only use this weapon prudently, on pain of destroying legal certainty.'

Thus, legal certainty was established as one of the general principles of Community law. The principle was invoked by the Court in *Defrenne* v *Sabena (No 2)* Case 43/75 [1976] ECR 455 as a major grounds for refusing to allow retrospective direct effect to art 141 EC (formerly art 119).

The principle would appear to embody the concept of respect for legitimate expectations and the principle that European Community measures may not have retrospective effect: see *Council* v *European Parliament* Case 34/86 [1986] ECR 2155 and *R* v *Kirk* Case 63/83 [1984] ECR 2689. In *Officier van Justitie* v *Kolpinghuis Nijmegen BV* Case 80/86 [1987] ECR 3969 the Court stated that national courts must interpret national law to comply with EC law in a manner that was 'limited by the general principles of law which form part of Community law, and in particular, the principles of legal certainty and non-retroactivity.'

It must be noted, however, that where the purpose to be achieved demands it, and where the legitimate expectations of concerned parties are respected, a measure may be held to be retroactive: *G R Amylum NV* v *Council* Case 108/81 [1982] ECR 3107.

### Protection of legitimate expectations

Advocate-General Trabucchi in *Deuka* Case 5/75 [1975] ECR 759 explained that 'trust in the Community's legal order must be respected' and consequently legitimate expectation became the basis of a rule of interpretation. However, it may in addition, be a ground for annulment. In *Mulder* v *Minister of Agriculture and Fisheries* Case 120/86 [1988] ECR 2321 the Court held that a farmer entering into an undertaking not to supply milk for five years to the market organisation which distributed milk throughout the European Community was entitled to resume production upon the expiry of the commitment. The European legislation that deprived the farmer of this right was void on the ground that it impinged upon the principle of legitimate expectation. Therefore, the principle of legitimate expectation facilitates the provision of a fair process.

In order for an expectation to be legitimate it must meet a number of conditions. First, the expectation must be legitimate in that it is reasonable: *Union Nationale des Coopératives Agricoles de Céréales* Cases 95–98/74, 15 and 100/75 [1975] ECR 1615. Second, it must not be established that the claimant was attempting to take advantage of any weakness or loophole in the Community system: *EVGF* v *Mackprang* Case 2/75 [1975] ECR 607.

The most common use of legitimate expectation is as a ground for an action of damages for non-contractual liability under art 288 EC. In such cases, the applicant must also prove that acted in reliance of the expectation and suffered loss as a result of the Community measure: *CNTA* v *Commission* Case 74/74 [1975] ECR 533.

However, the principle of legitimate expectation must not be used in a manner that fetters the freedom of action for the European Community. Should this occur then a balance of interests will need to be made and, in some instances, Community freedom of action will prevail: see *R* v *Ministry of Agriculture, Fisheries and Food, ex parte Hamble (Offshore) Fisheries Ltd* [1995] 2 All ER 714 and *O'Dwyer and Others* v *Council* Cases T–466, 469, 473, 474 and 477/93 [1995] ECR II–2071.

## Equality

The application of the principle of equality may be seen most frequently in cases involving discrimination on grounds of nationality and gender. The EC Treaty prohibits three types of specific discrimination:

1. Article 12 discrimination on grounds of nationality;
2. Article 34(2) discrimination between producers and consumers in relation to the operation of the Common Agricultural Policy (CAP); and
3. Article 141 that men and women are entitled to equal pay for work of equal value.

In broader terms, art 2 EC, as amended by the ToA, now includes the general goal of 'equality between men and women', rather than the previous confining of this principle to the workplace solely. As already explained in the previous chapter, the Council of Ministers may now take the action it considers appropriate to combat 'discrimination based on sex, racial or ethnic origin, religion, belief, disability, age or sexual orientation': art 13 EC. It is hoped that the Council will use this power to reverse the effects of such decisions by the ECJ as *Grant* v *South Western Trains Ltd* Case C–249/96 [1998] ECR I–621. In this case the Court failed to grant same-sex partners the same entitlement to employment benefits as spouses and cohabitees under art 141 EC. Further developments in relation to this issue are considered in Chapter 12.

The ECJ has, however, concluded that there is, in addition, a general principle of non-discrimination in EC law: see, for example, *Frilli* v *Belgium* Case 1/72 [1972] ECR 457, *Ferrario* Case 152/81 [1983] ECR 2357 and *Ariola* v *Commission* Case 21/74 [1975] ECR 221.

## Natural justice

This concept, often closely linked with 'equity', is derived from English administrative law, where the principle may be simply broken down to two basic rules:

1. the right to an unbiased hearing; and
2. the right to be heard before a potentially adverse decision is made.

However, the European Court has often referred to it simply as 'fairness'. There are express provisions in Community law requiring that this principle be observed, such as those requiring Member States to protect the principle when exercising their derogations from the free movement of workers under the grounds of public policy, security or health: see Council Directive 64/221, arts 5–7. Hence, according to these provisions Member States must provide full reasons for decisions. However, the ECJ has also made reference to the principle in light of its nature as one of the fundamental principles protected under EC law. In *Transocean Marine Paint Association* v *Commission* Case 17/74 [1974] ECR 1063 the Advocate-General argued that the right to a hearing was a general principle of Community law (by reference to the national laws of a considerable number of the Member States) that should be binding on the Commission. The Court concluded that 'a person whose interests are perceptibly affected by a decision taken by a public authority must be given the opportunity to make his point of view known'. In *UNECTEF* v *Heylens and Others* Case 222/86 [1987] ECR 4097 the Court stated:

> '[W]here ... it is ... a question of securing the effective protection of a fundamental right conferred by the Treaty on Community workers, the latter must ... be able to defend that right under the best possible conditions and have the possibility of deciding, with a full knowledge of the relevant facts, whether there is any point in their applying to the courts.'

### Legal professional privilege

In *AM & S Europe Ltd* v *Commission* Case 155/79 [1982] ECR 1575, it was acknowledged that the principle whereby written communications between lawyer and client are privileged would be upheld in Community law. The principle is, however, confined to communications between an independent lawyer and their client and does not extend to in-house lawyers or lawyers from non-Member States. (See Chapter 17 for discussion of this in the context of competition law.)

## Public international law

The extent to which public international law may be regarded as a source of Community law is determined by the dual nature of the European Community. There are, on the one hand, entities established by treaties under international law and, on the other hand, autonomous bodies with quasi-sovereign powers creating their own autonomous legal order that is distinct from both international and national law.

This first aspect implies that to the extent to which the EC possesses legal personality under international law it is in principle subject to the rules of that law. It is international law that governs external relations, whether by treaty or other relations with third countries and international organisations, for in the exercise of external powers, such as treaty-making, and of internal powers with an external effect, the European Community must conform with public international law. So public international law forms part of the 'law', the observance of which it is the task of the ECJ to ensure.

## *The principle of subsidiarity*

Article 5 EC provides:

> 'The Community shall act within the limits of the powers conferred upon it by [the EC Treaty] and of the objectives assigned to it therein.
>
> In areas which do not fall within its exclusive competence, the Community shall take action, in accordance with the principle of subsidiarity, only if and in so far as the objectives of the proposed action cannot be sufficiently achieved by the Member States and can therefore, by reason of the scale or effects of the proposed action, be better achieved by the Community.
>
> Any action by the Community shall not go beyond what it necessary to achieve the objectives of the ... Treaty.'

It should be noted at the outset that this principle applies only when the European Union is acting within its competencies under the EC Treaty, as amended, and not under its newly acquired competences such as those provisions on common foreign and security policy. Subsidiarity will also not apply where the Community has exclusive competence, although the delimitation of situations where this is the case remains vague.

The functioning of this principle requires the European Commission to demonstrate that there is a genuine and legitimate need for every initiative or proposal. Three preliminary issues must be settled before a proposed measure or policy satisfies this test:

1. identification of the Community dimension of the subject matter to be regulated;
2. isolation of the most effective means of regulating the matter given the means available under the EC Treaty to the European Community and the Member States respectively; and
3. confirmation of some tangible and identifiable real added value of common action as opposed to isolated national action on the part of the Member States.

Once these assessments have been made, the principle of subsidiarity requires that the measures must be proportionate to the aim or objective sought to be achieved. In many respects, this is akin to the general principle of proportionality created by the European Court as a general rule of Community law; the major difference is that the principle has been transformed into a fundamental constitutional principle of European Community law.

The Treaty of Amsterdam inserted a Protocol dealing with the application of the principle of subsidiarity to the EC Treaty. This Protocol defines the application of the principle in far more detail, although it does not define the boundaries of exclusive Community competence referred to above.

The Protocol provides that for Community action to be justified it must meet both conditions set out in art 5. In other words it must be established that the objectives of the proposed action cannot be sufficiently met by Member States and that they can be better achieved by Community action. The guidelines laid down in the Protocol for assessing whether the conditions are met are as follows:

1. the issue under consideration has transnational aspects which cannot be satisfactorily regulated by action by the Member States;
2. actions by Member States alone or lack of Community action would conflict with the requirements of the Treaty (such as the need to correct distortions of competition or avoid disguised restrictions on trade or strengthen economic and social cohesion) or would otherwise significantly damage Member States' interests;
3. action at Community level would produce clear benefits by reason of its scale or effects compared with action at the level of the Member States.

The Commission has offered some guidance on what constitutes an area of exclusive Community competence. In its opinion this will occur when the Treaties impose an act on the Community since it is regarded as having exclusive responsibility for the performance of a particular task, such as, for example, the removal of barriers to the free movement of goods, services, capital and persons; the Common Commercial Policy; the common organisation of agricultural markets; the conservation of fishing resources; the essential elements of transport policy; and the general rules on competition.

An applicant may challenge a Community measure under art 5, but to do so will have to establish the measure's objectives and prove that those objectives could be sufficiently met through action by the Member States. To date the ECJ has not struck down any legislation on the ground of subsidiarity.

# 4

# Enforcement Actions against Member States

4.1 Introduction

4.2 Actions by other Member States

4.3 Actions by the Commission

4.4 Breaches of Community law under art 226 EC

4.5 Defences to an enforcement action

4.6 Interim measures

4.7 The consequences of a successful action

4.8 The future of enforcement action under art 226 EC

## 4.1 Introduction

The Member States of the European Community are under a duty, imposed by art 10 EC, to ensure that all appropriate measures are taken at national level to comply with their Community obligations. This obligation requires Member States not only to adopt Community measures into national law, but also to eliminate any obstacles that would impair the effectiveness of Community law. This is particularly so where such obstacles would deny the proper exercise of Community rights by private individuals.

To ensure the Member States do not evade this obligation, the EC Treaty creates a structure to allow Member States to be brought before the European Court of Justice for alleged infringements of EC law. The primary means of enforcing Community obligations against Member States is by means of a 'direct action'. All Member States and the Commission are empowered to bring direct actions against any Member State accused of failing to comply with the legal requirements of their Community obligations.

Private individuals have no standing to bring direct actions against Member States. Under the EC Treaty, this right is the exclusive prerogative of other Member States and the Commission. Therefore, if a private party believes that its rights have been infringed by the national measure that contravenes Community law, it cannot initiate proceedings directly in the European Court. However, this omission in the EC Treaty has been partially compensated for by two factors. First, as we shall see later, individuals may challenge national measures as contrary to EC law and seek a ruling from the European Court through the art 234 preliminary reference procedure. This is an 'indirect' means of challenging the measure; the process allows the dispute to be brought to the attention of the ECJ via legal proceedings in a national court. The European Court has frequently declared that national measures brought to its attention through this procedure are incompatible with EC law (see Chapter 6).

The second mechanism is that national courts are now subject to a duty to provide redress to private parties who are successful in establishing injury caused by the failure of national authorities to comply with their Community obligations. Private parties may now claim damages from national authorities, in domestic courts, for breaches of Community law when certain conditions are satisfied. This is also an indirect procedure, which acts as a substitute for the inability of private parties to bring direct actions. This aspect of Community law will be the focus of Chapter 7.

In this chapter, discussion will focus on the rights of other Member States and Community institutions to initiate proceedings against Member States in the European Court. These proceedings are referred to as direct actions because they involve bringing the proceeding at first instance to the attention of the ECJ. The only other form of direct action is that brought against Community institutions, often referred to as judicial review or review of legality (see Chapter 5).

## 4.2 Actions by other Member States

Article 227 EC allows Member States to bring actions directly before the European Court if they believe another Member States has failed to meet its obligations under EC law. The Court exercises exclusive jurisdiction over all disputes between Member States arising out of the subject matter of the Community Treaties. Under art 292 EC, Member States are expressly prohibited from resolving such disputes by any other means or in any other forum.

Initiating proceedings against another Member State is perceived, in diplomatic terms, as a confrontational course of action, and to mitigate this impact art 227 contains a number of procedural steps designed to avert such confrontation. The purpose behind such steps is to bring the matter to the attention of the Community authorities, and inside the arena of concern of the Community, thereby interposing the interests of the Community between those of the two Member States involved in the actual dispute.

The steps that must be exhausted before a Member State may bring a dispute to the attention of the European Court are as follows:

1. the Member States alleging the violation must bring the dispute to the attention of the Commission;
2. the Commission is required to deliver a reasoned opinion on the subject-matter of the dispute after permitting the parties an opportunity to submit arguments;
3. only after the Commission has delivered this opinion, or has failed to do so within the prescribed period of three months from notification of the matter, can the Member State bring the matter to the attention of the European Court; and
4. if the Commission indicates that it has no attention of pursuing the matter further, the complaining State may initiate proceedings itself.

In the event that these steps are not exhausted, it is extremely unlikely that the Court would be prepared to recognise the standing of the Member State trying to bring the matter to its attention by this route.

In practice this right has been rarely exercised. In the one completed action to date, France brought proceedings against the United Kingdom for violations of Community law caused by the introduction of conservation measures without proper consultation with the Commission: *France* v *United Kingdom (Re Fishing Mesh)* Case 141/78 [1979] ECR 2923. The European Court found against the UK and ordered the repeal of the offending measure. Since this case only three other actions have been brought under art 227. However, action taken by Ireland against France was settled before recourse to the European Court, and the action against the UK by Spain was also discontinued. In *Belgium* v *Spain* Case C–388/95 [2000] ECR I–3121 the European Court rejected Belgium's action against Spanish legislative requirements that Rioja wine be bottled where grown and be subject to a ban on bulk exportation.

The common reason cited for the infrequent recourse to direct actions before the Court between Member States is the effect that such actions have on the diplomatic relations between the States involved. Generally, it is diplomatically preferable to have the Commission institute proceedings on the basis of a complaint from another Member State than it is for the complaining State to confront the accused State directly in the European Court. For this reason actions against Member States are most frequently raised by the Commission, either acting on behalf of Community interests in its capacity as 'guardian of the Treaties' or on the basis of a complaint received by one or more of the Member States.

However, in reality, the Member States are not averse to threatening such a course of action. For example, in 1990 the United Kingdom threatened to take France to the European Court under the inter-state procedure after the French government claimed that it would restrict imports of cars manufactured in the UK by Japanese companies. France claimed that the cars in question failed to satisfy the Community rules of origin and were therefore not Community goods entitled to unrestricted access into the French and Community markets. The French government also argued that Japanese investment in the UK was in reality an indirect means of circumventing French quotas on the importation of Japanese vehicles.

In reply, the British government claimed that at least 80 per cent of the costs of the vehicles in question were incurred in the UK, a proportion that clearly satisfied the rules of origin adopted under the EC Treaty. Eventually the French government backed down, a decision that may have been largely due to the fact that, had the matter been brought to the attention of the ECJ, they would have failed.

In 1993–4 the German government unilaterally threatened to introduce import restrictions on consignments of beef from the UK on the grounds of the threat posed by so-called 'mad cow disease' or BSE (Bovine Spongiform Encephalitis). The British government countered this with the threat of bringing a direct action in the ECJ. The European Commission eventually agreed with the UK and informed the German government that if it adopted unilateral measures, without adequate scientific evidence of the dangers posed by BSE, it would bring proceedings in the ECJ on behalf of the European Community. The irony of this decision, of course, rests in the fact that the Community recognised a potential threat to human life through consumption of contaminated beef, and imposed a Community-wide ban on the export of British beef that was not lifted until the year 2000.

## 4.3 Actions by the Commission

Article 226 EC provides that:

> 'If the Commission considers that a Member State has failed to fulfil an obligation under this Treaty, it shall deliver a reasoned opinion on the matter after giving the state concerned the opportunity to submit its observations. If the state concerned does not comply with the opinion within the period laid down by the Commission, the latter may bring the matter before the Court of Justice.'

The duty of the Member States to fulfil obligations arising from or under the Treaties is derived both from the general rule of international law, pacta sunt servanda, and from specific provisions of Community law itself.

The duty to carry out Community obligations falls upon the Member States as such and not upon their various internal organs and agencies, since it is the Member States, each taken as a whole, that are the subjects at Community level. It follows that a Member State cannot justify its failure to fulfil its Community obligations by invoking the provisions, procedures and practices of their internal legal or constitutional orders: see section 4.5.

### *The preliminary procedure*

Before instituting proceedings against a Member State in the European Court, the Commission must comply with the requirements of a compulsory preliminary procedure. Failure to do so will result in the Commission's action being held inadmissible. The procedure has three purposes: first, to enable the Commission to ascertain the precise nature and extent of the infringement alleged; second, to provide the Member State concerned with an essential guarantee in respect of its right of defence; and, finally, the process gives give both parties the opportunity of clarifying, in co-operation with one another, complex legal solutions, thus reaching an amicable solution.

The procedure is as follows:

1. The Commission is required to communicate to the Member State concerned a written statement of complaints clearly specifying the grounds on which the Commission considers that State to have failed to fulfil an obligation under the Treaties and the actual obligation broken.
2. At the same time the Commission must invite the State to submit its observations. This constitutes the Member State's guarantee of the right of defence, which need not be taken up by the State concerned, but which is an essential formal requirement. This right has the consequence that where the Commission changes the subject matter of its complaint it must set in motion the preliminary procedure again.
3. Following any dialogue between the Commission and the Member States, and assuming that no solution is found, the Commission delivers a reasoned opinion on the matter, fixing a period of time within which the Member State is required to comply. This reasoned opinion sets out the legal and factual grounds on which the Commission considers the Member State at fault and specifies the measures required to end the infringement.

As a matter of general practice, the Commission takes some care to provide exhaustive reasoning in its opinion. However, the opinion need not, as a matter of law, contain more than a certain minimum of information.

A Member State that is subject to an investigation by the Commission is required to co-operate at every stage in the investigation. In particular, Member States are required to respond promptly to preliminary enquiries dispatched by the Commission and to questionnaires sent in the more formal parts of the investigation. They must also respond to the formal, pre-litigation reasoned opinion. This duty of co-operation stems from art 10 EC and failure to co-operate is in itself a breach of Community law, even if the investigation, or the proceedings before the ECJ, do not reveal the existence of any actual substantive violation of Community law.

Member States are entitled to limited legal protection when the Commission initiates proceedings under this authority. The Commission must, for example, follow the correct pre-litigation procedure, with due respect for time limits, or the action will be inadmissible. Further, the scope of the application under art 226 is circumscribed by the pre-litigation notification intimated by the Commission to the Member State. New matters that are not included in the notification cannot be brought into the proceedings by the Commission at the contentious stage of the proceedings: see, for example, *Commission* v *Denmark (Re Taxation of Imported Motor Vehicles)* Case C–52/90 [1992] ECR I–2187.

## The enforcement procedure

If the Member State concerned does not comply with the reasoned opinion within the period laid down by the Commission, the latter may initiate proceedings against the State before the ECJ. The application made by the Commission to the Court must be based on the same facts, grounds and issues on which the reasoned opinion has been based, and in respect of which the Member State has been given an opportunity to present its observations.

The judicial proceeding is necessarily an objective proceeding, the sole purpose of which is to obtain a declaration to the effect that the State has failed to fulfil a certain obligation within a given period of time. It follows, from an objective concept of default, that the ECJ has to establish its existence without examining the question of culpability on the part of the Member State. This will be identified irrespective of any political, economic, social or legal difficulties that the Member State may have had, justified or unjustified, in fulfilling its obligation.

## The Commission's discretion

It appears that the Commission has discretion both in the decision to deliver a reasoned opinion and its decision to bring proceedings before the European Court. This is the case even though art 226 states that the Commission 'shall' deliver a reasoned opinion, whilst only stating that it 'may' bring the matter before the Court. In legal terms the European Court is not concerned with the motives or reasoning of the Commission. Hence, in *Commission* v *Greece* Case C–200/88 [1990] ECR I–4299 the Court concluded that it was not able to decide whether the Commission had exercised its discretion 'wisely', but could only examine whether there was indeed a breach of any Community obligation.

Member States have also argued that there are time limits on when proceedings should be brought. However, in *Commission* v *Italy* Case 7/68 [1968] ECR 423, the ECJ concluded:

'It is for the Commission ... to judge at what time it shall bring an action before the Court; the considerations which determine its choice of time cannot affect the admissibility of the action ...'

The situation though is different in relation to the time period in which it takes the Commission to bring proceedings in relation to a specific infringement. In *Commission* v *The Netherlands* Case C–96/89 [1991] ECR I–2461, the ECJ held:

'... in certain cases the excessive duration of the pre-litigation procedure ... is capable of making it more difficult for the Member State concerned to refute the Commission's arguments and of thus infringing the rights of the defence. Therefore, although [art 226] contains no specified time limits, the Commission must not create an excessive delay, since that may prejudice the Member State's defence. The outcome of such a delay could therefore render the proceedings inadmissible.'

The Commission must also provide the Member State with a 'reasonable' time period in which to respond to the reasoned opinion: see *Commission* v *Ireland* Case 74/82 [1984] ECR 317. However, the length of time considered 'reasonable' will depend on the facts of the case. In other words, if the Member State is fully aware of the situation because, for example, it has received the Commission's view beforehand, or the matter is of some urgency, then it may be given a shorter time period in which to respond.

## Remedying the breach before judicial proceedings

It appears that if the Member State fails to rectify the breach within the time period specified by the Commission in the reasoned opinion, but yet does so before legal proceedings, it may still find the case admissible. The crucial factor is whether the breach existed at the time the Commission initiated proceedings before the Court. Therefore, the European Court has admitted cases even though the breach has indeed been rectified. The ECJ has provided a number of reasons as to why it allows the case to still be admissible:

1. The Court has stated that the Commission may still have an interest in bringing the action. In *Commission* v *Italy (Re Pigmeat)* Case 7/61 [1961] ECR 317 the Court held:

   '... the Commission ... still has the highest interest in having the Court settle the issue whether the failure indeed occurred ... the opposite argument would allow a State which so desired to denude the action of its purpose by bringing its illegal conduct to an end just before the judgement, thereafter remaining safe to carry on with its improper conduct in the absence of any judgment finding that it was in breach of its obligation.'

2. The Court has also stated that it may need to rule on the legality of breaches of short duration. In *Commission* v *Greece* Case 240/86 [1988] ECR 1835 the Court held:

   'Since the duration of conduct which is contrary to the Treaty is no indication of the gravity of the infringement it must be possible to bring proceedings even in relation to a breach of the Treaty which is limited in time.'

3. The Court also concluded in the above case that there remains an interest in 'establishing the basis for a liability which a Member State may incur, by reason of its failure to fulfil its obligations, towards those to whom rights accrue as a result of that failure.'

## 4.4 Breaches of Community law under art 226 EC

Article 226 EC only includes reference to failing to fulfil 'an obligation under this Treaty'. Such breaches may therefore include both positive actions, and failure to act. The most common forms of breach are as follows:

### *Failing to co-operate under art 10 EC*

The Commission has shown an increased willingness to use this as grounds for enforcement action under art 226. In *Commission* v *The Netherlands* Case 96/81 [1982] ECR 1791 the ECJ concluded that art 10 placed an obligation on all Member States to aid the Commission in achieving its tasks. This includes the provision of requested information: see also *Commission* v *Greece* Case 272/86 [1988] ECR 4875. Failure to provide requested information impedes the ability of the Commission to ascertain whether there is indeed a breach, and may in itself lead to an enforcement action.

### *Inadequate implementation of EC law*

In *Commission* v *France (Re French Merchant Seamen)* Case 167/73 [1974] ECR 359 the French legislature had failed to repeal the French Maritime Code. The Code provided that for every non-French sailor there should be three French sailors. The Commission concluded that this contravened the Treaty's obligation that there should be no discrimination on the basis of nationality. The French government argued that they had issued instructions that Community nationals should be considered to be French nationals and that therefore, in practice, there would be no such discrimination. The ECJ concluded that this constituted inadequate implementation of the provisions establishing free movement for workers. The result for those that wished to rely on these provisions was 'an ambiguous state of affairs by maintaining ... a state of uncertainty as to the possibilities available to them of relying on Community law'.

Directives, a secondary form of Community legislation, require implementation by the Member State, ie a choice of form and method is available to them to meet the objectives of the directive. This discretion may, of course, lead to inadequate implementation methods being adopted, and this may be examined by the European Court. In *Commission* v *The Netherlands* Case 96/81 [1982] ECR 1791, the Court concluded:

> 'It is true that each Member State is free to delegate powers to its domestic authorities as it considers fit and to implement the directive by means of measures adopted by regional or local authorities. That does not however release it from the obligation to give effect to the provisions of the directive by means of national provisions of a binding nature.'

In this case, the Court concluded that the measure that had been adopted to implement the directive was a 'mere administrative practice'. This could be altered easily at any point in the future and was therefore a practice not sufficient to constitute 'the proper fulfilment of the obligation deriving from that directive'. The State may not be required to take any further legislative measures if national law exists providing for the full effect of the directive and persons are fully aware and able to enforce the law in national courts: *Commission* v *Germany (Re Nursing Directive)* Case 29/84 [1985] ECR 1661. This will be the case regardless of whether the national law is constitutional or administrative.

### Failure to give the correct effect to EC law

The Court held in *Commission* v *Greece* Case 68/88 [1989] ECR 2979 that a Member State may breach its obligations under art 10 EC if it fails to provide the same penalty for infringement of EC law as it does for infringement of national law. Conversely, in some cases it may be a requirement that infringement of EC law requires a more effective penalty than that offered by national law: *Commission* v *Denmark* Case 143/83 [1985] ECR 427. Penalties should also be imposed where the State fails to take measures. This was the conclusion in an enforcement action against France for failing to prevent internal disturbances/protests by French farmers, which in turn had prevented the free movement of goods contrary to art 28 EC: *Commission* v *France* Case C–265/95 [1997] ECR I–6959 (see Chapter 14).

## 4.5 Defences to an enforcement action

As stated at the beginning of this chapter, the European Court has been unwilling to uphold defences pleaded by the Member States, especially when they relate to political, administrative, institutional or technical difficulties. The following identifies some of the defences used by Member States against an enforcement action.

### The Community measure is illegal

In *Commission* v *Greece* Case 226/87 [1988] ECR 3611 the Greek government argued that the Community measure allegedly breached was illegal. The ECJ held that there were Treaty provisions available to challenge the validity of a Community measure, a process that Greece had failed to take. In the opinion of the ECJ, without a Treaty provision stating to the contrary:

'… a Member State cannot plead the unlawfulness of a decision addressed to it as a defence in an action for a declaration that it has failed to fulfil its obligations.'

## Force majeure

In a relatively early judgment the European Court was faced with the argument of the Belgian government in an enforcement action, that its constitutional doctrine of separation of powers had made it unable to comply with its obligations: *Commission* v *Belgium* Case 77/69 [1970] ECR 244. The ECJ considered the argument and concluded that the obligations of Community law resulted in the State incurring liability under art 226 EC regardless of the agency of the State responsible and regardless of whether the State body was a constitutionally independent organ.

In the case of failing to implement a directive, the Court has also stated:

'... a Member State may not plead provisions, practices, or circumstances existing in its internal legal system in order to justify a failure to comply with obligations and time limits laid down in Community directives': *Commission* v *Italy* Case 280/83 [1984] ECR 2361.

## Other Member States commit the same breach

This has traditionally been one of the most common pleaded defences, but one that has met with little success in the ECJ. In *Commission* v *United Kingdom* Case C–146/89 [1991] ECR 3533 the Court explicitly stated the following:

'... a Member State cannot justify its failure to fulfil obligations under the Treaty by pointing to the fact that other Member states have also failed, and continued to fail, their own obligations.'

The basis of the Member States' argument rests in public international law; they argue that Treaty rules are binding on a basis of reciprocity. The Court has not concurred with this, and has made considerable efforts to point out that Community law is a sui generis system with its own rules: see *Van Gend en Loos* Case 26/62 [1963] ECR 1. Therefore, the 'implementation of Community law by Member States cannot be made subject to a condition of reciprocity': *Commission* v *United Kingdom* (above).

## That the State did not oppose the EC law

In *Commission* v *Belgium* Case 301/81 [1983] ECR 467 the Belgian government were accused of failing to implement Directive 77/780 and argued, inter alia, that they had in no way opposed the Community law. The Court held:

'it must be observed that the admissibility of an action based on art [226] ... depends only on an objective finding of a failure to fulfil obligations and not proof of any inertia or opposition on the part of the Member State concerned.'

## 4.6 Interim measures

In cases involving enforcement actions there may be some considerable delay between the initial complaint to the Commission and the hearing before the European Court. In such cases, the Court may be prepared to grant interim measures. Article 243 EC provides:

'The Court of Justice may in any cases before it prescribe any necessary interim measure.'

The Court will take three main considerations into account when deciding whether to grant interim measures:

1. the likelihood of the proceedings being successful;
2. there must be urgency arising from the facts; and
3. the Commission will usually be required to establish that there will be irreparable damage to the Community interest unless the order is granted.

The following cases provide examples of the application of interim measures.

### *Commission* v *Ireland* Case 61/77R [1977] ECR 937

The Commission initiated proceedings on the basis that Ireland had conservation measures that were contrary to the EC Treaty. The Commission also made an application for interim relief requiring the Irish government to suspend the offending legislation. The ECJ gave judgment and ordered the Irish government to suspend the legislation within five days, on the basis that it believed the legislation to be discriminatory.

### *Commission* v *United Kingdom* Case 246/89R [1989] ECR I–3125

This case involved the now infamous Merchant Shipping Act 1988. This Act was passed by a British government keen to reserve fishing stocks from fishing by vessels from other Member States which would operate under what are termed as 'flags of convenience'. The Act required that in order to obtain the necessary fishing licence the company had to be registered in the United Kingdom and its owners or shareholders had to British or ordinarily resident in the UK. The Commission considered the Act to breach of both art 12 EC (formerly art 6), which prohibits discrimination on the grounds of nationality, and those Treaty provisions providing for freedom of establishment. The Act was challenged by a number of Spanish ship-owners/companies and they argued that, whilst the case was pending, they were making substantial losses.

The ECJ found that there was a prima facie case in support of the companies right to establishment and that there was the necessary element of urgency given the facts. In relation to the need for irreparable harm or damage, the Court stated:

'... for the fishing vessels ... the cessation of their activities entails serious damage. There is no ground to believing that, pending delivery of the judgment in the main proceedings, these vessels can be operated in the pursuit of alternative fishing activities. The aforesaid damage must also, should the application in the main proceedings be granted, be regarded as irreparable.'

The European Court therefore ordered the British government to suspend the relevant provisions of the Act. Unfortunately the British government failed to comply until the Spanish ship-owners had proceeded through the English courts to the House of Lords which, after a preliminary ruling, ordered an injunction against the Secretary of State for Transport preventing him from removing the companies from the fishing register. The eventual substantive hearing found that the Merchant Shipping Act 1988 was discriminatory: see *R v Secretary of State for Transport, ex parte Factortame Ltd and Others* Case C–221/89 [1991] ECR I–3905. As we shall see in Chapter 7, the plaintiffs then sued the British government under the principle of State liability for failing to suspend the Act on the order of the Court.

### *Commission* v *Belgium* Case C–87/94 [1994] ECR I–1395

This case offers an example of where the application for interim relief failed on the basis that there was no urgency. The facts of the case involved the awarding of contracts to replace old buses. The Commission claimed that the contracts had been awarded contrary to the provisions laid down in Directive 90/531. The contracts had already been awarded and it appeared that the first delivery of buses would occur before the full hearing. The Commission argued that this would result in a serious and immediate threat to Community law. The European Court concurred that the failure to comply with a directive was a serious breach of EC law. However, they found that whilst the Commission had been informed of the situation, they had waited over two months before applying for relief. The ECJ held that this failed to denote the necessary urgency and that since the contract had been concluded, relief would not be awarded.

## 4.7 The consequences of a successful action

Under the original terms of the EC Treaty, if the European Court finds against a Member State it does not, strictly speaking, pass a sentence but delivers a purely declaratory judgment that merely notes the fact that a Member State is in default. This judgment had no executory force and neither the Commission nor the Court was able to impose sanctions to compel the offending State to redress its behaviour. The Member State was, though, obliged to comply with the judgment under art 228(1) EC which states that:

'If the Court of Justice finds that a Member State has failed to fulfil an obligation under this Treaty, the State shall be required to take the necessary measures to comply with the judgement of the Court of Justice.'

However, this was insufficient to compel States to modify their behaviour in breach of Community law.

In the past, therefore, the Commission was continually compelled to bring proceedings against Member States failing to implement the Court's decisions, as violations of their Community obligations under art 10 EC (which requires Member States to respect their Community obligations). This position was not effective in the enforcement of EC obligations, and has since been radically altered by the amendments made to art 228 EC by the Treaty on European Union.

After the European Court has ruled against a Member State in a direct action brought by the Commission, the Commission is empowered to specify a fine for non-compliance if the terms of the judgment are not implemented within a time period specified by the Commission.

The Commission has considerable control in the exercise of this power. In particular, it is responsible for:

1. determining that the Member State has failed to comply with the terms of the decision and commencing the second proceedings for enforcement of the judgement;
2. deciding the time limits within which a Member State should implement a decision; and
3. quantification of the fine to be imposed by the ECJ which should be 'appropriate in the circumstances'.

In the event that the Court does confirm the determination of the Commission, which will happen in the majority of such cases, the Court is authorised to impose either a lump sum fine or a penalty payment. The Commission has adopted guidelines on how these fines will be calculated ([1997] C332 COM (97) 299). Three principles will be applied to this determination:

1. the seriousness of the violation;
2. the duration of the infringement; and
3. the need to achieve a deterrent effect by preventing the repetition of the violation. Penalties, therefore, may not be merely symbolic.

The starting point for calculation of the fine is a basic flat-rate amount of 500 euros per day, which applies for every day beyond the deadline for compliance. This sum is then multiplied by two co-efficients. The first relates to the seriousness of the violation, which is evaluated on a scale of one to twenty. The second relates to the duration of the violation. In this context, the Commission will judge the degree of goodwill demonstrated by the State on a scale of one to three.

As a final stage, this amount will be multiplied by a constant factor designed to express a Member State's ability to pay the fine. This factor is determined by reference to each Member State's gross domestic product and the number of votes that it can cast in the Council of Ministers. These constants vary from 1.0 for Luxembourg to 26.4 for Germany. The UK has been given a factor of 17.8, while France and Italy have been given the figures of 21.1 and 17.7 respectively. Consequently, the range of level of fine that could be imposed ranges from a maximum of 30,000 euros per day for Luxembourg, up to 791,293 euros per day for Germany.

In 1996 and 1997 the Commission initiated proceedings under art 228(2) EC for financial penalties against Germany, Spain, France, Italy, Belgium and Greece for breaches of environmental obligations. Some of the cases were settled during 1997 and 1998, but proceedings against Greece were continued.

The original direct action, *Commission* v *Greece* Case 45/91 [1992] ECR I–2509, had concerned the Waste Framework Directive (75/442). The claim was that Greece had failed to comply with art 4 of the Directive by permitting the uncontrolled disposal of waste at a tip situated at the mouth of a river in Crete. The evidence established that the tipping had included hazardous waste and that the tip had been burning, uncontrolled, for over a decade. The Court held that Greece had failed to fulfil its obligations.

After the direct action, the Greek government failed to provide any notification to the Commission on how it intended to remedy the situation, except for outline approval for new waste-disposal sites and recycling facilities. The Commission set in motion the Treaty procedure, alleging that there had been insufficient compliance with the judgment. The Commission's proposed penalty was 24,600 euros per day of delay in complying with the judgment.

The Court held (*Commission* v *Greece* Case C–387/97 [2000] ECR I–5047) that Greece had failed in it obligations under the Directive, and concluded that the 'incomplete practical measures' and 'fragmentary legislation' were not sufficient to comply with the obligations. However, the Greek government did prove that there were changed practices in relation to the dumping of toxic wastes at the site. This resulted in the Court reducing the level of the penalty payment from the Commission's suggested figure to 20,000 euros per day. This penalty would apply for every day from the date of the judgment until such time as the breaches of EC law were remedied.

The Court established that the Commission had acted within its competence to provide guidelines on the level of fines/penalties and that this ensured both transparency and equality. The ECJ also stated that the purpose of such a penalty was to ensure the compliance of the Member State in remedying the breach as soon as possible, and therefore it should be proportionate and appropriate to the circumstances of the case. In the case at hand, the Court concluded that art 4 of the Waste Framework Directive rested at the very heart of EC environmental policy and therefore was a sufficiently serious enough breach to warrant the imposition of a penalty.

It should be noted, however, that problems remain in the effectiveness of this new system. There is no coercive mechanism to actually secure payment of the penalties, and there remains no injunctive remedy available to the Court to require an illegal practice to stop.

## 4.8 The future of enforcement action under art 226 EC

Between 1953 and 1982 there were a mere 166 enforcement actions, but by 1998 there were 118 in just one year. Those Member States with the better compliance records are Denmark, the United Kingdom and The Netherlands. Between 1953 and 1998 the States with the worst compliance records were Italy and Belgium, with 355 and 225 actions against them respectively. However, it is perhaps interesting to note that France was the State with the most cases pending at the formal notice stage for every year from 1998 to 2000. The best indicator, though, of the States that are the best and/or worst at complying with Community obligations are the number of formal notices that they receive. Between 1992 and 1996 this can be summarised as follows, in descending order:

| | |
|---|---|
| Italy | 537 |
| Portugal | 506 |
| Greece | 504 |
| France | 493 |
| Spain | 462 |
| Germany | 461 |
| Belgium | 437 |
| United Kingdom | 392 |
| Luxembourg | 362 |
| Ireland | 358 |
| Netherlands | 314 |
| Denmark | 233 |

Whilst preliminary references do constitute the vast bulk of the Court's workload (see Chapter 6), enforcement actions do impose on the Court's limited time. It remains to be seen whether the imposition of fines, such as that against Greece discussed above, and the application of State liability (see Chapter 7), will be influential in promoting greater compliance by the Member States with their Community obligations.

# 5

# Judicial Review in the European Community – Direct Actions against Community Institutions

5.1 Introduction

5.2 Article 230 EC actions

5.3 Grounds for review under art 230 EC

5.4 Procedure for initiating review under art 230 EC – time limits

5.5 Consequences of successful action – art 230 EC

5.6 Actions for failure to act under art 232 EC

5.7 Consequences of successful action – art 232 EC

5.8 Actions for damages – art 288 EC

## 5.1 Introduction

To safeguard the rights of both Member States and private individuals, and to protect the rights of Community institutions relative to each other, an extensive system of judicial review for the acts of Community institutions was created under the EC Treaty. The function of this system is to ensure that the Community institutions operate within their respective competencies, as specified in the Treaty.

In order to provide effective remedies against any abuse of competence, relief is provided in the form of direct actions for the review of measures adopted by Community institutions. In other words, a Member State, another Community institution and, in certain circumstances, private individuals can apply directly to the European Court for review of such actions.

This system for judicial review is complex and elaborate, but it may be broken down, for the sake of simplicity, into three separate types of action.

1. actions for the review of the legality of acts of Community institutions under art 230 EC;

2. actions for failure to act under art 232 EC; and
3. actions for damages under art 288 EC.

Judicial review under art 230 is by far the most significant type of action. This provision forms the basis for the vast majority of actions brought against Community institutions.

## 5.2 Article 230 EC actions

Article 230 EC states:

> 'The Court of Justice shall review the legality of acts adopted jointly by the European Parliament and the Council, of acts of the Commission and of the European Central Bank, other than recommendations and opinions, and of acts of the European Parliament intended to produce legal effects vis-à-vis third parties.
>
> It shall for this purpose have jurisdiction in actions brought by a Member State, the Council or the Commission on grounds of lack of competence, infringement of an essential procedural requirement, infringement of this Treaty or any rule of law relating to its application, or misuse of powers.
>
> The Court shall have jurisdiction under the same conditions in actions brought by the European Parliament, by the Court of Auditors and by the European Central Bank for the purpose of protecting their prerogatives.
>
> Any natural or legal person may, under the same conditions, institute proceedings against a decision addressed to that person or against a decision which, although in the form of a regulation or a decision addressed to another person, is of direct and individual concern to the former.
>
> The proceedings provided for in this article shall be instituted within two months of the publication of the measure, or of its notification to the plaintiff or, in the absence thereof, of the day on which it came to the knowledge of the latter as the case may be.'

The above provision has two major roles:

1. it provides a judicial means of controlling the legality of the binding acts of the Community institutions; and
2. it offers legal protection to those who are subject to the legislative and executive competence of the Community, especially those individuals whose rights and interests may be adversely affected by the illegal conduct of the institutions.

The action, therefore, displays elements of judicial review of the 'constitutionality' of legislation and judicial review of executive action. The former is achieved by requiring the ECJ to check the objective conformity of secondary Community law with the Treaties. The latter is realised by empowering the Court to annul Community measures within the framework of individual fact-related complaints brought by a defined set of plaintiffs. The former allows the Court to act as the guardian of legality, the latter as the defender of private interests deemed worthy of protection.

The scope of measures that are subject to review depends, in the first place, on the identity of the party bringing the proceedings. For this purpose, applicants can be classified as either:

1. Member States and Community institutions; or
2. private parties.

## Member States and Community institutions

The ambit of Community acts that are actionable is, to a certain extent, determined by the identity of the person bringing the action. If the applicant is a Member State, the Council or the Commission, the acts that are subject to review are not specified by the article. The ECJ is, however, given jurisdiction to review the legality of all acts of the Council and the Commission, other than recommendations and opinions. Two considerations must be borne in mind: first, the act generally complained of must be binding on the applicant; and, second, in order to determine whether this is so, the Court will look at the substance of the act, its subject matter, context and legal effect, rather than its form and designation.

This can be witnessed in the judgment of the Court in *Commission* v *Council (Re ERTA)* Case 22/70 [1971] ECR 263, where it held that

'... an action for annulment must ... be available in the case of all measures adopted by the institutions, whatever their nature and form, which are intended to have legal effects.'

Thus the ECJ may review regulations, directives and decisions (defined under art 249 EC) but this list is not exhaustive – other acts that have binding force or produce legal effects can also be reviewed: *Commission* v *Council* Case 22/70 [1971] ECR 263.

Hence, for example, the Court held in *Council* v *European Parliament* Case 34/86 [1986] ECR 2155 and *Council* v *European Parliament* Case C–284/90 [1992] ECR I–2277 that a declaration, made by the Parliament's President at the conclusion of the Parliament's debate on the budget, had the character of a legal act and was therefore subject to annulment. This can be contrasted with the decision in *IBM Corporation* v *Commission* Case 60/81 [1981] ECR 2639, where the Court held that a letter initiating the competition procedure was merely a preparatory step in the process and that the actual decision, which could be subject to review as a decision producing legal effects, would be made at a later stage in that process.

It seems, therefore, that any measure designed to lay down a course of action binding on any of the Community subjects in Member States may be challenged by the Member States; the Member States are presumed to have an interest in the legality of all Community acts. In *Italy* v *Council* Case 166/78 [1979] ECR 2575 it was held that every Member State may, regardless of its position at the time of adoption, challenge a Council regulation, and presumably every other act too. (It should be noted that under art 35 TEU the Court has also been granted the ability to review the legality of framework decisions and decisions made in relation to PJCC (Pillar 3). Such actions must be brought by the Commission or a Member State within two months of the measure's publication.)

It should be noted at this point that, although acts of the Council are reviewable, the representatives of the Member States in the Council must be acting as the Council for art 230 to be applicable. The Parliament did attempt to challenge a decision of the Council granting special aid to Bangladesh in *European Parliament* v *Council and Commission* Cases C–181 and 248/91 [1993] ECR I–3685. However, the Court concluded that the act was adopted by the government representatives acting as just that, and not as members of the Council. The acts were consequently not subject to judicial review under art 230.

According to the original terms of art 230, Member States, the Council and the Commission were, and remain, privileged applicants, and their standing to bring actions to challenge such measures is presumed. No reference was made in the original provision to the right of the European Parliament to bring such actions against the Community institutions, and in a series of cases the Parliament was refused standing to do so by the European Court: see, for example, *European Parliament* v *Council (Re Comitology)* Case 302/87 [1988] ECR 5615.

The Court, however, subsequently reversed this decision in *European Parliament* v *Council (Re Chernobyl)* Case C–70/88 [1990] ECR I–2041. Having regard to the institutional balance within the Community, and by using its power of purposive interpretation, the Court held that the Parliament was able to proceed under art 230, if two conditions were satisfied:

1. the Parliament must demonstrate a 'specific interest in the proceedings'; and
2. the action must seek to safeguard the powers of the Parliament and must be based exclusively on the infringement of those powers: see also *European Parliament* v *Council (Re Student Rights)* Case C–295/90 [1992] ECR I–4193.

This formula was adopted into the revisions made to art 230 by the Treaty on European Union. The Treaty of Nice has further amended art 230 so that it now includes the European Parliament as one of the privileged applicants.

## Private parties

In order to establish standing to bring a direct action to the attention of the European Court to challenge a Community measure, private individuals must establish the existence of three separate facts:

1. the measure must be 'a decision';
2. the measure must be of individual concern to the applicant; and
3. the measure must be of direct concern to the applicant.

Under the fourth paragraph of art 230 EC, all of these conditions must be satisfied before the private party will have standing to challenge a Community measure.

However, it should be noted that Community law has encountered some considerable difficulty in defining who has sufficient interest to be recognised by the Court.

## A decision

Only 'decisions' of Community institutions may be challenged by private parties, but the concept of a 'decision' in this context is not identical to that contained in art 249 EC, namely a measure 'binding in its entirety upon those to whom it is addressed'. Rather, the concept has a broader definition. For example, measures that take the form of regulations may be considered decisions if certain conditions are met. In other words, a measure need not take the strict legal form of a decision to be challenged under art 230(4). For example, the decision of the Commission to close the file on a complaint alleging breach of art 82 EC on competition law was held in the case of *SFEI and Others* v *Commission* Case C–39/93P [1994] ECR I–2681 to be a decision reviewable under art 230.

## Individual concern

The Court first considered the meaning of the phrase 'direct and individual concern' in *Plaumann and Co* v *Commission* Case 25/62 [1963] ECR 95, where the act challenged was a decision addressed to a Member State. The Court decided, for no readily apparent reason, to consider the individual concern first. It held:

> 'Persons other than those to whom a decision is addressed may only claim to be individually concerned if that decision affects them by reason of certain attributes which are particular to them by reason of circumstances in which they are differentiated from all other persons and by virtue of these factors distinguishes them individually just as in the case of the person addressed. In the present case the applicant is affected by the disputed decision as an importer ... ie by reason of a commercial activity which may at any time be practised by any person and is not therefore such as to distinguish the applicant in relation to the contested decision as in the case of the addressee.'

Hence, although an undertaking may be adversely affected by a decision, if it is not of 'individual concern' to them that undertaking will not be considered as having sufficient interest.

Two features of the above criteria require further attention. First, there is the repeated reference to the importance of showing that the applicant is affected in the same way as the addressee of the decision. Second, there is a clear allusion to the comparison with the objective application of regulations, by reason of a commercial activity that may at any time be practised by any person.

Nothing in the later cases suggests that the ECJ intended anything other than assimilation of the notion of direct and individual concern with the criteria for defining a decision. Indeed, it seemed to regard them as interchangeable, sometimes looking first at the nature of the act, sometimes looking first to the question of 'individual concern'. From the cases where the latter approach was adopted, it might well be deduced that the Court necessarily had assimilated the two ideas. What would have been the point in examining the potentially broader notion first, coming to an affirmative decision on that point, and then rejecting the appeal because the act nevertheless did not amount to a decision because of the narrower definition of 'individual' for that purpose?

### Direct concern

The concept of direct concern has a somewhat different meaning and significance according to whether the contested measure is a decision addressed to a Member State, a decision addressed to another natural or legal person, or a decision taken in the form of a regulation. In all cases, however, it is clear that the criterion of 'directness' is not used simply to measure the gravity of the impairment of the applicant's rights of interests. Nor is it intended to refer merely to a casual connection, which may be both direct and indirect, between the challenged act and the rights or interests impaired. Rather, it expressed the fact that the decision produced immediate, automatic and inevitable – not merely possible – disadvantageous legal effects upon the applicant.

Thus, the difference between direct and indirect concern is characterised, on the one hand, by the absence or presence of an intermediary with an independent power of decision between the authority taking the measure and the results that follow from it and, on the other hand, by the inevitability or mere probability with which those results follow from that measure.

Generally, a decision will concern the applicant directly if:

1. it imposes a disadvantage on, or denies an advantage to, a class of persons of which the applicant is a member; or
2. it grants an advantage to, or terminates a disadvantage which had been imposed on, the applicants competitors, but only if these results follow automatically and necessarily from the decision. Where, however, the results are merely likely to follow, but depend upon the intervention of certain persons or upon the fulfilment of certain conditions, there will be no direct concern.

For example, where a number of companies apply for licences to import goods into the EC, and the Commission then makes a decision on these licences, the companies are directly and individually concerned: *L'Etoile Commerciale* v *Commission* Cases 89 and 91/86 [1988] 3 CMLR 564, *ARPOSOL* v *Council* Case 55/86 [1988] ECR 13 and *Sociedade Agro-Pecuaria Vincente Nobre Lda* v *Council* Case 253/86 [1990] 1 CMLR 105. On the other hand, where the allocation of such licences is at the discretion of national agencies, allocating future quotas to companies not traditionally importing these products, direct concern is more difficult to prove: see *Calpak* v *Commission* Cases 789 and 790/79 [1980] ECR 1949.

It is extremely important to note that private parties who can demonstrate direct and individual concern in a Community measure, and who decline to initiate direct proceedings against the Community institution on this basis, cannot later challenge the validity of the measure by bringing proceedings in a national court. In such circumstances, the ECJ will decline to answer a preliminary reference from the national court. This is because private individuals who have direct rights of action should exercise these rights, as opposed to indirect rights exercised by way of proceedings through a national court: *TWD Textilewerke Deggendorf GmbH* v *Germany* Case C–188/92 [1994] ECR I–833.

The Court it seems has been generally wary in defining those with sufficient interest. The reason for this may be an unwillingness to 'open the floodgates' to claims by the many bodies that may be adversely affected by Community legislation. There is, in addition, some inconsistency in the case law. The Court has itself stated that the situation perhaps requires reconsideration. In its Report to the Intergovernmental Conference 1996 the Court stated:

> 'It may be asked ... whether the right to bring an action for annulment under [art 230] ... which individuals enjoy only in regard to acts of direct and individual concern is sufficient to guarantee for them effective judicial protection ...'

However, it did not appear that the Court would indeed alter its restrictive approach to determining standing. This may now change with the focus given to this issue by Advocate-General Jacobs in what has the potential to be a landmark case. In *Unión de Pequeños Agricultores* v *Council* Case C–50/00P [2002] 3 CMLR 1 the Advocate-General's Opinion questioned the fact that justifying the restrictive interpretation of standing by referring to the provisions available under art 234 EC (the preliminary reference procedure) was satisfactory in providing 'full and effective protection against general measures'. In the opinion of Advocate-General Jacobs, the 'only satisfactory solution' was:

> '... to recognise that an applicant is individually concerned by a Community measure where the measure has, or is liable to have, a substantial adverse effect on his interests.'

He went on to explain why such a basis would be more beneficial, and these points can be summarised as follows:

1. such a test would provide a 'true right' of direct access to a court that would be able to grant a remedy, thus possible situations of a denial of justice would be avoided and overall judicial protection would be enhanced;
2. the complex and unpredictable rules on standing would be replaced by a much simpler test; and
3. re-interpreting the test would bring it into line with other judicial developments that have sought to extend the scope of judicial protection to counter the enhanced powers of the Community institutions.

This heralds a considerable change of approach and would, of course, result in the case law that already exists, and which has done so for some time, being rendered effectively 'redundant'. Whether the European Court of Justice is prepared to do this remains to be seen. The Court of First Instance, though, has shown willingness to travel down this route and this may encourage the ECJ to adopt the same approach. In *Jego-Quere et Cie SA* v *Commission* Case T–177/01 Judgment of 3 May 2002 (not yet reported), the CFI held that a person would be individually concerned by a Community measure of general application that concerns them directly, if that measure definitely and immediately affects their legal position by restricting their rights or by imposing obligations on them.

## 5.3 Grounds for review under art 230 EC

In direct actions for annulment the Court has been granted jurisdiction to declare acts void only where the alleged defect(s) correspond to one or more of the following four specified grounds of illegality upon which the annulment can be based:

1. lack of competence;
2. infringement of an essential procedural requirement;
3. infringement of the Treaties or of any rule of law relating to their application; and/or
4. misuse of powers.

Broadly speaking, the first and second grounds enable such formal and procedural defects to be invoked as are neither negligible nor so grave as to lead to absolute nullity, while the third ground provides the means for questioning the act's substantive legality. It is, therefore, the most important and most general of all grounds. By contrast, the fourth ground relates not to the act's objective formal or material legality but to the subjective intention of the institution in adopting it.

### *Lack of competence*

Lack of competence as a ground of action gives effect to the general principle that a measure is invalid if it originates from a body that does not possess the requisite power for its adoption (equivalent to substantive ultra vires in English law). The Community institutions will act outside their competence whenever they exercise a power that has not been conferred upon them by Community law. This may arise in three different circumstances:

1. where an institution (Council or Commission) exercises a power not transferred to the Community from the Member States or acts in an area not placed under Community competencies;
2. where an institution exercises a power conferred upon another institution, or upon two institutions jointly and is exercised without the other; and/or
3. where an institution exercises a Community competence in relation to a non-Member State or its subjects in circumstances not authorised by general international law.

An example of where an institution exercised a power not transferred to the Community arose in the cases of *Germany, France, The Netherlands, Denmark and the United Kingdom* v *Commission* Cases 281, 283–285 and 287/85 [1987] ECR 3203. The Commission in this case had adopted a decision under which Member States were required to consult the Commission on measures relating to the integration of workers from non-Community States. The ECJ held that the basis for the decision – art 137 EC – was confined to measures affecting migrants from other Member States. It did not extend to measures affecting only migrants from non-Community States, and therefore the Commission had acted without the necessary competence.

It should be noted that few challenges are successful under this ground. However, a successful action was made in *France* v *Commission* Case C–327/91 [1994] ECR I–3641. In this case the Commission had concluded an agreement with the United States that was intended to promote co-operation and co-ordination in competition law. The Court held that the Commission lacked the necessary competence to conclude the agreement – under art 228 (prior to amendment by the TEU) the Commission could negotiate the agreement, but it had to be concluded by the Council.

## Infringement of an essential procedural requirement

This ground of action gives effect to the general requirement that in the preparation, adoption, presentation and communication of their measures, public authorities must observe certain basic rules as to form and procedure. Infringement of these rules may have the consequence, depending upon the nature and degree of seriousness, either that no binding measure will come into existence at all, or that the measure will suffer from such a defect as to lead to its absolute nullity, or more usually to its annulment. This is equivalent to procedural ultra vires in English law.

In order to have an effect on the validity of the measure, the infringement must be of an 'essential' procedural requirement. What amounts to an 'essential requirement' depends to a large extent both on the nature and purpose of the measure and on the degree of legal protection required by its addressee. Thus, more detailed and stricter requirements apply to individual measures affecting the legal position of private persons.

Generally speaking, procedural requirements where infringement usually constitutes a ground for action may be divided into the following three groups.

### Preparation

There are two main types of infringement. The first is failure to consult the various consultative bodies where consultation is required by a provision of primary or secondary Community law. The second is the failure to give parties whose interests may be perceptibly affected by a measure the opportunity to make their point of view known before the measure is fully adopted: see *SA Roquette Frères* v *Council* Case 138/79 [1980] ECR 3333.

An illustration of a measure being annulled for reasons of inadequate preparation occurred in *Germany* v *Commission (Re Constructive Products)* Case C–263/95 [1998] 2 CMLR 1235. Council Directive 89/106 sets down procedures for the attestation of the conformity of certain constructive products to mandatory technical specifications. This is carried out by a standing committee of representatives of each Member State, acting in conjunction with the Commission. Under the terms of the Directive, the Commission submitted proposals for approval to the Permanent Representation offices of the Member States as well as the committee representatives.

Germany sought the annulment of an approval decision on the grounds that the German version of the draft measure had not been sent to its Permanent Representative nor the German member of the Commission within the time period specified. The Commission had acknowledged the delay in sending the German version but had circulated the English version of the draft decision in time to the German delegation. On this basis, it proceeded to adopt the approval decision, exercising its powers to do so under delegated powers.

The Court held that the failure to send the German version to the German delegation, within the appropriate time limits, constituted an infringement of an essential procedural requirement justifying the annulment of the Commission's approval decision. The English version of the proposed measure could not be considered as an adequate substitute for the German language version. The Commission was bound to strictly adhere to the procedural requirements specified in the Directive granting it delegated powers.

## Form

As regards the form of the measure, while insignificant formal irregularities are irrelevant, the giving of no, or insufficient, reasons for the adoption of a measure will always constitute an infringement of an essential procedural requirement. Inadequate reasoning is treated for this purpose as equivalent to the total absence of reasoning. Reasons are required under art 253 EC.

## Communication of the measure

Generally, a statement of reasons is deemed adequate when it sets out, in a concise but clear and relevant manner, all the essential legal and factual considerations upon which the operative part of the measure is based. It will thus enable both the parties concerned and the Court to discover the principal reasons that have led the institution to adopt the measure. General considerations which apply without distinction to other cases, or which are limited to repeating the wording of the Treaties, or refer to 'information collected' without specifying it, or which are otherwise vague and inconsistent, are not enough. In other words, the statement of reasons must be such as validly substantiate the measure. It must enable the Court to clearly recognise the facts and considerations held by the institution to be decisive and to determine whether on the basis of those facts and considerations the measure is well-founded or unfounded in law. In short, it must be capable of being judicially reviewed.

## Infringement of the Treaties, or any rule of law relating to their application

Undoubtedly this is the most general and the most important of the four grounds of action. The main difference between this ground and the others is that this ground provides the only legal basis for reviewing the objective and substantive legality of Community measures. In other words, their material conformity with the rules and principles of Community law may be examined.

The broad reference to the Treaties and to any rule of law relating to their application, virtually encompasses the whole body of written and unwritten Community law. In order to ascertain the rules whose infringement constitutes a ground for annulment, one must look into the primary, secondary and tertiary sources of Community law: see Chapter 3. While there is no problem in identifying the basic Community Treaties, certain difficulties may arise in defining the concept of 'rules of law relating to their application'. Broadly speaking, this concept refers to general and abstract rules that are binding upon the institutions, generally arising from secondary legislation.

## Misuse of powers

It follows from both the functional nature of the Community's legal existence and the attributed nature of the institutions' competencies that the powers conferred upon the latter are strictly purpose-bound – they can be exercised only for the general and particular purposes for which they have been granted. Misuse of powers occurs if the institutions use their powers for a purpose other than the one for which those powers have been given. In order to establish misuse of powers it is necessary first to uncover the real intentions of the institutions, that is, the subject pursued by them in taking the measure challenged. Second, it must be shown that this object is different from the one that they ought to have pursued under the Treaties. (This ground is equivalent to using a power conferred for an improper or illegitimate purpose in English law.)

Misuse of powers must be distinguished from the other grounds of action, especially from lack of competence and infringement of the Treaties. Such a distinction is easy to make if it is borne in mind that misuse of powers can only exist if the following two conditions are cumulatively fulfilled:

1. the institutions must be in possession of the requisite powers to act in the given case; and
2. those powers must be discretionary.

Where the requisite power is missing, the institutions cannot 'misuse' it. Where it is present, but can only be used in a certain way strictly specified by the Treaties, it cannot be misused either, it can only be used illegally or not at all. The former restriction, where power is missing, constitutes a case of lack of competence; the latter, where the conditions laid down by the Treaties are disregarded, one of infringement of the Treaties.

By its very nature, it is difficult to prove misuse of powers. On the one hand, the institutions enjoy the presumption of innocence, being presumed to have pursued legitimate objectives in their actions unless and until the opposite is proved. On the other hand, what needs to be proved is their substantive interests and motives, which are not usually recognisable from the act itself; nor are they easily ascertainable by any other usual means, especially by private individuals who may not have access to the relevant documents.

## 5.4 Procedure for initiating review under art 230 EC – time limits

The final paragraph of art 230 EC states:

> 'The proceedings provided for in this article shall be instituted within two months of the publication of the measure, or of its notification to the plaintiff, or in the absence thereof, on the day on which it came to the knowledge of the latter, as the case may be'.

This is supplemented by art 81(1) of the Rules of Procedure of the European Court of Justice:

> 'The period of time allowed for commencing proceedings against a measure adopted by an institution shall run from the day following the receipt by the person concerned of notification of the measure or, where the measure is published, from the fifteenth day after publication thereof in the Official Journal of the European Communities.'

No problem is raised in identifying the limitation period for actions for the annulment of regulations. This is because art 254 EC renders the publication of regulations obligatory, and it has been held that the publication of a regulation has immediate effect.

Following the TEU, directives and decisions under the co-decision procedure, and directives issued to all Member States, must be published. Time will run from their specified date of entry into force or on the twentieth day following publication: art 254 EC. Any other directives or decisions will be notified to those to whom they are addressed and take effect on such notification.

If the applicant is not an addressee time will run from the date of their knowledge of the measure (its precise content and basis).

The limitation periods may be extended in recognition of the distance between applicants and the ECJ: art 81(2) Rules of Procedure. As regards applicants resident in the United Kingdom, ten days are permitted.

The expiry of the time period allowed for bringing an action though will not be fatal if the applicant can prove 'the existence of unforeseeable circumstances or of force majeure': art 42 Protocol on the Statute of the Court. However, the Court has generally been unwilling to permit applications outside of the time limits.

The Court of First Instance considered the effect of procedural irregularities in the notification of decisions, excusable error in delaying to initiate proceedings and unforeseeable circumstances or force majeure in the case of *Bayer AG* v *Commission* Case T–12/90 [1993] 4 CMLR 30. In this case the applicant argued each of these grounds as justifying its delay in initiating proceedings within the time limits set in art 230(5). According to the decision of the CFI, a delay may only be justified on the grounds of irregularity of the notification if fault for the irregularity lies with the relevant Community institution.

The second plea, that of excusable error, was also rejected by the CFI as being inapplicable unless the applicants could satisfactorily demonstrate that they took all steps within their power to avoid any error causing the delay. Finally, on appeal, the ECJ considered that, for the concept of force majeure to apply, there must exist abnormal difficulties, independent of the will of the person seeking to rely on the plea and apparently inevitable, even if all due care is taken: *Bayer AG* v *Commission* Case C–195/91P [1994] ECR I–5619.

It may be gathered from the above that delay in initiating action after notification has been dispatched is difficult to justify to the Court, and the Court itself is rigorous in the application of this requirement.

## 5.5 Consequences of successful action – art 230 EC

Continuity of legislation and administrative action requires that acts of the institutions that are formally in force shall, in principle, be carried out as long as a judgment of the ECJ has not held them illegal.

If the action is well founded, the Court may declare the act concerned to be void, thus reversing the legal position: art 231 EC. The annulled act is regarded as if it had never existed in law, and the parties to the dispute must be restricted to their original position.

When a particular provision is severable from the rest of the measure, partial annulment is possible, even to the extent of deleting certain words from the challenged act. In the case of a regulation, if the Court considers it necessary, the EC Treaty authorises it to state which of the effects of the regulation it has declared void: art 231 EC. Where there is partial annulment, the unannulled parts of the act must be regarded as confirmed by the Court. If the unannulled parts are reproduced in a subsequent measure they have the benefit of res judicata and, if reproduced, cannot be contested by a further action for annulment. In the case of annulment of the provisions of a regulation or directive, the Court will frequently declare that they will remain effective until a new one is adopted. For example, the ECJ made such a declaration in relation to the annulment of Directive 90/366 on student rights in *European Parliament* v *Council* Case C–295/90 [1992] ECR I–4193.

The obligation of the institutions to comply with the Court's judgement does not include an obligation on the part of the Communities to make good any damage that may have been caused by the annulled act. Under art 233 EC the institution(s) 'whose act has been declared void or whose failure to act has been declared contrary to the Treaty shall be required to take the necessary measures to comply with the judgement of the Court of Justice'.

Any damage may be recovered by means of separate action under arts 235 and 288 EC (considered in detail at section 5.8). Although illegality of a Community act as established by a judgment of annulment may be an important factor in establishing the Community's non-contractual liability, it ensures in itself neither the admissibility nor the success of such an action for damages. In addition, the Court cannot order the Commission to adopt a measure to replace the annulled one: *British American Tobacco (BAT) & R J Reynolds Industries Inc* v *Commission* Cases 142 and 156/84 [1987] ECR 4487.

Although the obligation to give effect to the Court's judgment of annulment is imposed by the Treaties only on the institution whose act has been declared void (art 233 EC), the erga omnes effect of such a judgment may require third parties to take appropriate actions. The annulment of a Council regulation may entail, for the Commission or the Member States, the obligation to no longer apply the measure adopted by them in its implementation, and even to formally repeal such measures in the interests of legal certainty. The same obligation may arise for a Member State in respect of a Community dictate or decision annulled by the Court that has been implemented by national measures. These implementing measures, having lost their legal foundations, must be regarded as illegal.

## 5.6 Actions for failure to act under art 232 EC

It would obviously be unsatisfactory if Community institutions were subject to judicial control only in respect of their positive actions, whilst they could evade the obligations imposed upon them by simply failing to act. An action for annulment provides adequate remedy only against the illegal positive conduct of the institutions and is not suitable to compel an institution to act. For this purpose the action for failure to act is available. These two forms of action may, in fact, be envisaged as two sides of the same coin: they constitute, in a broader sense, the two aspects of the same general remedy, a review by the European Court of the legality of the institution's conduct.

In order to afford effective protection they should, in principle, form a 'watertight' system in the sense that any illegal behaviour of the institutions can be challenged through one procedure or another. Thus an action for a failure to act should in theory be always available where an action for annulment is not. In practice, however, such a watertight system does not exist under the provisions of the EC Treaty. This is due to the fact that an institution may prevent an action for failure to act by adopting an informal act that is not, at the same time, subject to annulment. This arrangement considerably weakens the legal protection that the action for failure to act ought, by its nature, to afford.

On the other hand, the two procedures are mutually exclusive of each other; the range of application of one ends where that of the other begins. An action for failure to act cannot be made parallel to, or in substitution for, an action for annulment for a purpose for which the latter is the proper remedy. For example, to bring about proceedings because the time limit for the latter has expired. Similarly, an action for failure to act is no longer available where the institution requested to act responds within the proper time limit by a formal, even though adverse or unsatisfactory, measure. Against this, an action for annulment is the appropriate remedy.

The position of 'privileged applicants', that is the Member States and the Community institutions, is that they may bring a claim under art 232 without being required to have any special interest. Legal and natural persons must establish that they have a special interest in that they are directly and individually concerned. The conditions under which this is established are the same as those under art 230.

### Concept of failure to act

Under the EC Treaty, a failure to act by the Council or Commission is subject to judicial review only in so far as it constitutes an infringement of the Treaty. Accordingly, failure to act means the omission of an act, the application of which is obligatory upon the institution: *Borromeo* v *Commission* Case 6/70 [1970] ECR 815. The institution must be under a clear legal obligation to take a certain action so that the failure to take such action constitutes a breach of duty. A failure to exercise mere discretionary power, or to take a measure dictated by mere considerations of expediency, is not sufficient. This type of negative conduct is not subject to judicial control, as was held in the case of *Eridania* v *Commission* Case 10/68 [1969] ECR 459. The failure to act must, in other words, be illegal.

In practice, in order for an action to succeed, it is not enough to refer in general terms to a violation of the Treaty. The applicant must specify the exact provision of Community law that requires the Council or Commission to take the measure sought. The provisions founded on must impose upon the institutions a particular obligation to take, and at the same time create a corresponding subjective right in the applicant to demand, the requested measure. The general duty of the Commission under art 211 EC, to ensure that Community law is observed by all those subject to it, is too general an obligation to serve as a basis for an action for failure to act. It does not confer upon individuals enforceable rights to demand particular measures. Reliance on art 211 alone will not, therefore, ensure admissibility of action. It is, moreover, doubtful whether interested parties possess an abstract right, enforceable by action for failure to act, to demand prompt and due consideration, as distinct from, or in addition to, the taking of a specified measure, whenever they make a complaint to an institution.

The categories of measures that are the subject matter of the obligation to act, and whose omission constitutes an actionable failure to act, differ according to whether the applicant is a Member State or Community institution, or a private party. The ECJ has stated that the concept of an act as the subject of an action is the same for the purposes of both actions for annulment and actions for failure to act, since both actions are in fact only different aspects of one and the same legal remedy. It is, however, thought that this statement is correct only where the applicant is a private party. In the case of Member States and institutions as applicants, while an action for annulment is not available against non-binding acts such as recommendations and opinions, no such limitation exists for failure to act. The latter is thus open in respect of any act, binding or non-binding, which the Council or Commission has failed to take, provided that the inaction constitutes an infringement of Community law.

Action for failure to act is admissible only if the requirement for an obligatory preliminary procedure has been complied with. Briefly, as a first step, the institution concerned has to be called upon to act. In this respect it is necessary that the prospective applicant should put the institution formally on notice to act. This is achieved only by indicating to it with unequivocal clarity the acts which it is required to take, and by advising it of the applicant's intention to go to Court, or at least to use 'all means of appeal', should it refrain from acting. Requests that do not amount to this will not suffice.

The Treaties do not specify a time limit within which this procedure should be initiated, but the Court in *Netherlands* v *Commission* Case 59/70 [1971] ECR 639 stated that it must be initiated within a 'reasonable' time period. However, once the request to act has been made, the relevant Community institution has two months within which to 'define its position', and should it fail to do this the applicant can bring the action under art 232 within a further two-month period.

## Definition of position

The definition of position, in this context, means an express declaration of the view taken by the institution of the subject matter of the request and the merits of the case. For example, the Commission's reply to a request asking it to initiate art 226 proceedings against a violated law, amounts to a definition of position and, if notified within the prescribed time limit, is sufficient to prevent an action. That is so even if the reply itself is not a binding act and is, therefore, not subject to annulment. It follows that a reply, which in the final analysis constitutes a refusal to act in the way requested, may indeed amount to a declaration of position and may stop an action.

Nevertheless, an interim reply that merely informs the applicant that his request is being studied, and which does not involve any clarification of attitude on the substantive issues of the request, does not amount to a definition of position. Even an indication to the effect that, in the Commission's view, there is no possibility of bringing an action on the basis of the applicant's request amounts in itself to a mere statement of an opinion, and does not constitute a taking of position in response to the request. That is so even if such an indication implies a refusal to act on the part of an institution. An implied refusal does not equal a taking of position; rather it is the typical case for which the action for failure to act is provided.

In contrast, a brief statement to the effect that the Commission is 'not under any obligation to adopt any measure' with respect to the request does, even if not reasoned, constitute, as an express refusal to act, a definition of position. A clear distinction must be made between an express refusal to act and a failure to act – ie between an expressed intention (even though negative) and the total lack of any expression of intention. The former does, and the latter does not, constitute a definition of position.

The failure to offer a definition of position can be seen in the case of *Ladbroke Racing (Deutschland) GmbH* v *Commission* Case T–74/92 [1995] ECR II–115. In this case Ladbroke alleged a breach by German and French companies of arts 81 and 82 EC by their refusal of access to the televising of horse racing. Ladbroke had made their complaint to the Commission, the institution responsible for the enforcement of Community competition law. The Commission did decide to investigate the complaint, but 16 months later had still not defined its position as to the alleged breach of art 82. The CFI held that the Commission had failed to define its position, even though it had a range of options open to it, such as establishing a breach of art 82, formally communicating with Ladbroke and dismissing the complaint, or producing a reasoned decision not to pursue the complaint on the basis that there was insufficient Community interest. The CFI therefore held that there had been a breach of art 232.

It should be noted that the adoption of an act different from the one sought, or deemed necessary by the interested parties, or the adoption of a negative decision, does not fall within the concept of failure to act: *National Carbonising* v *Commission* Cases 109 and 114/75 [1977] ECR 381.

## 5.7 Consequences of successful action – art 232 EC

There have been few successful actions brought under art 232. In *European Parliament* v *Council (Re Common Transport Policy)* Case 13/83 [1985] ECR 1513 the Parliament brought proceedings against the Council for failure to act. This was on the basis that the Council was required to adopt a common transport policy under arts 70 and 71 EC, but after 20 years had failed to do so. The Parliament had requested the Council to provide the policy on a number of occasions, and the ECJ recognised this. However, the Court also concluded that arts 70 and 71 did not provide an enforceable obligation to act and the Parliament's action failed.

The consequences of any successful action are as follows. An action for failure to act is not an action for annulment – that is, annulment of an implied decision of refusal inferred from the silence of the institutions – but an action for a declaration. The Court is asked to establish, first, the dilatoriness of the institution in defining its position with regard to the applicant's request, and, second, that this constitutes an infringement of Community law. All that the Court can do is examine whether the Treaties or secondary legislation impose a clear obligation to take the requested measure and whether, if so, that obligation has been fulfilled. It follows that the applicant cannot request, and the Court cannot order, specific measures to be taken by the Council or the Commission. In fact, the indication of such measures in the application is inadmissible, and still less can the Court's judgment itself be regarded as a substitute for such measures. Nevertheless, the applicant will attain practically the same result, since in the case of a successful action the institution whose failure to act has been declared contrary to Community law is required by the Treaties to take the necessary measures to comply with the judgment of the European Court.

Since the legal effect of the judgment flows from the operative part and the decisive grounds on which it is based, the institution must take the judgment as a whole into account, including any relevant observations made by the Court, in establishing what measures are necessary to comply with it. A mere reading of the judgment will indicate the measures by the adoption of which alone it is possible to terminate the infringement. Should the institution still fail to take the required measures, another action for failure to act is the only remedy. The obligation of the Council and the Commission to comply with the Court's judgement is clearly separated from the obligation of the Communities to make good any damage that may have been caused by the institution's inaction. This obligation is governed entirely by the principles laid down by art 288(2) and forms no part of the institution's duty to execute the Court's judgment rendered in the action for failure to act.

## 5.8 Actions for damages – art 288 EC

Article 288 EC provides for compensation for damages, but distinguishes between contractual and non-contractual liability. Article 288(1) states that contractual liability will be determined by the national law applicable to the particular contract in the relevant national court.

Article 288(2) EC provides:

'In the case of non-contractual liability, the Community shall, in accordance with the general principles common to the laws of the Member States, make good any damage caused by its institutions or by its servants in the performance of their duties.'

It is apparent that, in the course of the normal performance of their duties, Community institutions may commit certain acts or omissions which cause material damage to those subject to their jurisdiction, and to third parties. This is particularly so where such activities take place predominately in the economic sphere, where even a limited measure of improper intervention may have far-reaching and harmful consequences.

The Treaty has deliberately separated, both substantially and procedurally, the power of the European Court to review the legality of Community action or inaction, from the power to establish liability for the consequences of such action. Hence, the action for damages should be seen as a distinct and independent form of judicial recourse. Under art 235 EC the ECJ has exclusive jurisdiction over non-contractual damages claims against the institutions.

Any person may bring an action under art 288(2).

## General conditions for liability

The EC Treaty does not determine in precise terms the general conditions for, and the limits of, the Communities' non-contractual liability, which forms the legal basis for an action for damages. Article 288 refers, generally, to the non-contractual liability of the Communities, which is to be determined 'in accordance with the general principles common to the laws of the Member States'.

This reference is to the various national laws concerning administrative (governmental) liability, rather than to general (civil law) liability. It is clear that by referring to the broad concept of common general principles, the Treaties deliberately left it to the Court to determine, by a combination of comparative and creative activity, the general conditions for non-contractual liability.

Generally, four conditions must exist before liability for damages may be established: see *Lütticke (Alfons) GmbH* v *Commission* Case 4/69 [1971] ECR 325. These are as follows:

1. an injury must exist;
2. there must be a causal connection between the injury alleged and the conduct with which the institutions are charged;
3. the conduct of the institutions must be illegal; and
4. the conduct of the institutions must be culpable (wrongful).

## Nature, proof and assessment of injury

In order to establish the liability of the Community, there must exist damage that is certain, specific, proved and quantifiable. The damage must have crystallised by the time that the claim for compensation is made, and must be clearly specified by the applicant: *Lesieur* v *Commission* Cases 67–85/75 [1976] ECR 391. Not only must the damage be certain but it must also be specific, affecting the applicant's interests in a special and individual manner. The normal disadvantages of a financial arrangement or scheme set up for the benefit of all Community undertakings operating in a particular sector, or for the benefit of the public at large and affecting all commercial operators by virtue of general and objective criteria, cannot constitute 'injury' giving a right to compensation. It would otherwise be possible for individual undertakings to virtually cancel the effects of the scheme by claiming as damages the amount whereby they are disadvantaged by its operation.

Generally, the onus to prove an injury allegedly suffered rests with the injured party. They must provide conclusive evidence as to the existence and exact amount of the damage, to enable the Court to make the necessary assessment and award appropriate compensation.

## Causal connection

The existence of an injury cannot in itself establish the liability of the Community. It is also necessary that the injury should have been caused by the conduct of the Community's institutions or servants. The causal connection between the wrongful acts or omission and the damage alleged must be direct, immediate and exhaustive, and be proved by the applicant. In the absence of such proof the action will be dismissed as unfounded: *P Dumortier Frères SA* v *Council* Cases 64 and 113/76, 167 and 239/78 and 27, 28 and 45/79 [1982] ECR 1733

## Illegality of institutions' conduct

The non-contractual liability of the Community covers damages caused by their institutions or servants 'in the performance of their duties'. The institutions perform their duties basically in two different ways:

1. by carrying out ordinary official activity necessary for the putting into operation or supervision of legal measures; or
2. by enacting legal measures in the exercise of their quasi-sovereign powers.

The different methods of performance give rise to two different types of liability. In relation to the first method, the claim for compensation will be founded upon the restricted concept of official fault involving negligent or defective administration, bad organisation or lack of supervision. In such situations the question of liability can be, and usually is, disengaged from that of legality and is examined separately.

The position is complex where the damage alleged has occurred as a direct result of a binding Community measure or a failure to take such a measure. In such a case the question of liability is usually dependent upon, and therefore inseparably linked to, that of the legality of the measure or default.

Under the EC Treaty there is, in principle, nothing to prevent the question of the illegality of an act or a measure on which an action is based from being raised within the framework of such an action or, alternatively, in an action for annulment brought simultaneously.

In terms of claiming loss as a result of the acts of Community servants there have been some difficulties, since it is not comprehensively clear what types of act will be considered as coming within the 'performance of their duties'. The situation is further complicated by the fact that officials and servants of the Community are granted immunity from legal proceedings in respect of acts 'performed by them in their official capacity' under art 12 of the Protocol on the Privileges and Immunities of the European Communities. In *Sayag* v *Ludec* Case 9/69 [1969] ECR 329 the Court concluded that the Community is only liable for acts of its servants where 'by virtue of an internal and direct relationship' those acts are 'the necessary extension of the tasks entrusted to the institutions'. Consequently, a servant's use of a private car for transport during the course of their duties did not fall into this definition. In such circumstances, where the Community cannot be held liable, the servant may find themselves subject to an action brought in national courts under the relevant national law, although the Protocol referred to above may well offer them some protection.

## Culpability of institutions' conduct

Generally, the system of Community liability created by the Treaties is based on the concept of subjective, not objective liability. This means that, in addition to the objective illegality of the injurious act or omission, the subjective criteria of culpability on the part of the institution in committing it must also be shown to exist. The illegal act or omission must constitute an official fault, a wrongful conduct, on the part of its author. It is precisely the factor of culpability that endows the illegal act or omission with an element of default. Were it otherwise, the circumstances in which liability can be invoked and those in which illegality may be alleged would become indistinguishable. As a result, an action for damages could be brought on exactly the same grounds as an action for annulment or for the failure to act, despite their very different legal consequences and despite the very different limitations imposed on the right of private parties to institute each action.

A culpable conduct may consist of, for example:

1. the enactment of an improper Community measure;
2. the incorrect application of an otherwise lawful provision, in a situation or in a way that is unjustified because the requisite conditions have not been fulfilled; and
3. inadequate supervision of the execution of Community provisions by the Member State or other institutions set up for that purpose.

It must be added that if the damage complained of results from legislative measures, which involve choices of economic policy, the institution concerned will only be liable if there is a serious or flagrant breach of a 'superior rule of law for the protection of the individual': *Zuckerfabrik Schoppenstadt* v *Council* Case 5/71 [1985] ECR 975.

To be a serious enough breach, the applicant has to prove that the effects were serious and that the breach itself was arbitrary, in that an institution manifestly and gravely disregarded the limits of its power: see *Bayerische HNL Vermehrungbetriebe GmbH & Co KG* v *Council and Commission* Cases 83 and 94/76 and 4, 15 and 40/77 [1978] ECR 1209 and *Amylum NV and Tunnel Refineries Ltd* v *Council and Commission* Cases 116 and 124/77 [1979] ECR 3497.

However, the ECJ has, since these cases, adopted a less restrictive approach. A serious breach was defined in *Brasserie du Pêcheur SA* v *Federal Republic of Germany; R* v *Secretary of State for Transport, ex parte Factortame Ltd and Others* Joined Cases C–46 and 48/93 [1996] ECR I–1029. Although dealing with the conditions for State liability the Court in these cases based its test on the conditions for Community institutional liability under art 288 EC. The Court emphasised that the seriousness of a breach would be determinable by consideration of a number of factors. These include the relative clarity of the rule breached, the measure of discretion in the hands of the institutions, whether there was an excusable error of law and whether the breach was intentional or voluntary. The Court held that once it has been established that the breach is sufficiently serious, there is no need to determine fault. (For further discussion see Chapter 7.)

In addition, the following should be noted.

## Time

Proceedings are time-bound five years after the occurrence giving rise to the action, but the applicant must become aware of the occurrence before time starts to run: *Adams* v *Commission (No 1)* Case 145/83 [1985] ECR 3539. According to *De Franceschi SpA Monfalcone* v *Council and Commission* Case 81/81 [1982] ECR 117 the time period will begin only when the conditions for liability exist.

## Contributory negligence

This will not generally be considered by the Court, although it was in *Adams* (above) when the ECJ reduced the plaintiff's damages by half for failing to take measures to protect themselves.

Any applicant for damages must mitigate their loss. Hence, damages may be reduced, as in *Mulder* v *Commission and Council* Cases C–104/89 and 37/90 [1992] ECR I–3062, if they are unable to do so.

## Recoverable damage

Both actual and imminent damages are recoverable, although in the case of the latter it must be proved that the imminent damage is sufficiently foreseeable. Economic loss may be recoverable, but it must be specifically identifiable, and losses that could have been passed on to consumers are not recoverable: *Interquell Stärk-Chemie GmbH* v *Commission* Cases 261 and 262/78 [1979] ECR 3045.

# 6

# The Preliminary Reference Procedure

## 6.1 Introduction

Article 234 EC sets out the European Court's jurisdiction to give preliminary rulings. This jurisdiction fulfils two different but important functions.

### Legal integration

Legal integration within the Community is directly relevant to the attainment of fundamental Community objectives. Since this latter process is to take place within a strictly defined legal framework, it can only be successful if accompanied or preceded by corresponding legal integration. This has two aspects, namely, that Community law should be uniformly applied and that it should be uniformly interpreted throughout the Member States. To ensure this, the Treaties have placed the interpretation of Community law and the determination of the validity of the

118

acts of the institutions within the exclusive jurisdiction of the Court. At the same time they empower and, in the case of courts and tribunals of last resort, require national courts to invoke that jurisdiction whenever this becomes necessary in the course of the application of Community law by them.

Although the procedure is primarily aimed at avoiding divergences in the interpretation of EC law, it also tends to ensure uniformity and effectiveness in its application by providing the national courts with a means of eliminating any obstacles that might undermine such differences within the legal systems of Member States. As the European Court has stated, the purpose of the preliminary reference procedure is to prevent 'a body of national case law not in accord with the rules of Community law from coming into existence in any Member State': *Hoffman–La Roche* v *Centrafarm* Case 107/76 [1977] ECR 957.

The procedure for preliminary rulings, although designed to channel to the Court any dispute concerning the interpretation and validity of Community law that may arise in the national courts, should not superimpose the ECJ upon the national courts. The system implies a spirit of collaboration between the judicial systems, requiring joint efforts to ensure the uniform interpretation and effective application of Community law. Therefore, it is the national court that decides whether a reference is required or appropriate; the Court that rules on the issues raised in the reference; but the national court which applies the ruling to the facts of the case. In *Costa* v *ENEL* Case 6/64 [1964] ECR 585 the Court talked of there being a 'clear separation of functions between national courts and the Court of Justice'. However, as we shall discover, this original relationship, which is often described as 'horizontal and bilateral' – meaning that neither court has superiority and that the effect of rulings exists only in relation to the national court requesting it – has been somewhat manipulated and altered by the ECJ itself.

In exercising its preliminary ruling jurisdiction the ECJ is strictly limited to the interpretation of Community law and to the determination of the validity of the acts of institutions. It is required to leave the application of that law to the national courts. However, we shall witness that the Court has somewhat blurred the distinction between 'interpretation' and 'application'.

The task of the ECJ under the preliminary ruling procedure should be to assist the national courts, within the framework of the questions put to it, in resolving a particular dispute.

## Legal protection of individuals

The second function of preliminary rulings is that of affording legal protection to individuals by complementing and completing the system of remedies made available to them in the form of direct actions.

For this purpose they can be used both in situations where no other remedies exist, and in situations where other remedies do exist but fail to afford adequate protection. The former is the case where redress is sought against a Member State violating the Community rights of individuals by adverse national measures or practices. The latter arises where the complaint is directed against a Community institution but the bringing of an action is excluded for one reason or another.

The importance of preliminary rulings may be shown by the fact that by far the majority of cases come before the European Court on references from the national courts. In addition, the Court has formulated some of the most fundamental concepts and principles of Community law in the framework of the preliminary reference procedure, such as, for example, the doctrines of the supremacy and direct effect of Community law (Chapter 8) and, more recently, State liability (Chapter 7).

## 6.2 Jurisdiction of the European Court of Justice

Under art 234 EC, the ECJ has jurisdiction to give preliminary rulings concerning three distinct areas: first, the interpretation of the Treaties and the acts of the institutions; second, the determination of the validity of the acts of the institutions; and, third, the interpretation of the statutes of bodies established by acts of the Council.

The Court will therefore provide interpretation of Community law in relation to the following:

1. the 'basic Community Treaties – as amended by the SEA, the TEU, the ToA and the ToN;
2. treaties concluded between the Member States that have been expressly brought within the jurisdiction of the ECJ, such as, for example, the Convention on the Mutual Recognition of Companies and Legal Persons 1968, interpretation of which is entrusted to the ECJ by means of a separate protocol;
3. the interpretation of treaties and agreements concluded with third States and international organisations; and
4. the interpretation of all acts of the Community institutions, regardless of whether or not they have binding force. This embraces regulations, directives, decisions, recommendations and opinions of the Council and the Commission; the judgment and orders, as well as the rules of procedure, of the Court of Justice; and joint acts of the Council and the representatives of the governments of the Member States.

The ToA granted the ECJ jurisdiction to also deal with certain measures under the third pillar (justice and home affairs). Article 68 EC provides that measures adopted by the Council under Title IV EC Treaty (visas, asylum and immigration etc) may be referred under art 234 by a national court against whose decision there is no judicial remedy. Under the third paragraph of art 68 EC the Council, Commission or Member State may also request a ruling on the interpretation or validity of such measures. The ToA also extended the ECJ's jurisdiction to Title IV TEU (police and judicial co-operation) to examine the validity/interpretation of framework decisions (harmonising national laws) but not to consider operations/ actions of any national law enforcement agencies, such as the police. The Court has no jurisdiction in relation to common foreign and security policy to provide preliminary references.

The provisions of art 234 place a double limitation upon the jurisdiction of the Court of Justice. First, the Court should only consider the interpretation and validity of Community law, not domestic or general international law. However, the European Court has in some cases provided such a detailed ruling, explaining the national measure in hypothetical terms, that it, for all practical purposes, informs the national court that the national measure contravenes Community law.

Second, the Court should be concerned with an abstract 'interpretation' and 'determination' of the validity of Community law. It should not be concerned in the application of the law to particular facts, cases and situations. That task should be the sole province of the national courts. Thus, questions are posed and answered in the abstract. However, since the abstract interpretations of Community law always take place in the context of concrete cases that are the subject of litigation, the distinction between interpretation and application is a particularly delicate one, and one that some suggest has been 'blurred' by the Court.

The European Court also has jurisdiction to decide whether the requirements of the preliminary reference itself satisfy the terms of art 234. In particular, the Court deals with the following matters:

1. whether a body is a court or tribunal for the purposes of art 234;
2. whether a reference is premature or may have the effect of precluding a later reference from the same court in the same case;
3. whether the question asked is too vague or general or involves questions of national law; and
4. whether the preliminary ruling was competent in the event that a higher court had already ruled on the matter: see *Society for the Protection of Unborn Children (Ireland)* v *Grogan* Case C–159/90 [1991] ECR I–4685.

In general, the Court has demonstrated a great deal of flexibility in these matters, and has been willing to accept references from even the lowest courts, tribunals, or, as we shall see, quasi-tribunals. Similarly, until recently, if the Court found the reference too vague or general, it would reword it, and when questions were asked involving the interpretation of national law the Court skilfully elicited the Community law issues from the reference to provide an answer.

## 6.3 The definition of court or tribunal for the purposes of art 234 EC

The wording of art 234 refers to 'any court or tribunal of a Member State', which could be read to imply that only such bodies within the judicial system of a Member

State would be included. However, the interpretation of such bodies able to make a preliminary reference is in fact much wider.

The case of *Politi* v *Italian Ministry of Finance of the Italian Republic* Case 43/71 [1971] ECR 1039 establishes that the national law's determination of the body is not conclusive for the purposes of determining whether it is a court of tribunal for the purposes of making a preliminary reference. The Court will consider a number of factors in determining if the body is a court or tribunal, including whether:

1. the body is established by law;
2. it is a permanent body;
3. it has compulsory jurisdiction;
4. its procedure in inter pares;
5. it applies rules of law; and
6. it is independent.

There have been some problems in relation to determining whether an arbitral body, or arbitrator, comes within the ambit of art 234. An arbitration body may be a court or tribunal for the purposes of art 234 as, for example, the disciplinary body in *Broekmeulen* v *Huisarts Registratie Commissie* Case 246/80 [1981] ECR 2311 was concluded to be. This was because it

> '... operates with the consent of the public authorities and with their co-operation, and which, after an adversarial procedure, delivers decisions which are recognised as final ...'

An arbitrator, however, has been concluded to lack the official recognition to make 'judicial' decisions, and is therefore unable to make a preliminary reference under art 234: *Nordsee Deutsche Hochseefischerei GmbH* v *Reederei Mond Hochseefischerei Nordstern AG* Case 102/81 [1982] ECR 1095. In respect of the United Kingdom, references have been accepted from Employment Appeal Tribunals, Social Security Commissioners, VAT tribunals and the National Insurance Commissioner.

## 6.4 Optional references – the discretion to refer

Generally, the power of a court or tribunal to which art 234 applies to make a preliminary reference is optional, or discretionary. This is so except for the case of courts or tribunals against whose decisions there is no judicial remedy under national law, where it is compulsory: see section 6.5.

The power to refer is largely unfettered. The national courts may freely decide whether to refer or not, the legal issues and at what stage of the proceedings to refer. This means that a reference may be made before a full hearing, during the interlocutory stage, or even when the case is being heard in the absence of one of the parties. The Court has stated, though, that it prefers an inter pares hearing to take place before the reference if that is possible: *Eurico Italia Srl* v *Ente Nazionale Risi* Cases C–332, 333 and 335/92 [1994] ECR I–711. The Court will expect the case to have reached a stage where the facts have been established, and the issues requiring the Court's assistance identified: *Irish Creamery Milk Suppliers Association* v *Ireland* Cases 36 and 71/80 [1981] ECR 735. However, the Court has been known to accept references where it felt that it had sufficient information, even though it did not have all the relevant facts: see, for example, *Vaneetveld* v *Le Foyer SA* Case C–316/93 [1994] ECR I–763.

The only prerequisites on the discretion of a national court or tribunal to make a reference are: first, that a question involving interpretation or consideration of the validity of provisions of Community law should be raised before them; and, second, they should consider a preliminary ruling on that question to be necessary to enable them to give judgment. Such a question is raised as soon as plausible arguments are put forward which raise prima facie reasonable doubt upon the meaning, scope, effect or validity of a Community provision or upon the compatibility with it of a national measure or practice.

A preliminary reference on a question therefore becomes necessary where a court assesses that the clarification of the question is essential to the determination of the issue before it, and that it would be unable to perform that without the help of a ruling: see *Bulmer (HP) Ltd* v *J Bollinger SA* [1974] Ch 401; [1974] 3 WLR 202.

## 6.5 Compulsory references

If a question concerning the interpretation or the validity of Community provisions is raised in a case pending before a court or tribunal of a Member State, against whose decision there is no judicial remedy under national law, that court or tribunal is obliged to bring the matter before the European Court. The problem may be in defining such courts or tribunals of 'last resort'. The situation will obviously apply to those courts or tribunals that are placed at the top of that Member State's judicial hierarchy, such as the House of Lords in English law. However, the question arises as to whether the obligation to refer also relates to courts or tribunals from which there is no right to appeal in the case at hand.

The Court of Justice dealt with just such a situation in the case of *Costa* v *ENEL* Case 6/64 [1964] ECR 585. In this case the amount claimed was so small that there was no appeal allowed from the magistrate's decision. The ECJ concluded that, in such cases, there was an obligation to refer under art 234. In *Hoffman-La Roche* v *Centrafarm* Case 107/76 [1977] ECR 957 the Court considered the question of whether the highest appeal court in the case, or the highest appeal court in the national legal system, should be the court 'against whose decisions there is no judicial remedy under national law'. The case concerned interlocutary judgments, which were later found not to be final, but in so finding, the Advocate-General argued for the obligation to rest on the highest court in the actual case (sometimes known as the 'concrete theory'):

'It seems to me therefore that, in order that the Court may fully and effectively discharge its task of protecting the rights which the Community legal system has created in favour of individuals, it is reasonable to regard the courts, at every level, as under a duty to seek a preliminary ruling in the course of any proceedings which must of necessity result in a final decision.'

Initially, decisions in the UK courts appeared to follow a different line, in that the only courts from which a reference was compulsory were those from which there was no appeal in national law – the highest court in the land. However, in England, a party who wants to appeal to the House of Lords must obtain leave to proceed there. That leave may be refused. What then is the position of the Court of Appeal? In other words, if leave is granted the Court of Appeal is not the final court, but if leave is not granted, it becomes the court of last resort in that particular case.

The situation that the Court of Appeal may find itself in, and the application of the obligation to refer under art 234 in relation to the English judicial system, has been defined by Balcombe LJ in *Chiron Corporation* v *Murex Diagnostics Ltd* [1995] All ER (EC) 88, as follows:

'Except in those cases ... where the Court of Appeal is the court of last resort, the Court of Appeal is not obliged to make a reference to the ECJ ... If the Court of Appeal does not make a reference to the ECJ, and gives its final judgment on the appeal, then the House of Lords becomes the court of last resort. If either the Court of Appeal or the House of Lords grants leave to appeal, then there is no problem. If the Court of Appeal refuses leave to appeal, and the House of Lords is presented with an application for leave to appeal, before it refuses leave it should consider whether an issue of Community law arises which is necessary for its decision (whether to grant or refuse leave) ... If it considers that a reference is requisite, it will take such action as it may consider appropriate in the particular case.'

The recent case of *Lyckeskog* Case C–99/00 [2002] ECR I–4839 involved the Swedish judicial system, in which context the Court concluded that the Swedish appeal court was never obliged to make a reference. However, the Swedish Supreme Court was obliged to make a reference either when deciding to grant leave to appeal or when hearing the appeal after having granted leave. Such a situation should, by implication, also apply to the Court of Appeal and the House of Lords in the English legal system.

## 6.6  The need for a question

Article 234 only needs to be used by the national courts if there is a question of Community law. There may not be such a question if the Court has already ruled on the matter. However, the original relationship envisaged between the ECJ and the national courts was merely a bilateral one – in other words, the 'effect' of the ruling would only relate to the court that had answered the question. This relationship, whilst preserving the autonomy of the national courts, is, in practical terms, unwieldy since the European Court then receives numerous questions, from numerous national courts, many of which relate to the same point of Community law. The ECJ recognised this early in the Community's development and commented on the obligation to refer in the case of *Da Costa en Schaake NV* v *Nederlandse Belastingadministratie* Cases 28–30/62 [1963] ECR 31 in the following terms:

> '... the authority of an interpretation ... already given by the Court may deprive the obligation of its purpose and thus empty it of its substance. Such is the case especially when the question raised is materially identical with a question which has already been the subject of a preliminary ruling in a similar case.'

Indeed, the facts of *Da Costa* were materially identical to those of the previous case of *Van Gend en Loos* Case 26/62 [1963] ECR 1, with no new facts. Therefore, the Court in its judgment in *Da Costa* simply repeated the previous judgment and specifically referred the requesting court to that judgment. In *Da Costa* the ECJ also expressly recognised the ability of a national court or tribunal to make a reference, should it so wish, but that should they do so they should include some new fact or argument, or they would simply be referred to the previous judgment.

In practical terms, therefore, the obligation or the need to refer may be removed if the ECJ has already dealt with the point of Community law and, from the above case, the facts are materially identical. The Court, though, has since expanded on its judgment in *Da Costa*.

In the case of *CILFIT* v *Ministry of Health* Case 283/81 [1982] ECR 3415 the Court concluded that the obligation or need to refer could be removed if:

> '... previous decisions of the Court have already dealt with the point of law in question, irrespective of the nature of the proceedings which led to those decisions, even though the questions at issue may not be strictly identical.'

In relation to preliminary references on the validity of Community legislation, the Court has also specifically stated that:

> '... although a judgment of the Court given under [art 234] of the Treaty declaring an act of an institution ... to be void is directly addressed only to the national court which brought the matter before the Court, it is sufficient reason for any other national court to regard that act as void for the purposes of a judgment which it has to give': *ICC* v *Amministrazione delle Finanze dello Stato* Case 66/80 [1981] ECR 1191.

It should be noted at this point, that the ECJ has exclusive jurisdiction to declare an act of a Community institution invalid, and that national courts or tribunals cannot exercise such jurisdiction. The Court addressed this matter in *Firma Foto-Frost* v *Hauptzollamt Lubeck-Ost* Case 314/85 [1987] ECR 4199. It pointed out that, although art 234 allowed national courts and tribunals to make a reference (and to consider previous rulings), it did not provide for the national courts or tribunals to declare acts of the Community institutions invalid. Article 234 was designed to facilitate the uniform application of Community law, and this requirement is most acute when the validity of a Community act is in question. Divergences between courts in the Member States as to the validity of Community measures would place in jeopardy the unity of the Community legal order and detract from the fundamental requirement of legal certainty. This conclusion was supported by the system of judicial protection established by the Treaty, which allowed challenges to Community measures under a separate provision – art 230 EC. The Court has subsequently confirmed that national courts and tribunals do not have the power to declare an act of a Community institution void without intervention of the Court under the preliminary reference procedure (or by relying on a previous judgment of the Court): *Angelopharm GmbH* v *Freie und Hansestadt Hamburg* Case C–212/91 [1994] ECR I–171.

## 6.7 The development of the acte clair doctrine

The need to refer may be removed by the fact that the national court believes that the answer to the reference is clear, even though there is no direct precedent as in the cases above. In the case of *CILFIT* Case 283/81 (above), the Court held:

> '... the correct application of Community law may be so obvious as to leave no scope for any reasonable doubt as to the manner in which the question raised is to be resolved. Before it comes to the conclusion that such is the case, the national court or tribunal must be convinced that the matter is equally obvious to the courts of the other Member States and to the Court of Justice. Only if those conditions are satisfied may the national court of tribunal refrain from submitting the question to the Court of Justice and take upon itself the responsibility for resolving it.'

The Court also established criteria to aid the national courts in legitimately applying what is known as the acte clair doctrine. Special considerations require the national court to take account of the following factors:

1. European legislation is drafted in several different languages, all of which are equally authentic, and proper interpretation often involves comparison of texts with different language versions;
2. Community law has acquired its own terminology and legal concepts do not necessarily have the same meaning in Community law as in national law; and
3. every provision of Community law has to be placed in its proper context and interpreted in light of the system established by the Treaties having proper regard to both its objectives and to the state of the law at that particular point: see *Lister* v *Forth Dry Dock and Engineering Co* [1989] 1 All ER 1134 (HL).

The Court of Justice has therefore created an informal doctrine of precedent (or de facto precedent). By handing back power to the national courts to decide if they need to make a reference, whilst simultaneously providing strict guidelines for them to follow, the ECJ has asserted a position dominant to that of the national courts. In other words, the de facto precedent formulated in *Da Costa* increases the authority of the ECJ's rulings, and the Court assumes, in *CILFIT*, the ability to devolve power back to the national courts. Both of these factors enhance the position and authority of the Court of Justice, moving it away from being a player in a horizontal and bilateral system, to one where it is at the pinnacle of the judicial system. De facto precedent and acte clair have therefore altered the original relationship envisaged under art 234 to one that is both vertical and multilateral. In practical terms, these developments also relieve the Court of some of its considerable workload.

The decision of a national court on whether a point of Community law is acte clair can be a difficult one and, whilst the Court in *CILFIT* offered guidance, there is obviously the potential for abuse. Such abuse could threaten the uniformity of interpretation so essential for the supremacy of Community law to be maintained. Some national courts have recognised this responsibility and have responded to it positively. In *Customs and Excise Commissioners* v *Samex* [1983] 3 CMLR 194, Bingham J clearly expressed the opinion that the ECJ was in a more advantageous position than he was in determining the meaning and scope of Community law. Such an understanding of the complexities of Community law by a national court means that acte clair will be used wisely by them. Unfortunately, not all national courts have been as careful in recognising what they are truly capable of in relation to the interpretation of Community law.

Probably the most infamous English case dealing with this aspect of Community law is that of *Bulmer* v *Bollinger* (above), in which Lord Denning MR provided a set of guidelines on when a reference was, in his opinion, necessary. The guidelines are as follows:

1. the point must be conclusive;
2. previous rulings should be considered;
3. acte clair may apply; and
4. the facts should be decided first.

These guidelines will establish when the reference is 'necessary', but Lord Denning went on to provide guidelines on whether the discretion to refer in such situations should be exercised in the given case. These are as follows:

1. the time taken to get a ruling (in that it may be 'unreasonably' long);
2. to avoid overloading the European Court;
3. that the question must be clearly formulated;
4. the difficulty and importance of the question;
5. the expense that may be incurred; and
6. the wishes of the parties.

The criteria offered by Lord Denning have been applied in the courts. They have, however, been criticised, especially since their application has resulted in cases with a Community dimension not being referred to the Court of Justice: see, for example, *R* v *London Boroughs Transport Committee, ex parte Freight Transport*

*Association* [1991] 3 All ER 915. Other courts have been unwilling to refer because of the time that such rulings take to be returned: see, for example, *Johnson* v *Chief Adjudication Officer* [1994] 1 CMLR 829 and *R* v *Ministry of Agriculture, Fisheries and Food, ex parte Portman Agrochemicals Ltd* [1994] 1 CMLR 18. Generally, however, English courts, whilst still making reference to the *Bulmer* guidelines, have shown themselves increasingly willing to make proper references or apply the acte clair doctrine appropriately: see, for example, *R* v *Secretary of State for Employment, ex parte Equal Opportunities Commission* [1994] 1 All ER 910 (HL).

Modern guidance on when a reference under art 234 is 'necessary' is provided in the judgment of Bingham MR in the case of *R* v *International Stock Exchange, ex parte Else* [1993] QB 534:

> '... if the facts have been found and the Community law issue is critical to the court's final decision, the appropriate course is to refer the issue to the Court of Justice unless the national court can with complete confidence resolve the issue itself. In considering whether it can ... the national court must be fully mindful of the differences between national and Community legislation, of the pitfalls which face a national court venturing into what may be an unfamiliar field, of the need for uniform interpretation throughout the Community and of the great advantages enjoyed by the Court of Justice in constructing Community instruments. If the national court has any real doubt, it should obviously refer.'

## 6.8 The form and procedure for a reference

To enable the European Court to arrive at a useful interpretation, the referring court is generally expected to indicate the factual and legal context which has given rise to the request for the reference, and into which the interpretation is to be placed. Originally the Court of Justice was prepared to accept those references that were not properly framed: see, for example, *Costa* v *ENEL* Case 6/64 [1964] ECR 585. The ECJ was also not prepared to criticise why the reference had been requested by the national court since, because of the separation of functions under art 234, the decision was that of the national court alone: *Simmenthal SpA* v *Ministero delle Finanze* Case 35/76 [1976] ECR 1871. This flexibility encouraged national courts to request preliminary rulings, thereby ensuring the uniformity of interpretation so essential to the Community legal order.

However, the European Court has since adopted a much more rigorous approach in deciding whether or not to accept a reference from a national court. The Court has become increasingly intolerant of lax references, probably due to its increasing workload. This process began in 1980 in *Foglia* v *Novello* Case 104/79 [1980] ECR 745, in which the ECJ declined to give a ruling on the basis that the request was 'artificial' in the sense that there was no real dispute between the parties. This judgment was followed by *Foglia* v *Novello (No 2)* Case 244/80 [1981] ECR 3045, in which the Court stressed:

'... the duty assigned to the Court by [art 234] is not that of delivering advisory opinions on general or hypothetical questions but of assisting in the administration of justice in the Member States.'

Furthermore, the Court felt that it was in a position to:

'... make any assessment inherent in the performance of its own duties in particular in order to check, as all courts must, whether it has jurisdiction.'

In other words, the Court of Justice asserted that it had the jurisdiction to check the validity of the references requested by national courts. It claimed that it had the ultimate ability to control those cases that it heard, reaffirming its place at the top of the judicial hierarchy. So, for example, in *Meilicke v ADV/ORGA FA Meyer* Case C–83/91 [1992] ECR I–4871, the Court rejected a reference from a German court. This was because it involved a dispute that had not yet arisen between the parties but which had been the subject of proceedings in the national court to resolve a hypothetical and abstract point of law. In *Pretore Di Genoa v Banchero* Case C–157/92 [1993] I–ECR 1085 the Court refused to provide a reference on the basis that the facts specified in the request were inadequately stated for them to provide a useful interpretation of Community law.

The European Court has since formulated some guidance for national courts. *The Guidance Notes on References by National Courts for Preliminary Rulings* (1996) instruct the national court to provide reasons for their request, and that such reasons need to be comprehensive enough to provide the Court with an understanding as to why the request is being made. In addition the request should also include the following:

1. the essential facts;
2. the relevant national legal provisions; and
3. a summary of the parties' arguments (if appropriate).

## 6.9 The distinction between interpretation and application

As already stated, the provisions of art 234 create a separation of functions; it is the responsibility of the European Court to provide the interpretation of Community law, and the national court to apply that to the facts of the case in the national court.

However, the ECJ has somewhat blurred the distinction between the two duties by providing such detailed rulings that all the national court is required to do is to simply apply it to the case. For example, in *Cristini v SNCF* Case 32/75 [1975] ECR 1085, a case dealing with the 'social advantages' available to workers' families under Regulation 1612/68, art 7(2) (see Chapter 9), the ECJ was asked whether rail cards providing for reductions for large, French families were included. The Court provided a detailed ruling and specifically stated that:

'... in view of the equality of treatment which the provision seeks to achieve, the substantive area of application must be delineated so as to include all social and tax advantages, whether or not attached to the contract of employment, *such as reductions in fares for large families*' (emphasis added).

In other words, instead of defining the meaning of social and tax advantages, and to whom they apply, and leaving the national court to apply that to the facts of the case, the Court specifically said that the rail card did come within the Community provision. This left the national court with nothing to do except to apply the European Court's ruling.

One field of Community law in which the European Court has been prepared to provide extremely detailed rulings is that of State liability (see Chapter 7). This may however be explained by the Court's perceived need to retain control over a new development in Community law. Conversely, there are numerous areas of Community law in which the ECJ has merely provided guidelines, and the national courts are responsible for their application and future development.

In broad terms, the willingness of the Court of Justice to provide such detailed rulings, in certain circumstances, offers yet another example of it asserting its position above that of the national courts.

## 6.10 The situation pending the reference

Unfortunately, because of the heavy workload of the Court of Justice, it can take up to two years for the ruling to return to the national court. To compensate for this, the European Court, under art 243 EC, may order any interim measure that it considers appropriate. This is primarily the case if the reference concerns the legality of a measure. For example, if a provision of national law conflicts with Community law, the Court may require its suspension. Alternatively, there may be some dispute over the validity of a Community measure that has provided the basis for implementing national measures. In *Zucherfabrik Süderdithmarschen* v *Hauptzollamt Itzehoe* Case C–92/89 [1991] ECR I–415 the ECJ concluded that national courts had the power to grant interim relief, but that this should only be done in 'exceptional circumstances'. Such circumstances would include protecting Community law rights and protecting against irreparable damage: see, for example, *R* v *Secretary of State for Transport, ex parte Factortame Ltd and Others* Case C–213/89 [1990] ECR I–2433, and applied by the House of Lords ([1990] 3 CMLR 59).

## 6.11 The legal effects of preliminary rulings

The judgments of the Court of Justice given in reference proceedings are, in principle, subject to the normal operation of the res judicata rule. Accordingly, a preliminary ruling is binding on the national court that requested it, including all lower and higher courts that may be called upon to adjudicate in the same case, but, strictly speaking, only to the particular case and in respect of the parties to that case. This is subject to the concepts of de facto precedent and acte clair discussed above. Thus, the court before which the main action is pending is required to defer to the ruling as regards the points of law in which the European Court has given its decision.

Nevertheless, elements of the original separation of functions in terms of equality between the ECJ and the national courts remain. It follows from the nature and the purpose of the preliminary reference system, and from the special relationship between the European Court and the national court, that the latter remain free to draw from the ruling the relevant legal conclusions necessary for a definitive settlement of the case. It remains free even to the extent of not drawing any conclusions at all, for example, if it discovers afterwards that the consultation was not necessary and that it can give a decision on other grounds. Also, the national court remains free to assess whether it is sufficiently enlightened by the ruling of the Court, or whether certain doubts still remain which necessitate the re-submission of the same or further questions to the European Court (for example, the Sunday Trading Cases discussed in Chapter 14).

Generally, there is nothing to prevent a court, if it so desires, from making a new reference even though the issues involved have already formed the subject of a preliminary ruling in the very same proceedings or in a similar case. But, as already explained, unless some new factor is presented the ECJ will refer the national court to the previous judgment.

Over the last few years the European Court has attempted to reduce its workload by, as we have seen, refusing those references that fail to offer a new factor, or which are inadequately framed. It has also rendered judgments in similar or related cases by issuing one principal judgment and cross-referencing to that judgment in subsequent decisions. For example, in *Rochdale Borough Council* v *Anders* Case C–306/88 [1993] 1 All ER 520, the Court declined to issue a fresh judgment in the case, which was virtually identical in terms of both fact and law to an immediately preceding case. Even though the UK court had informed the ECJ in the reference that at least one point remained unsettled, the Court of Justice considered that all four points raised has been adequately settled. In the circumstances, the ECJ felt that it was appropriate to cite its earlier judgment and declined to issue a full report.

Although in theory the effect of the preliminary ruling is strictly inter pares, as we have discussed, in practice it may have an erga omnes effect. For example, an interpretative ruling that defines the meaning, scope and effect of a Community rule is in practice, because of acte clair, authoritative even beyond the individual case that has given rise to it.

When the preliminary reference procedure deals with the direct effect of a Community measure (ie that it creates rights for individuals that they may enforce in their national courts), once established that rule cannot change and the ruling must necessarily have a definitive effect. On the other hand, where the Court is concerned with the validity of an act the legal consequences may be strictly inter pares. As a rule, the Court does not examine and confirm the validity of an act in general, but strictly in relation to the specific arguments and complaints raised in the reference, as amplified by the submission of the parties.

If the Court confirms the validity of the act, then the effect is inter pares. If the Court declares an act invalid, although the ruling does not make the act in question null and void, this is the usual practical consequence. A measure that is invalid with respect to one person must be regarded as invalid with respect to all. It is inconceivable that such an act could ever be enforced, either by the Community institutions or by the national authorities, in any future situation.

## 6.12 Reforming the preliminary reference procedure

The extremely heavy workload of the Court of Justice has led to considerable delays in its ability to give judgments. Much of the Court's workload is derived from requests for preliminary references. The Court has attempted to assert some control over the process, to reduce the number of requests that it receives, by the creation of de facto precedent, the acte clair doctrine, and the assessment of the way in which the reference is framed and its basis. In addition, the Court of First Instance provides the European Court with valuable help.

However, the workload of the European Court has not been reduced to any great degree, and there remain delays in national courts receiving rulings. It could be expected that this situation will only worsen should the Union proceed with further expansion. As a response to the perceived problems in the preliminary reference procedure, a number of reforms have been suggested. The main suggestions for reform are as follows.

1. *To permit the ECJ to exercise control over those references it wishes to hear.* This would enable the Court to relieve its workload by hearing only those cases of significance to the Community legal order. In other words, the national court would be required to request the leave of the European Court before it would be able to receive a ruling. The perceived problems with such a reform include the lack of appeal should the ECJ decline such leave, and the creation of what would be tantamount to a federal legal system, similar to that of the United States. This would be a concrete development that the Member States are perhaps not yet ready for, a fact witnessed in the demands of the British government for the creation of a right of appeal from the ECJ itself.

2. *To create a lower tier of European courts, spread geographically throughout the European Union.* This would result in national courts accessing their regional European Court, before being able to appeal to the ECJ. The ECJ disliked this

suggestion, on the basis that it may destroy the essential uniformity required for the supremacy of Community law to be maintained.

3. *To prescribe the national courts able to make a reference.* Again, however, the ECJ has rejected this idea, on the basis that the preliminary reference procedure provides the 'cornerstone' of the development and success of the Community legal order. This is most evidently witnessed in the fact that many of the most important Community legal concepts have been both created and developed under the reference procedure – who is to say that there are not future, important legal concepts that may be created in such a way? Such a reform may also have detrimental consequences for the success of Community law in relation to any 'new' Member States who will undoubtedly encounter problems in the interpretation and application of Community law.

4. *To create a 'fast-track' procedure for some types of case.* There would, however, be problems in assessing which cases would be decided under such a process.

5. *To reduce the element of oral proceedings and improve the general quality of references.* Whilst this is a practical solution, it fails to recognise that the present procedure is already weighted in favour of written proceedings, and that national courts have been provided with guidance on the content of their references.

6. *To require the national courts and tribunals to whom art 234 applies to exercise greater discretion before requesting the ruling.* This suggestion requires clear guidance for national courts, since to do otherwise could result in abuse of the system, with detrimental knock-on effects for the uniformity of Community law. In addition, courts and tribunals in any new Member State may find it extremely difficult to assess those cases that required a reference, leaving the potential for disastrous consequences not just for the success of Community law, but also for individuals attempting to access their Community law rights.

7. *To create specialised courts.* This suggestion, supported by the ECJ itself, would provide for specialised bodies to deal with specific issues, with the ability to appeal to the ECJ. This solution is extremely practical, whilst retaining the original Community legal order envisaged under the Treaties. It is a suggestion that has been adopted under the Treaty of Nice (see Chapter 2) but the Community must wait to see whether it is a viable means of resolving the current problems.

8. *To extend the bodies able to hear preliminary references.* This suggestion has always been highly controversial and immediately rejected by the ECJ. However, the Treaty of Nice will extend the jurisdiction of the CFI so that it can hear the majority of direct actions (although enforcement action under arts 226–227 EC will remain in the hands of the ECJ) which may relieve the Court of some of its workload. More significantly, the CFI will be granted the jurisdiction to hear preliminary references (see Chapter 2).

# 7

# State Liability – the Creation of a Community Remedy

7.1 Introduction

7.2 The original approach

7.3 The *Francovich* case

7.4 The *Brasserie/Factortame* Cases

7.5 Post *Brasserie* – the application and development of State liability

7.6 Extending liability in the future

7.7 Conclusion

## 7.1 Introduction

The Treaties do not include any general provisions providing for remedies should European Community law be breached. The EC Treaty also did not envisage the possibility of individuals bringing direct actions against Member States, and there is no express provision to allow such actions to be brought immediately to the attention of the Court of Justice. The original approach by the ECJ was therefore to consider remedies as a matter for the national legal systems to determine. Hence, in English law, actions against the United Kingdom government and its agencies in the English courts could only be brought under the traditional heads of tortious injury, such as breach of a statutory duty. Infringements of Community law by the British government and its agencies were widely believed not to give rise to such liability.

This chapter will assess the original approach of the Court of Justice to the issue of remedies for breaches of Community law, and will trace its development through to the creation of a Community-wide remedy by the European Court in the early 1990s.

## 7.2 The original approach

In the early 1960s the Court stated that the provision of remedies for an infringement of Community law was to be determined by the national courts. In *Rewe-Zentralfinanz eG and Rewe-Zentral AG* v *Landwirtschaftskammer für das Saarland* Case 33/76 [1976] ECR 1989 the Court stated:

> '... in the absence of Community rules on this subject, it is for the domestic legal system of each Member State to designate the courts having jurisdiction and to determine the procedural conditions governing actions at law intended to ensure the protection of the rights which citizens have from the direct effect of Community law, it being understood that such conditions cannot be less favourable that those relating to similar actions of a domestic nature.'

Consequently, the discretion on the provision and type of remedy rested with the national courts, with the Court of Justice merely requiring two basic conditions:

1. the remedy for a breach of EC law was to be available under the same conditions as it was for a breach of national law. In other words, there was to be no discrimination between an applicant seeking a remedy for a breach of national law and one seeking a remedy for a breach of Community law; and
2. that no national 'conditions' or 'time limits' made it impossible in practice to gain the right to a remedy.

There was, in addition, no obligation on the national courts to create any new national legal remedy for infringements of European Community law, as long as they complied with the above two conditions. Thus, each Member State applied its own procedures and remedies to cases involving infringement of EC law. The resulting lack of uniformity, and potential for disproportionate punishment for relatively minor breaches, led the Court of Justice to expand on the conditions required for an 'adequate' remedy.

In *Sagulo, Brenca and Bakhouche* Case 8/77 [1977] ECR 1495 a German court wished to impose penal sanctions for breaches of the rules in relation to the free movement of workers. In this case it was the failure to comply with the necessary formalities for entry into the territory of a Member State and acquisition of a residence permit. The Court of Justice held:

> '... it is for the competent authorities of each Member State to impose penalties where appropriate on a person subject to the provision of Community law ... but that penalty must not be disproportionate to the nature of the offence committed.'

Furthermore, in the case of *Von Colson and Kamann* v *Land Nordrhein-Westfalen* Case 14/83 [1984] ECR 1891, the Court concluded that any remedy provided should, in addition to the above conditions, be 'effective' and 'adequate'. Effective in the sense that it provided a 'deterrent effect' and adequate in the sense that any compensation was not merely nominal but reflected the 'damage sustained'.

The potential for conflict between the need for effective and adequate remedies, and the reliance on pre-existing national remedies, came to a head in *R* v *Secretary of State for Transport, ex parte Factortame Ltd and Others* Case C–213/89 [1990] ECR I–2433. The facts of the case centred on the Merchant Shipping Act 1988, which required fishing vessels to re-register for licences to fish in British waters. The problem was that certain Spanish ship-owners failed to meet the new registration conditions. Whilst the Commission had already initiated a direct action against the UK government (see Chapter 4), the Spanish owners brought proceedings in the High Court challenging the new requirements as breaching Community law. In this case the breaches were in relation to the freedom of establishment and the prohibition of discrimination on the basis of nationality, since one of the new requirements was that 75 per cent of directors and shareholders of company-owned fishing vessels were nationals. The Spanish owners requested interim relief (in the form of an injunction against the Secretary of State for Transport) until the final judgment was awarded, since they were encountering considerable financial loss as a result of the denial of a licence.

The House of Lords held ([1990] 2 AC 85) that they were unable to grant interim relief on the basis that common law prohibited grant of an interim injunction against the Crown. The House of Lords also believed that the doctrine of parliamentary supremacy prevented the courts from enquiring into the validity of an Act of Parliament. The validity of such an Act, based on the doctrine of implied repeal, was presumed, unless and until a case established that the Act was in breach of Community law. The House of Lords, though, felt it necessary to request a preliminary reference under art 234 EC to request clarification as to whether they were indeed obliged to provide interim relief in such a situation. The Court of Justice held that:

> '... any provision of a national legal system and any legislative, administrative or judicial practice which might impair the effectiveness of Community law by withholding from the national court having jurisdiction to apply such law the power to do everything necessary at the moment of its application to set aside national legislative provisions which might prevent, even temporarily, Community rules from having full force and effect are incompatible with those requirements, which are the very essence of Community law ...'

In particular, the Court of Justice concluded that the effectiveness of Community law would be impaired if interim relief was not available and that any national rule or law that created such a situation must be set aside by the national court. The ECJ based its decision on art 10 EC, which provides that:

> 'Member States shall take all appropriate measures, whether general or particular, to ensure fulfilment of the obligations arising out of this Treaty or resulting from action taken by the institutions of the Community. They shall facilitate the Community's tasks.
>
> They shall abstain from any measure which could jeopardise the attainment of the objectives of the Treaty.'

The problem with the judgment in relation to the provision of remedies in national courts rests with the insistence of the Court of Justice that the remedy be effective. It did not, however, tackle the previous conclusion that Member States were not obligated to create any new remedies. The UK government argued that the practical result of the European Court's judgment in this case was the need for the creation of a 'new' remedy to resolve the need for protection of Community rights. Therefore, whilst the Court of Justice insisted that new remedies were not required, its insistence on effective remedies obligated the States to create new ones. This development contradicted the original approach, which had intended the national legal systems to have procedural autonomy in the way in which remedies were applied and enforced.

Further developments included the Court's insistence that procedural rules could not merely make the remedy 'impossible in practice' but 'excessively difficult' to obtain: see *Peterbroeck, Van Campenhout & Cie* v *Belgium* Case C–312/93 [1995] ECR I–4599. The developments of the law in this field created uncertainty for both the national legal systems of the Member States and those Community citizens seeking redress for infringements of Community law: see, for example, *Marshall* v *Southampton and South-West Hampshire Area Health Authority (No 2)* Case C–271/91 [1993] ECR I–4367.

Whilst such uncertainty was perhaps relieved a little by the Court of Justice taking a more restrained view of the need for effectiveness in national remedies after the cases of *Factortame* and *Marshall (No 2)* the element of uncertainty remained. There is no objective method available of assessing the validity of a particular national procedural rule, but to consider it in the light of each set of case facts and circumstances. Cases will, therefore, need to be referred to the European Court: see, for example, *Cotter and McDermott* v *Minister for Social Welfare and Attorney-General* Case C–377/89 [1991] ECR I–1155; *Emmott* v *Minister for Social Welfare* Case C–208/90 [1991] ECR I–4269; and *R* v *Secretary of State for Social Security, ex parte Sutton* Case C–66/95R [1997] ECR I–2163. However, in 1991, the ECJ provided for the creation of a new, Community-wide remedy in relation to claims for damages resulting from infringements of Community law by the Member States.

## 7.3 The *Francovich* case

In the landmark joined case of *Francovich and Bonifaci* v *Italian Republic* Cases C–6 and 9/90 [1991] ECR I–5357, the European Court upheld the existence of a duty in European law to make reparation for injury caused by a Member State failing to comply with its obligations.

The facts of this case were, essentially, that Italy had failed to transpose a directive (Council Directive 80/987) requiring the setting up of a scheme to compensate individuals in the event of the insolvency of their employers. The directive was intended to provide a minimum level of protection in the event that employers became insolvent and were unable to pay the wages of their employees.

The plaintiffs were made unemployed and were unable to recover their unpaid wages. They were also unable to claim under the scheme envisaged under the Directive since Italy had not incorporated the Directive into Italian law. In fact, Italy had already been found in breach of Community law for its failure to comply with Community law in an earlier direct action: *Commission* v *Italy (Re Failure to Implement Directives)* Case 22/87 [1989] ECR 143.

The plaintiffs raised an action in the Italian courts against the government to establish liability for failure to implement the Community directive, and for causing injury as a result of the omission. The Italian courts referred the question of State liability for failure to comply with Community law to the European Court under the art 234 preliminary reference procedure.

The Court held that Member States were under an obligation to ensure the full effect of Community law, under art 10 EC, and to guarantee the rights of private individuals under Community law. The Court stated that the effectiveness of these rights would be significantly undermined if individuals were denied compensation when their rights had been infringed by the illegal actions of Member States. Therefore, the Court concluded, Member States were liable to compensate individuals for any injury sustained for violations of Community law where the breach of duty could be imputed to the behaviour of the Member State:

> '... the full effectiveness of Community rules would be impaired and the protection of the rights which they grant would be weakened if individuals were unable to obtain compensation when their rights are infringed by a breach of Community law for which a Member State can be held responsible.
>
> The possibility of compensation by the Member State is particularly indispensable where, as in this case, the full effectiveness of Community rules is subject to prior action on the part of the State and consequently individuals cannot, in the absence of such action, enforce the rights granted to them by Community law before the national courts.
>
> It follows that the principle of State liability for harm caused to individuals by breaches of Community law for which the State can be held responsible is inherent in the system of the Treaty.'

The Court, however, stated that this liability was not unlimited, and that three conditions had to be demonstrated before it could be established. Those three conditions were that:

1. the purpose of the Community measure must have been to create rights conferred on private individuals;
2. the content of those rights must be identifiable from the content of the measure; and
3. there must exist some causal link between the failure by the Member State to comply with Community law and the injury sustained by the private individual.

The Court left open the exact mechanism in each Member State for the vindication of such rights. Each Member State is responsible for ensuring the existence of a mechanism of compensation but has a certain degree of discretion in selecting the most appropriate method. As a minimum requirement, the Court stated that the substantive and procedural conditions for establishing liability on this basis could not be less favourable than for similar claims under national law. At the same time, the procedure itself should not be organised in such a fashion as to render it excessively difficult, or practically impossible, for these rights to be exercised (see above).

Confirmation of whether the first two of the three requirements for establishing liability are satisfied may be obtained by a national court through the preliminary reference procedure; by requesting a ruling from the ECJ, a national court can confirm the compatibility of the national measure with Community law. Thereafter, it is for the national court to decide whether, on the basis of the facts presented, a causal connection exists between the violation of Community obligations and the injury sustained by the parties: see, for example, *Faccini Dori* v *Recreb Srl* Case C–91/92 [1994] ECR I–3325.

There were, however, a number of outstanding questions not elaborated on by the European Court. They included the following:

1. Although the Court held that the State was liable, it offered no explanation as to what bodies would be considered 'State organs'.
2. There was no indication as to whether State liability was 'an act of last resort'. In other words, if other forms of action would have to be attempted before liability could be established.
3. The Court only considered the breach of Community law in the case at hand – the non-implementation of a directive. There can, however, be numerous types of breach of Community law, such as the faulty implementation of a directive, breach of a Treaty article, or failure to abide by a judgment of the European Court. The *Francovich* case did not appear to consider whether liability would also extend to other such breaches of Community law obligations.
4. The Court's test in *Francovich* was somewhat vague, and could itself be open to interpretation by the national courts. This would result in a supposed Community law remedy being applied in a non-uniform way by national courts. This would undermine its effectiveness in securing adequate protection for individuals whose rights had been infringed by the State.

The majority of these outstanding questions were addressed in *Brasserie du Pêcheur SA* v *Federal Republic of Germany; R* v *Secretary of State for Transport, ex parte Factortame Ltd and Others* Joined Cases C–46 and 48/93 [1996] ECR I–1029.

## 7.4 The *Brasserie/Factortame* cases

The applicant in *Brasserie du Pêcheur* was a French company claiming damages against the German government because the company was forced to discontinue exports after the German authorities ruled that the product was not in conformity with German beer purity law. This law required all beer products to be manufactured using only four ingredients, and prohibited the use of additives in the production of beer. In *Commission* v *Germany (German Beer Purity Law)* Case 178/84 [1988] ECR 1227 the Court held that the statutory requirements were incompatible with art 28 EC, which provides for the prohibition of all quantitative restrictions, and measure of equivalent effect, on imports: see Chapter 14. The French brewery then brought an action against Germany for the damages that it had suffered whilst unable to export its beer for sale in Germany.

In *Factortame* the applicants claimed that the UK government was liable to them in damages because of injury sustained as a result of the application of the Merchant Shipping Act 1988. This statute (as discussed above) had tightened the requirements for registering vessels in the UK shipping register, mainly to prevent so-called quota-hopping by non-UK, European Union fishermen. The effect of the statute was to discriminate against non-UK nationals, contrary to the EC Treaty. The UK had also failed to abide by a previous ruling of the European Court in a direct action brought by the Commission: *Commission* v *United Kingdom* Case C–246/89R [1989] ECR I–3125. The fishermen had been unable to fish for approximately seven months between the President of the ECJ's order in the direct action and their eventual success in gaining interim relief in the House of Lords ([1990] 3 CMLR 59 (HL)).

In *Brasserie*, the Court was asked to clarify the conditions under which Member States would incur liability in light of the principles first developed in *Francovich*. The European Court first reiterated the basic rule that, in principle, Member States may be liable to private individuals for damage sustained as a result of an infringement of a provision of Community law. The right to reparation was, in the eyes of the Court, simply the 'necessary corollary' of the denial of these rights. The Court then went on to answer many of the questions left unanswered in the *Francovich* judgment.

### What organs of the State are liable for breaches of Community law?

According to the European Court in *Brasserie*, State liability could attach to a Member State as a result of both acts and omissions by any organ of the State, including the legislature, regardless of any constitutional division of power. This reasoning is similar to that used in actions under art 226 EC: see Chapter 4. In *Haim* v *Kassenzahnärztliche Vereinigung Nordrhein* Case C–424/97 [2000] ECR I–5123 a legally independent public body was concluded to be liable. As a general rule, the definition of the 'State' offered under those cases involving direct effect may provide guidance: see Chapter 8.

### Is State liability an 'act of last resort'?

Advocate-General Tesauro concluded that State liability was both alternative and additional to other courses of action, such as direct effect: see Chapter 8. However, *Brasserie* also concluded that should an individual fail to take appropriate action to secure the grant of their rights (through enforcing, say, their directly effective rights), if such action were available to them, they would have difficulty mitigating their loss. This could potentially leave a plaintiff with their damages reduced to a nominal amount. This conclusion provides protection against non-genuine litigation – any genuine plaintiff would wish to secure their denied right(s), rather than monetary compensation. Once they have secured their right(s), they would then seek compensation for damages suffered in the interim. This is effectively what had occurred in both *Brasserie* and *Factortame*. Finally, the Court made it clear that there is no prerequisite that the Community law breached be directly effective, ie create rights for individuals that they may enforce in their national courts – non-directly effective Community law, if breached, may also incur State liability.

### What types of breach of Community law may incur liability?
The *Francovich* decision had only considered liability in the context of a non-implemented directive. *Brasserie* confirmed that State liability extends to any breach of Community law, regardless of whether that measure has direct effect. Liability may also extend to both positive acts and omissions.

### What are the conditions required for State liability?
Following suggestions by Advocate-General Tesauro, the European Court concluded in *Brasserie*, that:

> '... the conditions under which the State may incur liability for damage caused to individuals by a breach of Community law cannot ... differ from those governing the liability of the Community in like circumstances.'

Thus, the Court based the principle of State liability on the same conditions as the liability of the Community itself under art 288 EC (formerly art 215), as well as on art 10 EC. Consequently, the cases that had developed the principle of Community liability under art 288 EC are relevant to the application and development of the principle of State liability: see Chapter 5.

The Court provided a three-part test to establish when State liability could be imposed, using the same principles established under art 288, stating that:

1. the rule of law infringed must be intended to confer rights on individuals;
2. the breach must be 'sufficiently serious'; and
3. there must exist a direct causal link between the breach of the obligation and the damage sustained.

The Court defined a 'sufficiently serious' breach as one in which the Member State 'manifestly and gravely disregarded the limits on its discretion'. In order to ascertain whether this is the case, the national court must consider the following:

1. the clarity and precision of the rule breached;
2. the measure of discretion left by the rule to the authorities;
3. whether the infringement and damage were intentional or involuntary;
4. whether there was any excusable or inexcusable error of law;

5. whether a Community institution contributed to the breach; and
6. whether there was any retention or adoption of national measures or practices contrary to Community law.

When delivering its ruling on the *Brasserie* reference (which took two years), the European Court gave clear guidance to the national courts, an example of the blurring between its role and the role of the national courts: see Chapter 6. The Court held that neither breach was excusable. In the case of Germany's breach, it was concluded that it was sufficiently serious, especially since previous case law had already established that the action had infringed Community law. In the case of the UK, the nationality restrictions imposed under the Merchant Shipping Act 1988 were manifestly contrary to Community law. In these circumstances, both countries were held liable.

The Court also held, however, that national courts were responsible for assessing the actual levels of reparation that had to be paid as a result of an infringement of Community law by the Member State. The criteria applied for this assessment must be no less than for similar claims based on domestic law and must not make a successful claim impossible or excessively difficult.

On receiving the ruling from the European Court, the German national court concluded that there had been no causal link between the breach and the damage suffered by Brasserie du Pêcheur, so awarded no damages: [1997] 1 CMLR 971. In *R v Secretary of State for Transport, ex parte Factortame Ltd and Others* [1998] 1 CMLR 1353 the High Court considered that the Merchant Shipping Act 1988 was a sufficiently serious breach of Community law, particularly since the Commission had always opposed its introduction. The Court of Appeal and the House of Lords ([1999] 3 CMLR 597 (HL)) were to agree, and both applied the ECJ's test laid down in *Brasserie*. Lord Slynn, though, offered the opinion that the Commission's view of a measure should not be considered as conclusive proof that there had been a breach of Community law or that it was necessarily sufficiently serious to merit the liability of the State.

## 7.5 Post *Brasserie* – the application and development of State liability

Since *Brasserie*, the test for State liability has been applied in a number of cases, although not always in a consistent manner. The European Court appears to have taken two different approaches in assessing whether a particular infringement of Community law incurs the liability of the State.

### *Consideration of the clarity and precision of the infringed Community measure/rule*

In *R v Her Majesty's Treasury, ex parte British Telecommunications plc* Case C–392/93

[1996] ECR I–1631 BT claimed that the UK government had incorrectly implemented Directive 90/351 (which deals with public procurement in relation to water, transport, energy, and telecommunications). Basing its claim on *Francovich*, BT argued that it had suffered financial loss as a result of the incorrect or faulty implementation of the directive.

The approach of the European Court was to concentrate on whether the breach was sufficiently serious, as per the test set out in *Brasserie*. The Court concluded that the UK's approach to implementation was contrary to the Directive, but that the Directive itself had been so unclear and 'imprecisely worded' so as to excuse the approach taken by the UK government. Consequently, the Court held that the UK had acted in 'good faith' on the basis of a reasonable interpretation of the Directive. The UK's approach was given additional credence by the fact that other Member States had adopted a similar interpretation of the Directive.

More generally, the Court held that the methods of implementing a directive should be assessed in terms of State liability in a restrictive manner. The Court justified such an approach on the basis that to do otherwise would potentially lead to the hindering of legislative functions, exercised in the general interest, by the 'prospect of actions for damages'.

The approach of the European Court in *ex parte British Telecommunications plc* can also be witnessed in *Denkavit International BV* v *Bundesamt für Finanzen* Cases C–283, 291 and 292/94 [1996] ECR I–5063. This case concerned the alleged faulty implementation of a directive by the German government, in this case Directive 90/435 on the taxation of parent companies and subsidiaries in different States. The Court again applied the test in *Brasserie*. As with *ex parte British Telecommunications plc*, the Court concluded that the Directive lacked clarity and precision. It also stated that Germany had had no previous case law on which to rely and, consequently, its breach had not been sufficiently serious.

In the case of *Brinkman Tabakfabriken GmbH* v *Skatteministeriet* Case C–319/96 [1998] ECR I–5255 it was argued that the Danish authorities had incorrectly implemented Directive 79/30. This directive concerned taxation on the consumption of manufactured tobacco. The Danish authorities had adopted a definition of the product imported by the applicant (namely tobacco rolls) which placed it in a higher tax bracket. The Court concluded that the Danish authorities had not manifestly breached the Directive since its was unclear in its wording as to what constituted a 'cigarette' and what constituted a 'tobacco product', on which the different tax rates were based. The Danish claim was further supported by the fact that the Commission supported the classification they had made, as did Finland.

The faulty implementation of a directive was also the basis for the claim for State liability made in *Rechberger and Greindl* v *Austria* Case C–140/97 [1999] ECR I–3499. The applicants alleged that Austria had incorrectly implemented Council Directive 90/314, on protection for consumers when travel organisers went insolvent. On considering the Directive, the European Court concluded that it was clear and precise in defining the level of protection required and that Austria had failed to provide that level of protection for consumers. The Court also established that Austria had set a date from when claims could be made, but that this had been some time after the required implementation deadline in the Directive. In such circumstances, the European Court felt that the breach was sufficiently serious enough to incur liability.

However, in other preliminary references during this period, the European Court adopted a different approach in cases involving a claim of State liability. In such cases, the Court considered that the 'mere infringement' was sufficient to incur the liability of the State, regardless of the clarity of the actual rule breached. The Court appears to have done this where the Member State was not required to make legislative choices or had little or no discretion in relation to the Community measure.

### 'Mere infringement' as a basis for State liability

In *R* v *Ministry of Agriculture, Fisheries and Food, ex parte Hedley Lomas (Ireland) Ltd* Case C–5/94 [1996] ECR I–2553, the applicants (an export company) claimed that they had suffered financial loss as a result of the UK's refusal to grant licences for the export of live sheep to Spain. The UK government argued that its decision to ban such exports was made because Spain had failed to comply with Directive 74/577 on the stunning of animals before slaughter. The UK had complained to the Commission that Spain had failed to provide any mechanism or sanctions for securing the compliance of its slaughterhouses with the provisions of the Directive, although Spain had actually implemented the Directive. The Commission concluded that it would take no direct action against Spain under art 226 EC.

The UK government conceded that the refusal to grant licences (an effective ban) breached art 29 EC on the free movement of goods: see Chapter 14. However, they argued that such action was justified under art 30 EC on the basis of protecting the life and health of animals. The UK government, though, could provide no substantive evidence of any breach of the Directive.

The European Court concluded that the breach of art 29 by the UK was not justified under art 30. The UK's position was not helped by the failure to 'produce any proof of the non-compliance with the Directive'. The Court did not apply the *Brasserie* test but held:

> '... where, at the time when it committed the infringement, the Member State in question was not called upon to make any legislative choices and had only considerably reduced, or even no, discretion, the mere infringement of Community law may be sufficient to establish the existence of a sufficiently serious breach.'

The Court adopted this basis for establishing liability – the assessment that the 'mere infringement' was a sufficiently serious breach – in the case of *Dillenkoffer and Others* v *Federal Republic of Germany* Cases C–178, 179, 188, 189 and 190/94 [1996] ECR I–4845. This case centred on the failure of Germany to implement Directive

90/314 on package holidays (the same Directive as in *Rechberger* above). The Court concluded that the failure to implement the Directive by the stated deadline was per se a sufficiently serious breach of Community law, and that this had been indicated in the *Francovich* ruling. As in *Hedley Lomas*, the European Court did not apply the *Brasserie* test.

This approach was also used in *Norbrook Laboratories Ltd* v *Minister of Agriculture, Fisheries and Food* Case C– 127/95 [1998] ECR I–1531, which concerned the implementation of directives dealing with veterinary products. The applicants claimed that the directives had been implemented incorrectly, which the ECJ examined before confirming that there had been clear breaches. The Court repeated the conclusion in *Hedley Lomas* – that where the State was not required to make legislative choices, or had no or little discretion, the mere infringement was sufficient to establish the sufficiently serious breach of Community law required for liability to exist.

An alternative approach used by the European Court is to require the national courts to assess whether the breach or infringement of Community law is sufficiently serious, using the guidelines the Court has provided: see, for example, *Klaus Konle* v *Austria* Case C–302/97 [1999] ECR I–3099 and *Haim* Case C–424/97 above.

In the *Brasserie* ruling the ECJ emphasised that State liability was a Community concept, the principles of which were to be determined by the Court. However, the Court also pointed out that those principles are to be applied by the national courts within the framework of their national legal systems. This results in a variety of procedural rules (in relation to, for example, time limits, mitigation, causation and assessment of levels of damages) being applicable.

The national rules that may apply must, according to the European Court, be equivalent and effective (as discussed above at section 7.2). In *Brasserie* and *Factortame* the Court concluded that legal provisions in both Germany and the UK would make it 'excessively difficult' to secure effective reparation.

According to *Brasserie*, the extent or level of reparation must be 'commensurate with the loss or damage sustained'. National laws imposing restrictions on the extent or level of damages are permitted, but only insofar as they also comply with requirements of equivalence and effectiveness: see also *Bonifaci and Berto* v *Istituto Nazionale della Previdenza Sociale* Cases C–94–95/95 [1997] ECR I–3969 and *Palmisani* v *Istituto Nazionale della Previdenza Sociale* Case C–261/95 [1997] ECR I–4025.

## 7.6 Extending liability in the future

One major issue remaining is whether the principle of liability will be extended to cover damage caused by private parties who breach Community law. This has been the subject of both academic and judicial debate (see, for example, the comments of the Advocate-General in *Banks* v *British Coal* Case C–128/92 [1994] ECR I–1209).

The ECJ did not deal specifically with the issue until the case of *Courage Ltd* v *Crehan* Case C–453/99 [2001] ECR I–6297. In this case the Court emphasised that the law in question – art 82 EC in relation to competition law – contained a fundamental prohibition, and that national courts were well acquainted with the fact that they were required to protect individuals' rights conferred by such rules and ensure that they had 'full effect'. The Court went on to state:

> 'The full effectiveness of art [82] of the Treaty, and in particular, the practical effect of the prohibition laid down in art [82(1)] would be put at risk if it were not open to any individual to claim damages for loss caused to him by a contract or by conduct liable to restrict or distort competition'.

The Court justified extending liability to the acts of private parties by concluding that 'actions for damages before the national courts can make a significant contribution to the maintenance of effective competition in the Community'.

Whilst this is most certainly an important ruling, it is made only in the context of the highly developed, and directly effective, Community rules on competition, and it remains to be seen whether the Court will extend such liability to other areas of EC law. The following comment of the Court in *Brasserie* certainly implies that it will:

> '... the full effectiveness of Community law would be impaired if individuals were unable to obtain redress when their rights were infringed by a breach of Community law.'

## 7.7 Conclusion

The creation of the State liability in the *Francovich* case may do much to enforce Community law obligations, and it may also to a certain extent rectify the problems encountered in the application of direct effects to certain provisions of Community law: see Chapter 8. Indeed, in some cases the European Court has identified that applicants may rely on the alternative course of action available under *Francovich*, since its application does not depend on the pre-existence of direct effect: see, for example, *Wagner Miret* v *Fondo de Garantia Salarial* Case C–334/92 [1993] ECR I–6911. This, obviously, is of some considerable benefit to those individuals who may have suffered some loss due to the infringement of Community law.

However, State liability as created by *Francovich* is not necessarily the ultimate solution to the problems in enforcing Community law obligations. In terms of relying on the principle, problems remain in relation to the burden of proof on the applicant. They are required to establish that the measure was intended to confer rights on individuals; that those rights are clearly defined; that the breach was 'sufficiently serious'; that there was a causal link between the breach and the damage suffered; and the damage itself.

In certain circumstances it may appear that this burden in a relatively light one; those infringements occurring in situations in which the Member State was not required to make legislative choices, or had little or no discretion, will, it appears, incur the liability of the State. This is perhaps most evident in relation to the failure to implement a directive by the prescribed deadline – this 'mere infringement' will most likely be considered as sufficiently serious: see *Francovich* and *Dillenkoffer*.

However, in other circumstances, particularly where the Community measure lacks clarity, the applicant will have greater difficulty in establishing liability. The cases discussed in this chapter reveal that the State may well be able to 'excuse' the breach or infringement by, for example, claiming that the action taken was done in good faith, or that a Community institution (primarily the Commission) was supportive of the measures taken. The need to therefore perhaps rely, additional to an action for State liability, on the principles of direct effect and/or indirect effect will remain, and will be discussed in the next chapter.

Finally, the European Court has provided the basic principles by which State liability may be established. These principles still have to be provided and applied within the individual legal systems of each of the Member States. Consequently there remain issues in relation to both the procedural and substantive national rules that may apply (such as causation, time limits, and levels of damages) which are discussed above. The compatibility of these national rules with the Community-wide remedy of State liability remains an issue that may require further additional clarification by the European Court or, indeed, the Community itself.

# 8

# Fundamental Principles of Community Law: Supremacy and Direct Effect

## 8.1 Introduction

European Community law operates on the basis of a number of principles that can accurately be described as fundamental to the operation of the Community legal system itself. These principles have played an orchestrating role in the evolution of Community law and lie at the heart of the present system. This chapter will deal with the following principles:

1. the supremacy of Community law over national law;
2. the principle of direct effect; and
3. the principle of indirect effect.

None of these principles were originally stated in the EC Treaty and have been developed in the jurisprudence of the European Court. These principles reflect the important role of the Court in developing and maximising the effectiveness of Community law. (An additional principle, that of direct applicability, is referred to in the EC Treaty and is discussed in Chapter 3 in relation to regulations.)

However, considerable political tension within the Community has been created by the development of these principles, and they have, in themselves, been highly controversial. Their development has encountered difficulties in terms of conflicts with national constitutions and application to the various sources of Community law.

This chapter will seek to identify the nature of these principles and will highlight problems, difficulties and issues in relation to them.

## 8.2 The supremacy of Community law

None of the original Treaties asserted that Community law was to have precedence over national law. The creation and development of this most fundamental of principles to the Community legal system was accomplished by the European Court in a series of important rulings, beginning with preliminary references made at the very beginning of the Community's existence.

In *Van Gend en Loos* v *Netherlands* Case 26/62 [1963] ECR 1 the Dutch court hearing the case felt that aspects of the case could not be dealt with by the ECJ, on the basis that they were questions of national constitutional law. The Court concluded that the then EEC (now EC) Treaty was not a mere agreement creating mutual obligations only between the Member States, especially since institutions had been created that had been 'endowed with sovereign rights'. The Court consequently came to the conclusion that

> '... the Community constitutes a new legal order of international law for the benefit of which the states have limited their sovereign rights.'

The Court avoided the problems inherent in describing Community law as international law, towards which Member States had differing approaches. Instead, the Court described Community law as an entirely new legal order (sui generis), different in nature from both international law and national law. The Court, though, considered the primacy of Community law only in broad terms – that the Member States had voluntarily transferred sovereignty to the institutions of the Community. The ruling itself concentrated on the issue of whether art 12 of the then EEC Treaty (now art 25 EC) created rights for individuals: discussed in detail at section 8.3. The Court however, did take the opportunity to expand on the principle of supremacy of Community law in *Costa* v *ENEL* Case 6/64 [1964] ECR 585.

In this case, an individual claimed before his local court – the guidice conciliatore of Milan – that the law nationalising production and distribution of electricity was incompatible with the then EEC Treaty. The local court referred several questions to the ECJ for a preliminary ruling under the then art 177 process (now art 234 EC). The Italian government maintained that the proceedings were totally inadmissible because, in the case in question, the Italian court was only entitled to apply the nationalisation law and not the Italian national law ratifying the EEC Treaty, since the latter law was earlier. This argument was based on a judgment given by the Italian constitutional court in a case between the same parties.

The Court in its judgment emphasised the unlimited duration of the Community, the autonomy of Community power, both internally and externally, and especially the limitation of competence or transfer of powers from the Member

States to the European Community. This was effectively a refashioning of powers, entailed in the establishment of the Community. Hence, primacy is the necessary corollary of the Court's conception of the Community legal order as being 'integrated into the legal systems of the Member States and binding on their courts'.

The Court was determined to show that the 'words and spirit' of the Treaty necessarily implied that:

> '... it is impossible for the States to set up a subsequent unilateral measure against a legal order which they have accepted on a reciprocal basis.'

The Court found the primacy of Community law confirmed by the wording of art 249 EC (formerly 189), under which regulations have binding force and are directly applicable to all Member States. In other words, regulations are automatically part of the corpus juris of the Member State: see Chapter 3. In so doing, the Court emphasised the connection between direct applicability and primacy, and between the latter and the legislative power conferred on the European Community. The Court pointed out that this provision, which was not qualified by any reservation:

> '... would be meaningless if a state could unilaterally nullify its effect by means of legislative measures which could prevail over European Community law.'

Any claim that a Member State might have to give precedence to a latter law over a regulation was moreover rendered absurd simply by the fact that a subsequent regulation could put an end to this inconsistency.

The Court was thus able to reach a conclusion in *Costa* in words that have become classic and have had considerable influence in national decisions:

> 'It follows from all these observations that the law stemming from the Treaty, an independent source of law, could not, because of its special and original nature, be overriden by domestic legal provisions, however framed, without being deprived of its character as Community law and without the legal basis of the Community itself being called into question. The transfer by the States from their domestic legal system to the Community legal system of rights and obligations arising under the Treaty carries with it a permanent limitation of their sovereign rights against which a subsequent unilateral act incompatible with the concept of the Community cannot prevail.'

The Court's ruling is addressed directly to national courts. Its decisions cannot be regarded as an expression of the practical necessity that had always led international courts to assert the superiority of the law they are applying over national law, the latter being sometimes treated as simply a question of fact. This dualism is not appropriate in the relations between the Community legal order and the national orders. It gives a poor idea of the co-ordination between them, which finds expression especially in the machinery for seeking preliminary rulings. Thus, when the Court rules that domestic law cannot override Community law, it is referring to proceedings before national courts.

This factor is even clearer in the case of *Simmenthal* v *Commission* Case 92/78 [1979] ECR 777. In this case the Court concluded:

'Every national court must, in a case within its jurisdiction, apply European law in its entirety and protect rights which the latter confers on individuals and must accordingly set aside any provision of national law which may conflict with it, whether prior or subsequent to the Community rule.'

Thus, primacy is not an obligation that is incumbent upon the founder of the constitution or the legislator to implement – it is a rule to be applied by the courts. This rule is unconditional. It is also absolute, in the sense that it applies to every rule of domestic law, whatever its standing, even if it is a constitutional rule. This last point can be witnessed in the Court's ruling in *Internationale Handelsgesellschaft GmbH v EVGF* Case 11/70 [1970] ECR 1125.

*Internationale Handelsgesellschaft* was concerned with a number of EC regulations setting up a system of export licences for certain agricultural products. The system required payment of a deposit, which was to be forfeited should the products not be exported during the validity of the licence. The plaintiffs had lost their deposit, and now argued that the system set up under Community law was contrary to the German constitution. In particular, the plaintiffs argued that the system was contrary to the right to proportionality of treatment – that the forfeit deposit system was not necessary to achieve the objectives of the system. The German courts were of the view that the system was unconstitutional, due to its infringement of the constitutional right to reasonable freedom to conduct a business. They also concluded that it contravened a German legal right not to be subject to the compulsory payment of money without fault on the part of the individual. The German court, however, felt it appropriate to make a preliminary reference to the European Court under what was then art 177 (now 234 EC).

The European Court concluded:

'The validity of a Community measure or its effect within a Member State cannot be affected by allegations that it runs counter to either fundamental rights as formulated by the constitution of the state or the principles of a national constitutional structure.'

The principle of the primacy of Community law applies regardless of the type of Community law. It will apply equally to a Treaty provision or secondary legislation, such as a regulation, as in the above case, a directive or decision: see, for example, *Ursula Becker* v *Finanzamt Münster-Innenstadt* Case 8/81 [1982] ECR 53 and *Salumificio di Cornuda* Case 130/78 [1979] ECR 867. General principles of Community law will prevail over national law (*Wachauf* v *Germany* Case 5/88 [1989] ECR 2609) as will any international agreements concluded between the EC and third countries: *Nederlandse Spoorwegen* Case 38/75 [1975] ECR 1439. The supremacy of Community law will also apply regardless of the nature of the national law that conflicts with it, even if it is an entrenched constitutional principle, or administrative, jurisdictional or legislative law. Furthermore, in *Commission* v *Council (Re ERTA)* Case 22/70 [1971] ECR 263 the Court concluded that Community law is supreme not only over domestic law but also over a Member State's obligations to other States.

The principle of the supremacy of Community law created both legal and political difficulties in a number of Member States, and it continues to do so to a certain extent. Whilst some Member States, such as the Benelux countries, accepted the principle with few problems, in other Member States the national courts only accepted the principle with reservations, such as Italy and Germany. In France the judiciary were divided, with only one branch accepting the primacy of Community over French national law. Such constitutional problems can be still witnessed, such as in, for example, Germany: see *Brunner* v *The European Union Treaty* [1994] 1 CMLR 57. In this case, Brunner challenged Germany's signing of the TEU as being unconstitutional. Whilst the Federal Constitutional Court of Germany concluded that the ratification process that had occurred was constitutional, they made specific comments about the sovereignty of Germany and its relationship with the Community. Such comments hold a resemblance to those made in English courts:

> 'The Federal Republic of Germany ... even after the Union Treaty comes into force, will remain a member of a federation of States, the common authority of which is derived from the Member States and can only have binding effects within the German sovereign sphere by virtue of the German instruction that its law be applied. Germany is one of the "Masters of the Treaties" which have established their adherence to the Union Treaty concluded "for a limited period" ... with the intention of long-term membership, but could ultimately revoke that adherence by a contrary act. The validity and application of European law in Germany depends on the application-of-law instruction of the Accession Act. Germany thus preserves the quality of a sovereign state in its own right.'

This chapter will focus on the judicial response to the supremacy of Community law in the United Kingdom. The explanation below is simplified, since the issues themselves are constitutional ones, and for further discussion and analysis reference should be made to a constitutional text.

## The United Kingdom

The United Kingdom's constitution is based traditionally on the fundamental principle that Parliament holds sovereignty, in that it may legislate on any matter it wishes, and that no other body may question the validity of a statute – known as the enrolled Act rule. Each successive Parliament is supreme and, consequently, no one Parliament may bind its successor by entrenching legislation. This is achieved through the process of implied repeal; in other words when two statutes conflict the latter one will prevail. Reconciling the doctrine of parliamentary sovereignty with that of Community law supremacy is therefore difficult, particularly since the choice of national measure to bring effect to Community law was to introduce an 'ordinary' statute. Under the traditional concept of parliamentary sovereignty, such an Act would be subject to implied repeal by any latter legislation.

The European Communities Act 1972, as amended by the European Communities (Amendment) Acts 1986, 1993 and 1998, makes all Community law provisions that are directly effective part of national law: s2(1) (see section 8.3 for analysis of the doctrine of direct effect). Further, s2(4) states that 'any enactment passed or to be passed, other than one contained in this Part of this Act, shall be construed and have effect subject to the foregoing provisions of this section.' This has been held by some to mean that the national courts must interpret national law 'in accordance with the principles laid down by and any relevant decision of the European Court' (s3(1)): see, for example, *Macarthys* v *Smith* [1979] 3 All ER 325 (CA). This process, sometimes referred to as a 'rule of construction', acknowledges the supremacy of Community law via a 'back door' route. The approach was accepted by the House of Lords in *Garland* v *British Rail Engineering* [1982] 2 All ER 402 (HL), where Lord Diplock stated that English courts were well used to the concept of interpreting national law so that it conformed with Treaty obligations.

It has been further contended by the European Court that all national courts are under a duty to interpret national laws so as to give effect to provisions of Community law. This proposition relies heavily on the judgment in *Von Colson and Kamann* v *Land Nordrhein-Westfalen* Case 14/83 [1984] ECR 1891. This ECJ decision relied on the obligation under art 10 EC to conclude that national courts are required to interpret national law in the light and wording and purpose of Community law: see section 8.6 for further details.

However, the doctrine of Community law supremacy requires more than simply interpreting national law to conform with Community obligations, particularly since this may not always be possible. The principle requires all directly effective Community law to be enforced, by the courts, and that any conflicting measure of national law, whatever its nature, be set aside. As regards this aspect of the principle of the supremacy of Community law, the English courts have tried hard to reconcile it with the principle of parliamentary supremacy. There was little doubt that Community law prevailed over pre-1972 British legislation, because the 1972 Act incorporated all existing Community law at that date into UK law. The courts were therefore prepared to accept that Community law overruled pre-1972 statutes: see *Shields* v *E Coomes (Holdings) Ltd* [1979] 1 All ER 456.

The problem was more complex in relation to whether a UK statute post-1972, that directly contravened Community law, would be applied, as per the implied repeal rule. This did not occur until the late 1980s. However, in *Felixstowe Dock and Railway Company* v *British Transport and Docks Board* [1976] 2 CMLR 655, Lord Denning concluded that all he would be able to do would be to apply such an Act, regardless of the obligation set out in the European Communities Act 1972 or Community law.

In *R* v *Secretary of State for Transport, ex parte Factortame Ltd and Others* [1990] 2 AC 85 the House of Lords was compelled to decide whether the application of an Act of Parliament, enacted after 1972, could be suspended pending an application to the European Court for a decision concerning the consistency of the legislation with Community law. The applicants were companies incorporated in the UK but owned mainly by Spanish nationals. These companies had been created for the purpose of acquiring ownership of fishing vessels registered in the UK. The statutory requirements for registering vessels as British were altered by the Merchant Shipping Act 1988 and the Merchant Shipping (Registration of Fishing Vessels) Regulations 1988. In particular, conditions relating to nationality were introduced in order for an applicant to register a vessel as a British ship. The applicants maintained that these conditions violated the principle of non-discrimination and deprived the applicants of enforceable Community rights.

The Divisional Court of the Queen's Bench decided to request a preliminary reference on the question from the European Court. On a motion by the applicants for interim relief, the court ordered that, pending a decision from the European Court, the contested parts of the statute were to be disapplied and the Secretary of State should be restrained from enforcing the legislation. The Court of Appeal, on appeal by the Secretary of State, set aside the order made by the Divisional Court for interim relief. The applicants appealed to the House of Lords.

In the House of Lords Lord Bridge of Harwich declared that, in the absence of an overriding principle of Community law allowing national courts to suspend the application of national law, the British courts would be unable to provide effective interlocutory relief to protect putative rights. No such doctrine existed in British constitutional law, and it was up to the European Court to establish such a principle if Community obligations were to be protected. The House of Lords therefore asked the European Court whether or not a national court was obliged to grant interim suspension of an Act of Parliament pending a decision by the European Court.

In reply to this reference the European Court stated:

> 'Any provision of a national legal system and any legislative, administrative or judicial practice which might impair the effectiveness of Community law by withholding from the national court having jurisdiction to apply such law the power to do everything necessary at the moment of its application to set aside national legislative provisions which might prevent, even temporarily, Community rules from having full force and effect, are incompatible with [the principles of Community law]': Case C–213/89 [1990] ECR I–2433.

Community law was therefore to be interpreted as meaning that a national court must set aside any measure of national law that precludes it from granting interim relief in order to protect rights under Community law.

Upon receiving this judgment from the European Court, the House of Lords reconsidered the issue and granted interim relief ([1990] 3 CMLR 59). Lord Bridge summarised the constitutional position in the following manner:

> 'If the supremacy ... of Community law over ... national law ... was not always inherent in the EEC Treaty it was certainly well established in the jurisprudence of the Court of Justice long before the United Kingdom joined the Community. Thus, whatever limitation of its sovereignty Parliament accepted when it enacted the European Communities Act 1972 was entirely voluntary. Under the terms of the 1972 Act it has always been clear that it was the duty of a United Kingdom court, when delivering final judgment, to override any rule of national law found to be in conflict with any directly enforceable rule of Community law.'

This conclusion achieves the supremacy of Community law, as desired by the European Court, but does so in a careful and deliberate way, so as to simultaneously maintain the doctrine of parliamentary sovereignty. The House of Lords has concluded that the need for the supremacy of Community law stems from Parliament's own voluntary action in passing the European Communities Act 1972. This statute expresses Parliament's intention to be bound by Community law obligations, and the courts therefore abide by that intention. This will be achieved either by the rather contrived method of interpretation referred to above, or simply by granting Community law precedence over the conflicting national provisions.

However, it should be noted that the courts recognise that if Parliament expressly states that the provisions of a statute are to stand, regardless of whether they conflict with Community law, they will simply apply the statute and follow Parliament's express intention: see *Macarthys* v *Smith* (above) and *Garland* v *British Rail Engineering* (above). The implications of such an action by the UK legislature would, of course, be great, particularly in the political context of continued membership, and it would have to be suggested that this is perhaps unlikely to occur. These final points are, however, interesting in that they to some extent conflict with the European Court's explanation of the transfer of sovereignty that each Member State undertook on membership, as explained in *Costa*. The UK has adopted a different explanation of the process, one that we can describe as a delegation of sovereignty, rather than a complete transfer. This discussion, though, is a relatively academic one – in practical terms, Community law achieves primacy in relation to conflicting national law in the United Kingdom.

## 8.3 Direct effect

### General

Direct applicability is the quality that enables a provision of Community law to become part of the national law of a Member State without the necessity of legislation. Such a provision will be incorporated directly into the corpus of national law: see art 249 EC and its reference to the direct applicability of regulations.

Direct effect describes a quality that a provision of Community law may have. It means that the provision can be interpreted by the courts as being capable of creating rights that any natural or legal person may enforce in their national courts. There may be two types of direct effect: first, vertical direct effect, which means that the provision may be enforced against the State; and second, horizontal direct effect, which means that the measure may be enforced against another natural or legal person. Once established, national courts must protect such rights. In *Luck* v *Hauptzollampt Köln-Rheinau* Case 34/67 [1968] ECR 115 the Court stated that the national court must not apply a national rule conflicting with a Community provision having direct effect. However, it is for the legal system in each State to decide the legal procedure by which this result is to be achieved.

Although the Court uses the terms direct applicability and direct effect interchangeably, it is proposed in the following discussion to adhere to the above definitions, for simplicity.

As a traditional principle, the effect of an individual international agreement has always been established by reference to the constitutional law of the State party to it. Consequently, in the United Kingdom, international agreements have not created rights for individuals unless and until implemented by the legislature, as seen, for example, in the Human Rights Act 1998 which implemented the European Convention on Human Rights. Other Member States, though, also believed that the Community Treaties were not capable of creating rights for individuals. This was not the belief of the European Court of Justice, which, with teleological interpretation as its aid, considered that the purpose and spirit behind the creation of the Treaties implied the need for a different approach. Without this different approach the Court believed that the effectiveness of the Community legal order would be undermined. This belief is perhaps most evident in the landmark decision of *Van Gend en Loos* v *Netherlands* Case 26/62 [1963] ECR 1.

## The rationale for the creation of direct effect

Van Gend en Loos, a company, sought to rely on what was then art 12 of the EEC Treaty (now art 25 EC). This provided that there would be no increases in import duties. The company had imported chemical substances from Germany into The Netherlands, but had been charged an increased import duty by the authorities. The national court requested a preliminary reference on the issue of whether art 12 of the EEC Treaty was capable of creating enforceable rights for individuals.

As part of the preliminary reference procedure, Member States are permitted to send their written observations to the European Court for its consideration. In this reference The Netherlands, German and Belgian governments submitted observations that the EEC Treaty was an international agreement that was to be determined only by reference to constitutional law by a national court, and that its provisions were not capable of creating enforceable rights for nationals.

The European Court referred to the 'objective' of the Treaty; its reference to 'peoples' as well as governments; the creation of 'institutions endowed with sovereign rights'; and the need for nationals to 'co-operate in the functioning of this Community'. Such factors, the Court believed, 'implies that this Treaty is more than an agreement which merely creates mutual obligations between the contracting States.'

The Court consequently felt able to conclude that:

> '... the Community constitutes a new legal order of international law for the benefit of which the states have limited their sovereign rights ... and the subjects of which comprise not only Member States but also their nationals. Independently of the legislation of Member States, Community law therefore not only imposes obligations on individuals but is also intended to confer upon them rights which become part of their legal heritage.'

The reasoning behind the Court's conclusion depended to a large extent on its willingness to explore the spirit and purpose of the Treaty, and this judgment marks the beginning of a long line of judgments in which the European Court has used this purposive or teleological interpretative method. The Court, though, did also point to substantive parts of the EEC Treaty, including the preamble and art 177 (now 234 EC) to support its conclusions. The creation of the preliminary reference procedure necessarily implies that individuals will be arguing and attempting to rely on Community law.

However, it has been suggested that the decision of the Court to grant individuals rights under Community law was perhaps based more on the need to enhance the effectiveness of the new legal system. The EEC Treaty included within it only a limited form of public enforcement (see Chapter 4) that was both politically orientated and not particularly effective, especially since its original inception did not include any sanction for non-compliance. It is suggested that the European Court recognised the problems inherent in the Treaty's public enforcement process and believed that it could maximise the effectiveness of Community law by also providing individuals with the ability to enforce Community rights in their own national courts via the concept of direct effect.

It should perhaps be noted that it is for the national courts to ensure that their subjects benefit from the legal protection arising from the direct effect of European Community law: see *Rewe-Zentralfinanz eG and Rewe-Zentral AG* v *Landwirtschaftskammer für das Saarland* Case 33/76 [1976] ECR 1989. In doing so, the national courts must apply the rules of domestic law. The absence of any co-ordination of domestic procedural rules necessarily entails the existence of different limitation periods, and therefore a certain divergence in the actual application of Community law. It is possible that similar observations might be made with respect to the system of national penalties for infringements of European Community law and the procedure for bringing actions: see Chapter 7. There is no doubt that in these matters there is a wide divergence, often rooted in history, between the various domestic systems. Only co-ordinating actions initiated by the European Community, or by the Member States, with a view to the approximation of national laws can, in the long term, reduce these differences.

## 8.4 The requirements for direct effect

In *Van Gend en Loos* the Court provided a strict test setting out the requirements that a measure of Community law was required to have before it was capable of creating enforceable rights for individuals. The test is as follows:

1. The provision being relied upon must be clear and precise: see *Gimenez Zaera* v *Instituto Nacional de la Seguridad Social* Case 187/85 [1987] ECR 3697.
2. The measure must be unconditional in that it does not depend on the discretion

or intervention of another body, be it the State or the Community institutions: *Sociaal Fonds voor de Diamantarbeiders* v *Brachfeld and Chougol Diamond Co* Cases 2 and 3/69 [1969] ECR 211.

3. The measure must be non-dependent, in that it requires no further legislative action to be taken by the State or by the Community institutions: see *Salgoil SpA* v *Italian Ministry for Foreign Trade* Case 33/68 [1968] ECR 453.

The original test in *Van Gend en Loos* was a strict one, perhaps to placate the Member States who believed that the Treaty did not create rights for individuals. However, over the years the Court has actively adopted the granting of direct effect, often as a policy choice, and the test has become far more relaxed (with an original fourth requirement being dropped). For example, the degree of clarity and precision required will, to a certain extent, depend on whom the obligation is imposed. If the obligation is imposed on an individual then a greater degree of clarity will be required. Alternatively, if the obligation is imposed on the Member State, which has far greater resources at its command, the degree of clarity required is less.

If a particular Community measure does require further legislative action, by either the Member State or the Community institutions, the Court has concluded (discussed below) that should the measure contain a time limit by which time such action must be taken, and that limit has expired without the further measures required being taken, then that measure may be become non-dependent. Thus, as long as the measure also meets the other two criteria, it will be capable of direct effect.

The Court's relaxation of the original test has a number of implications:

1. the European Court has adopted responsibility for ensuring the maximum effect for Community law;
2. granting of direct effect appears to have become a 'policy choice' for the Court;
3. the granting of direct effect can generally be regarded as the norm rather than the exception; and
4. direct effect will be denied if there are serious practical or political consequences: see, for example, *R* v *Secretary of State for the Home Department, ex parte Flynn* [1997] 3 CMLR 888 and *Banks* Case C–128/92 [1994] ECR I–1209.

The academic Hartley summarises the position as follows:

'... the test is of an essentially practical nature: it lays down the minimum conditions for the application of almost any legal rule. In other words, the test is really one of feasibility: if the provision lends itself to judicial application it will almost certainly be declared directly effective; only where direct effect would create serious practical problems is it likely that the provision will be held not to be directly effective.'

## 8.5 The sources of Community law capable of direct effect

### *The Treaties*

The decision in *Van Gend en Loos* concerned art 12 of the EEC Treaty (now art 25 EC). Consequently, from early on in the development of the principle, it could be concluded that Treaty provisions were capable of direct effect. Treaty articles are capable of vertical direct effect. Thus, such provisions may act as a means of establishing a defence to an action or as a grounds for an action in relation to the State: see *Brown* v *Secretary of State for Scotland* Case 197/86 [1988] ECR 3205.

However, the Court has also concluded that certain Treaty provisions are capable of creating horizontal direct effect, in that they may be invoked against other individuals. For example, Treaty provisions on the competition rules applicable to undertakings may be invoked before national courts by one undertaking against another: see *Nissan France* v *Garage Sport Auto* Case 309/94 [1996] ECR I–677 (see Part D).

Similarly, art 141 EC provides that 'each Member State shall ensure and subsequently maintain the application of the principle that men and women should receive equal pay for equal work'. It has also been held to apply 'not only to the action of public authorities, but also … to all agreements which are intended to regulate paid labour collectively as well as contracts between individuals': *Defrenne* v *Sabena (No 2)* Case 43/75 [1976] ECR 455 (see Chapter 12).

If the Treaty provision requires further legislative measures to be taken, then it fails the third criteria of the *Van Gend en Loos* test. However, the Court has concluded that once the time period set within that provision has elapsed, it may be capable of direct effect. For example, art 43 EC provides for freedom of establishment which appeared dependent on the issuing of directives, yet the decision in *Jean Reyners* v *Belgium* Case 2/74 [1974] ECR 631 grants art 43 EC (formerly art 52) direct effect (discussed in detail in Chapter 10).

It is clear that the Court makes up for failures on the part of the institutions and the Member States by giving direct effect to provisions when the period within which they *should* have been implemented has expired. At the same time, it sets limits by refusing to accord this effect to provisions it considers too general or indeterminate in scope for any clear rules to be inferred.

A limitation on the principle of giving direct effect to Treaty provisions is that the Court has, in certain cases, refused to adopt the principle of allowing retroactive application of direct effect. Thus, in *Defrenne*, the Court held that the direct effect of art 141 EC applied only from the date on which the judgment was rendered, except as regards those litigants who had already instituted legal proceedings: see also *Barber* v *Guardian Royal Exchange Assurance Group* Case C–262/88 [1990] ECR I–1889 (discussed in Chapter 12).

In *Blaizot et al* v *University of Liège* Case 24/86 [1988] ECR 379 the European Court outlined its policy towards the non-retroactive application of Treaty articles.

This case involved the payment by the State of university fees, which the Belgian government refused to allow in the case of a French national studying in a Belgian university. The student challenged this decision on the basis of the prohibition on discrimination on the grounds of nationality contained in art 12 EC. The Court held that the non-payment of the fees of European Community nationals was contrary to art 12 but, as regards the retroactive payment of fees to other Community nationals by the Belgian government, it observed:

> '... in determining whether or not to limit the temporal effects of a judgment it is necessary to bear in mind that, although the practical consequences of any judicial decision must be weighted carefully, the Court cannot go so far as to diminish the objectivity of the law and compromise its future application on the grounds of the possible repercussions which might result, as regards the past, from a judicial decision.'

In the given circumstances the Court precluded any re-opening of investigations into this matter, thereby effectively preventing the retrospective application of the principle. Hence, the Court will consider other factors, such as the financial burden that may be placed on the Member State, before necessarily granting the Treaty provision retroactive direct effect.

### Regulations

Article 249(2) EC reads as follows:

> 'A regulation shall have general application. It shall be binding in its entirety and directly applicable in all Member States.'

In the case of *Politi* v *Italian Ministry of Finance of the Italian Republic* Case 43/71 [1971] ECR 1039 the Court recognised that by 'reason of their nature and their function in the system of the sources of European Community law, regulations have direct effect and are ... capable of creating individual rights which national courts must protect.' Thus, regulations have both vertical and horizontal direct effect, which means that they may impose obligations on individuals as well as the State.

A note of warning must be sounded here, however, as the fact that regulations have direct applicability does not necessarily mean that they are directly effective. This is because, on occasion, Community regulations confer on Member States discretion as to the method of implementation and sometimes even a choice of obligations. Similarly, regulations that require penal sanctions often do not specify a particular penalty and this is left to individual Member States. In such cases national legislation is enacted to support the regulation with the necessary measures. Such a situation was pointed out by Advocate-General Roemer in the case of *Leonesio* v *Italian Ministry of Agriculture and Forestry* Case 93/71 [1972] ECR 287. Hence, the exact legal effect of a regulation will depend on whether any implementation discretion was left to national authorities and to what extent the provision had to be completed by national provisions.

Where Member States are required to implement national legislation to supplement a regulation, they are obliged to implement the regulation unless otherwise instructed. Thus, in *Commission* v *United Kingdom (Re Tachographs)* Case 128/78 [1979] ECR 419, the European Court held the United Kingdom to be in violation of its Community obligations by failing to incorporate a regulation in its entirety. Community regulations are intended to be directly applicable, and Member States are prohibited from implementing such measures in an incomplete and selective manner so as to render abortive those aspects of the legislation which the Member States oppose.

## Decisions

A decision is defined in art 249 EC as 'binding in its entirety upon those to whom it is addressed'. A decision will be an individual measure and will be specifically addressed, but it does not have direct applicability. The European Court, though, has concluded that decisions are capable of having direct effect, as long as they are clear and precise, unconditional and non-dependent. This was confirmed in the case of *Franz Grad* v *Finanzamt Traunstein* Case 9/70 [1970] ECR 825, where the Court, asserting the need to maximise the effectiveness of such measures, stated:

> 'It would be incompatible with the binding effect attributed to decisions ... to exclude in principle the possibility that persons affected may invoke the obligation imposed by a decision ... the effectiveness (l'effet utile) of such a measure would be weakened if ... nationals ... could not invoke it in the courts and the national courts could not take it into consideration as part of Community law.'

## International agreements concluded by the Community

The Court, given its view of the need for direct effect, was logically bound to admit that the provisions of international agreements concluded by the Community could be invoked by courts and tribunals. It did so in *Bresciani* v *Amministrazione delle Finance* Case 87/75 [1976] ECR 129, a judgment concerning the scope of an article in the Yaoundé Conventions I and II referring to a provision in the EC Treaty, which itself has direct effect.

The Court did not merely point to the existence of the particular article. It set the provision in the context of the association agreements to which it belonged. It observed that the provision on customs duties on imports was, for the European Community, an obligation unqualified by any reservation, either implicit or explicit. Only the associated States could ask for consultations on the subject to be opened, and this imbalance in the benefits, normal in agreements of this kind, did not have the result of robbing the provision of direct effect in the relations between the Member States and individuals.

The Court has also recognised the direct effect of provisions in international agreements similar to those contained in the EC Treaty. These can occur in agreements establishing free trade zones between the Community and non-Member States, such as the agreements concluded with European countries.

The Association Agreement between the EC and Portugal has been the subject of two cases that should be noted here. The first concerned provisions similar to arts 28–30 EC in the context of copyright, and the second concerned a provision similar to the prohibition on discriminatory internal taxation in art 90 in the context of port wine. In *Polydor* v *Harlequin Record Shops* Case 270/80 [1982] 2 ECR 329 the Court did not decide whether provisions similar to arts 28–30 were of direct effect. The Court held that its interpretation of arts 28–30 could not be transposed to the EC/Portugal Agreement since the objectives of the two treaties were different. The latter was only intended to establish a customs union while the former was designed to unite national markets into a single common market.

In *Haupzollamt Mainz* v *Kupferberg* Case 104/81 [1982] ECR 3641 the Court held that art 21 of the EC/Portugal Agreement was directly effective. This was because of its specific object and terms in the system of rules laid down by the Agreement, and not because of the nature or status of the Agreement. The Court did, though, give a more restrictive interpretation to art 21 than it has given to art 90 EC.

The British courts have also considered the doctrine of direct effect as it applies to international agreements entered into by the European Community. In *R* v *Secretary of State for the Home Department, ex parte Narin* [1990] 2 CMLR 233 the Court of Appeal was asked to decide whether a provision in an additional protocol to an Association Agreement between the European Community and Turkey had direct effect. The plaintiff argued that a deportation order made out against him was inconsistent with a provision in this Agreement, analogous to art 39 EC, which creates the right of free movement of persons. If this provision were given direct effect, the deportation order could not be carried out since such action would interfere with the Community rights of the plaintiff.

Sir Nicholas Browne-Wilkinson observed that, according to the jurisprudence of the European Court:

> 'A provision in an agreement concluded by the Community with non-Member countries must be regarded as being directly [effective] when, regard being had to its wording and the purpose and nature of the agreement itself, the provision contains a clear and precise obligation which is not subject, in its implementation or effects, to the adoption of any subsequent measure.'

After consideration of the structure, evolution and content of the additional protocol, the Court concluded that the protocol did not have direct effect because the article upon which the plaintiff relied did not satisfy the necessary criteria. Therefore the provision did not confer rights on individuals that could be exercised in the English courts.

## 8.6 Directives

Directives are defined in art 249(3) EC as:

'... binding, as to the result to be achieved, upon each Member State to which it is addressed, but shall leave to the national authorities the choice of form and methods.'

Directives are not directly applicable, and the question of whether they are capable of direct effect has long been a contentious and complex issue in Community law.

Directives are clearly dependent, in that they require the Member State to implement them to achieve the stated objective. They consequently, on face value, appear unable to create rights for individuals since their terms are not appropriate to do so. The discretion granted a Member State, however, has been consistently abused throughout the Community's history, with many of the States failing to meet their obligations and implement directives by the stated deadline, or to do so adequately. In this context, and given the importance of the role of this source of secondary legislation in the Community legal order and the somewhat ineffective public enforcement process, it is not difficult to appreciate why the European Court decided that directives were capable of granting right for individuals.

This decision was perhaps hinted at in the relatively early case of *Franz Grad* (above), a case that actually concerned the direct effect of a decision. In this case the Court held that:

'Although it is true that, by virtue of art [249], regulations are directly applicable and therefore by virtue of their nature capable of producing direct effects, it does not follow from this that other categories of legal measures mentioned in that article can never produce similar effects ...'

However, it was not until *Van Duyn* v *Home Office* Case 41/74 [1974] ECR 1337 that the Court gave a ruling on the direct effect of a provision in a directive taken in isolation. The Court was asked to give a ruling on the right of an individual before a national court to claim the benefit of art 3(1) of Directive 64/221, which co-ordinates provisions concerning the restriction of free movement. Article 3(1) states that 'measures taken on grounds of public policy or of public security shall be based exclusively on the personal conduct of the individual concerned'.

The case involved a European Community national, a member of the Church of Scientology, who had, on this ground, been forbidden access to British territory, where she wished to take up employment under the free movement of workers provided for by art 39 EC (formerly art 48). She claimed that she had the right, stemming from Council Directive 64/221, to ensure that the decision was based only on her personal conduct.

The Court explained that it would be incompatible with the binding effect attributed to directives by art 249 to exclude, in principle, the possibility that persons affected may invoke the obligations imposed by a directive. In cases where, for example, Community authorities issue directives to impose obligations on

Member States to act in a certain way, the effectiveness (l'effect utile) of such a measure would be weakened if the nationals of that State could not take it into consideration as part of Community law.

The Court based its decision to some extent on the preliminary reference procedure under art 234 EC. The Court stated that since the preliminary reference procedure empowered national courts to refer questions to the European Court on the validity and interpretation of all acts of the Community, without distinction, it necessarily implied that such acts could be invoked by individuals in their own national courts. The Court, however, did state that the Community measure would have to be evaluated in terms of its 'nature, general scheme and wording' before direct effect could be attributed to it. Applying these criteria to Directive 64/221, art 3(1) the Court held that it was capable of creating direct effects.

Whilst the Court recognised that directives may be capable of direct effect in principle in *Van Duyn*, they offered little in the way of reasoning. This was expanded on in the case of *Pubblico Ministero* v *Ratti* Case 148/78 [1979] ECR 1629. The key concept is the existence of discretionary powers with the Member States. The European Court made it clear that direct effect only exists in so far as there is no such discretionary power when the directive in question has not been implemented by the Member State within the period prescribed for its implementation. In other words, an individual may not rely on a directive, since it is dependent, until the date for implementation has expired. At this point the Member State has failed to comply with its obligations under the directive, and it is 'unable to rely on provisions of the internal legal order which are illegal from the point of view of Community law'. It is only at this point that the individual may be able to rely on the direct effects of the directive 'as against the defaulting State and acquire rights thereunder which national courts must protect'. It should be remembered that the directive provisions being relied upon must still be clear, precise and unconditional.

It is the defaulting action by the Member State that appears to be the basis of the Court's decision to grant directives direct effect; the Member State, by its own failure to implement the directive, is estopped from relying on national provisions that are incompatible with it. As the Court stated in *Ratti*:

> '... a Member State which has not adopted the implementing measures required by the directive in the prescribed periods may not rely, as against individuals, on its own failure to perform the obligations which the directive entails.'

An individual may therefore rely on the direct effect of a directive as a means of defending an action taken by the Member State that is relying on inconsistent national law, once the prescribed deadline has expired and as long as the directive meets the necessary criteria. Conversely, the European Court rejected an attempt by the Dutch authorities to prosecute a trader for stocking mineral water containing additives that were prohibited by a Council directive that the Dutch government had failed to implement: *Officier van Justitie* v *Kolpinghuis Nijmegen BV* Case 80/86

[1987] ECR 3969. In other words, a Member State may not rely on the principle of direct effect to impose duties upon individuals if the State in question has failed to implement the directive within the required period. However, an individual may also use the directly effective provisions of a directive as the basis of action and thereby gain their Community rights: see *Becker* v *Finanzamt Münster-Innenstadt* Case 8/81 [1982] ECR 53.

There is, though, one important limitation in the ability of an individual to rely on the direct effect of a directive. This limitation was identified in the case of *Marshall* v *Southampton and South-West Hampshire Area Health Authority (Teaching) (No 1)* Case 152/84 [1986] ECR 723. Ms Marshall worked for the Health Authority and was being dismissed at the age of 60, according to the Authority's policy, whilst men retired at 65. Whilst this was apparently permissible under the Sex Discrimination Act 1975, Marshall claimed that such action was in contravention of Council Directive 76/207 on equal treatment. The Court of Appeal requested a preliminary reference on whether she could rely on the provisions of Directive 76/207.

The European Court stated that a directive was incapable of imposing obligations on an individual. This was because it was addressed to Member States and was only published in the Official Journal as a matter of practice, which was 'a far too tenuous link with the individual concerned to create a legal obligation'. Thus, it was concluded that directives were incapable of possessing horizontal direct effect; if a directive conforms to all of the above criteria it may only possess vertical direct effect and may therefore only be enforced against the Member State. In the case at hand it was concluded that the Health Authority was the 'State' for the purposes of enforcing the directive (see below).

The reasoning of the Court appears to have been based on the fact that directives were not issued on individuals, but the State. Therefore, an individual had little chance of knowing what was in such directives, since they were only published in the Official Journal as a matter of practice. The Court's decision may have also been based on its desire to maintain a distinction between regulations and directives. Since *Marshall* directives have required publication, under the amendments to art 254 EC introduced by the TEU. This change of practice, and indeed the improved knowledge individuals have of Community law, has prompted some to suggest that directives should be capable of horizontal direct effect.

In *Faccini Dori* v *Recreb Srl* Case C–91/92 [1994] ECR I–3325 an individual attempted to claim against another individual under Directive 85/577 on consumer protection. The Italian authorities had not implemented the Directive. Advocate-General Lenz provided a compelling argument that directives should be capable of providing horizontal direct effects. His argument was based on the changes made by the TEU, referred to above, and in the need to meet the legitimate expectations of individuals seeking to rely on Community law. Such a decision would certainly have maximised the effectiveness of Community law, although the Advocate-General recognised that such a decision would have to be non-retrospective.

The European Court declined to accept the observations of the Advocate-General and repeated the conclusion of *Marshall*, that directives were not capable of such effects. The Court relied on art 249 which maintained a distinction between regulations and directives; if the Community wished to place immediate obligations on individuals it could and should do so through use of a regulation. The decision was probably more influenced by the problems encountered in the national courts, who had offered resistance to the concept of direct effect, especially for directives. In, for example, *Minister for the Interior* v *Cohn-Bendit* [1980] 1 CMLR 543, a supreme administrative court refused to grant direct effect to Council Directive 64/221, the same Directive as in the *Van Duyn* case.

The Court's decision not to grant directives horizontal direct effect does place limitations on the effectiveness of such Community measures. An individual may rely on the provisions of a non-implemented directive as against the 'State' but may not do so against a private party. In the context of Community directives providing for say employment rights, or consumer protection, or indeed environmental conditions, this may create an arbitrary and distinctly unfair situation. The European Court has attempted to resolve such problems in a number of ways.

## Defining the 'State'

Whilst the European Court defined the Health Authority as an emanation of the State in *Marshall*, the question, as pointed out by the Advocate-General in the case, is really a matter for the national courts. The European Court has offered guidance, albeit somewhat limited, on what may be considered an organ of the State. In *Fratelli Constanzo SpA* v *Commune di Milano* Case 103/88 [1989] ECR 1839, the European Court concluded that 'all organs of the administration, including decentralised authorities such as municipalities' were the State. (See also *R* v *London Boroughs Transport Committee* [1990] 1 CMLR 229 where it was held that since a local authority exercises governmental power it was an emanation of the State.)

In *Foster and Others* v *British Gas plc* Case C–188/89 [1990] ECR I–3313 the European Court considered the status of a nationalised industry, in terms of whether art 5(1) of Council Directive 76/207 could be relied on against British Gas. It was held that provisions of a directly effective directive may be relied upon against an entity that provides a public service under the authority of a State measure and under the control of the State and which has powers in excess of those which result from the normal rules applicable in relations between individuals. The legal form of the entity is irrelevant. The *Foster* criteria are helpful. However, it should be noted that not all of them are required for a body to be considered an organ of the State: see, for example, *National Union of Teachers* v *Governing Body of St Mary's Church of England (Aided) Junior School* [1997] 3 CMLR 630 (CA). The House of Lords, on receiving the preliminary reference in *Foster*, was responsible for applying the above test to the facts of the case. The conclusion was that elements one and two were present – British Gas, under statute, was responsible for the maintenance of an efficient system of gas supply for the entire State, and whilst the government did not have day-to-day control of the company, it did have the authority to issue directions. It also had special powers beyond those normally applicable since under statute it was granted a monopoly in the supply of gas.

In the United Kingdom the courts have concluded that Rolls Royce was not a public body within the *Foster* definition: *Doughty* v *Rolls Royce* [1992] 1 CMLR 1045. In contrast, a privatised water authority, in *Griffin* v *South West Water Services* [1995] IRLR 15, was held to be a public body. In terms of the first aspect of the *Foster* test, the High Court held that the test is not whether the body providing the service is subject to the control of the State, but whether the service itself is a public one under the control of, or regulated by, the State. The court also specifically stated that both the need for everyday control of the State over the body, and its legal form, were irrelevant factors: see *Kampelmann* v *Landschaftsverband Westfalenlippe and Others* Cases C–253–258/96 [1998] 2 CMLR 69 for a similar decision by the European Court.

## Limitations

The lack of clear guidance from the European Court has led to the possibility of a lack of uniformity throughout the Member States, as they each attempt to define what bodies are part of the State. In addition, individuals are left in a position of some uncertainty. The definition is a wide one, and encompasses the State in the role of employer (*Marshall*) as well as all decentralised governmental and administrative bodies (*Fratelli*) and certain public services (*Foster*). There is, though, a limitation to the extent to which the definition of the State may be broadened, and this, whilst obvious, solution is not sufficient to solve the problems created by the lack of horizontal direct effect granted to directives.

## *Indirect effect*

In *Faccini* (above) the Court refused to grant directives horizontal direct effect, for the reasons stated above. However, the Court did refer the individual to two further courses of action that they could pursue against a Member State that had failed to implement a directive. The first such action suggested by the Court was to use the principle of indirect effect.

Indirect effect was created in the early 1980s when two cases clearly revealed the full extent of the anomalous position created by the refusal to grant Council Directive 76/207 horizontal direct effect. Whilst *Marshall* had been concluded to work for a public body – an organ of the State – the situation was somewhat different in the cases of *Von Colson and Kamann* v *Land Nordhein-Westfalen* Case 14/83 [1984] ECR 1891 and *Harz* v *Deutsche Tradax GmbH* Case 79/83 [1984] ECR 1921. In these cases, Von Colson was employed by the prison service, whilst Harz was employed by a private company. Consequently, Von Colson would be successful, whilst Harz's action would fail. The European Court responded by taking an entirely different, and rather novel, approach.

Both cases concerned Directive 76/207, the Equal Treatment Directive, which had been the basis of the *Marshall* claim. Germany had implemented the Directive, but had done so in a way that provided only nominal compensation, rather than the proper compensation provided for under the Directive. This constituted improper or incomplete implementation of a directive: see, for example, *Marshall v Southampton and South-West Hampshire Area Health Authority (No 2)* Case C–271/91 [1993] ECR I–4367. In this case the European Court held that an upper limit for compensation on a claim brought in a national court by a private individual exercising their Community rights under a directive was tantamount to improper implementation of the measure. In the circumstances, the Court held that Member States were obliged to give full effect to Community measures by providing effective and real relief to those whose Community rights were infringed.

In *Von Colson* and *Harz*, though, the European Court concentrated not on the principle of direct effect, but on art 10 EC. Article 10 requires Member States to take 'all appropriate measures ... to ensure fulfilment of the obligations arising out of this Treaty'. The Court believed this obligation to be:

> '... binding on all the authorities of Member States including, for matters within their jurisdiction, the courts. It follows that, in applying the national law ... national courts are required to interpret their national law in the light of the wording and the purpose of the directive ...'

In other words, the German national court was obliged to interpret German national law so that it conformed with Community law, in this case a directive. As a result, there could be no limit on the compensation to which both Von Colson and Harz were entitled. The principle of direct effect was avoided, as were problems in horizontal effect and defining the State – such factors were entirely irrelevant.

In *Marleasing SA v La Comercial Internacional de Alimentacion SA* Case C–106/89 [1990] ECR I–4135 the European Court dealt, not with an improperly implemented directive as it had in *Von Colson*, but one that had not been implemented at all. In *Marleasing* the Court was required to answer the question whether Council Directive 68/151 on company law harmonisation, which had not been implemented by Spain, could be relied upon to override a provision of Spanish law allowing the nullity of a company on the ground of lack of consideration. The Directive exhaustively enumerated the grounds on which the incorporation of a company could be declared void. Spanish law therefore contradicted Community law, but the Directive remained non-adopted.

The Court held that the national law must be interpreted in conformity with the Directive, and any attempt to dissolve a company on grounds other than those set out in the Directive was incompatible with Community law. Furthermore, the Court also concluded that

> '... in applying national law, whether the provisions concerned pre-date or post-date the directive, the national court asked to interpret national law is bound to do so in every way possible in the light of the text and the aims of the directive to achieve the results envisaged by it and thus comply with ... the Treaty.'

National courts are therefore obliged to interpret all national law so that it conforms to Community law, regardless of when it was passed. It is also interesting to note that the date of implementation of the directive also becomes an irrelevant factor. Since a directive is a form of Community law, national law must be interpreted to conform to it. This proposition also finds support in Advocate-General Léger's comments in the case of *R* v *Ministry of Agriculture, ex parte Hedley Lomas* Case C–5/94 [1996] ECR I–2553. In his Opinion he stated that a directive could produce indirect effects even before the time for implementation has expired. However, this will be limited by the need not to operate the principle in a manner that is against the interests of someone facing criminal charges, in that it makes them liable or aggravates their liability: see *Kolpinghuis Nijmegen* Case 80/86 [1987] ECR 3969 and below.

Indeed, Hartley suggests that it would be wrong for a court to invoke indirect effect before the date for implementation has expired. In his opinion, such an obligation would only exist if the Member State had actually implemented the directive, at which point it could be assumed that the State intended the national law to comply with the terms of the directive, and indirect effect could be used in interpreting the provision of the national law to ensure they complied with the terms of that directive.

In conclusion, the impact of these decisions has been to give horizontal direct effect to directives in an indirect manner – indirect effect. While the Court has expressly rejected the possibility of directives having horizontal effect, its method of 'sympathetic interpretation' arrives at the same effect in practice.

## Limitations

There is an exception to the obligation to sympathetically interpret national law to conform with an unimplemented directive, and that occurs when the national measure, if interpreted in such a way, imposes criminal liability. The European Court has held that an unimplemented directive cannot impose obligations on individuals, and that no criminal liability could be imposed on persons who contravene the unimplemented directive: *Arcaro* Case C–168/95 [1996] ECR I–4705.

Another limitation to the principle of indirect effect can be found in the European Court's ruling in the *Faccini* case (above). In this case the Court made reference to the principle as an alternative course of action, but also commented that the obligation to interpret national law in accordance with Community law applied only so far as such an interpretation was possible.

The main limitation of this principle as an effective method of removing the problems created by the non-horizontal direct effect of directives is that the national courts themselves are required to undertake the process of interpretation: *Wagner Miret* v *Fondo de Garantia Salarial* Case 334/92 [1993] ECR I–6911. This creates the possibility of lack of uniformity both throughout the European Union and, indeed, within a Member State's judicial system. In addition, some judicial systems have had difficulties with such a purposive method of interpretation being imposed on them. Such problems have been particularly evident in the United Kingdom.

In *Duke* v *GEC Reliance* [1988] 2 WLR 359 the House of Lords held that it did not have to interpret the Sex Discrimination Act 1975 in line with Council Directive 76/207. The House concluded that it was Parliament's intention to permit discriminatory retirement ages for men and women, stating that it would 'distort' the Act to read it in the light of the Directive.

A similar approach was taken in the case of *Webb* v *EMO Air Cargo* [1993] 1 WLR 49, where Lord Keith referred to the decision in *Marleasing* (although this approach by the House of Lords in the case finds some justification in the European Court's ruling in *Faccini*, explained above). The national courts had been directed to interpret 'as far as possible, in the light of the wording and purpose of the directive'. The House of Lords believed that they could only do this when the national law was 'open to interpretation'. Consequently, the House of Lords appeared willing to substitute or perhaps add words, but felt unable to do more since that would be tantamount to legislating, a role that is in the hands of Parliament. Other British courts have shown similar discomfort with the obligation to sympathetically interpret national law: see, for example, *Finnegan* v *Clowney Youth Training Programme Ltd* [1990] 2 All ER 546 and the VAT tribunal in *Gould & Cullen* v *Commissioners of Customs and Excise* [1994] 1 CMLR 347.

There have, however, been circumstances in which British courts have taken a more positive approach. This can be seen in *Lister* v *Forth Dry Dock and Engineering Co* [1989] 1 All ER 1134 (HL), where the House of Lords was required to consider the compatibility between UK regulations on protecting workers dismissed in connection with business transfers and Directive 77/187. The European Court had already provided a number of decisions in relation to the Directive, and the House of Lords felt obliged to give effect to the UK regulations in a manner that was consistent with the decision of the European Court, via their interpretation of the British law.

## State liability

The alternative course of action mentioned by the European Court in *Faccini* was the principle of State liability. In *Francovich and Bonifaci* v *Italian Republic* Cases C–6 and 9/90 [1991] ECR I–5357 it was established that a party who had suffered damage through the non-implementation of a directive (now extended to other breaches of Community law) could sue the defaulting Member State for damages. This was discussed in detail in the preceding chapter, but it should be noted that some of the more recent decisions do perhaps make it more difficult for an individual to pursue this course of action. It may also be the case that damages are an inappropriate solution to some failures to implement a directive. For example, the failure to establish a system of environmental protection, where more than one individual may be affected and where the establishment of the rights themselves may be far more satisfactory in the long term than monetary compensation. However, this will require the European Court to finally decide that directives are capable of horizontal direct effect, and such a decision seems unlikely at present.

It seems, therefore, that should the Community measure, such as a directive, lack direct effect, or be inappropriate in the circumstances, in that it is being enforced against a private individual, then State liability as a course of action may be the most suitable and likely of success. This may be especially so given the uncertainty in whether national courts will adopt fully the obligation under indirect effect.

Finally, it must be noted that this relatively new course of action, combined with direct effect and indirect effect, attempts to place a heavy burden on Member State to comply with their Community obligations. In the case of directives, often still either unimplemented or inadequately implemented the principle of State liability may provide an effective 'deterrent' but others are not confident that this will be the case. For example, Tridimas and Hartley identify that all of the cases so far have originated from Member States that already have relatively good records for complying with their Community law obligations, including the correct implementation of directives. As Hartley points out,

'... those countries that show the least respect for Community law in general are unlikely to show any greater respect for the new remedy, the application of which will always remain in the hands of the national courts.'

# PART B

# Free Movement of Persons

The birth of the European Community was primarily concerned with promoting economic integration. As an integral part of this process, the Community needed to ensure the free movement of not only goods but other factors that are relevant in production, such as free movement of labour and services. This is provided for under art 3(1)(c) EC, which states that one of the activities of the Community will be to create 'an internal market characterised by the abolition, as between Member States, of obstacles to the free movement of goods, persons, services and capital.' (This provision lacks direct effect: *R* v *Secretary of State for the Home Department, ex parte Flynn* [1995] 3 CMLR 397.)

Part C of this book will examine in detail those Community provisions on the free movement of goods, whereas this Part will assess the free movement of persons and services. In addition to art 3(1)(c) there are additional Treaty provisions providing support for free movement (known as 'flanking measures'):

1. Articles 136–145 EC providing for greater uniformity in terms of worker protection; and
2. Article 141 EC providing for equal pay for equal work for men and women. This was the means by which a more level playing field was to be established in terms of the Community labour force. Article 141 will be considered in Chapter 12.

This area of Community law has been considered one of the cornerstones of the European Community and developments have moved the law away from its original economic basis to one perhaps better described as humanitarian. This process has been achieved by Treaty amendments, the introduction of secondary legislation and via the decisions of the European Court of Justice. This area of Community law now provides a rich and fertile source of rights for Community nationals, particularly since the majority of provisions are directly effective. We shall briefly examine the main Treaty developments in the area of free movement, the basic Treaty framework and the influence of the European Court in the general development of the law, before moving on to examine workers, the self-employed and equal pay in detail.

## Treaty developments

### European citizenship

One of the most important Treaty developments, clearly indicating the recognition of people as individuals rather than members of the labour force, was the introduction of European Citizenship by the Treaty on European Union: art 17 EC, which provides that:

> '(1) Citizenship of the Union is hereby established. Every person holding the nationality of a Member State shall be a citizen of the Union. Citizenship of the Union shall complement and not replace national citizenship.
> (2) Citizens of the Union shall enjoy the rights conferred by this Treaty and shall be subject to the duties imposed thereby.'

However, the actual benefits from being such a citizen are rather limited and could be described as merely symbolic.

The rights of EU citizens are provided under arts 17–22 EC. According to art 18(1) EC:

> 'Every citizen of the Union shall have the right to move and to reside freely within the territory of the Member States, subject to the limitations and conditions laid down in this Treaty and by the measures adopted to give it effect.'

In addition to rights of free movement, European citizens have the following rights:

1. to stand and vote in municipal (but not national) and European Parliament elections (art 19);
2. petition the Ombudsman and Parliament (the right to petition the Ombudsman is in fact open to any natural or legal person residing or having registered an office in a Member State: art 195(1));
3. have a right to diplomatic representation outside the Community from any other Member State when they are in territory where their own State has no embassy or consulate (art 20); and
4. a right of access to documents held by the Community institutions.

The ToA introduced the amendment to art 17 EC, so that it states that 'Citizenship of the Union shall complement and not replace national citizenship'. Hence, citizenship provides additional rights but does not remove or alter those provided by Member States to their own nationals. It remains the case, as provided by public international law, that a Member State is still free to determine who its nationals are: see *Micheletti* v *Delegación del Gobierno en Cantabria* Case C–369/90 [1992] ECR I–4239 and *R* v *Secretary of State for the Home Department, ex parte Kaur* Case C–192/99 [2001] ECR I–1237.

The Treaty of Nice has amended the second paragraph of art 18 EC and inserted an additional third paragraph, which provide that:

'(2) If action by the Community should prove necessary to attain the objective and this Treaty has not provided the necessary powers, the Council may adopt provisions with a view to facilitating the exercise of the rights referred to in paragraph 1. The Council shall act in accordance with the procedure referred to in Article 251.

(3) Paragraph 2 shall not apply to provisions on passports, identity cards, residence permits or any other such document or to provisions on social security or social protection.'

In 1997 the Commission stated that the concept of European citizenship was one that was a 'fundamental and personal right ... which may be exercised outside the context of en economic activity'. However, the political rights are somewhat limited, and the rights to free movement remain those of most significance. These rights are, in turn, subject to the limitations and conditions laid down in the Treaty and secondary legislation and the existence and validity of these limitations are protected by art 18(1). In other words, any rights to free movement and residence are subject to any limits or conditions laid down in the Treaty and any relevant secondary legislation.

The Community has extended rights of residence to other categories of persons (such as students under Directive 93/96, retired persons under Directive 90/364 and persons of independent means under Directive 90/365). Here, too, there are limitations, in that the right of residence will only be accorded to the person and certain family members if they are able to establish that they have adequate resources and are covered by sickness insurance. This limitation was introduced as a means of reflecting the financial concerns of the Member States. The practical consequence of such a limitation is that, whilst free movement extends beyond those who are economically active, it still requires those persons wishing to exercise the rights to be financially independent. This limitation is compatible with art 18(1), as discussed above.

As we shall see, the rights provided under the EC Treaty for workers and the self-employed do not relate to purely internal situations and require some inter-State movement. It was suggested that the introduction of European citizenship would remove this requirement. This has, however, not been the conclusion of the European Court, which has failed to allow the application of art 18 to purely internal matters: see, for example, *Kremzow* v *Austria* Case C–299/95 [1997] ECR I–2629 and *Land Nordrhein-Westfalen* v *Uecker; Jacquet* v *Land Nordrhein-Westfalen* Cases C–64 and 65/96 [1997] ECR I–3171.

A number of relatively recent cases have revealed that the ECJ is perhaps now more willing to expand the effect of art 18. In *Bickel and Franz* Case C–274/96 [1998] ECR I–7637 the Court ruled that art 12 EC had been breached by the Italian authority's refusal to permit Bickel and Franz to speak German in judicial proceedings, particularly since Italian German-speaking nationals were permitted to do so. The Court, however, also made reference to art 18, on the basis that the pair were not just seeking the receipt of certain services but were also exercising their rights to free movement as European citizens.

In *Maria Martinez Sala* v *Freistaat Bayern* Case C–85/96 [1998] ECR I–2691 the Court found that Ms Martinez was lawfully resident in Germany, where she had lived and worked since 1968. The German authority's decision not to grant her access to social benefits because they had failed to provide her with a residence permit was a limitation on her ability to access that right, which did not apply to nationals. The Court based its ruling simply on art 17 only – since she was lawfully resident, and a Community citizen, she was entitled to all rights granted under the Treaty:

> 'As a national of a Member State lawfully residing in the territory of another Member State, the appellant … comes within the scope … of the provisions of the Treaty on European citizenship.
>    Article [17(2)] … attaches to the status of citizen of the Union the rights and duties laid down by the Treaty, including the right, laid down in Article [12]…not to suffer discrimination on grounds of nationality …'

Further, in *Grzelczyk* v *Centre Public d'Aide Sociale d'Ottignes-Louvain-la-Neuve* Case C–184/99 [2001] ECR I–6193 the Court made the following statement:

> 'Union citizenship is destined to be the fundamental status of nationals of the Member States, enabling those who find themselves in the same situation to enjoy the same treatment in law irrespective of their nationality …'

Consequently, in this case, whilst Grzelczyk was not a worker, he was a Union citizen and as such was entitled to equality of treatment and the absence of discrimination on the basis of nationality, as laid down by art 12 EC.

### The Schengen Agreement, justice and home affairs and third-country nationals

Whilst the European Community was intended to be an area without internal frontiers, there was difficulty securing action to achieve this between the Member States. One particular thorny issue was the extension of free movement rights to third-country nationals. With lack of consensus on this issue, some Member States made their own agreement to remove all checks on people crossing their borders. This was known as the Schengen Agreement 1985 (later transformed into an implementing Convention in 1990), and the parties to it were Germany, France and the Benelux countries. The general success of the Agreement prompted other States to join, such as Italy, Portugal, Spain and Greece (although there were problems of a technical nature).

The Treaty on European Union introduced the justice and home affairs (JHA) pillar (see Chapter 1) but progress on developing this aspect of the Union and the treatment of third-country nationals was extremely slow. The JHA pillar was intended to deal with, inter alia, asylum policy, rules on border crossing, immigration and treatment of third-country nationals. The pillar was originally intended to be intergovernmental in nature, hence developments would be reached via the consensus of Member States' governments and the introduction of common policies or positions by unanimity. The Community institutions played only a minor role. The need for uniformity in such a politically sensitive area greatly hampered the development of this area of law, for example, a proposed Convention on the admission of third-country nationals was not adopted.

As a means of providing momentum in this field, the Member States agreed in 1996 to incorporate the Schengen Agreement into the EC Treaty. This was put into effect by the Treaty of Amsterdam, with the creation of a new Title IV (arts 61–69) in Part III of the EC Treaty. At the same time, immigration, visas, third country nationals, judicial co-operation in civil matters, administrative co-operation and asylum elements in the JHA pillar were moved to Title IV. (It should be noted that the United Kingdom, Ireland and Denmark refused to sign up to these provisions and their position was provided for by protocols attached to the ToA.) The provisions under Title IV (discussed in brief below) appear to extend to everyone. Article 62(1), which requires the elimination of controls on internal borders, benefits all persons 'be they citizens of the Union or nationals of third countries'. Some measures, such as that on visa policy, only extend to third-country nationals.

Article 61 EC states that the overall aim is the progressive establishment of an area of 'freedom, justice and security'. It also provides that the Council is to adopt measures to ensure 'the free movement of persons in accordance with art 14, in conjunction with directly related flanking measures with respect to external border controls, asylum and immigration'. The Council was required to take such action within a period of five years, and in order to achieve this, drew up a programme with the Commission in 1998.

Achieving these aims relies considerably on the approach taken in the Schengen Agreement. A protocol attached to the EC Treaty and amended by the ToA states that from the date of the coming into force of the ToA the entire Schengen acquis would apply to the Member States (unless they had opted-out). The Schengen acquis includes both the original Agreement and implementing Convention, and all those decisions and declarations adopted by the participating Member States. These were defined in a Council Decision in May 1999 and were provided with a formal treaty basis under either the EC Treaty or the JHA pillar of the TEU. Consequently, removing internal frontiers, the rights of third-country nationals to circulate within the Community, control of external borders and visa policy are now within the EC Treaty. A Council decision in June of the same year provided that the Schengen acquis would extend to both the UK and Ireland, after they made such a request, as provided for under the opt-out protocol.

Article 62 EC includes more detailed provisions in relation to internal and external border controls. It provides for:

1. the creation of the internal market in persons;
2. standards and procedures to be followed by Member States in respect of persons crossing external borders; and

3. granting third-country nationals rights to travel within the territory of the Member States for up to three months. (This was implemented via Council Regulation 1683/95, which provides that third-country nationals will be issued with a standardised EU visa and will be able to travel anywhere within the Union for a period of three months. Any Member State may issue the visa, but the form used is now standardised.)

There are, however, some problems related to this relatively new area of Community law. First, it appears that the provisions (especially art 62) will not have direct effect. The provisions also do not provide for anything more than the right to freely move. There are, presently, no corresponding rights of residence. Second, Steiner suggests that the Council may have difficulty in securing the unanimity it requires to proceed with its five-year plan. The Commission has put forward a range of proposals, but obtaining agreement may be a long and politically controversial process. There are also problems in relation to securing accountability in this area since the Parliament has only a consultative role and the European Court has limited jurisdiction. For example, it cannot consider any measure based on art 62 concerning internal law and order or national security and the Member States have only limited access to the Court through the art 234 preliminary reference procedure: art 68 EC.

However, this is not to say that the Community has not made some advances in the context of third-country nationals. Regulations have been enacted in the attempt to improve the ability of such people to enter and move within the European Union. Hence, for example, Regulations 539/2001 and 2414/2001 identify those third-country nationals that require a visa to enter an external border of the Union.

Generally, however, the position and treatment of third-country nationals within the EU is a difficult one. There is no body of law that extends protection to such peoples in their own right once they are located within the Union; instead they may gain rights through more indirect means, such as being a member of a worker's family. The position is not improved with the extension of European citizenship to Community nationals – indeed, it only draws closer attention to the distinction in treatment.

In terms of protecting third-country nationals, the situation looked promising when, at a European Council meeting in Tampere in 1999, there was a call for a codified set of rights for third-country nationals that was comparable to that offered to Community nationals. Some tentative steps have been taken to secure this, with the introduction of measures providing rights of residence for those with long-stay national visas (Regulation 1091/2001); and proposed directives dealing with, for example, the provision of cross-border services and granting equal status in relation to employment, education and social protection to those that are long-term residents. These developments are positive but they were overshadowed and to some extent overtaken by the tragic events in New York on 11 September 2001. Since then much of the focus has been on security and, at a national level, the issues of immigration and high numbers of asylum seekers has dominated the political scene, witnessed particularly in the run up to the 2001 general election in the UK. It is extremely unfortunate that this appears to be the current political ethos, particularly given the context behind the birth of the European Union. The academic Weiler neatly sums up the situation in the following comment:

> 'It would be ironic that an ethos which rejected the nationalism of the Member States gave birth to a new European nation and European nationalism ... We have made little progress if the Us becomes European (instead of German, French or British) and the Them becomes those outside of the Community or those inside who do not enjoy the privileges of citizenship.'

## The European Economic Area Agreement

The remaining States in EFTA (except Switzerland) were provided, under this agreement, with the same rights of free movement as those provided under the EC Treaty. The Agreement came into effect on 1 January 1994. Consequently, those citizens of the Union and their families enjoy all the rights of free movement in relation to those EFTA States, and citizens and their families of the EFTA States enjoy identical rights in relation to the Member States of the European Community.

In addition, there are limited rights held by those nationals of States that have entered into Association Agreements with the EC, such as those with Turkey, Morocco (see below), Tunisia, Algeria, the Czech Republic, Hungary, Poland, Romania, Slovakia and Cyprus. These Agreements may have direct effect. There are no rights to enter, but there are rights in relation to equal treatment in employment and social security after entry. Two examples of such Association Agreements creating such rights are the EC–Turkey Agreement and the EC–Morocco Co-operation Agreement: see respectively *Kazim Kus* v *Landeshauptstadt Wiesbaden* Case C–237/91 [1992] ECR I–6781 and *Bahia Kziber* v *ONEM* Case C–18/90 [1991] ECR I–199.

## The legislative framework and rulings of the European Court of Justice

The basic principles on the free movement of persons are contained within arts 39–42 EC, in relation to workers; arts 43–48 EC, in relation to establishment for the self-employed; and arts 49–55 EC, in relation to the provision or receipt of services. These provisions will be examined in detail in Chapters 9 and 10. In brief, the basic rights provided for are to freely leave, to enter or reside in a Member State for the purposes of work, establishment or to provide or receive services. These rights are limited in that they do not apply to the public service in the case of workers (art 39(4)) and activities connected with the exercise of official authority in the case of establishment and services: arts 45 and 55. Member States are also able to derogate from the rules on the grounds of public policy, security or health (arts 39(3) and 46 and Council Directive 64/221). One further limitation on the rights to free movement is that they may not be exercised in an internal context. In other words, there must be some element of inter-State movement. Any person who has not left, or has any intention to leave their home State, will not be able to benefit from the Community rules: *Iorio* Case 298/84 [1986] ECR 247.

The rights to free movement for workers and the self-employed were originally included in the Treaty with the economic objective of providing for shortages in labour in skills in one Member State being compensated for by surplus skills and labour in another. This approach, as mentioned above, has been modified by both the introduction of a considerable body of secondary legislation by the Community institutions and by the European Court of Justice. As a result, the rights to free movement are considered fundamental personal rights. The migrant worker is no longer to be considered as merely a source of labour but as a human being: see the comments of the Advocate-General in *Mr and Mrs F v Belgium* Case 7/75 [1975] ECR 679. They are aided in securing their rights by the fact that the law in this context (both the Treaty articles and the secondary legislation) has direct effect. In the context of the Treaty articles and regulations, the direct effect will be both vertical and horizontal: see *Walrave and Koch v Association Union Cycliste Internationale* Case 36/74 [1974] ECR 1405, *Union des Associations Européenes de Football v Jean-Marc Bosman* Case C–415/93 [1995] ECR I–4921 and *Angonese v Cassa di Riparmio di Bolzano SpA* Case C–281/98 [2000] ECR I–4139.

One of the most influential decisions of the European Court has been to extend art 39 on the free movement of workers, to include those searching for work: *Procureur du Roi v Royer* Case 48/75 [1976] ECR 497. This was the case even though the Treaty article expressly linked the right to accepting offers of employment actually made. The decisions of the Court to extend the rights to those searching for work remains one of the best examples of teleological interpretation and the proactive approach of the Court, and will be discussed at length in Chapter 9. Conversely, the European Court has narrowly interpreted those limitations on the right to free movement, as discussed in Chapter 11.

One of the most important principles in this area of law in that of the prohibition on discrimination on the grounds of nationality. This is provided for under the Treaty articles referred to above, but is further reinforced by art 12 EC, which states:

> 'Within the scope of application of this Treaty, and without prejudice to any special provisions contained therein, any discrimination on grounds of nationality shall be prohibited.'

In other words, this obligation, imposed on the Member States, extends to all activities within the scope of the EC Treaty, including those dealt with in this Part. The European Court has supported many of its decisions by reference to this most fundamental of provisions, and by doing so has extended equal employment and social treatment to both workers, the self-employed and their families (in addition to those rights provided under secondary legislation such as Regulation 1612/68). As we shall discover, both direct and indirect forms of discrimination are prohibited, although in the case of the latter the Court has provided for the discrimination to be objectively justified. The various tests laid down in each of the areas in which indirect discrimination may be objectively justified are relatively similar, and we will discuss the use of objective justification in relation to workers (Chapter 9), establishment and services (Chapter 10) and equal pay: Chapter 12.

Finally, the Treaty of Amsterdam introduced art 13 into the EC Treaty, which provides that the Council of Ministers has the power to adopt legislation to prohibit discrimination based on sex, racial or ethnic origin, religion or belief, disability, age or sexual orientation. The majority of these prohibitions are innovations as far as Community law is concerned.

# 9

# The Free Movement of Workers

9.1 Introduction

9.2 The definition of worker for the purposes of art 39 EC

9.3 The exclusion of workers in the public service

9.4 Directive 68/360 – rights of entry and residence

9.5 The right to equality

9.6 Regulation 1251/70 – the right to remain

9.7 The right of Member States to restrict free movement

9.8 The future

## 9.1 Introduction

Article 39 EC provides for the free movement of workers and that discrimination between workers of the Member States and those who originate from other Member States, regarding employment, remuneration and other conditions of work and employment, shall be prohibited. This is often referred to as one of the four fundamental freedoms of the Treaty. This chapter will consider the rights available to workers and their families, in the context of employed individuals, whereas the next chapter will deal with those rights afforded to the self-employed.

Article 39(3) provides that workers shall be entitled, subject to limitations justified on grounds of public policy, security and health, to:

1. accept offers of employment actually made;
2. move freely within the territory of Member States for this purpose;
3. stay in a Member State for the purpose of employment in accordance with provisions governing the employment of nationals of that State laid down by law, regulation or administrative action; and
4. remain in the territory of a Member State after having been employed in that State, subject to conditions that shall be embodied in implementing regulations to be drawn up by the Commission.

Article 39(2) is still extensively relied on to challenge national laws and practices that discriminate in the employment of workers on the grounds of nationality, notwithstanding the considerable secondary legislation that operates in this area of the law: for example, see *Allué* v *Universita degli Studi de Venezia* Cases C–259, 331 and 332/91 [1993] ECR I–4309 and *Spotti* v *Freistaat Bayern* Case 272/92 [1993] ECR I–5185. In addition, it should be remembered that one of the fundamental provisions of the EC Treaty is that discrimination on the grounds of nationality be prohibited: art 12 EC (see Chapter 3).

Article 39 itself contains its own provision for derogation in para 3, which allows limitations on free movement on the grounds of public policy, security and health. Additionally, the article does not apply to employment in the public service: art 39(4).

Article 40 provides that art 39 will be supplemented by secondary legislation, as indeed it has been by the following means:

1. Regulation 1612/68 providing for workers' rights;
2. Regulation 1251/70 on remaining after employment;
3. Directive 68/360 on entry and residence permits; and
4. Directive 64/221 on justifying exclusions.

The European Court's view of the rights available under this area of Community law is robust. In *Mr and Mrs F* v *Belgium* Case 7/75 [1975] ECR 679 Advocate-General Trabucchi stated that a migrant worker should not be considered as a mere source of labour, but as a human being. Community law should serve to remove all obstacles to the mobility of workers and especially obstacles to 'the integration of his family in the host country'. The Court has adopted this approach throughout its decisions in this area, giving a wide interpretation to those rights available and limiting the ability of Member States to derogate or use the exceptions to this fundamental freedom.

Article 39 has direct effect: *Kenny* v *Insurance Officer* Case 1/78 [1978] ECR 1489. In *Commission* v *France* Case 167/73 [1974] ECR 359 the Court stated that art 39 was 'directly applicable in the legal system of every Member State' and that any national law that is contrary to this (the French Maritime Code in this case) was, as a consequence, inapplicable. It has been held that art 39 has horizontal direct effect as well as vertical direct effect, in that the European Court has applied art 39 to the rules of private organisations and bodies that have the effect of restricting the movement of workers.

In *Walrave and Koch* v *Association Union Cycliste Internationale* Case 36/74 [1974] ECR 1405 the Court stated that art 39 did not just extend to the actions of public authorities, but to 'rules of any other nature aimed at regulating in a collective manner gainful employment and the provision of services'. Thus, art 39 extended to 'agreements and other acts adopted by private persons' since to decide otherwise would 'risk creating inequality' in the application of Community law.

In *Union des Associations Européennes de Football* v *Jean-Marc Bosman* Case

C–415/93 [1995] ECR I–4921 the Court ruled on the legality of the rules of football organisations and their compatibility with art 39 and the prohibition of discrimination on the grounds of nationality. This case dealt with both the horizontal direct effect of art 39, in other words its application against private bodies, and the question of whether the principles also apply to non–discriminatory measures.

The body in question, UEFA, is the organisation that regulates the national football associations of some 50 countries, including those of the 15 Member States of the European Union. It enacts rules that are implemented at national level by the individual national football associations. In this case the European Court reviewed two of these rules.

The first concerned the imposition of transfer fees that allowed national football clubs to impose a transfer fee when a player moved from one club to another. In the absence of such a fee, which was set by the transferring club, a player could not move from one club to another. These requirements were written into individual player's contracts. If a club refused to accept the fee offered by another club, it could prevent the player moving, in which case the player in question would be unable to break their contractual link.

The second regulation concerned restrictions on the number of non–national players that could be fielded by a club. The number of non–national players that could be fielded at any one time during a game was restricted to three. UEFA justified this rule on the basis that it preserved the national element in football clubs.

Bosman was a Belgian football player who had been prevented from transferring from a Belgian team to a French team because the fee offered by the French team was inadequate. As a result he was unable to transfer and his football career was destroyed. He sued the Belgian football team, the Belgian national football association and UEFA, claiming that these rules violated Community law. Both questions were referred to the European Court for a preliminary ruling.

The Court ruled first that the transfer fees contravened art 39 because they interfered with the right of free movement for football players. The Court accepted that the same rules applied inside Member States but held that the nature of these rules was too excessive and constituted a barrier to the cross–border movement of players inside the Community.

The Court also found that the nationality restrictions contravened art 39 and, in particular, the prohibition on discrimination on the grounds of nationality. The rules could not be justified as preserving the national identity of teams and violated one of the fundamental freedoms of Community law.

Article 39, therefore, may be applied in a horizontal as well as vertical manner and its terms may be breached by provisions that appear either non–discriminatory (as in *Bosman*) or a form of indirect discrimination. Indeed, the existence of discrimination is not the key factor – a breach of art 39 will occur where an obstacle to free movement exists, regardless of the way in which that obstacle applies to national and non-nationals. This development, the extension of art 39 to non-discriminatory measures on the basis that they impede access to the employment market, mirrors those developments that have occurred in other areas of Community law, such as establishment and services, and the free movement of goods: see, for example, *Keck and Mithouard* Cases C–267 and 268/91 [1993] ECR I–6097, discussed in Chapter 14. Consequently, the absence of any discrimination is not a bar to the application of art 39; what is required is the imposition of a barrier or obstacle to the ability to exercise the right of free movement: see also *F C Terhoeve* v *Inspecteur van de Belastingdienst Particulieren/Ondernemingen Buitenland* Case C–18/95 [1999] ECR I–345.

Both non-discriminatory provisions and indirect discrimination may be justified as being in the public interest, an open-ended means of justification, seen, for example, in *Groener* (discussed below) where a genuine linguistic requirement was acceptable. However, the Court will closely examine the validity of the justification, and may, as in *Bosman*, refuse to accept the justification offered. The justification will be assessed in terms of its appropriateness and proportionality and Member States may find the burden of proof difficult to meet: see, for example, *Finanzamt Köln-Alstadt* v *Roland Schumacker* Case C–279/93 [1995] ECR I–225; *Bachmann* v *Belgium* Case C–204/90 [1992] ECR I–249; and *Terhoeve* (above).

Finally, it should be noted that art 39 does not apply in a purely internal situation. Its provisions only operate where there is some element of movement from one Member State to another: see *R* v *Saunders* Case 175/78 [1979] ECR 1129.

## 9.2 The definition of worker for the purposes of art 39 EC

Neither the Treaty nor the secondary legislation offer any definition of the term 'worker'. This was not an oversight, but an attempt to ensure that the term 'worker' was given as broad an interpretation as possible. The European Court, though, has offered guidance on what constitutes a worker. In *Hoekstra* v *Bestuur der Bedrijfsvereniging voor Detailhandel en Ambachten* Case 75/63 [1964] ECR 177 the Court concluded that the freedom envisaged under art 39 would be:

> '... deprived of all effect and the ... objectives of the Treaty would be frustrated if the meaning of such a term could be unilaterally fixed and modified by national law.'

Hence, the term 'worker' is to be given a Community meaning and reference to national law and practice is irrelevant.

In *Levin* v *Staatssecretaris van Justitie* Case 53/81 [1982] ECR 1035, a part-time worker was held to be a worker. The Court provided a test to identify a worker: they must be pursuing an effective and genuine activity that is not marginal or ancillary, and the activity must be economic. Whether the test is satisfied is a matter for national courts.

*Levin* was followed in *Kempf* v *Staatsecretaris van Justitie* Case 139/85 [1986]

ECR 1741. A German national, Kempf had been earning a living in The Netherlands by giving music lessons for which he received very little money. He required social security payments to bring his income up to subsistence level. He had also drawn sickness benefit from the State. Dutch law provided that these benefits were only available to workers. On his application for a residence permit a reference was made to the European Court. Advocate-General Slynn reiterated the *Levin* test and, in discussing the drawing of state benefit in order to reach subsistence level, suggested that this would no more than raise a question as to whether genuine and effective activity was being pursued. It was held that Kempf was a worker and as such was entitled to a residence permit. It is therefore evident that the hours spent working and the wages received are simply factors to be taken into consideration in determining whether a person falls within the article; they are not conclusive factors.

The call for a broad interpretation of the term worker was taken up in *Lawrie-Blum v Land Baden-Württenberg* Case 66/85 [1986] ECR 2121. This case concerned a trainee teacher, a British national, who, as part of her training, took classes for which she was paid. The remuneration received was less than that of a qualified teacher. She subsequently applied for a post as a secondary school teacher but was refused because of her nationality. The reference by the national court elicited from the European Court the proposition that the term worker should 'receive as wide a meaning as possible'. The Court pointed out that art 39 provided a fundamental right and cited the following as requirements to be met to achieve the status of worker: that they were providing services for another over a given period of time; that they were under the direction of that other; and that they received remuneration/payment. The Court was satisfied that Lawrie-Blum met all the requirements and was further satisfied that she was pursuing a genuine and effective economic activity.

In the case of *Steymann v Staatssecretaris van Justitie* Case 196/87 [1988] ECR 6159 the European Court considered further the notion of receiving remuneration. Steymann, a German national, had worked in The Netherlands as a plumber. He joined a religious community and participated in the community by performing general household duties, and plumbing work. Whilst he received no salary for his work, all his material needs, such as housing and 'pocket money', were provided for by the community. On applying for a residence permit, he was informed by the authorities that he was not eligible. On his appeal a reference was made to the European Court.

The Court held that participation in a religious community could fall within the required economic activity and the meeting of Steymann's material needs as being an 'indirect quid pro quo for [his] work'. It was irrelevant that the work was perhaps rather unconventional in nature.

The Court considered the need for the work to be 'genuine' in *Bettray* v *Staatssecretaris van Justitie* Case 344/87 [1989] ECR 1621. Bettray undertook work as part of a drug-rehabilitation programme in The Netherlands. He was paid and therefore the Court concluded that he performed services for another and received remuneration – the low level of that remuneration was irrelevant. They also considered the need for the work to be genuine, as identified in *Levin*, and to do so examined the purpose behind it. The conclusion the Court came to was that 'work under the Social Employment Law cannot be regarded as an effective and genuine economic activity if it constitutes merely a means of rehabilitation or reintegration for the persons concerned.' Furthermore, the Court identified that:

'... persons employed under the Social Employment Law are not selected on the basis of their capacity to perform a certain activity; on the contrary, it is the activities which are chosen in the light of the capabilities of the persons who are going to perform them.'

Consequently Bettray's work was not of a sufficiently genuine nature to classify him as a worker for the purposes of art 39.

One major development in the application of art 39 is its extension, via the teleological interpretation of the European Court, to include those seeking work, otherwise referred to as 'migrant' workers. In *Procureur du Roi* v *Royer* Case 48/75 [1976] ECR 497 the Court concluded that art 39 extended to those who wished to search for work, and suggested that a period of three months should be permitted to do so.

In *R* v *Immigration Appeal Tribunal, ex parte Antonissen* Case C–292/89 [1991] ECR I–745 the applicant was a Belgian national who had entered the United Kingdom in 1984 and had unsuccessfully searched for work. He was imprisoned for a drug offence and the Home Secretary ordered his deportation. One of the grounds for deportation offered by the UK authorities was that art 39 only extended to those that had confirmation of employment. Antonissen appealed to the Immigration Appeal Tribunal, which made a reference to the European Court.

The Court examined the express wording of art 39(3)(a) and (b) and concluded that the right to free movement for Community workers extended only to accept offers of employment actually made. However, they believed that 'such an interpretation would exclude the right of a national of a Member States to move freely and to stay in the territory of the other Member States in order to seek employment there, and cannot be upheld'. The Court concluded that any strict or literal interpretation of art 39 would itself 'jeopardise' the full effectiveness of the rights envisaged under art 39; it would render the provision ineffective by providing an obstacle to the right of free movement.

Such a conclusion could have been of some concern to the Member States, especially when one considers the large number of rights to which a worker and their family are entitled. In response to such concerns the European Court made it clear that a migrant worker was not in the same position as a 'true' worker: see section 9.5. The onus is placed on the individual to prove that they are genuinely searching for work and that they have a genuine chance of finding employment. If they are unable to do so the Member State may be free to deport them without having to base their action on one of the three recognised grounds under art 39.

The individual must be given a 'reasonable' period of time within which to search for work; in the case itself six months was not considered to be too short a time period within which to find employment. However, the Court's assessment appears to leave an open-ended period of time within which an individual may find employment, and the final discretion rests in the hands of the national courts. The case law does specifically state that the migrant worker should be entitled to at least three months (see *Royer* above), and this was reasserted in *Commission* v *Belgium* Case C–344/95 [1997] ECR I–1035.

## 9.3 The exclusion of workers in the public service

Article 39(4) states that the provisions of art 39 do not apply to employment in the public service. This 'public service proviso' raises the rather thorny issue of what precisely the public service is. As an exception to the fundamental freedom of movement, it has been narrowly construed by the European Court. Whilst the Member States supported the idea of an institutional test to identify those jobs within the public service, positions they regard as instrumental in protecting their interests and an aspect of national sovereignty, the European Court has adopted a functional test.

In *Commission* v *Belgium (Re State Employees)* Case 149/79 [1980] ECR 3881, the Court declared that it was posts that involve direct or indirect involvement in the exercise of powers 'conferred by public law and duties designed to safeguard the general interests of the state and other public authorities', that would be considered as within the public service proviso. The Court went on to point out that such posts will usually involve some 'allegiance to the State' and consequently are best performed by nationals.

*Commission* v *France* Case 307/84 [1986] ECR 1725 involved proceedings brought by the European Commission against France. The French authorities insisted that only French nationals could be appointed as nurses in a public hospital. The European Court held that such a provision was contrary to art 39, saying that public service implied an occupation that involved safeguarding of the public interest. It is also evident from the case of *Lawrie-Blum* (above) that teaching in a State school is not employment within the public service.

In an attempt to clarify the public service the Commission produced guidance, in the form of a Notice, in the Official Journal in 1988, although this is non-legally binding. From this it can be deduced that the following are posts considered to be within the public service proviso: the armed forces, the judiciary, the police, tax authorities, and bodies preparing or monitoring legal acts. The following do not fall within the public service: teachers, nurses and non-military research in a public establishment (thereby implying that military research will).

Whilst the Commission has received suggestions that it should propose a Community measure to clearly define the public service, this has not been adopted, perhaps because to do so may permit the Member States to abuse the current case law. Some believed that the creation of European citizenship would reduce the interest of the Member States in identifying employment within the public service. This does not appear to have been the case, and in recent years there have been a number of enforcement actions against Luxembourg, Belgium and Greece on the basis of their application of art 39(4): *Commission* v *Luxembourg* Case C–473/93 [1996] ECR I–3207; *Commission* v *Belgium* Case C–173/94 [1996] ECR I–3265; and *Commission* v *Greece* Case C–290/94 [1996] ECR I–3285. Indeed, the Luxembourg argument was based strongly on the notion that the public service proviso permitted a State to preserve its national identity. The Court, whilst recognising the validity of the objective, was of the opinion that using the proviso in such a way was disproportionate.

## 9.4 Directive 68/360 – rights of entry and residence

Directive 68/360 provides for Community rules in relation to the entry and residence of workers into the State in which they wish to work. The Directive also applies to the workers family: see section 9.5 for discussion of who constitutes the worker's family.

To gain entry to a Member State a Community national need only produce a passport or valid identity card: art 3 of Directive 68/360. A Community national will not require a visa or any other permit: see *Sagulo, Brenca and Bakhouche* Case 8/77 [1977] ECR 1495. The European Court has held that the mere requirement of a stamp in a passport constitutes a formality equivalent to a visa: see *R* v *Pieck* Case 157/79 [1980] ECR 2171. Should the individual be unable to produce such documentation, their treatment must be proportionate to the administrative breach that has occurred and this does not include the ability to deport the individual: *Watson and Belmann* Case 118/75 [1976] ECR 1185 and *Royer* Case 48/75 [1976] ECR 497.

Article 4(2) provides that a document entitled 'Residence Permit for a National of a Member State of the EEC' shall be issued. This permit is simply proof of the right of residence. The worker may be employed prior to completion of the formalities for obtaining a permit: art 5. The permit must be valid for at least five years, be applicable to the entire Member States territory and be automatically renewable: art 6. In order to apply for such a permit, the worker must provide their entry documentation, and proof of engagement in employment from their employer. Family members need to show their entry documentation, and proof of their relationship with the worker. They may in addition have to show proof of 'dependency' should they have entered under such a basis as permitted by Regulation 1612/68: see section 9.5. The validity of the residence permit is not affected by breaks in residence of six consecutive months nor is it affected by military service: art 6(2). The validity of the permit is also not to be affected by the fact that the worker is no longer employed through illness, accident or through involuntary unemployment (although in the latter situation the onus is on the worker to prove that they were involuntarily made unemployed): art 7(1).

Article 8 extends the right of residence to those employed for less than three months, frontier workers – that is, those who return to their own Member State every day or week – and seasonal workers. They need not be required to apply for residence permits.

The question as to whether a worker's rights are conditional upon the issue of a residence permit by a national authority, or whether the rights were granted directly by art 39 EC, was the basis of *Procureur du Roi* v *Royer* Case 48/75 [1976] ECR 497. It was held that:

1. the right of nationals of a Member State to enter and reside in the territory of another Member State is conferred directly by the Treaty;
2. art 4 of Directive 68/360 entails an obligation for the Member States to issue a residence permit to anyone providing the proof required by the Directive; and
3. the mere failure by a national to comply with formalities concerning entry is not behaviour threatening to public policy and by itself cannot justify a measure ordering expulsion or imprisonment.

## 9.5 The right to equality

### General

A number of positive substantive rights are provided for by Regulation 1612/68. Part II of the Regulation includes detailed provisions relating to the need for employment agencies in the Member States to co-operate, and for similar co-operation in relation to employment and vacancies between the Member States' agencies, the Commission and the European Co-ordination Office. Part III of the Regulation attempts to ensure close co-operation by establishing an Advisory Committee and a Technical Committee (from Member States' representatives). However, the most important practical aspects of the Regulation are found in Part I, which has formed the basis of a considerable degree of litigation.

Article 1 of the Regulation provides that non-nationals may take up employment with the same priority as nationals of that State. Articles 3 and 4 prohibit direct or indirect discrimination in relation to certain practices. These include reserving posts for national workers, restricting advertising or applications and setting special recruitment or registration processes for non-nationals. There is, however, one exception to this. This was established in the case of *Groener* v *Minister for Education* Case 379/87 [1989] ECR 3967, which concerned a Dutch national working in Ireland. She applied for a permanent, full-time post at an Irish educational institution but was unsuccessful because she failed a test in the Irish language. The requirement that the candidate have adequate knowledge of the Irish language applied regardless of the nationality of the applicant, but was not actually required to perform the job. She appealed on the basis of art 3 of Regulation 1612/68.

The European Court held that 'the [EC] Treaty does not prohibit the adoption of a policy for the protection and promotion of a language of a Member State which is both the national language and the first official language'. However, the Court also stressed the need for the requirement not to be 'disproportionate in relation to the aim pursued and the manner in which they are applied must not bring about discrimination against nationals of other Member States'. In this case it was concluded that the requirement was not disproportionate.

Article 5 of the Regulation provides that non-nationals may seek employment and receive the same assistance as nationals from employment offices. In addition, art 6 provides that discriminatory vocational or medical criteria in relation to recruitment and appointment are prohibited.

Article 7 of the Regulation provides a rich source of rights: art 7(1) prohibits both direct and indirect discrimination. An example of indirect discrimination can be seen in the case of *Sotgiu* v *Deutsche Bundespost* Case 152/73 [1974] ECR 153. In this case an Italian national was offered employment with the German post office. As part of his package Sotgiu was paid a separation allowance, as were all employees separated from their families. The post office stated that it intended to increase the separation allowance for all employees that had been resident in Germany when they had been appointed. The European Court concluded that this was a form of 'covert' or indirect discrimination:

> '... criteria such as place of origin or residence of a worker may, according to circumstances, be tantamount, as regards their practical effect, to discrimination on the grounds of nationality, such as is prohibited by the Treaty and the Regulation.'

Article 7(2) of the Regulation provides that non-national must be granted the same social and tax advantages as nationals (this is discussed in further detail below). Article 7(3) provides for the worker to receive vocational education (although it should be noted that this does not include university education). Furthermore, under art 8, non-nationals must be entitled to membership of trade unions on the same basis as nationals, and under art 9 they are entitled to the same rights as nationals in relation to housing.

Three aspects of this Regulation will be discussed in further detail, namely, the worker's family, the entitlement to social and tax advantages under art 7(2) and educational rights.

## The worker's family

In addition to the above rights, the Regulation allows for workers to 'install' their family with them, although the worker must establish that they have adequate housing before entry is permitted. (Such a factor, though, is irrelevant once entry has been granted, and future lack of adequate housing may not be considered as valid grounds for the refusal to renew a residence permit: see *Commission* v *Germany* Case 249/86 [1989] ECR 1263.)

'Family' is defined under art 10(1) as the spouse and descendants under 21, or who are dependent, and dependent relatives in the ascendant line of both the worker and the spouse. The nationality of the family members is irrelevant, although if they are not nationals of one of the Member States they will require a visa. Dependency is a question of fact, not of law, and the particular circumstances of the case will have to be considered by the national court to determine whether a family member is indeed dependent: see *Centre Public de l'Aide Sociale de Courcelles* v *Lebon* Case 316/85 [1987] ECR 2811. Article 10(2) provides that other, additional dependent relatives (or those that were living under the same roof as the worker before they moved) may be permitted to join the worker, although the Member State is not obligated to accept them and is only required to 'facilitate' their entry.

The rights of the family are 'parasitic' on the worker – in other words, they cannot exercise their rights without the worker first exercising theirs. This can be seen in the cases of *Morson and Jhanjan* v *Netherlands* Cases 35 and 36/82 [1982] ECR 3723. This case involved two Dutch nationals working in The Netherlands, in other words they had not exercised any free movement. They both wished to bring their parents over to The Netherlands but it was concluded that they had no right to do so under Community law. This decision may be described as harsh, especially given the decision in *Singh* (see below) – if Morson and Jhanjan had moved to another Member State they would have had the right to bring their parents over to live with them and then could have returned to The Netherlands. The Court's insistence that the principles and rights under free movement in Community law do not apply to such purely internal situations creates a distinction in treatment, a form of reverse discrimination, and does little to promote the principle of moving towards ever closer union, or European citizenship.

The definition of spouse is that of someone legally married to the worker and this situation remains until the full and legal dissolution of the marriage. In *Diatta* v *Land Berlin* Case 267/83 [1985] ECR 567, on an art 234 EC reference, it was held that separated spouses who were non-nationals of a Member State (in this case Senegalese) could still enjoy the status of spouse notwithstanding the fact that they no longer cohabited with the worker.

A similar decision was rendered in *R* v *Immigration Appeal Tribunal and Surinder Singh, ex parte Secretary of State for the Home Department* Case C–370/90 [1992] ECR I–4265. In this case Mr Singh, an Indian national, married a British citizen in the United Kingdom in 1982. The couple then left the UK to work in Germany, where both obtained employment. They subsequently returned to the UK to start a private business. However, at no time during this period did Mr Singh acquire British nationality.

In 1987 a decree nisi of divorce (rather than a decree absolute) was pronounced against Mr Singh, and the date of the expiry of his temporary leave to remain in the UK was brought forward to September of that year. After the expiry of this period

Mr Singh remained in the UK without permission, and eventually a deportation order was made out against him.

The question of whether Mr Singh was entitled to exercise the right of free movement of workers to continue to reside in the UK, after initiating this right by travelling to Germany as the spouse of a Community worker, was brought before the Immigration Appeal Tribunal. The tribunal ruled in Mr Singh's favour. According to the decision of the tribunal, the right of free movement included the right to return to and reside in the country from which the party left to exercise the right of free movement in another Member State.

The matter was referred to the European Court, which upheld the ruling of the tribunal. Once an individual travels from one Community country to another for the purpose of obtaining employment, the whole gambit of Community rights under the principle of free movement of workers is activated. This includes the right of the spouse of a Community worker to return with his or her spouse to their original Member State.

The question of whether a cohabitee may be considered a spouse within the definition of art 10(1) Regulation 1612/68 was considered by the European Court in *Netherlands* v *Reed* Case 59/85 [1986] ECR 1283. Reed, a British national who was unmarried, sought work in The Netherlands, but then moved in with Mr W, another British national working in The Netherlands. Reed, though, remained unemployed. She subsequently applied for a residence permit, which was refused. Dutch law permitted non-nationals to extend their rights to residence permits to their cohabitees, but only if the relationship had been entered into prior to entry into The Netherlands. Dutch nationals, on the other hand, suffered no such restraint.

In the art 234 EC ruling, the European Court refused to extend the term spouse to include cohabitees. The Court instead relied on alternative provisions of Community law, namely art 12 EC, which prohibits discrimination on the grounds of nationality, and art 7(2) of Regulation 1612/68. The latter provision requires that non-nationals receive the same social and tax advantages as nationals (discussed in detail below). Hence, if Dutch nationals were permitted to live with cohabitees when the relationship had been instigated within The Netherlands, then non-nationals, such as Mr W, should be entitled to the same 'social advantage': to permit any other situation would be to discriminate on the basis of nationality. Hence, cohabitees may gain the right to join the worker on the basis that to prevent them would be discrimination on the basis of nationality, and that cohabitation is a social advantage to which nationals are entitled so, therefore, non-nationals must be entitled to the same.

This principle will probably also have to be applied to those relationships where the parties are of the same sex. Only Member States that desired to make such cohabitation illegal for their own nationals would be able to prevent non-nationals from living with a cohabitee of the same sex. However, Community law does not offer specific protection for non-traditional relationships, whether the cohabitee is of the same or opposite sex, and this remains an area that Community law should address as a matter of some priority, although the Commission has recognised the existence of the problem: see Chapter 12.

It is worth noting that, should Reed have gained employment, or have claimed that she was looking for work and had a reasonable chance of finding employment, then she would have been able to claim her own rights as a Community national under art 39 EC. This, of course, will only apply if the cohabitee is a Community national.

Article 11 allows those embraced by art 10 to take up employment in the State, witnessed in the case of *Singh* (above). The case of *Emir Gül v Regierungspräsident Düsseldorf* Case 131/85 [1986] ECR 1573 gives a further illustration of the Court's attitude to this provision. Gül, a Cypriot, was a doctor who, in 1971, married a British national. His spouse worked as a hairdresser in Germany. Dr Gül was given temporary leave to practise medicine in Germany provided that he returned to Cyprus on completion of that period. He eventually applied for permanent permission to practise. The point was raised as to whether the right granted under art 11 extended to the practising of medicine. The Court concluded that the only limitation envisaged on a spouse's right to work under art 11 was that they lacked the necessary and appropriate qualifications (see Chapter 10). Gül was accordingly entitled to practise.

## Article 7(2) Regulation 1612/68 – social and tax advantages

This is probably one of the most important provisions of the Regulation, and one that has been widely interpreted by the European Court. In *Fiorini (neé Cristini) v SNCF* Case 32/75 [1975] ECR 1085 the widow of an Italian worker claimed that she was entitled, under art 7(2), to a rail card offering reductions for large families. The French authorities argued that the benefits associated with art 7(2) were limited to those that were connected with the contract of employment only. Therefore, they asserted, family members were not entitled to such rights.

The European Court disagreed, stating that social and tax advantages offered to nationals should also be offered to non-national workers, including those not associated with their contract of employment. However, the European Court has since identified that in order to assess whether the worker is entitled to the social advantage one should consider three factors:

1. their status as workers;
2. their residence in the territory of the Member State; and
3. whether the benefit 'seems suitable to facilitate their mobility within the Community'.

Hence, in *Ministère Public v Even and ONPTS* Case 207/78 [1979] ECR 2019 it was concluded that deducting an early pension, since the worker was not a Belgian in receipt of a Second World War service invalidity pension, was not a breach of art

7(2) Regulation 1612/68. This was because it was not required to facilitate the worker's free movement but was received by virtue of the fact that Belgian nationals had rendered services to their country during wartime and had suffered hardships for their country.

Furthermore, in *Fiorini* the Court had concluded that art 7(2) Regulation 1612/68 extended not only to workers, but to family members too. However, family members are only entitled to such rights if they are of some direct or indirect benefit to the worker (see *Lebon* above) and if the family members of the nationals of that State are entitled to such rights: see *Belgium* v *Taghavi* Case C–243/91 [1992] ECR I–4401.

The following discussion provides examples of the extensive range of rights offered under art 7(2) of Regulation 1612/68. In *Castelli* v *ONPTS* Case 261/83 [1984] ECR 3199 the Court concluded that an old age pension available to nationals should also be available to the elderly mother of an Italian worker who had 'installed' herself with her son in Belgium. In *Hoeckx* v *Openbaar Centrum voor Maatschappelijk Welzijn, Kalmthout* Case 249/83 [1985] ECR 973 art 7(2) was held to include a minimum subsistence allowance paid to nationals. In *Frascogna* v *Caisse des Dépôts de Consignation (No 2)* Case 256/86 [1987] ECR 3431 a 'job seekers allowance' was held to be a social advantage and in *Commission* v *Luxembourg* Case 111/91 [1993] ECR I–817 childbirth allowance was also included within the ambit of art 7(2). Reference could also be made to the case of *Netherlands* v *Reed* (above), as an example of the expansive interpretation of this Community provision.

Indirect discrimination in relation to the receipt of both social and tax advantages may be objectively justified (see section 9.1), but the national measure must seek to achieve a legitimate ends and must be proportionate (ie no more than is necessary) to achieve that objective: see, for example, *O'Flynn* v *Adjudication Officer* Case C–237/94 [1996] ECR I–2617 and *Hans-Martin Bachmann* v *Belgian State* Case C–204/90 [1992] ECR I–249.

There is, however, one important limitation to the ability to receive social and tax advantages under this provision of Community law. In the case of *Lebon* Case 316/85 (above) the Court came to the following conclusion:

> '... the right to equal treatment with regard to social and tax advantages applies only to workers. Those who move in search of employment qualify for equal treatment only as regards access to employment in accordance with art [39] ... and arts 2 and 5 of Regulation No 1612/68.'

Thus, it is extremely important that the migrant worker gain genuine and effective employment within an economic activity, since without doing so they, and their family, will not be entitled to any of the social and tax advantages to which nationals are entitled. Obviously, a migrant worker would also not be entitled to install their cohabitee with them, since this in itself is a 'social advantage'.

Finally, it should be noted that an additional regulation complements and expands on art 7(2) Regulation 1612/68. This is Regulation 1498/71, which concerns the application of social security schemes to employed persons, to self-employed persons (see Chapter 10) and to members of their families moving within the Community. The Regulation is designed to ensure that, in the social security areas of sickness and maternity benefit, invalidity benefit, old-age benefit, survivor's benefit, benefits in respect of accidents at work and occupational diseases, unemployment benefits and family benefits, there will be no discrimination on grounds of nationality. Benefits will be paid notwithstanding that the recipient resides in another Member State.

## Rights to education

Community law has developed various rights to education in regards to three different categories of persons. These are workers, children of workers (and to a limited extent other family members) and students. The final category was created by the European Court dealing with students that had moved to another Member State to participate in an educational programme, but who failed to meet the necessary criteria to be considered 'workers'.

The worker gains educational rights under art 7(3) of Regulation 1612/68 which states that they 'have access to training in vocational school and retraining centres' on the same basis and according to the same conditions as nationals of that Member State. Whilst this appears fairly extensive, and would also include any financial incentives available to nationals, there is one important limitation in its scope.

According to the cases of *Lair* v *University of Hanover* Case 39/86 [1989] ECR 3161 and *Brown* v *Secretary of State for Scotland* Case 197/86 [1988] ECR 3205 art 7(3) of the Regulation does not extend to universities. The European Court believed that the scope of the vocational training to which the worker was entitled was 'a more limited one and refers exclusively to institutions which provide only instruction either alternating with or closely linked to an occupational activity.'

*Lair* and *Brown*, however, provided an alternative means for the worker to gain further educational rights. The European Court suggested that in such circumstances, should art 7(3) be inappropriate, the worker could rely on art 7(2) and claim these educational rights as a social advantage. There are, however, two limitations to this. First, there must be some link between the workers previous form of work or employment and the education that they wish to receive, although this is not necessary where the worker has been made involuntary unemployed and is required to retrain on order to re-enter the job market. Second, the Court examined whether the applicants were indeed workers in order to be entitled to such rights.

Advocate-General Slynn suggested that only an individual that had genuinely come to the Member State to work would be a worker for the purpose of gaining rights to education as a social advantage. He suggested that those who had entered for the purpose of becoming students, or had undertaken work experience prior to undertaking studies, would not be 'genuine' workers and would therefore not be eligible. In order to assess which of these was the case in a given situation, the Advocate-General suggested that the period of residence (a minimum of one year in his opinion), and the work that the individual had done, should be considered.

The European Court did not accept that any minimum period of residence was a requirement in assessing whether the individual was a true worker. They assessed the facts of both cases and concluded that Brown, who had accepted a place at Cambridge before working in Scotland, was not therefore a worker for the purposes of gaining educational rights as a social advantage – his work was merely 'ancillary' to the taking up of his studies. Lair's situation was somewhat different since she had been in Germany for some five years and had worked intermittently during that period. The Court stated that if they had become involuntarily unemployed then they were entitled to retrain, but that if they had given up their work for the sole purpose of taking up their studies they were only entitled to undertake a course that was linked to their previous employment.

The children of the worker are specifically granted rights to education under art 12 of Regulation 1612/68. This has been interpreted very broadly by the European Court. In *Michel S v Fonds National de Reclassement Handicapés* Case 76/72 [1973] ECR 457 the Court stated that art 12 extended equality for workers' children to all measures designed to facilitate education, in this case a national fund. In *Casagrande v Landeshauptstadt München* Case 9/74 [1974] ECR 773 the Court confirmed that art 12 entitled children to all measures designed to facilitate education, such as financial grants, and that it provided for equal access to all educational courses, including university level.

This was given further support in the cases of *Echternach and Moritz* v *Netherlands Minister for Education* Cases 389 and 390/87 [1989] ECR 723, which confirmed that all educational courses are within the ambit of art 12. The case also concluded that these rights continue even if the worker dies or decides to retire in the Member State. The child is also permitted to continue their education if the worker leaves the State, either to move on to another or to return to their host Member State. The Court, in this case, recognised that the educational systems of many of the Member States were not compatible. They asserted that a child's education was best if it had continuity – this, of course, would not be possible to achieve if a child was 'forced' to leave one educational system to re-enter another, given the marked difference in the systems throughout the Union. They also asserted the need to integrate the worker into the host Member State. This decision, therefore, perceives the potential for a child's education to be interrupted to be, in turn, a potential barrier to the worker exercising their right to free movement. It may also, in the long term, lead to more citizens of the European Union being multi-lingual and understanding of the various cultures and societies that make up the Union – a praiseworthy goal, although not one the European Court specifically stated that it had.

Furthermore, art 12 has been concluded to apply to children over the age of 21: *Landesamt für Ausbildungsförderung Nordrhein-Westfalen* v *Gaal* Case C–7/94 [1995]

ECR I–1031. The child in question was the son of a deceased Belgian worker, resident in Germany, but who was over 21 and not dependent on his family. The Court held that reference to the conditions in art 10(1) Regulation 1612/68 were not relevant in assessing whether a child was entitled to financial assistance in relation to their education.

Finally, it appears that members of the worker's family, although not specifically mentioned as having educational rights in the Regulation, are also entitled. However, their rights stem not from art 12 of the Regulation, but from either art 7(2) as a 'social advantage' or from art 12 EC, which prohibits discrimination on the grounds of nationality: *Forcheri* v *Belgium* Case 152/82 [1983] ECR 2323. In this case the spouse of a worker did not have to pay a fee to enrol on a course since nationals were not required to pay the fee.

The final category of those having educational rights are students. In *Gravier* v *City of Liège* Case 293/83 [1985] ECR 593 the Court examined the rights available to a French student in Belgium who had not worked nor had any family in Belgium. The Court concluded that access to vocational training fell within the ambit of the Treaty. It concentrated on art 150 EC (formerly art 128) which provides that the Council should identify general principles for implementing a common vocational training policy. The Court also concluded that:

> 'Access to vocational training is … likely to promote free movement of persons throughout the Community, by enabling them to obtain a qualification in the Member State where they intend to work and by enabling them to complete their training and develop their particular talents in the Member State whose vocational training programmes include the special subject desired.'

Consequently, since such vocational training was included within the Treaty, Gravier was entitled to freedom from discrimination on the grounds of nationality under art 12 EC and did not have to pay an enrolment fee unless nationals also had to pay that fee.

Given the financial concerns expressed by the Member States on the implications of such a ruling, the European Court placed two limitations on its scope. First, whilst vocational training was given a reasonably wide interpretation, as any education designed to facilitate the persons ability to enter a profession or trade, including university courses (see *Blaizot* v *University of Liège* Case 24/86 [1988] ECR 379), it did not include those courses designed to merely increase or expand knowledge. Furthermore, the Court limited the retrospective effect of *Blaizot* because of the financial implications on the Belgian educational system.

Second, whilst access to such vocational courses attracted equality, the conditions attached to that access were limited. In other words, the Court concluded that the student was only entitled to equality in relation to grants relating specifically to the vocational course, such as tuition fees and enrolment fees. The Court did not feel able, under Community law, to extend equality to the accessing of maintenance grants or other such financial aid.

The student will have a right of residence, as secured under both European Court case law (see *Raulin* v *Minister van Onderwijs en Wetenschappen* Case C–357/89 [1992] ECR I–1027) and under Directive 93/96.

There have been changes to the EC Treaty in relation to this area, with a new art 149 and an amended art 150, but the law already developed is to remain and be expanded on rather than replaced: art 3 TEU. This respects the Member State's position in having ultimate control over their educational systems, which in turn is a reflection of the principle of subsidiarity. Thus, the Community is more willing to adopt 'soft' law. This is witnessed in a variety of Action Programmes and Green and White Papers. The Community seems unwilling to take more strident action, being perhaps cautious of treading on what is considered by many Member States to be an important part of their cultural diversity or to create any serious financial implications.

## 9.6 Regulation 1251/70 – the right to remain

This Regulation provides that having been employed in a Member State the worker has the right to remain under art 2(1) if:

1. they have been employed and have reached pensionable age having worked for the previous 12 months and resided there continuously for more than three years; or
2. after continuous residence for more than two years they become permanently incapable of work.

These rights are extended by virtue of art 3 to the worker's family, subject to the conditions laid down in that article. Article 3(2) provides:

'If, however, the worker dies during his working life and before having acquired the right to remain in the territory of the state concerned, members of his family shall be entitled to remain there permanently on condition that:
(a) the worker, on the date of his decease, had resided continuously in the territory of that Member State for at least two years; or
(b) his death resulted from an accident at work or an occupational disease; or
(c) the surviving spouse is a national of the state of residence or lost the nationality of that state by marriage to that worker.'

The right to remain after ceasing employment also extends to employees and self-employed persons who have decided to retire. Council Directive 90/365, which came into effect in July 1994, requires Member States to grant the right of residence to nationals of other Member States who have been employed or self-employed and are recipients of an invalidity or early retirement pension, an old–age pension or a pension in respect of industrial accident or disease. Entitlement to this right requires the individual to prove to the national authorities that they receive sufficient income from these sources as not to be a burden on the social security system of the host State.

## 9.7 The right of Member States to restrict free movement

Article 39(3) EC provides that the rights are subject to limitations justified on the grounds of public policy, public security and public health. These grounds may also be used to justify refusal for those wishing to establish themselves of provide or receive services. The full extent of these rights, and the corresponding protection offered to individuals in such situations, will be considered in Chapter 11.

## 9.8 The future

The European Parliament and Council have jointly produced a new, general directive (Directive on the Right of Citizens of the Union and Their Family Members to Move and Reside Freely within the Territory of the Member States: COM (2001) 257 final) that will replace much of the existing secondary legislation referred to in this chapter. The rationale offered for the introduction of this new legislation is based on the need for harmonisation and a more direct link to the concept of European citizenship (discussed in the introduction to Part B). The proposed new Directive (under amendment by the European Parliament at the time of writing) is intended to apply from 1 July 2005. The principal provisions of the new Directive can be summarised as follows:

| | |
|---|---|
| Article 1 | provides for conditions governing the right to move and freely reside in a Member State, the right to permanent residence, and the limits imposed on the grounds of public policy, security and health. These conditions apply to both a Union citizen and their family. |
| Article 2 | offers the definition of a Union citizen as a person who holds the nationality of one of the Member States. Paragraph 2 provides a broader and more uniform interpretation of the family members so that it includes not only the spouse, but an unmarried partner too, although this is subject to the need for the host State to treat unmarried couples in the same way as it treats those that are married. |
| Article 4 | provides that there must be no discrimination on the basis of sex, race, colour, ethnic or social origin, genetic characteristics, language, religion or beliefs, political or other opinion, membership of a minority, property, birth, disability, age or sexual orientation. |
| Chapter II | provides that there is a general right to move and reside for up to six months for Union citizens and their family, irrespective of their |

particular nationality, if, under art 6, they have a valid passport or ID card.

Chapter III    provides for rights of residence for more than six months to both the employed and self-employed, if they have sufficient resources; to students admitted to a vocational course/training; and to family members of Union citizens that fall into one of these categories. Article 8 provides that, in such circumstances, such individuals will be issued with evidence of the right to reside in the form of a 'certificate of registration'. Article 13 also provides measures dealing with the implications of divorce, following the developments made by the ECJ.

Chapter IV    introduces for the first time a right of permanent residence, which will be formally awarded with the granting of a 'permanent residence card': art 17. This right only applies to those Union citizens that have legally resided continuously for a period of four years within that State and can be removed only if the individual is absent from that State for a period of four consecutive years.

Chapter V    Articles 20–21 provide for the members of the family to work and to equality of treatment, regardless of their nationality.

Chapter VI    provides for changes in relation to the derogations under the grounds of public policy, security and health (which will be discussed in Chapter 11).

# 10

# Freedom of Establishment and Services

## 10.1 Introduction

The EC Treaty provisions on the rights of freedom of establishment and the freedom to provide services are arts 43 and 49 EC respectively. These articles are reinforced by art 12 EC, which prohibits discrimination on the grounds of nationality. Taken together, these provisions ensure that restrictions on the self-employed on the right and the freedom to provide professional and commercial services, either from a fixed establishment or on a temporary basis, are to be 'progressively abolished'.

The right of establishment and the right to provide or receive services have been described by the European Court as fundamental Community rights. The primary principle applying to both is that there should be no discrimination on the grounds of nationality, whether such discrimination stems from legislation, regulation or administrative practices. This principle is binding on the Member States, competent bodies and legally recognised professional bodies: see *Steinhauser* v *City of Biarritz* Case 197/84 [1985] ECR 1819 and *Walrave and Koch* v *Association Union Cycliste Internationale* Case 36/74 [1974] ECR 1405 in relation to establishment and services respectively. On a number of occasions the European Court has held Member States in violation of Community law for discriminating in favour of their own nationals when regulating professional activities within their territories: see, for example, *Commission* v *Luxembourg (Re Access to the Medical Profession)* Case C–351/90 [1992] ECR I–3945.

Article 48(1) extends these rights not only to natural persons but also to companies, who may enjoy the same conditions. A company (or firm) includes those constituted under civil and commercial law including co-operative societies and other legal persons governed by public or private law, save for those which are non-profitmaking: art 48(2).

## Distinguishing between establishment and services

Articles 43 and 49 may appear to overlap, but in separating their application a rule of thumb may be employed: art 43 relates to the freedom to establishment. This entails the 'actual pursuit of an economic activity through a fixed establishment in another Member State for an indefinite period': *R* v *Secretary of State for Transport, ex parte Factortame Ltd and Others* Case C–221/89 [1991] ECR I–3905. According to the case of *Gebhard* v *Consiglio dell' Ordine degli Avvocati e Procuratori di Milano* Case C–55/94 [1995] ECR I–4165, establishment requires the activity to be carried out on a 'stable and continuous basis'.

Article 49 applies where a person simply conducts professional forays into another Member State without establishing a business presence there, or, as we shall see, wishes to receive services for a temporary period in another Member State. A Community national will therefore rely on this provision when their activities are to be temporary and, according to *Gebhard*, whether the activities are temporary will be decided by reference to 'not only the duration of the service, but also of its regularity, periodicity or continuity'.

In *Gebhard* the Court stated that those Treaty provisions on establishment, services and indeed, workers (see Chapter 9) were mutually exclusive, and therefore if there is any doubt as to which is the most applicable all should be pleaded. In relation to whether establishment or services is applicable, reference should be made to the above distinction. In practical terms, however, since the rights available under both are reasonably equivalent, there should be relatively little concern placed on distinguishing which to plead.

There are two issues of some significance to the development of the area of Community law. The first relates to the need for the recognition of the various qualifications throughout the Community that professionals may have. This has been an area of considerable controversy and tension between the Community institutions and the Member States and, as we shall see, between the political and judicial institutions of the Community. This chapter will consider the issue of qualifications in relation to establishment, although it should be noted that the need for relevant qualifications also applies should an individual wish to provide a service.

The second issue relates to whether the Treaty prohibits not only discriminatory national measures in relation to the freedoms of establishment and services, but whether it also extends to prohibiting non-discriminatory provisions. Member States have to, and continue to, impose measures to regulate the activities and standards of professionals, such as lawyers and doctors, claiming that they are done so in a non-discriminatory manner and are therefore not within the ambit of the Treaty provisions. This chapter will discuss the Court's approach to such measures and the various alternative approaches taken to tackling the problems inherent in the recognition of qualifications throughout the Community.

## 10.2 The exception to freedom of establishment and services – the official authority exception

Articles 45 and 55 EC provide that the provisions on establishment and services respectively shall not be available to those 'activities which in that State are connected, even occasionally, with the exercise of official authority'. This is simply the equivalent provision, for the self-employed, to art 39(4) EC in relation to workers: see Chapter 9.

The scope of this exception was considered in the case of *Jean Reyners* v *Belgium* Case 2/74 [1974] ECR 631, in which the Court was asked to consider whether the role of a lawyer fell within the exception. Whilst Luxembourg argued that the entire profession was exempt from the Treaty rules because it was closely connected with the exercise of official authority, the European Court concluded that the exception should be narrowly construed and have a Community definition. It concluded that the exception would not apply when 'within the framework of an independent profession, the activities connected with the exercise of official authority are separable from the professional activity in question taken as a whole'. In the case of the legal profession it was established that, whilst lawyers had professional contact with the judicial system of the Member State, their profession was not one that fell within the official authority exception. See also *Thijssen* v *Controledienst voor de Verzekeringen* Case C–42/92 [1993] ECR I–4047 in which the job of commissioner of insurance companies was not considered to be a post of official authority.

## 10.3 The right of establishment: art 43 EC and direct effect

Article 43 EC provides for the prohibition on restrictions on the freedom of establishment, which entails the right to be treated under the same conditions imposed on nationals. The right is a broad one, allowing the individual to 'participate on a stable and continuous basis in the economic life of a Member State other than [their] own': *Gebhard* (see above). Article 44 EC required the Council to draw up a General Programme (produced in 1961) to ensure the abolition of restrictions to the freedom of establishment. Article 47 EC required the Council to also draw up directives for the mutual recognition of qualifications.

The existence of the need for further legislative measures under arts 44 and 47 originally appeared to have prevented art 43 from acquiring direct effect. In other words, since further legislative action was required the provision on freedom of establishment was dependent and therefore failed the *Van Gend en Loos* test for direct effect (see Chapter 8). In addition, the Council had not successfully completed the necessary legislative action. The process had proved to be a difficult and time-consuming one: see section 10.4. The question of whether art 43 was nonetheless directly effective was answered in the case of *Reyners* (above).

The European Court, in yet another example of its desire to promote the effectiveness of Community law, concluded that since the transitional period had expired, and the obligation was sufficiently precise, art 43 was capable of producing direct effects in relation to the requirement that there be no discrimination. In the case at hand, Reyners had been refused access to the Belgian Bar not because of his qualifications but simply because he did not have Belgian nationality (he was Dutch). Hence, Reyners was able to rely on art 43 to secure his directly effective right not to be discriminated against in relation to establishing himself in another Member State.

The ability to rely on art 43 was therefore established in relation to challenging discriminatory national measures, such as the nationality requirement in *Reyners*, or a residence requirement. Discriminatory measures will breach art 43 if they impede access to the profession or if they impose restrictions on the performance of that activity: see *Steinhauser* v *City of Biarritz* Case 197/84 [1985] ECR 1819.

In *Reyners*, though, the European Court did believe that, in the case of recognising qualifications, the need for the necessary directives was still important. The Court therefore implied that art 43 would not have direct effect if the difference in treatment was based not on discrimination on the basis of nationality but related to the possession of differing qualifications to those held by nationals. This distinction was tested in a series of cases that followed *Reyners*.

In *Thieffry* v *Conseil de l'Ordre des Avocats à la Cour de Paris* Case 71/76 [1977] ECR 765 the Court considered whether art 43 could be relied upon when the difference in treatment was based on whether the non-national possessed adequate qualifications. Thieffry was a Belgian national with a doctorate in law awarded by a Belgian institution. He had also practised in Belgium. His qualifications were considered as acceptable by a French university, which decided to award him with a certificate of aptitude for the French profession of avocat. Whilst he possessed this certificate of equivalence, he was still refused access to the Paris Bar on the basis that he did not have a French law degree.

The European Court concluded that Thieffry was able to rely directly on art 43, regardless of the lack of any directive recognising his particular qualifications. The requirement for the drawing up of such directives, therefore, did not impede the ability of art 43 to possess directly effective rights that individuals could enforce in national courts. The same conclusion was reached in *Patrick* v *Ministre des Affaires Culturelles* Case 11/77 [1977] ECR 1199, where a British qualified architect was entitled to establish himself in France on the basis of art 43. His case had added weight since a French Ministerial Decree in 1964 had recognised the equivalence of his particular qualification.

The case of *UNECTEF* v *Heylens* Case 222/86 [1987] ECR 4097 concerned a Belgian national who possessed a football trainer's diploma. He was employed as a trainer for a French football team in Lille. He subsequently applied to have his Belgian qualification recognised as equivalent to the French, but was denied this by the French Ministry of Sport. Heylens was offered no reasons for the decision and, when he tried to continue coaching, was prosecuted by the French football trainer's union, UNECTEF.

The Court concluded that both Member States and professional bodies, such as UNECTEF, were obligated to ensure that freedom of establishment was not impeded and indeed to take positive steps to ensure that the right was obtained. The Court supported this conclusion by stating that the Treaty created such precise obligations, and that such obligations rested on both the Member State and professional bodies – in other words that art 43 had both vertical and horizontal direct effect. These obligations existed regardless of any need for further legislative measures.

Consequently, in terms of recognising the equivalence of qualifications, the Member State and its professional bodies had to at least consider the qualifications obtained by the non-national to assess whether they were equivalent; they could not merely refuse to recognise them. In doing so, the Court directed Member States and professional bodies to consider the following:

> '... the level of knowledge and qualifications which its holder can be assumed to possess in the light of that diploma, having regard to the nature and duration of the studies and practical training which the diploma certifies ... has been carried out.'

Furthermore, the Court stated that an individual, who required their qualifications to be assessed before being able to exercise their right to establishment, was entitled in Community law to both an appeal against the decision and to be furnished with the reasons for any decision not in their favour.

The European Court reasserted this obligation in *Vlassopoulou* v *Ministerium für Justiz, Bundes-und Europaangelegenheiten Baden-Württemberg* Case C–340/89 [1991] ECR I–2357. It was held that requirements in relation to qualifications for a regulated profession, such as the legal profession, even though applied to both nationals and non-nationals alike, could still prove an obstacle to the freedom of establishment contrary to the Treaty. This would be the case if the national authorities failed to consider the 'knowledge and qualifications already acquired by the person concerned in another Member State' and compare them to those obtained under their national qualifications. Moreover, the Court also referred to 'other evidence of qualifications', which in the case at hand was considerable practical experience by Vlassopoulou, a Greek national lawyer, in the field of German law.

This has since been extended by the European Court to include professions that are unregulated. In *Arantis* v *Land Berlin* Case C–164/94 [1996] ECR I–135 the Court required the relevant professional bodies to consider not only the individual's qualifications, but any work experience they had acquired in their home State.

The obligation on the national authorities is therefore as follows:

1. they are obligated to assess the equivalence of the qualification and must do so by comparing the nature, duration and content of the studies undertaken, along with the skills acquired, with the national qualification;
2. if there is any difference then the national authorities must identify whether any practical training or experience rectifies the discrepancy; and
3. an appeal against the decision must be available and the reasons for the decision must be provided.

## 10.4 The problem of qualifications

The European Court made considerable in-roads into the problem of differing national qualifications by deciding that art 43 did have direct effect. Individuals could, therefore, rely upon art 43 when seeking recognition of the equivalence of their qualification. However, the Council was also attempting to reach a solution to the problem as obligated under the Treaty.

### The original approach – harmonising qualifications

The Council originally took the approach of identifying various sectors/professions and attempted, through negotiation with the Member States, to identify the minimum requirements in terms of qualifications for each of them. Once consensus was reached directives would be issued, which would identify the level of qualifications and training required, and which would also state each of the recognised qualifications throughout the Community. If a Community national's qualifications were cited within the directives, they had an absolute right to have them recognised in any other Member State that they wished to establish themselves in or provide services. The provisions of such a directive cannot be relied on until the date for its implementation has expired: *Ministère Public* v *Auer* Case 136/78 [1979] ECR 437.

Unfortunately, whilst directives were issued in relation to a number of professions (such as nursing, pharmacy, veterinary practices, architecture and general practitioners) and on a range of industries (such as food and beverage, retail, wholesale, hairdressing, coal and small crafts) this approach was extremely slow and time-consuming. Problems were encountered in gaining the consensus of the Member States and, more importantly, the professional bodies regulating those professions within the Member State. This was particularly true of the legal profession. Member States and the relevant professional bodies seemed unwilling to release control on the issue of equivalent qualifications, and have often been accused of being protectionist. In 1974, in response to these problems, the Council decided to change the approach to the problem of recognising qualifications.

## Mutual recognition – Directives 89/48 and 92/51

The new approach to this thorny issue adopted by the Council was to produce only one directive, instead of concentrating on each and every profession and the qualifications that could be obtained in each and every Member State. The new directive, Directive 89/48, adopted a policy of 'mutual trust'. In other words, a Member State would have to trust the qualifications obtained by an individual in another Member State that entitled them to practise in that State as being equivalent to the qualifications they required. If the individual is adequately qualified in one Member State they are therefore presumed to be qualified in all Member States. The Directive relates only to professional activities regulated in at least one Member State.

Directive 89/48 applies only if the individual has been awarded a higher-education diploma on the basis of the completion of at least three years of professional education and training or has undertaken the profession for at least two years in a State that does not regulate that profession: art 3. They need not rely on the Directive if they are already covered by one of the sectoral directives referred to above, since they have an automatic right to have their qualification recognised and should not require recourse to Directive 89/48.

There are three limitations to the effectiveness of this approach (not including the fact that some Member States, such as Belgium, Greece and France, failed to implement the Directive within the prescribed deadline: *Commission* v *Belgium* Case C–216/94 [1995] ECR I–2155; *Commission* v *Greece* Case C–365/93 [1995] ECR I–499; and *Commission* v *France* Case C–285/00 [2001] ECR I–3801):

1. Directive 89/48 provides no automatic right to have the qualifications recognised, unlike the previous 'sectoral' directives. Persons only have the right to have their qualifications assessed for equivalence and cannot be denied the right to establishment merely on the basis that they do not have the national qualification.
2. If the education and training are at least one year less than that required in the State that the person wishes to establish themselves in, then they may require the State to consider their professional experience: art 4(a) – a requirement very similar to the European Court's decision in *Vlassopoulou* (above). No more than four years evidence should be required.

3. If there are 'major differences' in the education, training, or structure of the profession compared to the national requirement, or the activity was not regulated in the applicant's home State, or activities included within that profession are not undertaken by nationals in the applicant's home State, an individual may be required to undergo a 'compensation mechanism'. The mechanisms provided for under the Directive are either an aptitude test or an adaptation period: art 4(b). The adaptation period must not exceed three years. If the authorities require evidence of professional experience and an adaptation period, the total period of time cannot exceed four years. Which applies, aptitude test or adaptation period, will depend on the choice made by the individual, although many realise that aptitude tests may be significantly more difficult to pass successfully. The bodies that decide whether one of the compensation mechanisms are required are usually the professional bodies regulating that particular profession, which are therefore often criticised as inherently biased or protectionist against their profession being infiltrated by 'outsiders'. Consequently, a right to appeal against such a decision is provided under art 8. There is one exception to the right to choose, and that is where the profession requires precise knowledge of the national law. If this is the case then the right to choose falls in the hands of the host State, which will inevitably choose the more difficult aptitude test. Unfortunately, a considerable number of professions have been included within the ambit of this provision. (Directive 98/5 alters the application of this provision. Lawyers who have experience of at least three years within their home State of the law of the State in which they wish to establish themselves, or Community law, are now exempt from the need to complete any compensation mechanism.)

The deadline for the implementation of Directive 89/48 was 4 January 1991. From this date any clear, precise and unconditional provisions within the Directive were directly effective against a 'public body', which includes legally recognised professional bodies.

Directive 92/51 expands this system of recognising qualifications. It applies to both diplomas on completion of a post-secondary course of at least one year's duration, and certificates also of at least one year's duration given for education or training courses, or professional practice period or vocational training, if the diploma or certificate entitles the individual to pursue a regulated profession. A right to appeal is provided under art 12 of the Directive.

One final point to note is that the Treaty provisions and those of the Directives referred to above do not relate to non-Community nationals. In 1989 the Council passed a recommendation that Member States recognise qualifications obtained by Community nationals in non-Community States. However, even if a Community national has obtained a qualification from outside the Community, that is subsequently recognised by one Member State, they are not entitled to automatic recognition in any other Member State: *Tawil-Albertini* v *Ministre des Affairs Sociales*

Case C–154/93 [1994] ECR I–451. Whether their qualification is suitable will be a matter for the discretion of each Member State. If a Member State does decide to consider the equivalence of the non-Community qualification, according to *Haim* v *Kassenzahnärtzliche Vereinigung Nordrhein* Case C–319/92 [1994] ECR I–425, the authorities should also consider the work experience of the applicant.

Interestingly, the Court in *Hocsman* v *Ministre de l'Emploi* Case C–238/98 [2000] ECR I–6623 concluded that art 43 required the State to assess all of the qualifications held by an EC citizen, regardless of their origin, as well as their practical experience.

In 2001 a new, general directive introduced a range of changes to Directives 89/48 and 92/51 and the sectoral directives. Directive 2001/19, also known as the SLIM Directive, codifies some of the principles referred to above, such as, for example, requiring the State to examine the applicant's professional experience as compensating for any gap or lack of education/training and the recognition of a third-country qualification and experience in another Member State. The Directive also provides for rights of appeal and maximum time limits to decide on applications for qualification recognition.

To summarise, in relation to a Community national with Community qualifications seeking to have their qualifications recognised in another Member State in order to avail themselves of the right to establishment, we can state the following:

1.  They should first assess whether there is an individual harmonising directive on their profession which includes reference to their qualification. If this exists, their qualification should be automatically accepted as equivalent by all Member States.
2.  If there is no harmonising measure, and the individual is within a regulated profession, they should seek to rely on Directive 89/48 (as amended by the SLIM directive), as long as they have a minimum three years' higher education and training. If they have a diploma for post-secondary education or certificate of educational training course, professional practice period or vocational training of at least one year's duration, then they may rely on Directive 92/51.
3.  If the person's qualifications do not fall within the Directives they may rely on the direct effect of art 43. According to the case law, they should have their qualifications assessed, along with any experience, and be provided with the reasons for any decision and a right of appeal.

## 10.5 Relying on art 43 EC in an internal context

An initial and literal reading of art 43 reveals that Community nationals can invoke their rights when they wish to establish themselves in the territory of another Member State. Hence, it was thought that a Community national would not be able to rely on art 43 in their own State. The European Court concluded otherwise in the case of *Knoors* v *Secretary of State for Economic Affairs* Case 115/78 [1979] ECR 399. Knoors was a Dutch national who had trained and practised in Belgium. He wished to establish himself as a plumber in his home State, but the Dutch authorities refused to recognise both his training and experience, claiming that art 43 did not provide rights in such internal circumstances. He did, however, have qualifications recognised under Directive 64/427.

The European Court concluded that since Directive 64/427 included his qualification he was entitled, as a beneficiary of that Directive, to have his qualifications recognised, with 'no differentiation of treatment on the basis of ... residence or nationality'. The Court held that art 43 provided rights for those nationals that had lawfully resided in another Member State, and gained qualifications there, which they could exercise on return to their own State.

Reference to some cases appears to indicate that without being covered by some form of legislation in addition to art 43, such as a sectoral directive or the mutual recognition Directives referred to above, the applicant will not be able to rely on art 43 in their own State. The Member State is therefore free to regulate the profession in question as it thinks fit, as long as it does so in a non-discriminatory way: see, for example, *Ministère Public* v *Auer* Case 136/78 [1979] ECR 437 and *Bouchoucha* Case C–61/89 [1990] ECR I–3551. However, in the case of *Kraus* v *Land Baden-Württemberg* Case C–19/92 [1993] ECR I–1663 the European Court did solely rely on art 43 to give the national the right to use their qualification (an LLM degree from the United Kingdom) in their home State of Germany. However, one crucial factor remained – there was still an element of Community movement involved since Kraus had resided in another Member State to gain his qualification before returning to Germany. It remains the case that art 43 cannot be used in a purely internal situation.

## 10.6 Article 43 EC and non-discriminatory rules

A literal reading of art 43 EC would find that those wishing to establish themselves in another Member State may do so, but under the same conditions as applied to nationals. Such 'conditions' would therefore apply in a non-discriminatory manner, and would include, for example, conditions designed to secure and maintain professional standards and ethics. It was originally held by the European Court that such non-discriminatory conditions or measures would fall outside of art 43 EC: *Commission* v *Belgium* Case 221/85 [1987] ECR 719 and *Société Générale Alsacienne de Banque SA* v *Koestler* Case 16/78 [1978] ECR 1971. Direct discrimination, on the other hand, would require justification under the exhaustive grounds offered in art 46 EC of public policy, security and health: *Bond van Adverteerders* v *Netherlands* Case 352/85 [1988] ECR 2085 (see Chapter 11).

The European Court has departed from this literal interpretation of art 43 over a series of cases, beginning with assessing whether the measure was non-discriminatory but in fact prevented secondary establishment contrary to the Treaty. In *Ordre des Avocats* v *Klopp* Case 107/83 [1984] ECR 2971 a German lawyer was refused access to the Paris Bar. The Bar's conditions stipulated that lawyers, regardless of nationality, had to have only one office, within the district of the court served, whereas Klopp maintained another office outside of France.

The European Court concluded that this requirement, whilst not directly discriminatory in application, prevented the very essence of freedom of establishment protected under art 43. The whole intention of the rules was to offer Community nationals the ability to set up a secondary establishment, and the provision applied by the Paris Bar totally precluded this possibility. In turn, whilst the Paris Bar argued that such rules were necessary in order to ensure that there was adequate contact between the lawyer and their clients and with the courts, the European Court believed that the measure they had adopted for such a purpose was not proportionate. The Court suggested that, given communication and transport links, a less restrictive measure should have been adopted.

The European Court went further in the case of *Gullung* v *Conseil de l'Ordre des Avocats* Case 292/86 [1988] ECR 111. In this case the Court declared that a non-discriminatory measure would breach art 43 because it could hinder, or make less attractive, the right to free movement unless it were objectively justified. Furthermore, the Court has provided a test for national courts to apply to assess whether such measures are objectively justifiable. This test originates in the context of establishment from the case of *Gebhard* (above), but a similar approach may be seen throughout Community law in such fields as indirect discrimination in equal pay and the free movement of goods.

In *Gebhard* (above) the European Court provided a four-part test:

1. such measures must be applied in a non-discriminatory manner (any directly discriminatory measure will have to be justified under the Treaty grounds of public policy, security or health in art 46 (see Chapter 11));
2. they must be justified as being in the 'general good';
3. they must be 'suitable' to achieve that purpose; and
4. they must be proportionate, in other words, no more than is necessary.

A similar test may also be witnessed in the field of the freedom of services, and the types of objective reasoning offered by Member States will be discussed under that heading: see section 10.9.

## 10.7 The free movement of services – art 49 and direct effect

The freedom of movement for services entails not the permanent establishment of the individual, but their temporary provision or, as we shall see, receipt of services in another Member State than that in which they are established. Consequently, to partake of the right to free movement envisaged under art 49 EC, the individual must already be established in one of the Member States. If a company wishes to gain rights under art 49 they must be formed under the laws of one of the Member States. They must also have their centre of administration or main establishment within the Community. If all they have is a seat within one of the Member States, they will also have to prove that they have a 'real and continuous' link with the economy of the Community. This prevents companies from outside of the Community enjoying the freedom of movement for services without in some way contributing to the Community economy.

Services are defined in art 50 EC as those that are normally provided for remuneration and, in particular, include activities of an industrial character, of a commercial character and of craftsmen and the professions (although this is a non-exhaustive list). Such services, according to art 50, must be pursued under the same conditions as those imposed by a Member State on its own nationals. Economic activities considered as services within art 50 include professional football, professional pace-setting, cycling and abortion: see, respectively, *Donà* v *Mantero* Case 13/76 [1976] ECR 1333, *Walrave and Koch* v *Association Union Cycliste Internationale* Case 36/74 [1974] ECR 1405 and *Society for the Protection of Unborn Children (Ireland)* v *Grogan* Case C–159/90 [1991] ECR I–4685. The essence of an economic activity is that the services performed will be genuine and effective, not marginal or ancillary: *Deliège* v *Ligue Francophone de Judo et Disciplines ASBL* Cases C–51/96 and 191/97 [2000] ECR I–2549.

In a similar way to freedom of establishment, the provisions on services required the adoption of directives under art 52 EC. The Member States argued that art 49 was not capable of having direct effect. Furthermore, they believed that the very essence of the temporary nature of providing such services would imply that the State would need to offer tighter controls to ensure the protection of their nationals. However, in a similar judgment to that of *Reyners* (see above), the European Court decided that art 49 was capable of creating directly effective rights: *Van Binsbergen* v *Bestuur van de Bedrijfsvereniging voor de Metaalnijverheid* Case 33/74 [1974] ECR 1299. In this case a residence requirement before being able to provide services was considered a direct obstacle to the freedom envisaged under art 49.

As with establishment, the Treaty does not offer protection in purely internal situations: *Société Générale Alsacienne de Banque SA* v *Koestler* Case 16/78 [1978] ECR 1971. There must be some inter-State element in existence. This will occur when the provider is established in one Member State and the recipient is in another, although it should be noted that in this scenario the provider may rely on art 49 in their own State because the service they offer has the necessary inter-State element.

There must also be some element of remuneration. According to the European Court,

'... [t]he essential characteristic of remuneration ... lies in the fact that it constitutes consideration for the service in question, and is normally agreed upon between the provider and the recepient of the service': *Belgium* v *Humbel* Case 263/86 [1988] ECR 5365.

Therefore, if the State provides the remuneration for the service such as, for example, a vocational course within a publicly funded institution, then art 49 will not apply. Conversely, if the institution operates to make a profit, and receives some element of private funding, art 49 will apply: *Wirth* v *Landeshauptstadt Hannover* Case C–109/92 [1993] ECR I–6447.

A literal reading of both arts 49 and 50 EC reveal that they talk only of the provision of services. Whilst some of the secondary legislation in this field talks of the receipt of services, it is the European Court, via teleological interpretation, that has extended the Treaty provisions to include freedom to receive as well as provide services.

In *Luisi and Carbone* v *Ministero del Tesoro* Cases 286/82 and 26/83 [1984] ECR 377 the European Court held:

'It follows that the freedom to provide services includes the freedom, for the recipients of services, to go to another Member State in order to receive a service there, without being obstructed by restrictions.'

The Court concluded that this right to move to receive services would extend to education, training, vocational programmes, business services, medical services and even the general services afforded to tourists. Once an individual has exercised their right to free movement, they are also entitled to treatment free from discrimination on the grounds of nationality: art 12 EC. In *Cowan* v *Trésor Public* Case 186/87 [1989] ECR 195 a British citizen who was assaulted outside a Paris metro station was entitled to compensation from the French equivalent of the Criminal Injuries Compensation Board. This was because any laws or regulations that prevented him from receiving that service because of his nationality were discriminatory and prohibited under the Treaty:

'When Community law guarantees a natural person the freedom to go to another Member State the protection of that person from harm in the Member State in question, on the same basis as that of nationals and persons residing there, is a corollary of that freedom of movement. It follows that the prohibition of discrimination is applicable to recipients of services ...'

## 10.8 The freedom to provide or receive illegal or immoral services

Certain Member States consider some essentially economic activities to be illegal and/or immoral, and have argued that such activities should be outside of the scope of art 49 EC. The European Court has not adopted such a restrictive approach. In *Society for the Protection of Unborn Children (Ireland)* v *Grogan* (above) the European Court was asked to assess whether abortion was a service within art 49, even though it was considered illegal under Irish constitutional law.

The Court declared that it would not impose its judgement on the Member States where such activities were legal and hence abortion was a service. However, the Court also stated that since it could not impose its judgment, each State was free to regulate those activities considered as illegal or immoral, and could prevent the provision of those services within its territory. The Court refused to answer the question of whether the State could prevent its nationals from moving to receive the service of abortion in a State where is was legal. (This difficult and controversial issue in Ireland was the subject of a protocol under the TEU, which protects the relevant provision in the Irish Constitution.)

The Court clarified its approach to such types of services in the case of *Customs and Excise* v *Schindler* Case C–275/92 [1994] ECR I–1039. The case concerned two defendants, based in the United Kingdom, who worked for a German public body that organised lotteries. Lotteries were heavily regulated in the UK and the Schindlers were charged after their post was intercepted. As part of the written proceedings in an art 234 EC preliminary reference, five Member States expressed their belief that lotteries were not services within the Treaty because they were either illegal or regulated public bodies.

The European Court concluded that whilst lotteries were strictly regulated they were not prohibited and were indeed 'commonplace'. The Court was not therefore prepared to accept that lotteries were of a harmful nature, nor would it substitute its own assessment of them as being illegal activities in those Member States where they were legal. As a result, the provision of lotteries was concluded to be a service within art 49, since they were legal in at least one Member State. However, a State retains the ability to regulate the provision of receipt of that service, but only in so far as that regulation is proportionate and non–discriminatory.

## 10.9 Article 49 EC and non-discriminatory rules

As with establishment, discriminatory provisions in relation to the provision or receipt of services may only be justified under the grounds specified in the Treaty: art 55 EC on the grounds of public security, policy or health: discussed in detail in Chapter 11. Non-discriminatory measures may also be applied, and indeed have been advocated by the Member States as especially necessary given the temporary nature of providing a service. In other words, with the provider not resident in the State they would have the opportunity of causing considerable damage to the nationals of that State unless measures were imposed on them to ensure their professional standards.

The European Court has examined such non-discriminatory measures and has adopted the same approach as that indicated above in relation to establishment – they will breach the Treaty unless objectively justified. In the case of *Van Binsbergen* (above) the Court held:

'... taking into account the particular nature of the services to be provided, specific requirements imposed on the person providing the service cannot be considered incompatible with the Treaty where they have as their purpose the application of professional rules justified for the general good – in particular rules relating to the organisation, qualifications, professional ethics, supervision and liability – which are binding upon any person established in the State in which the service is provided ...'

Therefore, the following test to assess whether such measures are justifiable must be applied by national courts:

1. The measure must be designed to achieve a factor of legitimate public interest. The Court provides examples of such factors (see above quote) but the 'sound administration of justice' has also been accepted: *Reisebüro Broede* v *Sandker* Case C–3/95 [1996] ECR I–6511.
2. The measure must be applied equally to those persons established within that Member State.
3. The measure must be objectively justified. This entails the need for the measure to be proportionate and necessary. This may be assessed by considering whether the measure is also imposed by the Member State in which the provider is established. If this is the case then there is no genuine need for the measure since it merely duplicates protective measures that the individual has already been subjected to, and indeed places a double burden on them: see *Criminal Proceedings against Webb* Case 279/80 [1981] ECR 3305.

According to Advocate-General Slynn in *Webb*, whether the objective justification test has been met will be decided by the national courts. The European Court has used the test in enforcement proceedings: art 226 EC (see, generally, Chapter 4).

In *Commission* v *Germany (Re Insurance Services)* Case 205/84 [1986] ECR 3755 the Court examined rules imposed by the German authorities on the provision of insurance services. The Court reiterated the test in *Van Binsbergen* (above) in the following way:

'... requirements may be considered compatible with ... the [EC] Treaty only if it is established that in the field of activity concerned there are imperative reasons relating to the public interest which justify restrictions on the freedom to provide services, that the public interest is not already protected by the rules of the State of establishment and that the same result cannot be obtained by less restrictive rules.'

In the case itself, the Court agreed that the provision of insurance services required protection for the parties involved, and that there was therefore a public interest factor. The rules imposed by Germany constituted residence requirements, in that the provider of some insurance services had to be undertakings established in Germany, but they were applied in a non-discriminatory manner. The Court, however, applied the proportionality test and concluded that the residence requirement was, as in *Van Binsbergen*, able to deprive art 49 of its full effect. The

Court emphasised that the only circumstance in which such a residence requirement would be permitted was one in which it was 'indispensable' in terms of achieving the public interest objective. The Court held that in this case Germany had not proved the residence requirement to be indispensable.

These cases concern what appear to be non-discriminatory measures, but which in fact actually create indirect discrimination, in that they have the effect of making the provision of services by a non-national more difficult. If we take the above case as an example, whilst Germany may have argued that the residence requirement was applied equally, in fact the undertakings more likely to have established themselves in Germany, and therefore be able to provide temporary insurance services under German law, were German undertakings. The Court will therefore examine the actual effect of such measures and will require their objective justification.

The European Court's reaction to truly non-discriminatory measures has been similar. In *Säger* v *Dennemeyer* Case C–76/90 [1991] ECR I–4221 the Court was asked to examine a measure that was truly non-discriminatory – the reservation of certain activities to specified agents. Advocate-General Jacobs suggested that a non-discriminatory measure would not be precluded from possibly contravening art 49. He concluded that regard should be had to whether the undertaking wishing to provide the service had already complied with legislative requirements in the State in which it was established. If it had then it should be permitted to provide services throughout the remaining Community States. If a State wished to impose further regulation on that undertaking they would have to show that it was 'justified by some requirement that is compatible with the aims of the Community'. The Court held:

> 'The freedom to provide services may be limited only by rules which are justified by imperative reasons relating to the public interest and which apply to all persons and undertakings pursuing an activity in the State of destination insofar as that interest is not protected by rules to which the person providing the service is subject in the State in which he is established. In particular, these requirements must be objectively necessary in order to ensure compliance with professional rules and must not exceed what is necessary to attain those objectives.'

The Court has accepted some measures as being in the public interest and proportionate: see, for example, *Ramrath* v *Ministre de la Justice* Case C–106/91 [1992] ECR I–3351 and *Alpine Investments BV* v *Minister van Financiën* Case C–384/93 [1995] ECR I–1141. In the latter case, restrictions on telephone 'cold-calling' in relation to financial services were concluded to be justified in the public interest – protecting consumers and the reputation of the Dutch financial services market – and proportionate. Other measures have not been successful because they were disproportionate: see, for example, *Commission* v *France (Re Tourist Guide)* Case C–154/89 [1991] ECR I–659, where a licence requirement was required for tourist guides in France. This was granted on successful passing of an examination. Whilst the Court accepted the public interest factor, they believed that the measure itself was disproportionate. Alternatively, the Court may conclude that there is no 'overriding reasons in the public interest'. For example, in *Van der Elst* v *Office des Migrations Internationales* Case C–43/93 [1994] ECR I–3308 it was found that since third-country nationals seeking work in France already had permits from Belgium, there was no need to require them to also have French work permits.

It appears that the measure must also not restrict access to the providing or receiving of services. *Alpine Investments* (above) concluded:

> 'Although a prohibition such as the one at issue ... is general and non-discriminatory and neither its object not its effect is to put the national market at an advantage over providers of services from other Member States, it can ... constitute a restriction on the freedom to provide services ...
>
> It ... directly affects access to the market in services in the other Member States and is thus capable of hindering intra-Community trade in services.'

A similar approach may be witnessed in *Kohll* v *Union des Caisses de Matadie* Case C–158/96 [1998] ECR I–1931 where the Court concluded that art 49 prohibits measures which 'have the effect of making the provision of services between Member States more difficult'.

We may conclude that, whilst Community law in this field may originally have been applied as a means of preventing discrimination, and ultimately protectionism, it has now been extended beyond being solely concerned with discrimination on the basis of nationality. Instead, the measures providing for both services and establishment have been read in the light of the wider aim of securing the internal single market. Thus, even a measure that is non-discriminatory, but which hinders free movement and access for establishment and services, will be a measure that requires strong objective justification. (This approach is one reflective of principles developed in the free movement of workers and goods also.)

Finally, in relation to some professions, directives have been passed that harmonise and recognise professional rules in relation to that particular profession, and thus only those rules may be permitted. Each national measure is examined to ascertain whether it comes within the directive. If it does then it will have to comply with the provision of the directive. If it does not, it will have to meet the objective justification test above if applied in a non-discriminatory manner (see *Commission* v *Germany (Re Insurance Services)* Case 205/84 [1986] ECR 3755) or, if applied in a discriminatory way, will have to be justified under public policy, security or health: see Chapter 11. In the case of the legal profession, Directive 77/249 gives limited rights to provide legal services, whereas the relatively new Directive 98/5 (implementation deadline 14 March 2000) provides for establishment. Under this Directive, lawyers are able to establish themselves in another Member State using their home, professional title and are entitled to undertake certain activities. Furthermore, individuals who have in their home State undertaken 'effectively and regularly', for at least three years, activities in the law of the State in which they wish to establish themselves, or in Community law, may be able to claim exemption from art 4 of Directive 89/48 (see above).

## 10.10 Social benefits and arts 43 and 49 EC

The first thing to note is that those wishing to freely move to establish themselves or provide or receive services are not able to avail themselves of secondary legislation equivalent to Regulation 1612/68 for workers: see Chapter 9. However, the European Court has concluded that access to such rights may stem directly from the Treaty articles, but the rights must be connected to facilitating the pursuit of the activities in question, namely establishment or services.

In the context of establishment, in *Commission* v *Italy (Re Housing Aid)* Case 63/86 [1988] ECR 29 the Court stated that any restriction on various facilities that were granted to nationals to alleviate financial burdens (in this case housing) should also be available to non-nationals. To do otherwise would be to introduce an 'obstacle to the pursuit of the occupation itself'. Similarly, in *Commission* v *France* Case C–334/94 [1996] ECR I–1307 the Court held access to leisure facilities as a necessary corollary to the freedom of movement.

In the case of services, the Court has adopted a similar policy of identifying whether the social right claimed is linked to the ability to exercise and provide that self-employed service: *Commission* v *Italy* Case 63/86 [1988] ECR 29.

Alternatively, the Court has applied art 12 EC to such circumstances where self-employed persons have been denied access to social rights, concluding that they have been discriminated against on the basis of their nationality: see *Cowan* (above) and *Commission* v *Spain* Case C–45/93 [1994] ECR I–911. In *Hayes* v *Kronenberger GmbH* Case C–323/95 [1997] ECR I–1711 the Court concluded that a requirement that non-nationals pay a court security deposit was a breach of art 12 EC, since nationals were not required to make such a payment.

## 10.11 Rights of entry, residence and to stay

Similar to the free movement of workers, the Treaty provisions on establishment and services have been supplemented with secondary legislation in relation to the rights to enter, reside and stay.

Directive 73/148 provides the conditions of entry and residence. Its provisions apply to both those wishing to establish themselves or provide/receive services, and to their families. The latter is given the same definition as under Regulation 1612/68 (see Chapter 9). Directive 73/148 provides the following rights:

Articles 2–3     that rights of entry are guaranteed without the need for a visa, unless the individual is a non-Community national.

Article 4       that those establishing themselves are entitled to a permanent right of residence, with a residence permit, whilst those offering or receiving services are entitled to a temporary right of residence for the duration of their stay. This is known as a right to abode if the stay is to exceed three months.

Article 6          to apply for a residence permit or right to abode one must provide an identity card or passport and proof of being one of the persons covered under the terms of the Directive.

Directive 75/34 provides that persons who have exercised their right to work as a self-employed person in another Member State have the right to stay there, as do their family.

Finally, the right of establishment and the freedom to provide and receive services are subject to derogation on the grounds of public policy, security and health: arts 46 and 55 EC. The conditions on which such action may be taken, and analysis of the extent of the grounds themselves, will be discussed in the following chapter.

# 11

# Derogating from Free Movement for Workers, Establishment and Services

11.1 Introduction

11.2 Directive 64/221

11.3 The personal conduct of the individual

11.4 Criminal convictions

11.5 Justifying use of public policy or security

11.6 The procedural safeguards

## 11.1 Introduction

Article 39(3) EC provides that a Member State may derogate from the free movement for workers on the exhaustive grounds of public policy, security or health. Article 46 EC in relation to establishment provides that non-nationals may receive 'special treatment' on the same grounds, and this is also applied to services under art 55 EC. The burden of proof is on the Member State to justify the denial of rights by providing sufficient evidence.

These grounds have been narrowly construed by the European Court. Public health has created little litigation, as appears to be the case with public security. It is public policy that has proved to be difficult to define, and which forms the basis of many of the cases that will be discussed in this chapter.

Directive 64/221, which has direct effect, prescribes the conditions under which the grounds may be used and provides minimum levels of protection for those individuals affected by such action. The Directive applies to workers, those wishing to establish themselves as self-employed persons and those wishing to both provide and receive services, as well as their families. The Directive also applies to persons of independent means who exercise their right to free movement under Directive 90/364; students under Directive 90/366; and retired persons under Directive 90/365. The Directive also covers those nationals from EEA countries.

The Directive does not apply to companies, hence any 'special treatment' applied to them under art 46 need only comply with general principles of Community law.

It also does not apply to non-Community nationals, unless they are members of the worker's family. However, the introduction towards provisions providing for common immigration and asylum conditions (see Chapters 1 and 9) may provide third State nationals with some element of free movement.

In addition to Directive 64/221, Member States must ensure that the fundamental human rights of the person are not violated: *Elliniki Radiophonia Tileorassi* v *Dimotiki Etaria Pliroforissis* Case C–260/89 [1991] ECR I–2925 (for discussion of these principles see Chapter 3). This includes reference to the European Convention on Human Rights. In *Rutili* v *Minister for the Interior* Case 36/75 [1975] ECR 1219 the Court stated that the controls on Member States exercising these limitations were:

> '... a specific manifestation of the more general principle ... of the Convention for the Protection of Human Rights ... which provide in identical terms, that no restrictions in the interests of national security or public safety shall be placed ... other than such as are necessary for the protection of those interests 'in a democratic society.'

If one of the grounds are to be invoked they cannot be used in a way that provides for a partial prohibition on residence; invoking the grounds therefore applies to the entire territory of the Member State and must not be applied with reference to any 'internal subdivisions': *Rutili* (above). The only exception to this would be if nationals were subject to some limitation in terms of residence for the same reasons.

## 11.2 Directive 64/221

Directive 64/221 provides for harmonised conditions in relation to the use of 'measures' invoking one of derogations by the Member States. Such derogations will be invoked in a number of situations: refusing entry into the State; deporting a Community national from the State; or refusing to grant or renew a residence permit. A 'measure' has been defined as any action affecting the right of a person coming within the application of Community law in terms of free movement: *R* v *Bouchereau* Case 30/77 [1977] ECR 1999.

In brief, the Directive provides for the following:

| | |
|---|---|
| Article 2 | provides that none of the grounds may be used for economic purposes, such as refusal of entry to protect against the unemployment of nationals. The same will be the case if an individual has received welfare benefits, perhaps because they were involuntarily unemployed or unable to work through incapacity. To deport or expel for such a reason would be to 'service economic ends' contrary to the Directive. |
| Article 3 | provides that when using the grounds of public policy or security, the Member State must base its decision exclusively on the |

personal conduct of the individual. Criminal convictions are not sufficient grounds, nor is expiry of a passport or failure to apply for a residence permit (art 3(3)), although failure to provide one of these on entry may result in the application of a penalty, which will have to be proportionate: see Chapter 9.

Article 4    provides detail on the use of the public health grounds. If this ground is to be used it must be invoked on entry or before the issue of the first residence permit. The article refers to Annexes A and B of the Directive for those illnesses and disabilities that may justify use of this ground. There are two main categories of diseases and disabilities referred to. The first are those diseases that are a threat to public health (because of their contagious or infectious nature), which includes those identified by the World Health Organisation as being subject to quarantine, such as tuberculosis and syphilis. The Community has stated that Member States are not permitted to exercise this grounds on the basis of an individual having HIV or AIDS: Commission Communication 1999. However, if an individual with HIV/AIDS falls into one of the listed categories, they may be excluded on that basis. The second category are those diseases and disabilities that threaten public policy or security, such as drug addiction, profound mental illness, and manifest conditions of psychotic disturbance with agitation, delirium, hallucinations or confusion.

A Member State may not require that a routine medical examination be carried out to identify whether any of these conditions exist, since this would constitute an additional requirement on entry as prohibited under art 3(1) of Directive 68/360: *Commission* v *The Netherlands* Case C–68/89 [1991] ECR I–2637. The authorities are also not permitted to request medical certificates before entry is permitted since Directive 68/360 requires only the production of a valid ID card or passport: see Chapter 9. The only exception to this appears to be where the person is showing clear symptoms of one of the diseases or disabilities referred to in Directive 64/221: *Commission* v *Belgium* Case 321/87 [1989] ECR 997.

Articles 5–9    provide a range of procedural safeguards for the individual, which will be discussed in further detail at section 11.6.

## 11.3 The personal conduct of the individual

As stated above, a decision of the Member State to exercise derogation on the grounds of public policy or security must be based exclusively on the personal conduct of the individual: art 3 Directive 64/221. This was examined by the European Court in *Van Duyn* v *Home Office* Case 41/74 [1974] ECR 1337. In this case Van Duyn, a Dutch national, was offered a post working as a secretary for the Church of Scientology in the United Kingdom. She entered the UK on the 9 May 1973, but was refused entry by immigration officials on the grounds of public policy. The British government argued that the Church was anti-social and therefore harmful to the mental health of those involved. The organisation, however, had not been declared illegal. Van Duyn argued that her refusal of entry was based on the assessment of the Church, and not her personal conduct as required under the Directive. The European Court, under the preliminary reference procedure, considered, inter alia, whether association with an organisation was evidence of personal conduct and whether, to be contrary to public policy, that organisation had to be illegal.

In relation to whether membership of, or association with, an organisation was evidence of personal conduct the Court held:

> 'Although a person's past association cannot, in general, justify a decision refusing him the right to move freely within the Community, it is nevertheless the case that present association, which reflects participation in the activities of the body or of the organisation as well as identification with its aims or designs, may be considered a voluntary act of the person concerned and, consequently, as part of his personal conduct within the meaning of the provision.'

Thus, the Court clearly stated that past association was irrelevant, and that present membership had to be supplemented with active participation in, or support of, the aims of the organisation.

The Court then examined the scope of the public policy ground for derogation, and concluded that it had to 'interpreted strictly' in order to avoid its scope being 'determined unilaterally by each Member State'. Hence, the ground was 'subject to control by the institutions of the Community'. Nevertheless, the Court also held that:

> '... the particular circumstances justifying recourse to the concept of public policy may vary from one country to another and from one period to another, and it is therefore necessary in this matter to allow the competent national authorities an area of discretion within the limits imposed by the Treaty.'

With reference to whether the organisation had to be declared illegal before the grounds could be invoked, the Court declared that this was not necessary. What was required was for the competent national authorities of the Member State to have 'clearly defined their standpoint as regards the activities of a particular organisation'. If they considered the organisation to be socially harmful it could be regulated by 'administrative measures'. It was not necessary 'to make such activities unlawful if recourse to such a measure is not thought appropriate in the circumstances'.

The UK government had in fact expressed its disapproval of the Church in a ministerial statement in Parliament in 1968.

Thus, present membership of any organisation that is committed to activities that breach criminal law will fall within the concept of personal conduct, such as a terrorist organisation or certain animal rights groups. This will not be the case if the membership or participation was past, such as in *Proll* (cited and discussed below in section 11.4) and the individual no longer has an active role in the organisation or, as in the case of *Proll*, has proved that their political beliefs have changed.

If the organisation receives the full protection of the law, unlike the Church of Scientology in *Van Duyn*, then membership or participation in it will not constitute personal conduct for the purposes of Directive 64/221. To decide otherwise would most certainly breach the ECHR provisions on freedom of thought, religion and expression, to which any national court should make reference, as directed by the European Court in *Rutili* (above).

The fact that the person may have become involuntarily unemployed or is unable to work due to incapacity will not constitute evidence of personal conduct, whether they are the main beneficiary or a family member: *Lubbersen v Secretary of State for the Home Department* [1984] 3 CMLR 77.

## 11.4 Criminal convictions

Article 3 of Directive 64/221 stipulates that criminal convictions per se are insufficient to justify exercising either the public policy or security grounds. In *Bonsignore v Oberstadtdirektor of the City of Cologne* Case 67/74 [1975] ECR 297 the Court was requested, under a preliminary reference, to consider whether an individual could be deported as a general preventative measure. An Italian national worker, illegally in possession of a firearm in Germany, had accidentally shot and killed his brother. In other words, the Court was asked whether criminal convictions would justify exercising the derogations, on the basis of providing a deterrent to others.

The Court held that since the grounds were 'departures from the rules' on free movement, they could only be 'strictly construed'. Thus, the grounds could only be exercised on the personal conduct of the individual. Criminal convictions did not justify deportation as a general preventative measure; the Advocate-General doubted that any deterrent effect would result from deporting someone as 'an example' to others.

Past convictions were considered in the case of *R v Bouchereau* Case 30/77 [1977] ECR 1999. This case involved a French national working in the United Kingdom. He had been convicted twice of unlawful possession of drugs, the second offence occurring whilst he was still on a conditional discharge for the first. The national court had recommended to the Home Secretary that he be deported – a recommendation that was considered to be a measure and therefore within the ambit of Directive 64/221. The Court was requested to consider whether past criminal convictions could be considered in a decision to exercise derogation.

The Court stated that past criminal convictions could be used as evidence of personal conduct that was a present threat. In particular, the past criminal convictions would have to prove that the individual was a 'present threat to the requirements of public policy' in that there was a propensity to act in the same way in the future. Furthermore, the threat to public policy would have to be 'genuine and sufficiently serious' and affect 'one of the fundamental interests of society': see also *Rutili* v *Minister for the Interior* Case 36/75 [1975] ECR 1219.

In *Criminal Proceedings against Calfa* Case C–348/96 [1999] ECR I–11 the applicant appealed against a Greek law that required automatic deportation of those committed of, inter alia, possession of drugs. The European Court required the national authorities to look not only at the commission of any offence, but at the personal conduct of the individual too. Thus, it appears that each case will require an examination of the gravity of the offence or conduct of the person, in relation to both the past and the future propensity to act in the same manner. This should be done at the time the deportation is ordered, since there may have been some change in the time between the offending activity and the issuing of the order: see *R* v *Secretary of State for the Home Department, ex parte Santillo* Case 131/79 [1980] ECR 1585.

The fact that a person may no longer pose a present threat to public policy or security, since they have no propensity to act again, can be seen in *Proll* v *Entry Clearance Officer, Düsseldorf (No 2)* [1988] 2 CMLR 387. In this case a German citizen had been convicted in 1979 of offences resulting from her membership of a terrorist organisation. She had received a 12-month sentence since she had shown remorse at her hearing and had indicated that her political beliefs had changed. She applied for entry into the United Kingdom on three separate occasions, the last in 1985, but had been rejected. On appeal against the decision, the Immigration Appeal Tribunal found that she had remained changed in her political beliefs and that therefore her past conduct and conviction indicated no present threat to either public policy or security.

Finally, reference should perhaps be made to the comments of Advocate-General Warner in *R* v *Bouchereau* (above). In his Opinion the Advocate-General made the following comment:

> '... circumstances ... do arise, exceptionally, where the personal conduct ... has been such that, whilst not necessarily evincing any clear propensity on his part, has caused such deep revulsion that public policy requires his departure.'

However, the Advocate-General offered no examples of the type of offences or activity that may cause such 'deep revulsion' and the European Court failed to make any reference to such situations. No other cases have referred to such a concept and, indeed, the following words of warning offered by Advocate-General Mayras in *Bonsignore*, commenting on public reaction to offences committed by non-nationals, should prevent such a development in the law:

'... one cannot avoid the impression that the deportation of a foreign worker, even a national of the Common Market, satisfies the feeling of hostility, sometimes verging on xenophobia, which the commission of an offence by an alien generally causes or revives in the indigenous population.'

## 11.5 Justifying use of public policy or security

As stated above, the case of *Rutili* emphasised that there must be a genuine and sufficiently serious threat before use of public policy or security as grounds for derogation may be justified. Obviously, to deport a non-national for an offence considered 'minor' if committed by a national would in effect be tantamount to discrimination on the basis of nationality, prohibited under art 12 EC, and would undermine the argument that there was indeed any 'genuine' threat. In other words, if a person's conduct is such a threat to public policy or security, should their nationality be relevant? On the other hand, it is contrary to public international law for a State to deport its own nationals, so there cannot be identical treatment of nationals and non-nationals in such circumstances.

In *Adoui and Cornvaille* v *Belgian State* Cases 115 and 116/81 [1982] ECR 1665 the European Court provided a means by which the genuineness of the measure may be examined, and which also provides for as little discrimination on the basis of nationality as possible when exercising the grounds for derogation. Adoui, a French national, working in Belgium, applied for a residence permit but was rejected on the basis that she worked in a bar considered by the Belgian authorities as 'suspect from the point of view of morals', in other words, she was a prostitute. She was then served with a deportation order. The Belgian court requested a preliminary reference on the question of whether a non-national could be deported as a threat to public policy, whilst no repressive measures as such were taken against nationals who participated in the same activity.

The Court recognised that the principles of public international law made it impossible for States to deport their own nationals, and that there was therefore to be a difference of treatment between nationals and non-nationals. They also recognised that Community law did not impose on any Member State a 'scale of values' that could be used to assess whether the conduct of an individual was contrary to public policy – this was within the discretion of the State.

At the same time, the Court stressed the need for there to be no 'arbitrary distinction' to the detriment of non-nationals. The Court emphasised the following important point:

'... conduct may not be considered as being of a sufficiently serious nature to justify restrictions on the admission to or residence within the territory of a Member State of a national of another Member State in a case where the former Member State does not adopt, with respect to the same conduct on the part of its own nationals, repressive measures or other genuine and effective measures intended to combat such conduct.'

The Court, therefore, expressed the need for the Member State wishing to invoke the grounds of public policy, and presumably public security, to identify that there was some equivalence of treatment between non-nationals (who will be either refused entry, deported or refused a residence permit) and the treatment of nationals. Unfortunately, the Court did not offer any examples of equivalent repressive measures that could be imposed on nationals. Whether there is indeed equivalence of treatment, and therefore no discrimination, will have to be assessed on the facts of the particular case by the national court: see also the case joined with *Adoui, Cornvaille* v *Belgian State* Case 116/81 [1982] ECR 1665.

## 11.6 The procedural safeguards

Directive 64/221 provides an individual with a number of procedural safeguards that they may rely on should one of the grounds for derogation be exercised against them. These rules are somewhat comparable to the rules of natural justice in English administrative law. The following provisions of the Directive are relevant:

| | |
|---|---|
| Article 5 | provides for a six-month maximum time period when considering whether or not to grant the first residence permit. In the interim period a right of temporary residence should exist. This is backed up, in the context of Community nationals, by their status as European Union citizens, since they have rights of entry and residence under art 18 EC (see Introduction to Part B). |
| Article 6 | provides that the individual should receive notification of which of the three grounds have been applied. The reasons provided must be sufficiently clear, precise and comprehensive so that they may take effective steps to prepare their defence: *Rutili* (see above). Family members that are non-Community nationals should also be furnished with the reasons for any decision to refuse them a visa: Commission Communication 1999. If the communication to the individual does not provide sufficient grounds, in the eyes of the national court, then the decision will be invalidated: *R* v *Secretary of State for the Home Department, ex parte Dannenberg* [1984] 2 CMLR 456. |

The only exception to this requirement is if providing the reasons would prejudice national security. The Member State wishing to rely on this will probably have to provide some justification of why this was the case: see, for example, *Johnston* v *Chief Constable of the Royal Ulster Constabulary* Case 222/84 [1986] ECR 1651. Whilst this case dealt with this in the different context of sex discrimination, it provided that some indication of why disclosure was contrary to the interest of national security should be provided as part of the principle of effective judicial control. This need would also comply with art 6 of the ECHR.

Article 7     stipulates that the person must be officially notified if the decision is
              not in their favour. Unless the matter is urgent, the person must be
              given a minimum of 15 days leave should they not have a residence
              permit or a minimum of one month if they do possess one.

Article 8     provides that non-nationals being expelled are entitled to all legal
              remedies available to nationals. In English law, this will be satisfied
              by the availability of judicial review, even though a national whose
              immigration status was in doubt would be entitled to an appeal: *R* v
              *Secretary of State for the Home Department, ex parte Shingara and
              Radiom* Cases C–65 and 111/95 [1997] ECR I–3341.

Article 9     requires that if there is no possibility of appealing to court of law
              against an administrative decision, an appeal to a 'competent
              authority' should be provided. This body must not be the same
              body that made the original decision and should provide an effective
              remedy. As stated above, in English law this may be achieved
              through the process of judicial review.

According to the case of *Royer* Case 48/75 [1976] ECR 497, if a legal remedy is
available under art 8 of the Directive then any expulsion order cannot take effect
before the party has availed themselves of that remedy. If no such remedy is
available, or if it is one that has no suspensory effect, then the individual must be
given the opportunity to appeal to a competent authority under art 9. Again, they
cannot be expelled (except in cases of urgency which are decided by the
administrative authorities) until that body has reached a decision. If the individual,
though, does not have a residence permit they may be deported, but only if they
give their permission: *R* v *Secretary of State for the Home Department, ex parte
Gallagher* Case C–175/94 [1995] ECR I–4253.

In the above case it was also concluded that the individual had no right to know
the members that constituted the competent authority, and that those persons could
be appointed by the body making the original decision to expel. However, the
competent authority did have to be absolutely independent, and not subject to the
control, directly or indirectly, of the body able to make the order under the
Directive. The national court should determine whether this is the case.

In *R* v *Secretary of State for the Home Department, ex parte Santillo* Case 131/79
[1980] ECR 1585 an Italian national was convicted and sentenced for eight years for
a number of serious crimes, including rape. The court also recommended that at the
end of his sentence he be deported from the United Kingdom. The Home Secretary
acted on this recommendation five years later. Santillo applied for judicial review
and two questions were asked of the European Court under a preliminary reference
request.

The first question concerned whether the trial judge's recommendation that he
be deported was the opinion of a 'competent authority'. The European Court
concluded that it was. Second, the European Court was asked whether the five-year

period between the trial judge's recommendation and the Home Secretary's deportation order affected the validity of the opinion. The Court concluded that there needed to be sufficient proximity between the original recommendation and the decision to deport, or the safeguard provided under art 9 would be deprived of any real value. This would obviously also ensure that the original factors behind the recommendation still existed at the time of the order. In the case at hand the court concluded that there had been no change in the circumstances and therefore the original opinion was still valid.

There are examples of where the original circumstances have changed. In the case of *Monteil v Secretary of State for the Home Department* [1984] 1 CMLR 264 a Frenchman, convicted in the United Kingdom, served a 12-month prison sentence before being issued with a deportation order. He claimed that the reason for his crimes had been alcoholism, of which he was now cured, and appealed against the decision. The Immigration Appeal Tribunal accepted that he was no longer a present threat to public policy or security. As discussed above, criminal convictions may only be considered as evidence of personal conduct if they reveal a propensity to act in a manner contrary to public policy in the future – no such propensity was identified in this case.

Article 9 of Directive 64/221 does not state that the decision of the competent authority has to be binding. The European Court supported this in *Gallagher*. However, this should be contrasted with the decision in *UNCETEF* v *Heylens* Case 222/86 [1987] ECR 4097 (for the facts see Chapter 10), where the European Court examined the ability of the individual to have a remedy in relation to the recognition of their qualifications. The Court stated:

> '... the existence of a remedy of a judicial nature against any decision of a national authority refusing the benefit of that right is essential in order to secure for the individual effective protection for his right.'

If this is placed within the context of the ECHR provisions, art 13 ECHR provides that if a persons rights or freedoms have been violated they should be entitled to an 'effective remedy' even if the body violating those principles is 'acting in an official capacity'. In Community law an effective judicial remedy has been defined as a national court having the power 'to set aside national legislative provisions which might prevent ... Community rules from having full force and effect': *R v Secretary of State for Transport, ex parte Factortame Ltd and Others* Case 213/89 [1990] ECR I–2433. Consequently, the academic, Vincenzi, has suggested that it may be presumed that the decision of the competent authority will need to be binding on the administrative body to comply with both the ECHR and general principles of Community law. This, however, has still to be specifically decided in the context of art 9 of Directive 64/221.

As introduced in the earlier chapter on the free movement of workers, the law in this area is to be replaced with a new, general directive that will apply from 1 July 2005: see Chapter 9, section 9.7. In the context of the exercise of the derogations to free movement discussed in this chapter, the Commission had identified a number of problems that required addressing such as:

1. the role of previous convictions in the decision-making process;
2. a general failure to inform;
3. the use of measures in a general preventative context; and
4. the deportation/expulsion of long-term residents, second generation migrants and family members that were third country nationals.

The proposed directive will replace most of the relevant provisions of Directive 64/221 and also incorporates many of the decisions discussed above, such as *Adoui* and *Bouchereau*. More specifically, the directive will provide an absolute right of residence for those that enjoy the new status of 'permanent residence', and minors with family relationships in the host State. Further, should the State wish to consider expulsion, they must include analysis of the extent of the person's integration into the life of the State as an important factor, and expulsion can no longer be based on the failure to comply with administrative requirements. The directive will also alter the health ground by removing the annexes and replacing them with a new 'list', designed to be both narrower and more reflective of current medical practice.

# 12

# Equal Treatment for Women and Men

12.1  Introduction

12.2  Directive 75/117

12.3  The direct effect of art 141 EC

12.4  Indirect discrimination and objective justification

12.5  The definition of 'pay'

12.6  Equal treatment in employment

12.7  Equal treatment in social security

12.8  Equal treatment in occupational pension schemes

12.9  Equal treatment for the self-employed

## 12. 1 Introduction

Articles 136–148 EC contain the main provisions of the 'social policy' of the European Community, such as improving working conditions and equality between men and women. The Treaty of Amsterdam (ToA) incorporated the Social Policy Agreement (SPA) into the EC Treaty. In addition, art 3 EC was amended by the ToA so that it provides that 'the Community shall aim to eliminate inequalities, and to promote equality, between men and women'.

Whilst the original EEC Treaty only included the provision on equal pay (art 119) in response to French arguments that it was necessary to ensure a level playing field in the labour market, the European Court has emphasised that equal treatment of men and women is a fundamental general principle of Community law. It is a personal human right that Community law and the national courts must protect: see, for example, *Defrenne v Sabena (No 3)* Case 149/77 [1978] ECR 1365; *P v S and Cornwall County Council* Case C–13/94 [1996] ECR I–2143; and *Deutsche Telekom v Schröder* Case C–50/96 [2000] ECR I–743. In *Defrenne v Sabena (No 2)* Case 43/75 [1976] ECR 455, the Court stated that art 141 EC pursues a 'double aim'. First, it provides for an economic aim in that it avoids undertakings in States that have implemented equal pay from being at a competitive disadvantage as compared to those that have not. Second, art 141 has a social objective, in that there is to be social progress and the improvement of living and working conditions. Interestingly, in the case of *Deutsche Post AG v Sievers and Schrage* Cases C–270 and 271/97 [2000] ECR I–929 the Court concluded that the economic aim of art 141 is now secondary to its social aim. This reflects the decision that equal treatment is a fundamental human right within Community law.

In line with this reasoning, this area of law has expanded beyond any original economic intentions. This has been achieved in a number of ways. First, there has been the production of a wealth of secondary legislation, creating what has become a relatively complex area of law. Second, the European Court has adopted a proactive approach in interpreting the provisions, both of the Treaty and the secondary legislation.

This is seen in its attempt to move the law away from employment-related discrimination in cases dealing with the treatment of transsexuals: see *P v S* (above). This should, though, be compared to the less proactive approach taken in *Grant v South West Trains Ltd* Case C–249/96 [1998] ECR I–621 and *D v Council* Cases C–122 and 125/99P [2001] ECR I–4319, where it was concluded that Directive 76/207 (see below) did not extend to discrimination on the grounds or sexual orientation.

This somewhat controversial area of law was debated within the Community institutions, and in October 2000 agreement was reached in the Council to provide two directives and an Action Programme to prohibit discrimination on grounds of ethnic or racial origin, religion, disability, age or sexual orientation. Council Decision 2001/51 establishes a four-year action programme, to run from 2001 until 2005, on gender equality. The programme and the framework strategy focus on: gender equality in the fields of economic life; equal participation and representation; social rights; civil life; and gender roles and stereotypes. This should be considered a welcome development in Community law. Directive 2000/43, adopted in June 2000, prohibits discrimination on ethnic or racial grounds. Both direct and indirect discrimination are prohibited. The Directive applies to both public and private bodies. Matters covered by the Directive include, inter alia, access to employment. The Directive imposes the obligation on Member States to establish judicial or administrative procedures to enforce the law and provide remedies for its breach.

Third, there is soft law is the form of memorandums, resolutions and recommendations, and the Commission has adopted a number of Action Programmes (the Fourth one finishing in 2000 which was followed by the adoption in 2000 of the first 'framework strategy on gender equality' referred to above) and Annual Reports, a practice adopted in 1996. One example of the development of the law through such 'soft law' measures is a Commission recommendation, adopted in 1991, on the protection of the dignity of employees at work. This was subsequently annexed to a Code of Practice on measures designed to combat sexual harassment.

This has prompted further development of the law – Directive 76/207 (see below) will be amended so that it includes a definition of sexual harassment as a form of discrimination.

Briefly, this area may be summarised as providing for:

1. equal pay – under art 141 EC and Directive 75/117;
2. equal treatment – under art 141 EC and Directives 76/207, 86/613 and 96/34;
3. social security – under Directives 79/7, 86/378 and 96/97.

This chapter will focus to a large extent on the application and interpretation of art 141 EC. The ToA amended art 141 (which originally did not include any reference to equal pay for work of equal value only for equal work) and has added two further paragraphs, so that it now reads as follows:

> '(1) Each Member State shall ensure that the principle of equal pay for male and female workers for equal work or work of equal value is applied.
> (2) For the purposes of this art, "pay" means the ordinary basic or minimum wage or salary and any other considerations, whether in cash or in kind, which the worker receives directly or indirectly, in respect of his employment from his employer.
> Equal pay without discrimination based on sex means:
> (a) that pay for the same work at piece rates shall be calculated on the basis of the same unit of measurement;
> (b) that pay for work at time rates shall be the same for the same job.
> (3) The Council, acting in accordance with the procedure referred to in art 251, and after consulting the Economic and Social Committee, shall adopt measures to ensure the application of the principle of equal opportunities and equal treatment of men and women in matters of employment and occupation, including the principle of equal pay for equal work or work of equal value.
> (4) With a view to ensuring full equality in practice between men and women in working life, the principle of equal treatment shall not prevent any Member State from maintaining or adopting measures providing for specific advantages in order to make it easier for the under-represented sex to pursue a vocational activity or to prevent or compensate for disadvantages in professional careers.'

Not surprisingly, since art 141 was for a long time the keystone of the Community's Social Policy, it is directly effective: *Defrenne* v *Sabena (No 2)* Case 43/75 [1976] ECR 455. But the road to that conclusion was not an easy one. Unfortunately as identified by the Commission, a number of Member States failed to implement the objectives of the article, which led to the adoption of Directive 75/117, the Equal Pay Directive.

## 12.2 Directive 75/117

Whilst art 141 EC does now include the fact that equal pay must be provided for not only equal work, but work of equal value, the original art 119 did not. This was provided for by Directive 75/117, which is based 'on the approximation of the laws of the Member States relating to the application of the principle of equal pay for men and women'. Article 1 of the Directive restates art 119 and adds to the principle the meaning that there must be equal pay for the same work or for work to which equal value is attributed. Comparison may be made with non-contemporaneous employees within the same establishment or service, but not with the hypothetical male: *Macarthys* v *Smith* (below, section 12.3).

If a job classification system is used to determine pay, art 1(2) requires that the scheme is based on the same criteria for men and women and that it is drawn up in such a way as to exclude discrimination on grounds of sex. The criteria used must also be transparent: see *Handels-og Kontorfunktionærernes Forbund i Danmark* v *Dansk Arbejdsgiverforening acting on behalf of Danfoss* Case 109/88 [1989] ECR 3199, in which the Court held that the burden of proof will be on the employer to establish that the criteria used are not based on sex. However, using the criteria of 'muscle-demand' has been held to be an objective criteria permitted in job classification schemes: *Rummler* Case 237/85 [1986] ECR 2101. In *Brunnhofer* v *Bank der Österreichischen Postparkasse* Case C–381/99 [2001] ECR I–4961 it was established that the employer may not refer to the retrospective personal qualities and performance of the employee as a means of arguing that the employee was not undertaking similar work or work of equal value, if there was a pay difference from the beginning of the employment: see also *Angestelltenbetriebsrat der Wiener Gebietskrankenkasse* v *Weiner Gebietskrankenkasse* Case C–309/97 [1999] ECR I–2865.

In *Commission* v *United Kingdom (Re Equal Pay Directive) (No 1)* Case 61/81 [1982] ECR 2601 the United Kingdom was the subject of enforcement proceedings brought by the Commission for failing to ensure an adequate job-classification system, required in order to assess whether work really was of the same value. Under UK law, provided for by the Equal Pay Act 1970 and the Sex Discrimination Act 1975, a job-classification scheme could only be introduced if the employer gave their consent. The Court held that if there were problems in assessing whether the equal pay principle applied, individuals were entitled, as of right, to have their claim assessed by an appropriate authority. This authority would have to be able to produce a binding ruling as to whether the work was of equal value.

Article 2 of the Directive requires Member States to introduce such measures as are necessary to facilitate the bringing of claims by employees who consider themselves wronged, and art 5 provides that any complainants should be protected from dismissal. Member States should also ensure that provisions in collective agreements, wage scales, wage agreements or individual contracts contrary to the principle of equal pay are annulled or amended: art 4. Member States are obligated to ensure that effective measures are taken to ensure that the equal pay principle is observed under art 6 and, under art 7, that employees are aware of provisions adopted under the Directive.

At one point it was submitted that the Directive merely repeated what was already provided by art 141 and that a Member State could not be in violation of its Treaty obligations by failing to implement it: *Commission* v *Luxembourg* Case 58/81

[1982] ECR 2175. The Court did not uphold this proposition and stated that even if the Directive reiterated the provisions in the Treaty it was still valid.

*Defrenne* (above) acknowledged that Directive 75/117 did not affect art 141 but provided for 'further details regarding certain aspects of the material scope' of the article. The result of this is that the right to equal pay for work of equal value existed under art 141 (even before the amendments made by the ToA). The practical implication of this conclusion is that claims for equal pay for work of equal value, as well as equal work, could be bought under the Treaty, and not the Directive. This removes any potential problems inherent in the lack of directives having horizontal direct effect (see Chapter 8).

One final point worthy of note is that, should it be found that female employees are doing equal work, or work or equal value, to that of male employees, they are entitled to not be discriminated against in terms of pay. However, they are not entitled under art 141 to proportionate pay – pay reflecting the work that is undertaken. Hence, if the female employee does something more, or the male receives more pay for work of lower value, female employees are not entitled to claim any more pay than their male counterpart: *Murphy* v *Bord Telecom Eireann* Case 157/86 [1988] 1 CMLR 879.

## 12.3 The direct effect of art 141 EC

*Defrenne* v *Sabena (No 2)* (above) involved an action for compensation brought by Gabrielle Defrenne against her employer, the airline Sabena. She claimed that she was not paid the same as male air stewards. There was no question that they were doing the same/equal work, or that the pay they received was discriminatory. The case posed the following questions: did art 141 introduce, directly into the law of the Member States, the principle that men and women should receive equal pay for equal work so that workers were entitled to institute proceedings before their national courts? If art 141 did provide for this, from when had this been the case?

The Court ruled that art 141 could be relied upon before the national courts but could not be relied on to support claims prior to the judgment except by those who had already brought legal proceedings. This was justified as a necessary response to the claims of the Member States that they would otherwise incur a heavy financial burden and that art 141 had been previously incorrectly understood – a situation not helped by lack of involvement by the Commission. Consequently, art 141 did not have retrospective but only prospective effect. (See Chapter 8)

The Court also concluded that 'since Article [141] is mandatory in nature [it] applies not only to the action of public authorities but also … to contracts between individuals'. Thus, art 141 was concluded to have both vertical and horizontal direct effect. However, the Court also made the following point:

'For the purposes of the implementation of these provisions a distinction must be drawn within the whole area of application of [art 141] between, firstly, direct and overt discrimination which may be identified solely with the aid of the criteria based on equal work and equal pay referred to by the art in question, and, secondly, indirect and disguised discrimination which can only be identified by reference to more explicit implementing provisions of a Community or national character.'

In other words, the Court stated that direct or overt discrimination was identifiable through use of the criteria in art 141 and therefore, in such circumstances, the Treaty article had direct effect. In situations involving direct discrimination there can be no means of justifying the pay difference: see, for example, *Dekker v Stichting Vormingscentrum voor Jong Volwassenen* Case C–177/88 [1990] ECR I–3941. In situations where the discrimination was indirect or disguised, reference to the criteria in art 141 would be insufficient to include it within its ambit and the Treaty article would not have direct effect.

This was confirmed in *Macarthys v Smith* Case 129/79 [1980] ECR 1275. In this case a stockroom manageress discovered that a previous male employee doing the same job had been paid more. The Court held that in identifying whether there was discrimination in pay, comparison could be made between the work of done by employees of different sexes only if they were within the same establishment or service, although the work did not have to be contemporaneous. What could not be done, was any comparison with the hypothetical male, since this could not be achieved through the application of the criteria provided for in art 141.

This distinction created discomfort, not least for Advocate-General Warner who expressed dissatisfaction in his opinions in *Jenkins v Kingsgate (Clothing Productions) Ltd* Case 96/80 [1981] ECR 911 and *Worringham and Humphreys v Lloyds Bank* Case 69/80 [1981] ECR 767. He acknowledged that art 141 did not have direct effect in all circumstances, but he limited those circumstances where it was not directly effective to those where the national courts could not apply it simply by reference to the criteria laid down in the article. In such circumstances either Community or national legislation was required to establish any further rights. Hence, forms of indirect discrimination (discrimination occurring when the rule applies to both sexes but where it has the practical effect of disadvantaging a considerably higher percentage of one sex) could not be identified by the criteria within art 141 and it therefore had no direct effect in such situations.

Subsequent to *Defrenne* and *Macarthys*, the Court responded to the criticisms of such a distinction. The Court was to hold that indirect discrimination also came within the ambit of art 141, without the need to rely on further legislative measures of either a Community or national character. That art 141 also extended to indirect discrimination was finally established in the important case of *Jenkins v Kingsgate (Clothing Productions) Ltd* Case 96/80 (above). In this case Jenkins was a part-time employee paid a lower, hourly rate that full-time male employees, even though they were performing the same work. Kingsgate claimed that the difference was not based on sex but other material differences, in line with s1(3) of the Equal Pay Act 1970.

The Court held that art 141 could extend to such circumstances of indirect discrimination:

'... if it is established that a considerably smaller percentage of women than of men perform the minimum number of hours of weekly working hours required in order to be able to claim the full-time hourly rate, the inequality in pay will be contrary to [art 141] of the Treaty where, regard being had to the difficulties encountered by women in arranging to work that minimum number of hours per week, the pay policy of the undertaking ... cannot be explained by factors other than discrimination based on sex.'

In other words, indirect discrimination, such as paying full-time and part-time workers different hourly rates, would not be discrimination per se within the meaning of art 141, provided that the rates were applied without distinction based on sex. Any distinction between different rates of pay may therefore be 'attributable to factors which are objectively justified', bringing such differences outside the scope of art 141.

## 12.4 Indirect discrimination and objective justification

As a result of the decision in *Jenkins*, discrimination in relation to pay that is indirect or disguised may also come within the ambit of art 141. Such indirect discrimination will not be as a result of criteria based on sex per se and in those terms will apply equally, but the result will be one that detrimentally affects a considerably higher percentage of one sex. The starting point, therefore, in establishing the existence of a measure that is indirectly discriminatory is to identify that a predominant class of persons of one sex are affected by the measure. In *Jenkins* this was relatively easy since all except one of the part-time workers being paid 10 per cent less were women. The burden of proof in establishing that this is the case rests with the employee.

In *Enderby* v *Frenchay Health Authority and the Secretary of State for Health* Case C–127/92 [1993] ECR I–5535 the applicant was employed as a speech therapist by the Health Authority. She claimed that her profession was predominantly female, but were paid less than comparable jobs, such as pharmacists and clinical biologists, which were predominantly carried out by men.

The Court held that there was no de facto discrimination and that the system of pay was transparent as required under Directive 75/117. The Court then found that there would be the possibility of indirect discrimination if:

'... the pay of speech therapists is significantly lower than that of pharmacists and if the former are almost exclusively women while the latter are predominantly men, there is a prima facie case of sex discrimination.'

However, two requirements must exist before it may be established that there is a case of indirect discrimination:

1. It has to be established that the employment in question is of the same value. This was not the case in *Angestelltenbetriebsrat der Wiener Gebietskrankenkasse* v *Weiner Gebietskrankenkasse* Case C–309/97 [1999] 2 CMLR 1173. In this case institutions

in Austria employed three different classes of psychotherapists. Each class had received different training, knowledge and skills from different disciplines – general practitioners, graduate psychologists and those with general education but with specialised training in psychotherapy. The Court held that since they did not have the same qualifications, knowledge or skills from the same discipline, their work could not be considered the same within the ambit of art 141.

2. It must be established that the statistics, provided by the employee, are valid and accurate. The role of determining whether this is the case rests with the national courts. The Court's guidance in *Enderby* suggests that the statistics should be considered in light of any 'fortuitous or short-term phenomena, and whether, in general, they appear to be significant'. In *R v Secretary of State for Employment, ex parte Seymour Smith* Case C–167/97 [1999] ECR I–623 the European Court held that the best means of determining whether a measure has a disproportionate effect on women is to compare the relevant statistics by considering the proportions of each sex able to satisfy the measure.

This is confirmed in Directive 97/80 (Burden of Proof Directive, which applies to the directives on Equal Pay, Equal Treatment, Pregnancy and Parental Leave) which states that the employee only has to offer 'facts from which it may be presumed that there has been direct or indirect discrimination'.

Whilst satisfying the above criteria may establish that there is a case of indirect discrimination, the Court in *Jenkins* held that the discrimination may be due to objective factors other than sex. Consequently, the burden of proof will shift to the employer to show that there is in fact no discrimination or that the difference is indeed objectively justifiable. This is confirmed in Directive 97/80. Article 2(2) of the Directive states that:

> 'Indirect discrimination shall exist where an apparently neutral provision, criterion or practice disadvantages a substantially higher proportion of one sex unless that provision is appropriate and necessary and can be justified by objective factors unrelated to sex.'

In *Jenkins* the Court suggested that differences in rates for full-time and part-time workers could be justified by the legitimate aim of trying to encourage a greater number of full-time employees.

Obviously, without additional guidance on what constitutes objective justification, the national courts could have applied it in a non-uniform manner. Consequently, the European Court provided a test for objective justification in *Bilka-Kaufhaus GmbH v Karin Weber von Hartz* Case 170/84 [1986] ECR 1607. The Court confirmed that it is 'for the national court, which has sole jurisdiction to make findings of fact, to determine whether and to what extent the grounds put forward by an employer ... may be regarded as objectively justified economic grounds'. The test that the national courts should apply is as follows:

1. the measures adopted should correspond to a real need on the part of the undertaking;

2. the measures must be proportionate to achieve that need; and
3. the measures must be necessary.

In *Rinner-Kühn* v *FWW Spezial-Gebäudereinigung GmbH* Case 171/88 [1989] ECR 2743 part-time workers were excluded under national legislation from receiving sick pay. In this case the Court again stated that indirect discrimination could be objectively justified, but reworded the *Bilka* test. In *Rinner* the Court held that the measure had to be a necessary aim of social policy and had to be 'suitable and requisite' to achieve that purpose. In the case, Germany argued that the measure was justified because part-time workers were not as 'dependant' on their employer. This was concluded to be a generalisation about part-time workers, and was not an acceptable objective justification: see, also, *Nimz* v *Freie und Hansestadt Hamburg* Case 184/89 [1991] ECR 297.

In *R* v *Secretary of State for Employment, ex parte Equal Opportunities Commission* [1995] 1 AC 1 the House of Lords concluded that provisions in the Employment Protection (Consolidation) Act 1978, which excluded workers employed for less that eight hours a week, affected a disproportionate amount of women. They were not objectively justifiable. In the case of *Danfoss* (above) the Court examined indirect discrimination in the criteria used to establish supplementary payments. The Court accepted that training and length of service could be objectively justified criteria. The Court also accepted the criterion of 'mobility', but only in the context of whether it was an important factor for the performance of specific tasks assigned to the employee and not if it implied adaptability in terms of hours and place of work. It is in the hands of the national courts to examine the compatibility of such criteria with Community law.

It has also been concluded by the European Court that indirect discrimination stemming from collective bargaining agreements, as well as from national legislation, will breach art 141 unless objectively justified: see *Kowalska* v *Freie und Hansestadt Hamburg* Case 33/89 [1990] ECR 2591, *Nimz* and *Enderby* (above). In *Royal Copenhagen* Case C–400/93 [1995] ECR I–1275 the Court held that if different rates of pay had been concluded through a collective bargaining process at a local level, it was a factor that could be used in assessing whether there was indeed objective justification for the difference.

In the past there has been significant criticism of the European Court's approach to indirect discrimination and its ability to be objective justified. Such criticism was based on two primary objections – the fact that the concept of discrimination was based on a 'male norm' to begin with, and that employers appeared to be able to meet the objective justification test with the use of relatively broad economic grounds. However, when that objective justification is being offered by the State, rather than a private employer, the ECJ appears to be adopting a far more rigorous analysis of the claim. This can be witnessed particularly in the case of *Hill and Stapleton* v *Revenue Commissioners* Case C–243/95 [1998] ECR I–3739.

In this case indirect discrimination was established against job-sharers, the majority of whom were women, in the context of awarding pay increases. The

Revenue Commissioners argued that this was objectively justified because it was established practice, promoted staff morale and motivation, and avoided increased costs. None of these justifications were accepted by the Court. Indeed, in the Court's opinion the practices were considered to undermine the general principle of protecting women attempting to combine work and family life, since many attempted this through the practice of job-sharing.

Such a development can also be witnessed in *Seymour-Smith and Perez* Case C–167/97 [1999] ECR I–623, where the UK attempted to objectively justify indirect discrimination on the basis of social policy – the stimulation of recruitment by employers. Whilst the Court was prepared to accept that such a purpose was a legitimate aim of social policy, and that Member States had a wide measure of discretion in determining and achieving such policy aims, they could not adopt a policy that was far too generalised and that had the consequence of 'frustrating the implementation of a fundamental principle of Community law such as that of equal pay for men and women'.

## 12.5 The definition of 'pay'

Under art 141, women and men are entitled to the same 'pay', once it has been established that their work is equal or of equal value, and that either direct discrimination exists (which may not be justified) or that there is indirect discrimination, which cannot be objectively justified.

Article 141 provides that pay means the 'ordinary basic or minimum wage or salary or any other consideration, whether in cash or in kind, which the worker receives directly or indirectly, in respect of his employment from his employer'. This has formed the basis for the European Court's liberal interpretation of what constitutes pay. Examples of what may constitute pay are provided below.

### Perks (non-pay benefits)

In *Garland* v *British Rail Engineering* Case 12/81 [1982] ECR 359, the European Court concluded that special travel facilities to former employees were pay, even though there was no contractual entitlement to the facility. In this case a previous female employee and her dependants were not entitled to the facilities, whilst male employees were.

### Sick pay

In *Rinner* (above) part-time workers working less that ten hours a week were not entitled to sick pay. It was established that the measure disproportionately affected women and there was no objective justification (see above) and, in addition, that sick pay constituted pay within the ambit of art 141.

## Redundancy payments

These are also considered to be pay within art 141, regardless of whether such payment is made on a contractual or voluntary basis, or under national legislative obligations: see *Barber* v *Guardian Royal Exchange Assurance Group* Case C–262/88 [1990] ECR I–1889. Similarly, in *Commission* v *Belgium* Case C–173/91 [1993] ECR I–673 the Belgian government argued that redundancy supplements were a form of social security and therefore outside of the scope of art 141 (see below). The Court held that such redundancy payments did constitute pay.

## Supplementary payments

In *Worringham and Humphreys* v *Lloyds Bank Ltd* Case 69/80 (above) men under 25 were paid a supplementary amount to their gross salary so that they could contribute to the compulsory employee's occupational pension scheme. Women under 25 were not under any compulsory obligation to join the pension scheme and therefore did not receive the additional payment. Under Section 6(1)(a) of the Equal Pay Act 1970, it was argued that equality did not extend to provisions made in connection with death or retirement. The European Court held that the supplementary payment was pay within the terms of art 141, and that consequently equality was required:

> 'Although, where women are not required to pay contributions, the salary of men after deduction of the contributions is comparable to that of women who do not pay contributions, the inequality between the gross salaries of men and women is nevertheless a source of discrimination contrary to [art 141] of the Treaty since because of that inequality men receive benefits from which women engaged in the same work or work of equal value are excluded, or receive on that account greater benefits or social advantages that those to which women are entitled.'

## Maternity pay

The European Court has held that the amount of maternity pay must not be so low as to defeat the purpose of having maternity leave. The Court has also held that if pay increases are awarded during maternity leave, and the maternity pay is calculated by reference to the pay received before the leave is taken, then the increased pay should be awarded to the woman on leave: *Gillespie* v *Northern Ireland Health and Social Services Board* Case C–342/93 [1996] ECR I–475 (although this was heard before the introduction of the Maternity Directive: see below).

## Contributions under a statutory scheme used to calculate other benefits

In *Defrenne* v *Belgian State (No 1)* Case 80/70 [1971] ECR 445 the Court was asked to examine whether Belgian law on retirement pensions fell within the scope of art 141. Under the scheme, air stewards, such as Defrenne, were excluded. The pension was granted under the terms of a social security scheme financed by workers, employers and the State.

The Court held that the following were not within the concept of pay:

> '... social security schemes or benefits, in particular retirement pensions, directly governed by legislation without any element of agreement within the undertaking or the occupational branch concerned, which are obligatorily applicable to general categories of workers.'

The Court considered that such schemes were not determined by the employment relationship, but by 'considerations of social policy'. The benefits were provided under law because the recipient fulfilled the legal conditions necessary to receive the benefit, and not by reason of the employer's contribution. Consequently, there was no direct or indirect payment by the employer to the employee for the purposes of art 141.


## Pensions

This has proved to be a difficult and complex area of law, provoking tension between the Court and the political institutions of the Community and the Member States. The original position appeared straightforward under the decision in *Defrenne (No 1)* explained above – that retirement pensions were a form of social security benefit, which brought them outside the scope of art 141. This was because they were not determined by the employer but by the State as part of its social policy.

Equal treatment in social security is provided under Directive 79/7 (see below), although it should be noted that this Directive contains a number of exceptions within it. For this reason, it would seem beneficial for individuals that pensions, or some forms of them, come within art 141 since it contains no express exceptions. The political institutions of the Community were in the process of devising Directive 86/378, which was to provide that occupational pension schemes were social security and therefore outside of the scope of art 141. It is in this context that the European Court was faced with having to consider whether occupational pension schemes fell within the definition of pay.

In *Bilka-Kaufhaus* v *Weber von Hartz* Case 170/84 (above) Ms Weber challenged her employer's occupational pension scheme. The scheme was non-contributory and was financed entirely by the employer. Part-time workers, such as Ms Weber, were excluded from receiving benefits unless they had been employed by the firm for a minimum of 15 out of 20 years. This requirement did not apply to full-time workers. Since it was established that the majority of part-time employees were women (see above) she claimed that the scheme breached art 141.

The Court held that the employer's contributions to a occupational pension scheme under a contractual obligation did fall within pay for the purposes of art 141. This was because the contributions were paid by the employer to supplement existing statutory security schemes (which fall outside of art 141) so they were consideration paid by the employer to the employee. The essential difference between statutory and occupational pension schemes was that the latter was a scheme devised and regulated as an 'integral part of the contracts of employment':

> 'It must therefore be concluded that that the scheme does not constitute a social security scheme governed directly by statute and thus does not fall outside the scope of [art 141].'

Such a decision, of course, removed the need for Directive 86/378, but it was nevertheless adopted. It was thought that *Bilka* would only apply when the occupational pension scheme supplemented the statutory scheme, and that occupational pension schemes that were a direct substitute for a statutory scheme (a contracted-out occupational pension scheme) would be considered as social security and therefore outside of art 141. This was, however, before the landmark and controversial decision of the European Court in *Barber* v *Guardian Royal Exchange Assurance Group* Case C–262/88 (above). It was this decision that was to render the practical effect of Directive 86/378 redundant.

Mr Barber was a member of a pension fund set up by Guardian Royal Exchange (GRE). The scheme was contracted-out, in other words, it was a private, non-statutory scheme approved under United Kingdom legislation as a substitute for the earnings-related part of the State pension scheme, and was non-contributory. The scheme provided that the standard retirement age was 57 years of age for women and 62 for men. This reflected the ages provided for under the UK's national statutory social security scheme. Under the terms of Mr Barber's employment contract, if he was made redundant he was entitled to an immediate pension on reaching 55 years of age. The same provision applied to women, but they would receive the pension at the age of 50.

In 1980 Mr Barber was made redundant. He was 52 years old. GRE provided severance pay under the terms of his contract and an ex gratia payment. He also received statutory redundancy pay (see above). However, GRE refused to pay him his pension until he reached the full pensionable age of 62. Mr Barber brought an action before an industrial tribunal claiming that there was discrimination contrary to UK and Community law. His claim failed in both the industrial tribunal and the Employment Appeals Tribunal. Unfortunately, Mr Barber died but his action was taken over by his widow. The Court of Appeal decided to make an art 234 EC preliminary reference to the European Court, one of the questions asked being whether a private, contracted-out occupational pension scheme constituted pay within art 141. This was important, since if it was social security it fell outside of art 141 and was governed by the terms of Directive 79/7, which permits different pensionable ages, whereas no such exception exists under art 141.

The Court held that the contracted-out occupational pension fell within the definition of pay. The Court came to this conclusion after examining the characteristics of the scheme. It found that for the following three reasons the scheme was not social security but pay:

1. the scheme was agreed and entirely financed by the employer and was not imposed by statute. Although it should be noted that in *Coloroll Pension Trustees Ltd v Russell* Case C–200/91 [1994] ECR I–4389 the Court held that all benefits paid to an employee under an occupational pension, regardless of whether it was partly financed by contributions from employees, would constitute pay;
2. the scheme was not compulsory, unlike a statutory social security scheme, and was regulated by its own rules; and
3. the provisions of the scheme allowed for additional benefits beyond those provided under social security schemes.

Since the occupational pension scheme was pay, the Court held that:

'... it is contrary to [art 141] to impose an age condition which differs according to sex in respect of pensions paid out under a contracted-our scheme, even if the difference between the pensionable ages for men and that for women is based on the one provided for by the national security scheme.'

It is worth noting that a similar decision was reached in relation to the setting of different retirement ages in supplementary pension schemes, such as that in *Bilka*: see *Moroni v Firma Collo GmbH* Case C–110/91 [1993] ECR I–6591.

However, facing considerable pressure from the Member States in relation to the huge number of claims for past discrimination in relation to such schemes, the European Court concluded that its decision had no retrospective effect (unless proceedings had already been initiated). Therefore, the direct effect of art 141 in such circumstances was limited in that it would not apply to claims prior to the date of the *Barber* judgment: 17 May 1990. It was not made clear in the decision whether this applied to periods of service prior to this date where the person had not yet actually received their pension benefits.

This was clarified by the addition of a protocol, attached to the EC Treaty by the TEU. The protocol provides that only pay attributable to periods of service after 17 May 1990 will constitute pay within art 141, except for those who had already brought their claim. However, the limitation in the protocol only relates to the benefits from an occupational scheme and does not apply to the right to actually join an occupational pension scheme in the first place.

Many women had been deprived of the simple right to even join an occupational pension scheme, often because they were only provided for full-time workers or because married women were excluded. The European Court has held that, since occupational pension schemes are pay, such discriminatory practices could have been challenged from the date of *Defrenne (No 2)*: *Fisscher v Voorhuis Hengelo BV and Stichting Bedrijfspensioenfonds voor de Detailhandel* Case C–128/93 [1994] ECR I–4583 and *Vroege v NCIV Institut voor Volkshuisvesting BV and Stichting Pensioenfonds NCIV* Case C–57/93 [1994] ECR I–4541. However, should a woman wish to challenge her exclusion from an occupational pension scheme, and gain her right to have belonged to it from the date of *Defrenne* (or when she began employment and in theory had the right to join), she must pay all the back-dated contributions required. As Craig and de Burca point out, it is highly unlikely that many female part-time workers will be able to afford this opportunity.

In addition to the non-retrospective effect of *Barber*, there are other limitations to its impact. In *Neath* v *Hugh Steeper Ltd* Case C–152/91 [1993] ECR I–6935 the Court held that differentiation by the employer in contributions paid under a defined benefit scheme as a result of actuarial factors (such as life expectancy in this case) were outside of art 141. In *Van den Akker* v *Stichting Shell Pensioenfonds* Case C–28/93 [1994] ECR I–4527 the Court held that, between the date of the *Barber* decision (17 May 1990) and the date of the adoption of equality measures as required under that judgment, equalisation had to be achieved without reducing the previously existing entitlements: see, also, *Smith* v *Advel Systems Ltd* Case C–408/92 [1994] ECR I–4435. However, the equalisation measures actually adopted did not have to be fixed at any particular level and could indeed be set at less favourable measures than had previously existed. In other words, instead of bringing the male entitlement age down to the same as a woman's, such as in the *Barber* case, the ages could both be set at the higher age applied previously only to men, or indeed at a higher age altogether.

## 12.6 Equal treatment in employment

### General

Equal treatment in employment is provided for under Directive 76/207– the Equal Treatment Directive. This Directive was based on art 308 EC under the general powers of the Community institutions. Hence, unlike Directive 75/117, claims within its scope cannot be brought under art 141 and must be confined to use of the Directive and the implementing national legislation.

Article 1(1) of the Directive provides that there must be equal treatment of men and women in relation to access to employment, promotion and vocational training, as well as equal treatment in relation to working conditions and social security. The latter was provided under Directive 79/7 in relation to statutory schemes and Directive 86/378 in relation to occupational schemes (see below).

Article 2 defines equal treatment as prohibiting all direct or indirect discrimination on grounds of sex, particularly that in relation to marital or family status. This has been extended to include discrimination against transsexuals: see *P* v *S* (above). Derogation from this general prohibition is available under art 2(2), and is discussed below. The Directive has been invoked in numerous cases, but has been most often used in relation to protecting mothers at work, part-time workers, retirement ages, dismissal and pregnant women.

## Pregnancy and maternity

It was held in *Dekker* v *Stichting Vormingscentrum voor Jong Volwassenen* Case C–177/88 [1990] ECR I–3941 that refusing to give a woman a job as a training instructor because she was pregnant was direct discrimination: see also *Mahlburg* v *Land Meckleburg-Vorpommern* Case C–207/98 [2000] ECR I–549. In *Webb* v *EMO Air Cargo* Case C–32/93 [1994] ECR I–3567 the Court found that a woman employed on an indefinite basis but then dismissed because of pregnancy was also direct discrimination.

These decisions should be contrasted with that in *Hertz* v *Dansk Arbejdsgiverforening* Case 179/88 [1990] ECR I–3979. In this case the woman had given birth and was on maternity leave but was ill due to complications in her pregnancy. Her subsequent dismissal was held to be indirect discrimination and therefore capable of objective justification. Indeed, Directive 76/207 does not cover dismissal after the expiry of the maternity leave at all. Hence, if a woman is absent from work after the expiry of her maternity leave, even if it is due to illness or complications associated with childbirth, she is to be considered on the same basis as a sick man. She may consequently be dismissed without breaching the equal treatment provisions: *Brown* v *Rentokil* Case 394/96 [1998] ECR I–4185.

It was originally thought the protection against dismissal for pregnant women would only apply where they were employed for an indefinite period, as in *Webb*. This has been resolved by the introduction of Directive 92/85 on pregnant workers and working mothers. Under this Directive pregnant women are protected from dismissal regardless of the contractual status of their employment. However, this Directive also does not apply to women suffering complications after the expiry of their maternity leave, as discussed above.

## Determination of retirement and redundancy ages

The Directive has also been used to challenge the imposition of age limits for compulsory redundancy. In *Burton* v *British Railways Board* Case 19/81 [1982] ECR 555 Mr Burton applied for voluntary redundancy but was rejected since he was two years younger than the minimum 60-year limit set for male employees. Since female employees could apply for voluntary redundancy at the age of 55 he brought a claim for unequal treatment under Directive 76/207 (art 5 of which applies the principle of equal treatment to conditions of work and dismissal).

The ECJ held that the different ages reflected those in the national statutory security scheme. This was exempted from having to have equality in terms of pensionable age by Directive 79/7, art 7. The Court held that the same conditions could apply to differing ages for voluntary redundancy. The conclusion appearing to be that redundancy did not constitute dismissal within the terms of art 5 of Directive 76/207.

In *Roberts* v *Tate & Lyle Industries* Case 151/84 [1986] ECR 703 the situation was slightly different in that Ms Roberts belonged to an occupational pension scheme that resulted in compulsory retirement at 65 for men and 60 for women. Under its compulsory redundancy terms the scheme also provided that men and women would receive an early pension at 55 if made redundant. Roberts was made redundant at the age of 53 and was subsequently awarded no early pension. She brought a claim arguing that the scheme was in breach of Directive 76/207. This was because men could receive an early retirement pension ten years before the normal retirement age, but women were only entitled to one five years beforehand.

In this case the European Court changed its approach to that in *Burton*. Instead of considering the redundancy scheme as tied to the statutory retirement scheme and outside of the scope of the need for equal treatment in relation to the determination of ages, the Court held that redundancy conditions, including the setting of ages, came within the concept of dismissal. This meant that art 5 of Directive 76/207, providing for the need for equality, applied to Robert's situation. In other words, the Court found that if compulsory redundancy (rather than the voluntary redundancy in *Burton*) was dismissal, which it was, any receipt of a pension on redundancy was merely a condition of that dismissal and such conditions under art 5 had to reflect the equality principle. In the case, since the ages were set at identical levels for men and women, there was no breach of the Directive.

A similar decision was reached in *Marshall* v *Southampton and South-West Hampshire Area Health Authority (Teaching) (No 1)* Case 152/84 [1986] ECR 723, but in relation to compulsory retirement rather than redundancy. Even though the compulsory retirement ages reflected those of the statutory security scheme, as in *Burton*, the Court nonetheless held the compulsory retirement to be dismissal. Therefore, the differing ages were not permitted under art 7 of Directive 79/7, and the compulsory retirement had to comply with conditions of the Equal Treatment Directive.

However, since these decisions the Court has again changed its approach. This has resulted from decisions in cases such as *Bilka* and *Barber* (above) that redundancy payments and payments from occupational pensions schemes come within the scope of art 141. Hence, in relation to retirement ages, the decision of *Barber* now means that the calculation of pensionable age for the purpose of redundancy is governed by art 141, in total contrast to the decision previously held in *Burton* (above). Discriminatory ages for compulsory and voluntary redundancy and for occupational pensions all breach the Treaty. There is no need to use art 5 of Directive 76/207 in such situations, and such situations are not covered by the exception in art 7 of Directive 79/7, since they are not forms of statutory social security.

### Derogation under art 2 of Directive 76/207

Article 2 sets out three situations that may be excluded from the principle of equal treatment:

**Article 2(2) – that in occupational activities and training, there may be exemption from equal treatment where the sex of the worker constitutes a 'determining factor'**

In *Commission* v *United Kingdom (Re Equal Treatment for Men and Women)* Case 165/82 [1983] ECR 3431 the Commission brought an enforcement action against the UK government for failing to comply with Directive 76/207. This was based on the Sex Discrimination Act 1975 having exempted the need for equal treatment in private households and firms employing less than six staff. The Court concluded that the exemptions under art 2 of Directive 76/207 could not be applied in a blanket manner.

However, in the same case, the Commission had also challenged the decision of the UK government to limit the access of men to the profession of midwife under s41 of the Sex Discrimination Act 1975. The British government claimed that this was to respect 'personal sensitivities' between patient and midwife. The Court held that the UK's action in this respect came within the scope of the exemption provided in art 2(2).

In *Johnston* v *Chief Constable of the Royal Ulster Constabulary* Case 222/84 [1986] ECR 1651 a female member of the Royal Ulster Constabulary (RUC) challenged the decision to refuse to renew her employment contract. The RUC had made a policy decision not to employ any woman as a full-time member of the RUC Reserve because they were not trained in the use of firearms. The RUC argued that if they were permitted to carry firearms they would be at a greater risk of being assassinated.

The Commission argued that the occupational activity of an armed police officer was not one where sex was a determining factor. The European Court, however, did not agree, and held that the sex of police officers could be a determining factor when conducting certain types of policing. It is this latter point which appears to be important – that certain activities within the type of employment generally may have sex as a determining factor.

Hence, in *Sirdar* v *The Army Board and Secretary of State for Defence* Case C–273/97 [1999] 3 CMLR 559 the Court held that the general management of the armed forces should comply with the principle of equality of treatment. However, the Royal Marines, as a special combat force, could be exempt under art 2(2) since sex was a determining factor. The exclusion of women from the Royal Marines was therefore upheld. Similarly, in *Commission* v *France* Case 318/86 [1988] ECR 3559 the Court held that the French police's separate recruitment processes for men and women was contrary to the Directive, but recognised that some duties performed by the police could involve sex as a determining factor. Finally, in *Kreil* v *Bundesrepublik Deutschland* Case C–285/98 [2000] ECR I–69, the European Court held that permitting women to join medical and musical sections of the armed forces, but excluding them from military posts involving the use of arms, was not within the art 2(2) exception.

**Article 2(3) – the protection of women in pregnancy and maternity**

This provision has been held not to extend to the need to provide equal benefits to men. In *Hofmann* v *Barmer Ersatzkasse* Case 184/83 [1984] ECR 3047 Hofmann had taken unpaid leave to look after his child. Under German law the mother was not permitted to work for eight weeks after birth, and was permitted a further period of maternity leave until the child was six months old. Hofmann took his unpaid leave after the eight-week period since the mother had returned to work. He claimed that the fact that he was not entitled to pay during this period, whereas the mother would have been, was a breach of the Equal Treatment Directive.

The Court dismissed the claim and held that the provision in the Directive was not concerned with the 'organisation of the family' or the 'division of responsibility between parents' but was designed to protect women. The protection it offered was to ensure that the biological condition of the woman could return to normal after childbirth and to prevent disturbing the relationship between mother and child after childbirth from the 'multiple burdens which would result from the simultaneous pursuit of employment'.

This area of law has now been expanded upon by the Pregnancy Directive (92/85), which imposes a requirement to provide minimum employment protection for pregnant women, those who have recently given birth and those that are breast-feeding. However, the Directive also provides that Member States are free to offer greater protection should they so wish. In brief the Directive provides for the following:

| | |
|---|---|
| Article 5 | employers are required to take appropriate action to ensure that women in the above categories are not exposed to certain risks (to be defined by the Commission) and that action such as adjusting working hours and conditions, granting leave or movement to another job may constitute such appropriate action. |
| Article 6 | pregnant and breast-feeding women cannot be required to undertake duties involving risk of exposure to certain substances. |
| Article 7 | prohibits any obligation to undertake night work (for a period to be determined by national law) and alternatively day work or extended maternity leave must be made available. |
| Article 8 | provides for the minimum of 14 weeks of continuous maternity leave before and/or after confinement and this must include at least two weeks of compulsory maternity leave. |
| Article 9 | pregnant workers must be entitled to time off work without loss of pay to attend ante-natal treatment, where necessary. |
| Article 10 | prohibits the dismissal of workers during the period of maternity leave except in exceptional circumstance not connected with the pregnancy. |
| Article 11 | the right to maintenance of pay and other employment rights must be provided for those on leave as defined under arts 5–7. Those |

on maternity leave defined in art 8 must be entitled to an 'adequate allowance' that must be no less than the amount paid under statutory sick pay.

Article 12     requires access to a judicial remedy.

Leave after birth has also now been covered under Community law by Directive 96/34 on parental leave. The Directive implements the 1996 Framework Agreement on Parental Leave, the main aim of which was to grant male and female workers a minimum of three weeks' parental leave on the birth or adoption of a child. This leave can be taken up to a point to be defined by the Member State, but no later then eight years after the birth or adoption of the child. The Framework Agreement does provide Member States with the discretion to determine the conditions on which this leave is granted, such as whether it can be on a full- or part-time basis, whether it can only be granted after a certain minimum level of employment, and the period of notice required. The Framework Agreement also permits special arrangements for small undertakings and requires the drawing-up of necessary measures to ensure that workers can take leave on the basis of what is described as 'force majeure for urgent family reasons in cases of sickness or accident'.

### Article 2(4) – measures giving a 'specific advantage to women with a view to improving their ability to compete on the labour market and to pursue a career on an equal footing with men'

This provision states that it is 'without prejudice to measures to promote equal opportunity for men and women, in particular, by removing the existing inequalities which affect women's opportunities in areas referred to in art 1(1)'. The first case to examine such 'positive discrimination' (sometimes referred to as affirmative action) was *Kalanke* v *Freie Hansestadt Bremen* Case C–450/93 [1995] ECR I–3051. The action in question had been taken by the German government, which had produced measures requiring women to be given priority when applying for employment in areas where women were under-represented, even though men were as equally qualified.

On a preliminary reference, the European Court held that art 2(4) of Directive 76/207 permitted a Member State to give 'specific advantage to a woman with a view to improving their ability to compete in the labour market and to pursue careers on an equal footing with men'. However, it did not provide for women to be given a clear priority over men, or visa versa.

This has since been enshrined in the EC Treaty, within the Social Agreement annexed to the TEU and the amending of art 141 by the ToA. Article 141(4) EC now reads:

'With a view to securing full equality in practice between men and women in working life, the principle of equal treatment shall not prevent any member state from maintaining or adopting measures providing for specific advantages in order to make it easier for the under-represented sex to pursue a vocational activity or to prevent or compensate for disadvantage in professional careers.'

In *Marschall* v *Land Nordhein-Westfalen* Case C–409/95 [1998] 1 CMLR 547 the Court held that a national law requiring that preference be given to promoting a woman in sectors of the public service where there were fewer women than men at that level was justifiable. There was, however, the proviso in this case that a man could still receive the promotion if, on an objective assessment of all candidates, their personal attributes and situation made them the best candidate for the promotion. This has since been followed in *Georg Badeck* Case C–158/97 [2000] All ER (EC) 289 where the Court held that candidates must still be objectively assessed and that national courts have the responsibility to ensure that this is the case.

In the case of *Abrahamsson* v *Fogelqvist* Case C–407/98 [2000] ECR I–5539, the Court was required to examine Swedish legislation. The legislation permitted the preferred appointment to a public post of someone from the under-represented sex that possessed 'sufficient' qualifications where it was 'necessary to secure the appointment of a candidate from the under-represented sex and the difference between the respective merits of the candidates is not so great as to give rise to a breach of the requirement of objectivity in making appointments'. The Court concluded that the 'selection method of the kind at issue' was 'disproportionate to the aim pursued'. A positive action measure will only be permitted if it meets the following criteria:

1. it is designed to 'reduce de facto inequalities that may arise in society' and prevent or compensate for 'disadvantages in the professional career of persons belonging to the under-represented sex'; and
2. the measure's application is based on 'transparent' criteria and 'amenable to review in order to obviate any arbitrary assessment of the qualifications of candidates'.

## Remedies

Reference should be made to Chapter 8 on the direct effect of directives, such as Directive 76/207. It should be noted that art 6 of the Directive requires Member States to provide a mechanism of enforcement. In the case of *Von Colson* (above) it was concluded that this would be achieved through imposing an obligation on the national courts to sympathetically interpret their national law to conform to the Directive.

## 12.7 Equal treatment in social security

The equality principle in matters of social security is provided under Directive 79/7, which according to *Netherlands* v *FNV* Case 71/85 [1986] ECR 3855 and *Borrie Clark* v *Chief Adjudication Officer* Case 384/85 [1987] ECR 2865 is directly effective. Article 1 of the Directive states that its aim is the progressive implementation of the principle of equal treatment in the field of social security. Hence, Member States have had some considerable time to ensure the adaptation of national law The Directive extends to 'self-employed persons, workers and self-employed persons whose activity is interrupted by illness, accident or involuntary unemployment and persons seeking employment' as well as to 'retired or invalided workers and self-employed persons'. Unless the work has been interrupted by one of the 'risks' dealt with under art 3(1) of the Directive (see below), it will not extend to those who have not been employed or who are not seeking work: *Achterberg-te Riele and Others* v *Sociale Verzekeringsbank* Cases 48, 106, and 107/88 [1990] 3 CMLR 323. Article 3(2) provides that survivor and family benefits are excluded from the Directive's provisions unless they are designed to increase the statutory benefits from schemes identified in art 3(1).

The Directive secures equal treatment in relation to statutory schemes (art 3(1)) providing for protection against the 'risks' of sickness, invalidity, old age, accidents at work, occupational diseases and unemployment. It also extends to social assistance intended to supplement or replace the above statutory schemes. It has been held, for example, that the Directive extends to providing equal treatment in relation to receiving winter fuel payments provided in the UK: *R* v *Secretary of State for Health, ex parte Taylor* Case C–382/98 [2000] 1 CMLR 873. It also extends to exemptions provided in relation to prescription charges: *R* v *Secretary of State for Health, ex parte Richardson* Case C–137/94 [1995] ECR I–3407.

In order to benefit from the protection provided under this Directive, the benefit claimed must be 'directly and effectively' linked to the protection provided against one of the risks under art 3(1). In *R* v *Secretary of State for Social Security, ex parte Smithson* Case C–243/90 [1992] ECR I–467 this was held by the Court not to extend to housing benefit. In the case of *Atkins* v *Wrekin District Council* Case C–228/94 [1996] ECR I–3633 the Court held that it also did not extend to travel concessions paid by public authorities. Supplementary allowances intended to replace a wage are not covered: see *Jackson* v *Cresswell* Cases 63 and 64/91 [1992] ECR I–4737. 'Child-raising' allowances also do not fall within the Directive: *Hoever and Zachow* v *Land Nordrhein-Westfalen* Cases C–245 and 312/94 [1996] ECR I–4895.

Article 4(1) prohibits both direct and indirect discrimination on grounds of sex by reference to either marital or family status (although art 4(2) provides that this must be without prejudice to measures protecting women on grounds of maternity) and, in particular, in relation to the following:

1. the scope of schemes and the conditions of access to them;
2. any obligation to contribute and the calculation of those contributions;
3. the calculation of any benefits in respect of spouses and dependants; and
4. conditions on the duration and retention of entitlement to any benefits.

Indirect discrimination may be objectively justified (art 4(1)) such as on grounds of social policy: see, for example, *Teuling* v *Bedrijfsvereniging voor de Chemische Industrie* Case 30/85 [1987] ECR 2497 and *Laperre* v *Bestuurcommissie Beroepszaken in de Provincie Zuid-Holland* Case C–8/94 [1996] ECR I–273.

The Directive also provides that five specific matters are excluded from the equal treatment principle: art 7. These include the determination of pensionable ages; pension benefits or entitlements granted to those having brought up children; old age or invalidity benefits deriving from a wife's entitlements; increases in benefits granted to any dependant wife; and consequences from the option not to gain rights/incur obligations under any statutory scheme. However, art 7(2) also provides the obligation on Member States to re-examine these excluded matters to determine whether changes mean they should no longer be permitted exceptions.

In relation to pensionable ages, use of the Directive cannot justify discriminatory ages in relation to early retirement: *Marshall* Case 152/84 [1986] ECR 723. At pensionable age, however, discrimination is justifiable under art 7: *Burton v British Railways Board* Case 19/81 (above). It will also extend to justifying any discrimination in relation to the number of payments required for a full pension: *R v Secretary of State for Social Security, ex parte Equal Opportunities Commission* Case C–9/91 [1992] 3 All ER 577. Article 7, though, cannot be used to justify linking the receipt of other benefits (such as exemption from prescription charges and invalid care allowance) to pensionable ages: see *R v Secretary of State for Health, ex parte Richardson* (above) and *R v Secretary of State for Social Security, ex parte Thomas* Case C–328/91 [1993] 3 CMLR 880.

## 12.8 Equal treatment in occupational pension schemes

This is provided for under Directive 86/378, which had an implementation deadline of July 1989, although Member States were given until 1 January 1993 to take all the necessary measures to ensure that the occupational pension schemes operating within that State were compatible with the equal treatment principle. Consequently the Directive only has direct effect from 1 January 1993, from which date claims may be made in national courts. The effect and scope of the Directive has been much undermined by the European Court's decision in *Barber* (above), in the context that occupational pensions are considered to be pay within the ambit of art 141 EC. A significant effect of this decision is that, in relation to matters such as discriminatory retirement ages (intended to be excluded from the equal treatment principle under art 9 of the Directive) or the amount of the benefits paid out, individuals may now rely on the full force of art 141. The Directive, to bring it in line with the decision in *Barber*, was amended by Directive 96/97.

Directive 86/378 closely follows the provisions of Directive 79/7. It extends to occupational pension schemes supplementing or replacing statutory schemes and relates to the same persons and the same risks as provided for under Directive 79/7: arts 3 and 4 of Directive 86/378. Under this Directive, survivors and family benefits provided as part of the consideration paid by an employer are not excluded: art 4. The Directive provides ten examples of the types of discrimination that are prohibited as incompatible with equal treatment because they discriminate on the basis of sex or marital/family status: art 6.

## 12.9 Equal treatment for the self-employed

This is provided for under Directive 86/613. The implementation deadline was 30 June 1989, except where Member States were required to alter their national law on matrimonial rights and rights to form a company (see below), in which case the deadline was 30 June 1991.

Article 1 provides that equal treatment shall extend to those engaged in a self-employed capacity or who are contributing to the pursuit of such an activity as regards those aspects not already covered by Directives 76/207 and 79/7. Article 2 extends the Directive to spouses of self-employed persons if they participate in the activities of the self-employed person by performing the same or ancillary tasks. Such spouses are also entitled to the right to join a contributory social security scheme, if not protected via the self-employed worker's scheme: art 6.

Article 3 defines prohibited discrimination in the same terms as the other directives (direct or indirect discrimination on the grounds of sex by reference in particular to marital or family status) and again provides that this shall be without prejudice to measures protecting women during pregnancy or maternity. Article 4 of the Directive extends the obligation on Member States to eliminate all discrimination contrary to Directive 76/207 to the ability to establish oneself, to equip or extend the business, and to launching or extending any form of self-employed activity with financial facilities. Article 5 provides that Member States must not make it more difficult for spouses to form companies than for those that are unmarried. Article 9 requires Member States to provide access to judicial redress for infringements of the Directive, although this may also include the requirement to apply to competent authorities beforehand.

# Part C

# European Community Economic Law

The internal market is defined under art 14 EC as 'an area without internal frontiers in which the free movement of goods, persons, services and capital is ensured in accordance with the provisions of this Treaty.' The term internal market was introduced by the Single European Act 1986 to replace the term 'common market'. The creation of an internal market develops through the following processes:

1. the creation of a free trade area which involves the parties removing their customs duties and system of quotas as between themselves;
2. the creation of a customs union whereby the parties agree to also apply a common tariff on goods entering from third states – known as the Common Customs Tariff in Community law;
3. the creation of a common market which requires not only the free movement of goods but other factors relevant to the production of goods such as capital and labour; and
4. the creation of full economic union, which requires complete monetary union, with a common currency and a single fiscal policy.

Part III of the EC Treaty contains those provisions designed to facilitate this process. This includes the provisions designed to secure the customs union and the fundamental freedoms to ensure the free movement of goods and other factors of production, such as labour. The latter have already been considered in Part B. As we have seen, they have since been interpreted to have not just economic objectives but social ones too.

Whilst it would be inaccurate to suggest that the free movement of goods is the most important principle, it has been described as one of the fundamental freedoms, and remains one of the strongest reasons why many new States wish to join the European Community.

In essence, the free movement of goods implies that products manufactured or produced in one Member State can move throughout the Community without having to pay customs duties or charges having an equivalent effect to customs duties. They will also not be subject to unfair restrictions when sold in a country, other than the country where they were manufactured or produced.

The purpose of this principle is to promote efficiency in production by removing artificial barriers to trade between Member States, allowing producers in different countries to compete directly with each other. As well as efficiency being improved, consumer choice widens and businesses within the Community improve their position in the world market. This objective is also reinforced by the Community's competition policy, an indispensable element to the creation of a true internal market among the Member States. This will be discussed in detail in Part D.

In order to achieve these objectives it was necessary for the then EEC to begin the process of creating an internal market. This was achieved in the following ways:

1. Article 23 EC provided for the creation of a customs union. This entailed the prohibition of customs duties between Member States on imports and exports and the prohibition of all charges with equivalent effect to customs duties. It also required the creation of a single, common customs tariff in relation to third countries. These aspects are discussed in further detail in Chapter 13.

2. Articles 28 and 29 EC required the elimination of quantitative restrictions and all measures having an equivalent effect. These provisions are discussed in further detail in Chapter 14.

3. Article 31 EC required the adjustment of State monopolies of a commercial character to be accomplished by the end of the transitional period. This would ensure that there was no discrimination in relation to the procurement and marketing of goods between the nationals of the Member States. *Costa* v *ENEL* Case 6/64 [1964] ECR 585 defines such monopolies as those bodies having as their object transactions of a commercial product capable of being the subject of trade between Member States, and who play an effective part in such trade. Such monopolies are not to be prohibited or abolished but 'adjusted' so that they do not operate on a discriminatory basis, which would obstruct the free movement of goods and distort competition. Hence, a State can regulate who sells a product, but not the supply of those products, which must be left free: *Banchero* Case C–387/93 [1995] ECR I–4663. An exclusive right to import or export a particular product will fall within the ambit of art 31. It does not apply to services, which will come within the ambit of art 12 EC; the Treaty provisions on free movement of services (see Chapter 10); or art 82 EC which prohibits abuse of a dominant position: see Chapter 16.

The term 'good' is not defined in the Treaty, nor is the term 'product'. The European Court has held that they include anything capable of a monetary valuation and of being the object of a commercial transaction: *Commission* v *Italy (Re Export Tax on Art Treasures)* Case 7/68 [1968] ECR 423. This will include those goods and materials supplied in relation to providing a service, insofar as their supply is an ends in itself: *Commission* v *Ireland (Re Dundalk Water Supply)* Case 45/87R [1987] 2 CMLR 197 (discussed in further detail in Chapter 14). It will not include those goods provided as part of a service, for example, a ticket for a train or a lottery, since they are covered by those provisions relating to the freedom to provide and receive services: see Chapter 10.

As a general rule, the European Court has interpreted the provisions in this field of Community law in a very strict manner. The exceptions that exist under the Treaty have been given very little scope. This is also an area of considerable judicial activism and some of the most important and influential of ECJ decisions. One theme that we will witness in the case law is that the European Court will not merely examine the name of a measure or the reason why it was introduced, but will concentrate on the actual or potential effect that the measure may have on the internal market.

It is not only the European Court that has been busy in this field of Community law. It became clear reasonably early on in the development of the common market, that there was, in addition to the above rules, a need for the Community to actively seek to harmonise Community rules, particularly since many of these rules were designed, at national level, to protect certain interests.

## Completing the single market

Such a programme was adopted under the Single European Act 1986. The legislative process was speeded up by not requiring unanimity, but qualified majority voting, when it came to harmonising or approximating the laws of the Member States that had the object of establishing and functioning the internal market: art 95 EC. The deadline for the achievement of the internal market was set as 31 December 1992.

The internal market programme was designed to remove the major physical, technical and fiscal barriers to trade. The programme involved the adoption of 282 Community measures designed to remove barriers to trade in the area of customs tax, public procurement, capital movements, company law, employment, transport and safety standards. The existing disparities in the national laws in these areas were seen as being the primary impediment to the free flow of goods.

From a legal perspective, the greatest obstacle to trade was the existence of many technical barriers. These included: the diversity of national regulations and standards for testing products for the safety of the consumer; the duplication of product testing and certification (for example, in the pharmaceutical industry); and the reluctance of public authorities in certain Member States to open procurement procedures to the nationals of other Member States.

Substantial Community legislation on the harmonisation of technical standards, mostly in the form of directives, has been passed to approximate technical standards on products ranging from the alcohol content of certain wines to the level of noise emissions from vehicles. The most heavily Community-regulated sectors are the food and drink, chemical and pharmaceutical industries.

It should be pointed out that the internal market programme was not solely confined to the practical realisation of the free movement of goods. Measures have also been enacted in relation to the free movement of persons, services and capital. However, of the measures adopted under the programme, a large number were designed to procure the free movement of goods.

As noted above, the target set for the enactment of all 282 proposals was 31 December 1992. While the Council was unable to adopt all the measures proposed by the Commission under this programme, around 95 per cent of this total were enacted. Further, while the record varies from Member State to Member State, the vast majority of measures adopted have been implemented into national law.

Article 14 EC does not have direct effect, notwithstanding that the programme was due to be completed by December 1992. Consequently, the obligation to implement the measures required to complete the internal market programme cannot be enforced at the instance of private individuals: see *INPS* v *Baglieri* Case C–297/92 [1993] ECR 5211.

Council Regulation 2679/98 was adopted to remove further obstacles to free movement within the internal market, particularly in respect of goods. Under the system established by the Regulation, when an obstacle occurs or a threat thereof emerges, any Member State that has relevant information can transmit this to the Commission. The Commission will then immediately transmit to the Member States that information and any information from any other source that it may consider relevant. If the Commission considers that the obstacle exists, it will notify the Member State concerned and request it to take all necessary and proportionate measures. The Member States shall, within five working days of receipt of the text, either inform the Commission of the steps it has taken, or intends to take, or communicate a reasoned submission as to why there is no obstacle constituting a breach of arts 28–30 EC. (For discussion of these provisions see Chapter 14.)

In addition, Member States undertook to do all within their power to maintain the free movement of goods and to deal rapidly with actions that seriously disrupt free movement. They must ensure that effective review procedures are available for any person who has been harmed as a result of breaching the rules on the free movement of goods.

The process of expanding and enhancing the internal market continues, with, in particular, continued harmonisation and constant revision needed of technical barriers to trade. The future for this area of Community law may be one that continues to involve controversial issues; issues ranging from the British beef scandal over 'Mad Cow' disease to the creation of the Single Currency, a development that eliminates monetary barriers to trade thereby freeing the internal market further. Such issues remain hotly debated, often because of the negative impact they are assumed to have on the concept of national sovereignty, but perhaps because they also impact greatly on the lives, thoughts and general fears of the citizens of Europe.

This Part will examine the following:

1. the creation of the customs union, with discussion of the Common Commercial Policy and the external trading relations of the Community, the Common Customs Tariff, the prohibition on customs duties and measures of equivalent effect, and the prohibition on discriminatory internal taxation in Chapter 13; and
2. the elimination of quantitative restrictions and measures having equivalent effect to quantitative restrictions and the ways in which they may potentially be justifiable in Chapter 14.

# 13

# The Free Movement of Goods I: The External Trading Relations of the European Community and the Customs Union

13.1   Introduction

13.2   The Common Commercial Policy

13.3   Trade protection laws

13.4   The Common Customs Tariff

13.5   The elimination of customs duties and charges having equivalent effect

13.6   The prohibition on discriminatory taxation – art 90 EC

## 13.1 Introduction

The customs union was achieved by two primary measures: first, the adoption of a Common Customs Tariff in relation to third countries and, second, the prohibition of customs duties on imports and exports and all measures of equivalent effect to a customs duty: art 23. In addition, a Common Commercial Policy (CCP) was to be established in relation to third countries: art 3(1)(b) and arts 131–134 EC. This chapter will also consider the powers the Community has to impose measures on imports from non-EC countries to protect industry and commerce within the Community from unfair foreign trade practices.

## 13.2 The Common Commercial Policy

The Common Commercial Policy (CCP) is the Community's commercial instrument for regulating its trade relations with other non-Community states. Article 133 EC is the constitutional basis for this instrument and provides:

'The Common Commercial Policy shall be based on uniform principles, particularly in regard to changes in tariff rates, the conclusion of tariff and trade agreements, the achievement of uniformity in measures of liberalisation, export policy and measures to protect trade such as those to be taken in the case of dumping or subsidies.'

This list of relevant subjects is not exhaustive; the Community's competence in matters covered by the CCP extends to all matters within the purposes and aims of the Community.

The procedure for the formulation of the CCP is similar to the normal decision-making processes within the Community, with the principal exception that the European Commission is responsible for conducting negotiations with third States. While the Commission almost invariably has its negotiating mandate set by the Member States, on occasions there have been splits between the Commission and the Member States in the conduct of negotiations.

The creation of the CCP was a primary goal of the EC Treaty: see art 3(1)(b) EC. The Treaty transfers exclusive authority to formulate trade policy to the Community institutions. Individual Member States no longer retain authority to act in matters in which the Community has adopted measures in pursuit of the CCP: see *Donkerwolcke* v *Procureur de la République* Case 41/76 [1976] ECR 1921. This means that Member States cannot legislate in fields covered by Community measures nor can they enter into international obligations that would restrict the powers of the Community.

Despite the expiry of the transition period for the completion of the CCP, Member States have continued to express reluctance to transfer complete authority to the Community to formulate a comprehensive and coherent commercial policy. This reluctance may be attributed to two factors. First, the institutional structure for the formulation and administration of the policy is inadequate. Second, the actual objectives of the policy are fragmented and not stated with a sufficient degree of precision in the Treaty to encourage a transfer of competence to the Community.

The consequence is that the CCP is not a continuous, unbroken superstructure. It consists of a complex framework of international agreements and Community measures, and in those areas of policy not yet covered by Community measures Member States may continue to act: see *Bulk Oil* v *Sun International* [1986] 2 All ER 744. The failure to enact Community measures to cover all aspects of the policy has left loopholes for Member States to restrict, prohibit or limit imports from non-EC countries. This practice has been considered by the European Court to be lawful in a number of cases: see *Tezi Textiel* v *Commission* Case 59/84 [1986] ECR 887.

Neither the SEA nor the TEU significantly amended the CCP provisions of the Treaty. The ToA amended art 133 EC to include the conferral of express competence to conclude international agreements on services and intellectual property.

## 13.3  Trade protection laws

The Community also has a number of powers to impose measures on imports from non-EC countries in order to protect industry and commerce within the Community from unfair foreign trade practices. In brief, these measures may be classified into four categories:

1. anti-dumping measures;
2. anti-subsidy measures;
3. safeguard measures; and
4. measures under the Trade Barrier Regulation.

### Anti-dumping measures

The Community authorities are able to impose anti-dumping duties on foreign products that are deemed to have been dumped within the Community and which have caused injury to a Community industry: Council Regulation 384/96. A foreign product has been dumped inside the Community if it has been introduced into the internal market at a price less than the comparable price for the product in the country of origin.

A dumping complaint may be lodged by any legal person (an individual, firm or company) or by an association not having legal personality acting on behalf of a Community industry. Investigations of such complaints must normally be concluded within one year from the initiation of the complaint.

The basic substantive elements of an anti-dumping investigation are the existence of dumping, injury and 'Community interests' requiring intervention.

The procedure for determining the existence of dumping in the Community is deceptively simply. It involves four basic steps:

1. the determination of the normal value of the goods on the market of their country of origin;
2. the determination of the price at which the goods are sold in the Community after adjustments;
3. comparison of the normal value with the Community price; and
4. the calculation of the 'margin of dumping' (the normal price minus the export price).

Normal value is the price of the goods in the country of origin, while the export price is the price of the goods inside the Community. The margin of dumping is the difference between these two figures and is also the measure of the anti-dumping duty, which will be levied to neutralise the unfair competitive advantage enjoyed by the foreign product.

In addition to establishing the existence of dumped products, it is also necessary to prove that these products have caused material injury to an industry within the

Community. In other words, the efficiency, productivity or profitability of the Community industry must be damaged by the imports.

Finally, before anti-dumping duties may be imposed, it must be established that the interests of the Community call for such intervention. No list of Community interests is provided in the basic Regulation. The concept will cover a wide range of factors, the most important being the protection of the consumer; protection of foreign investment; employment; and the interests of Community users of the imported products in production of other goods.

If all these elements are established after the Commission's investigations, the imported product may be subject to anti-dumping duties which are assessed on each product according to their country of origin.

## Anti-subsidy measures

Anti-subsidy duties are imposed on foreign products that have benefited from subsidies from foreign governments during their manufacture, distribution or export, but again, only if these products cause injury to Community industries producing similar goods. The authority under which the Community imposes such duties is Council Regulation 2026/97.

Again, anti-subsidy measures are imposed only after a Commission investigation. The investigation must establish that:

1. a subsidy has been paid by a foreign government to the producers of the goods;
2. material injury is being caused by these imported goods to a Community industry; and
3. Community interests call for intervention.

Anti-subsidy and anti-dumping investigations are similar in their nature, with the exception that in an anti-subsidy investigation the illegitimate practice being countered is subsidisation, whereas in anti-dumping the unfair practice is the dumping itself.

## Safeguard measures

Imports into the Community may also be subject to safeguard measures under the relevant provisions of Council Regulation 3285/94. If foreign products are being imported into the Community in such increased quantities as to cause, or threaten to cause, serious injury to a Community industry, safeguard measures may be imposed to protect that industry, regardless of the cause or source of the increase in the volume of imports. The standard is that of serious risk, not material injury or merely injury. This is a higher threshold than that in the case of anti-dumping and anti-subsidy investigations.

If the existence of increased imports and serious injury are both established the

Community may impose additional duties, tariffs or quotas on the importation of such products to protect Community industry.

## Measures under the Trade Barrier Regulation

The Commission is empowered to investigate allegations of obstacles to trade erected by non-EC countries under the Trade Barrier Regulation: Regulation 3286/94. Under this Regulation companies or industries may lodge a complaint with the Commission requesting the examination of foreign trade practices that impede EC exports. If these allegations are found true, and if the complainant can show injury, the Commission is required to enter into discussions with the third State with a view to removing the obstacle to trade. If a negotiated settlement proves ineffective, the matter may be brought to the attention of the World Trade Organisation's dispute settlement body for resolution.

## 13.4 The Common Customs Tariff

As provided for under arts 26–27 EC, goods entering the Community from non-Community states are subject to the Common Customs Tariff (CCT), which is a comprehensive Community regime to regulate the levying of duties on non-EC goods. The CCT supersedes the individual tariff schedules and customs laws of the Member States, although national customs officials enforce its provisions. The Community has exclusive competence to regulate the CCT and measures enacted by the Member States that conflict with its provisions are void: see *Sociaal Fonds voor de Diamantarbeiders* v *NV Indiamex* Cases 37 and 38/73 [1973] ECR 1609.

The CCT specifies a particular tariff for each product imported into the Community, according to its description. These take three forms.

1. ad valorem tariffs are calculated as a percentage of the value of the goods imported and are the more common form of tariff;
2. fixed tariffs apply a duty rate according to the quantity or volume of the products imported regardless of their value; and
3. mixed tariffs are applied by a formula that combines both fixed and ad valorem elements.

The tariff nomenclature for each product is set out in Council Regulation 2658/87, as amended by Commission Regulation 2261/98. The rules setting out the actual procedure, determination of origin and valuation are contained in the Community's Customs Code which is Council Regulation 2913/92, as supplemented by Commission Regulation 2454/93.

Rates of duty are assessed according to the origin of the imported product. Where the country of origin is a member of the World Trade Organisation (WTO), the Most-Favoured-Nation (MFN) rate is applicable, unless the country benefits from a preferred rate specified for developing countries under the Lomé Convention scheme or the General System of Preference (GSP). If the country of origin is not a member of the WTO or entitled to preferred treatment, the standard rate of duty applies. Rates of duty may be amended on a country-by-country basis by the negotiation of a free trade or association agreement.

Liability to duties depends on the classification of the goods in the scheme of the CCT, which in turn depends on the description given to the goods. The nomenclatures stated in the CCT do not invariably correspond to all types of imported products or goods. In such cases, products that are not covered by any tariff heading must be classified under the heading for the products for which they are most analogous. This assessment is made not only on the physical characteristics of the goods but also their intended purpose and commercial value: see *Huber* v *Hauptzollamt Fränkfurt-am-Main-Flughafen* Case 291/87 [1990] 2 CMLR 159.

Where customs duties are calculated on an ad valorem basis, the value attributed to the goods is important to determine liability. The fundamental principle is that goods should be given their actual commercial value at the port of entry into the European Union. This is known as the 'arm's length sales price'. Where an export sale is made to a Community purchaser and the parties are commercially unrelated, the invoice price represents the value of the goods as long as:

1. the purchaser remains free to dispose of the goods at their discretion without restrictions other than those imposed by law;
2. no additional payment is required under the transaction; and
3. no part of the consideration involved remains unquantifiable: see *Brown Boveri & Cie AG* v *Hauptzollamt Mannheim* Case C–79/89 [1993] 1 CMLR 814.

As noted above, determination of the origin of the goods is essential for the proper application of the CCT, since rates vary according to the country that the goods originated from. For this purpose, the country of origin is the state that produced the goods and not the country from which the goods were shipped to the EU.

Council Regulation 2913/92, as amended, specifies the general rules for establishing the origin of goods. Goods originate in the country in which they were wholly obtained or produced or, alternatively, where the last economically justified and substantial processing occurred. Goods wholly produced in a territory include minerals and agricultural commodities. Manufactured goods present greater problems in this respect.

In general, the country of origin of manufactured goods is either where the last substantial economic process occurred to them, resulting in a transformation of the component parts, or where a major stage of manufacturing occurred. The Regulation specifically prohibits the assessment of origin based on economic processes undertaken simply for the purposes of obtaining a lower duty rate. The Commission has enacted a number of regulations to clarify this distinction. Further, the European Court has subjected these regulations to a test of objectivity and in at least one case has held that a stricter concept of origin was applied than was necessary in the circumstances: see *SR Industries* v *Administration des Douanes* Case 91/86 [1988] ECR 378.

Article 24(1) EC provides that products from a third country shall be considered to be in free circulation in the Community if the import formalities connected with the CCT have been satisfied. Thus, they are considered to be in free circulation if:

1. the relevant import formalities have been completed;
2. any customs duties having an equivalent effect have been levied; and
3. the goods have not benefited from a total or partial drawback of such duties or charges.

According to art 23(2) EC, once non-EC goods are in free circulation they may not be subject to quantitative restrictions, or measures having an equivalent effect for the purposes of intra-Community trade, if they cross the border of one Member State into the territory of another: *Grandes Distilleries Paureux* v *Directeur des Services Fiscaux* Case 86/78 [1979] ECR 975 (see Chapter 14). This has significant consequences – most importantly, no additional import requirements may be imposed on goods originating from third States if they are in free circulation in another Member State.

## 13.5 The elimination of customs duties and charges having equivalent effect

### Customs duties

The six original Member States of the Community agreed to reduce customs duties among them in progressive phases immediately after the EEC Treaty came into effect. This involved a series of staggered reductions in the duties that were applicable at that time, eventually culminating in the elimination of all duties, on both import and export transactions, on 1 July 1968.

The nine Member States that have subsequently joined the Community have been required, as a condition of membership, to eliminate all customs duties between them and other Member States over negotiated transitional periods. Any new members in the future will be similarly obligated to remove such barriers to trade. The exact terms of these reductions are specified in the treaties of accession entered into by these States with the Community. Hence, the last remaining customs duties for intra-Community trade, in respect of the accessions of Spain and Portugal, were removed on 1 January 1993. Austria, Finland and Sweden were given no additional transition time to remove customs duties because these were to have been eliminated as part of the EEA Agreement. Member States were also required not to re-introduce any customs duties on imports or exports of goods passing between Community States. The original provisions made distinctions between both imports and exports and existing and new duties, but this has since been removed. Consequently the main Treaty provision in this context is art 25 EC which provides that:

> 'Customs duties on imports and exports and charges having equivalent effect shall be prohibited between Member States. This prohibition shall also apply to customs duties of a fiscal nature.'

This article has direct effect: *Van Gend en Loos* v *Netherlands* Case 26/62 [1963] ECR 1 (see Chapter 8). It provides no derogation and is interpreted very strictly by the Court. For example, in *Sociaal Fonds voor de Diamantarbeiders* v *Brachfeld and Chougol Diamond Co* Cases 2 and 3/69 [1969] ECR 211, the Belgian authorities imposed a duty on diamonds in order to raise money to benefit Belgian diamond workers. Belgium defended itself by stating that the duty was not imposed for protectionist reasons and therefore art 25 was not applicable; Belgium is not a diamond producer. It was held that the duty came within art 25 and was prohibited:

> 'It follows ... that customs duties are prohibited independently of any consideration of the purpose for which they were introduced and the destination of the revenue obtained therefrom. The justification for this prohibition is based on the fact that any pecuniary charge – however small – imposed on the goods by reason of the fact that they cross a frontier constitutes an obstacle to the movement of such goods.'

Therefore, it is irrelevant how low the charge is, or its purpose: see also *Commission* v *Italy* Case 7/68 [1968] ECR 423, concerning what was then art 16 EEC, now covered by art 25 EC, where it was emphasised that the application of the article depends upon the effect of the charge or duty and not its intended purpose.

The case of *Société Cadi Surgélés* v *Ministre des Finances* Case C–126/94 [1996] ECR I–5647 identifies that this prohibition also applies to additional charges on goods imported into a particular region, but which originated from a third country.

## Charges having equivalent effect

Member States are also obliged to eliminate all 'charges having an equivalent effect to customs duties', again both on imports and exports, and also refrain from re-introducing such charges on intra-Community transactions.

No definition of charges having an equivalent effect can be found in the EC Treaty and interpretation of this term has been left to the European Court of Justice. In *Commission* v *Italy (Re Statistical Levy)* Case 24/68 [1969] ECR 193 the Court defined the term as follows:

> 'Any pecuniary charge, however small and whatever its designation and mode of application, which is imposed unilaterally on domestic and foreign goods by reason of the fact that they cross a frontier, and which is not a customs duty in the strict sense, constitutes a charge ... even if it is not imposed for the benefit of the state, is not discriminatory or protective in effect and if the product on which the charge is imposed is not in competition with any domestic product.'

This definition has been repeatedly stated by the Court, and requires no reference to the purpose behind the imposition of the charge, or where the revenue is to go: see *Procureur du Roi* v *Dassonville* Case 8/74 [1974] ECR 837 and *Sociaal Fonds voor de Diamantarbeiders* (above). In the latter case the Court held:

> 'It follows from the system as a whole and from the general and absolute nature of the prohibition of any customs duty applicable to goods moving between Member States that customs duties are prohibited independently of any consideration of the purpose for which they were introduced and the destination of the revenue obtained therefrom.'

Consequently, there is no requirement to consider the name of the charge; the reason behind the introduction of the charge, since it is irrelevant whether or not it was created to achieve a protectionist goal; or whether it is applied in a discriminatory manner. The Court will instead examine the effect that the measure has. In other words, is it imposed because of the fact that the goods or products cross a frontier? The Court will not be influenced by the name given to the charge. Hence, in *Commission* v *Luxembourg (Re Import Duties on Gingerbread)* Cases 2 and 3/62 [1963] CMLR 199, the Court examined a charge on imported gingerbread. Luxembourg claimed this was a 'compensatory' measure designed to offset the disadvantage domestic producers of gingerbread faced because they had to pay a high internal, domestic tax on rye. The Court concluded that the effect of the compensatory measure, albeit indirectly, was equivalent to a customs duty. The Court expressed a Community definition of such equivalent charges, based on their effects rather than their terminology or the manner in which they were imposed. To do otherwise would be to permit unilateral imposition of such compensatory measures, which in turn would damage free competition and the internal market.

The charge may take the form of a number of things but is often called a 'tax'. If the measure is a genuine tax then it will be governed by art 90 EC: see section 13.6. A genuine tax is defined as one that relates 'to a general system of internal dues applied systematically to categories of products in accordance with objective criteria irrespective of the origin of the products': *Commission* v *France (Re Levy on Reprographic Machines)* Case 90/79 [1981] ECR 283. Any genuine taxes will not breach art 25, but may be examined under art 90 to assess whether they breach Community law, which prohibits discriminatory taxation. Conversely, in *Fratelli Cucchi* v *Avez SpA* Case 77/76 [1977] ECR 987 the Court held that internal taxation would constitute a charge equivalent to a customs duty if:

> '... it has the sole purpose of financing activities for the specific advantage of the taxed domestic product; if the taxed product and the domestic product benefiting from it are the same; and if the charges imposed on the domestic product are made good in full.'

It appears that a charge levied on an importer for a service is a type of measure that may not breach art 25. However, to come within these terms the service must provide something of tangible benefit to the importer. Hence, in *Commission* v *Italy* (above) the Court examined a charge placed by the Italian authorities on exports which they claimed permitted them to collect statistical data to aid in assessing trade patterns. This information, the Italian government claimed, would then aid importers of products into Italy. The Court held:

'Even if the competitive position of importers and exporters were to be particularly improved ... the statistics still constitute an advantage so general, and so difficult to assess, that the disputed charge cannot be regarded as the consideration for a specific benefit actually conferred.'

The charge must not be based on the value of the products or goods being imported and must be no more than the actual value of the service provided, or be proportionate: *Commission* v *Denmark* Case 158/82 [1983] ECR 3573 and *Rewe-Zentralfinanze GmbH* v *Direktor der Landwirtschaftskammer Westfalen-Lippe* Case 39/73 [1973] ECR 1039. Whether this is the case will be a matter for the national courts. In order to be permitted to impose the charge for the service on the importer the following should be noted.

1. A charge for the service of an inspection test in the general interest (for example, health, safety or quality purposes) or an administrative formality will not be justified, regardless of the body providing the service, be it customs officials or private firms: see *Rewe-Zentralfinanz* (above) and *Dubois et Fils SA and General Cargo Services SA* v *Garoner Exploitation SA* Case C–16/94 [1995] ECR I–2421. A medical examination was considered in the case of *Bresciani* v *Amministrazione Italiana delle Finanze Case* 87/75 [1976] ECR 129. In this case the Court was requested to examine whether a charge imposed on raw cowhides as part of a compulsory veterinary and public health inspection was a charge having an equivalent effect to a customs duty. The Court held:

'The activity of the administration of the state intended to maintain a public health inspection system imposed in the general interest cannot be regarded as a service rendered to the importer such as to justify the imposition of a public charge.'

2. If such inspections are permissible under Community law a charge cannot be imposed since this will not be considered as a service for the benefit of the importer: *Commission* v *Belgium* Case 314/82 [1984] ECR 1543.
3. A charge may be imposed if the service provided is mandatory under Community law. However, the charge levied must be proportionate to the actual cost of providing the service: *Bauhuis* v *Netherlands* Case 46/76 [1977] ECR 5. In this case a fee was imposed by Dutch authorities for a veterinary inspection on pigs, which was in part to meet requirements under Community law. It was concluded that this was permissible since the test was mandatory under Community law, but that the charge, to not fall under art 25, also had to be proportionate to the cost of actually providing the inspection. The same conclusion was reached in *Commission* v *The Netherlands* Case 89/76 [1977] ECR 1355 on a charge levied for plant inspections conducted under requirements stemming from the International Plant Protection Convention 1951, an international agreement to which all Member States were party.

In *Commission* v *Germany (Re Animals Inspection Fees)* Case 18/87 [1988] ECR 5427 the Court examined a charge imposed by the German authorities on imported live animals. Inspections of such animals were obligatory under Council Directive 81/389 and the charges were imposed to cover costs. The Court cited the cases of *Bauhuis* and *Commission* v *The Netherlands* and held that such fees may not be charges having an equivalent effect to a customs duty if the following strict conditions are satisfied:

a) they do not exceed the actual costs of the inspection in connection with which they are charged;
b) the inspections in question are obligatory and uniform for all the products concerned in the Community;
c) they are prescribed by Community law in the general interest of the Community; and
d) they promote the free movement of goods, in particular by neutralising obstacles which could arise from unilateral measures of inspection.

The Court will sometimes examine, along with whether the charge is within this exception from art 25, whether the charge is a tax coming within the prohibition on discriminatory taxation under art 90. The inter-relationship between these two provisions can be seen in *Haahr Petroleum Ltd* v *Abenra Havn* Case C–90/94 [1997] ECR I–4085, in which the Court examined a Danish import surcharge of 40 per cent levied on imported goods. This was imposed in addition to goods duties, and applied to all imported goods loaded or unloaded within commercial ports or deep-water channels to those ports. The Danish government argued that this was a charge equivalent to a customs duty imposed on importers for the service of using Danish commercial ports and general facilities. The Court concluded that the levy was part of a general system of internal taxation and, even if it was lawful under art 25, still had to comply with the prohibition against discriminatory taxation under art 90 EC: see section 13.6.

Non-discriminatory charges are treated differently under Community law. In other words, charges imposed on products, regardless of their origin, may not breach art 25. In order to benefit from this, the charge must be identical (ie imposed under identical criteria and by the same body: see *Marimex SpA* v *Italian Finance Administration* Case 29/72 [1972] ECR 1309) regardless of the origin of the product it is being imposed on. It must also be part of a general system of taxation and the proceeds from the charge must not be used to benefit only the domestic product. If this is the case the charge will be considered as a fiscal measure and will instead come within the ambit of art 90 EC: see section 13.6.

Finally, it should be noted that there are no derogations for imposing a customs duty or equivalent charge, unlike the imposition of a quantitative restriction or measure of equivalent effect (see Chapter 14): *Commission* v *Italy (Re Export Tax on Art Treasures)* Case 7/68 [1968] ECR 423. It should also be noted that the payment of a sum breaching art 25 will be recoverable under the specific conditions and national law of the Member State imposing the duty: *Amministrazione delle Finanze dello Stato* v *San Giorgio* Case 199/82 [1983] ECR 3595. National laws in this context must not make recovery impossible or excessively difficult: *Dilexport Srl* v *Amministrazione delle Finanze dello Stato* Case C–343/96 [1999] ECR I–579. There is one exception to this, and that is when the charge has been passed on to the consumer, by increasing the price of the product. In such cases, the trader may have made up their loss and not have suffered any damage and is, therefore, not entitled to any repay of the charge since that would constitute unjust enrichment.

## 13.6 The prohibition on discriminatory taxation – art 90 EC

Article 90 EC, which has direct effect (*Mölkerei-Zentrale Westfalen/Lippe GmbH* v *Hauptzollamt Paderborn* Case 28/67 [1968] ECR 143), provides:

> 'No Member States shall impose, directly or indirectly, on the products of other Member States any internal taxation of any kind in excess of that imposed directly or indirectly on similar domestic products.
>
> Furthermore, no Member State shall impose on the products of other Member States any internal taxation of such a nature as to afford indirect protection to other products'.

This measure supplements those that provide for no customs duties or charges of equivalent effect. Whilst such levies are prohibited when a product crosses a frontier, as previously discussed, the prohibition on discriminatory internal taxation prevents such products from incurring additional charges once within the territory of the Member State.

The obligation on Member States is not that they must adopt a uniform system of internal taxation, but that whatever system they do adopt should be one that is entirely non-discriminatory (including the manner in which it is imposed and collected) in its treatment of domestic and imported goods. For example, *Hansen* v *Hauptzollamt Flensburg* Case 148/77 [1978] ECR 1787, in which German tax relief was not provided equally for imported products.

Article 90 also makes reference to the prohibition extending to indirectly discriminatory taxation. This includes a tax which, whilst appearing non-discriminatory, actually has the effect in practice of being discriminatory on imports. (The concept of indirect discrimination is a recurrent theme in Community law, and one that has been discussed in the context of equal pay: see Chapter 12.) Such indirectly discriminatory taxation was defined in the case of *Humblot* v *Directeur des Services Fiscaux* Case 112/84 [1985] ECR 1367 as a system that although 'embodies no formal distinction based on the origin of the products ... manifestly exhibits discriminatory or protective features' contrary to art 90.

Indirectly discriminatory taxation may be objectively justified, and therefore not be held in breach of art 90. The test that the Member State must prove has been complied with has been explained by the European Court in the following terms:

'... Community law does not restrict the freedom of each Member State to lay down tax arrangements which differentiate between certain products on the basis of objective criteria, such as the nature of the raw materials used or the production process employed. Such differentiation is compatible with the requirements of the Treaty and its secondary law and if the detailed rules are such as to avoid any discrimination, direct or indirect, in regard to imports from other Member States or any form of protection of competing products': *Chemical Farmaceutici* v *DAF SpA* Case 140/79 [1981] ECR 1.

Objective justification may include reference to social as well as economic objectives: *Commission* v *Greece* Case C–132/88 [1990] ECR I–1567. In order to be objectively justifiable, the measure must comply with the following, cumulative requirements:

1. the tax must be based on objective criteria;
2. it must be non-discriminatory; and
3. it must not be protectionist.

On closer examination of art 90, it can be seen that there are two scenarios covered by the prohibition. The first is provided by art 90(1), which examines discriminatory taxation in relation to similar products. Article 90(2), on the other hand, prohibits discriminatory taxation not as between similar products, but products that are in competition with each other. Thus, they need not in actual fact be similar but there will be competition between them:

'The function of the second paragraph of [art 90] is to cover ... all forms of indirect tax protection in the case of products which, without being similar within the meaning of the first paragraph, are nevertheless in competition, even partial, indirect or potential, with certain products of the importing country': *Commission* v *France* Case 168/78 [1980] ECR 347.

Whether the first or second paragraphs will apply can be a difficult assessment, and the national court will have to carefully examine the facts of the case before it. The European Court itself has experienced some problems in identifying whether the products concerned are in competition with each other and whether art 90(2) has been breached, but has developed some general guidelines to establish whether this is the case. These are as follows:

1. To examine whether there is a competitive relationship between the products. This should be assessed with reference to the inter-changeability of the products. In other words, would a consumer consider the goods as substitutable – if they could not have one would they choose the other? However, this must be seen in the context of the particular time of the facts, since consumer choices may change over time: *Commission* v *United Kingdom* Case 170/78 [1980] ECR 415.
2. Analysis should then be made of whether the tax system imposed is protective of the domestic product.

Thus, in *Commission* v *Italy* Case 184/85 [1987] ECR 2013 the Court was required to examine an Italian consumption tax on fruit. Whilst Italy itself produced large quantities of a wide range of fruits, it did not produce significant quantities of bananas which were imported primarily from France. Other fruit were generally not subject to the consumption tax but bananas were. The Court concluded that the products in question, fruit and bananas, were not similar because bananas did not have the thirst-quenching properties of other fruit and because consumers perceived bananas to have a better nutritional value. The Court then went on to examine whether there was a competitive relationship between the two products, which it concluded there was, since consumers considered bananas as an additional choice in the general fruit market. On further examination the Court concluded that the tax system imposed was protective of the domestic product since the level of tax imposed on the bananas was half of its import cost, whereas most other fruit was not subject to the tax at all. This was concluded to be clearly protectionist, and a breach of art 90(2): see also *John Walker* v *Ministeriet for Skatter* Case 243/84 [1986] ECR 833.

# 14

# The Free Movement of Goods II: The Prohibition on Quantitative Restrictions and Equivalent Measures

14.1 Introduction

14.2 Defining QRs and MEQRs

14.3 Justifying QRs and distinctly applied MEQRs

14.4 Indistinctly applied (non-discriminatory) MEQRs

14.5 Application of the *Cassis de Dijon* rule of reason

14.6 Applying *Cassis* – the problems

14.7 Selling arrangements

## 14.1 Introduction

This aspect of Community law attempts to remove non-fiscal barriers to trade. A quantitative restriction is a national measure designed to restrain the volume or amount of imports or exports. This is achieved, not by artificially raising the direct cost of importing or exporting (as would be the case with a tariff or duty), but by placing direct or indirect limits on the physical quantity of imports or exports that may enter or leave a country.

Quantitative restrictions were to be gradually phased out between the original six Member States and new Member States must observe the same obligation. Article 28 EC applies this obligation to imports, whilst art 29 EC provides for the same prohibition in relation to exports. Article 30 EC provides for express Treaty derogations, although, as we shall discover, this is one field of Community law the European Court has been extremely proactive in developing.

The explicit prohibition on the introduction of quantitative restrictions (QRs) and measures equivalent to quantitative restrictions (MEQRs) has been consistently broken by the Member States, particularly by imposing such measures on imports. For example, in 1978 the United Kingdom restricted imports of Dutch potatoes, whilst in the same year France imposed an embargo on sheepmeat from the United Kingdom: see *Commission* v *United Kingdom (Re Imports of Dutch Potatoes)* Case 231/78 [1979] ECR 1447 and *Commission* v *France (Re Sheepmeat from the United Kingdom)* Case 232/78 [1979] ECR 2729. Such violations continue today and this area of Community law has generated a considerable amount of litigation, in no small part due to the fact that the Treaty articles have direct effect: see *Ianelli & Volpi SpA* v *Meroni* Case 74/76 [1977] ECR 557.

The obligations in arts 28 and 29 EC rest on the Member States not to adopt such 'measures'. This has, however, been given a broad interpretation (similar to that witnessed under the direct effect of directives: see Chapter 7) and will extend to legislative, judicial and administrative bodies, as well as semi-public bodies that exercise powers conferred from public law. The body does not need to be able to make binding measures. For example, the definition will extend to those bodies that have a regulatory function and whose powers are conferred by statute: *R* v *Royal Pharmaceutical Society of Great Britain, ex parte Association of Pharmaceutical Importers* Cases 266 and 267/87 [1989] ECR 1295. In *Commission* v *Ireland (Re Buy Irish Campaign)* Case 249/81 [1982] ECR 4005 the Court examined whether the Irish Goods Council was the State for the purposes of applying art 28. The Court identified that the Irish government:

> '... appoints the members of the Management Committee of the Irish Goods Council, grants it public subsidies which cover the greater part of its expenses and ... defines the aims and the broad outline of the campaign conducted by that institution ... In the circumstances the Irish government cannot rely on the fact that the campaign was conducted by a private company in order to escape any liability it may have under the provisions of the Treaty.'

In ascertaining whether or not a particular body exercises sufficient authority to establish measures having an equivalent effect to a quantitative restriction, the Court suggests consideration of, inter alia, the legal status of the body; the requirement of mandatory enrolment; the power to enact rules of ethics; the existence of disciplinary powers; and the sanctions that may be invoked in the event of failure to respect the rules and regulations of the organisation.

It also appears that the Member State is not simply responsible for refraining from introducing any QR or MEQR. The Member States must also take positive action should they find that the free movement of goods is being restricted by, for example, their own nationals demonstrating and blockading the free movement of goods. This obligation extends from a combination of arts 28 and 29 EC and art 10 EC, which requires Member States to take all necessary and appropriate measures to ensure that the objectives of the Treaty are fulfilled: see *Commission* v *France* Case C–265/95 [1997] ECR I–6959.

The academic, Steiner, suggests that the Member States are only actually required to react proportionately, given the circumstances and the resources available and that they should not be required to do more. However, the additional burden on the Member State is that they may be potentially liable for damages under the principle of State liability: see Chapter 6. This potential may promote a more positive reaction in such circumstances, and, indeed, greater adherence to the rules in arts 28 and 29 generally: see *Brasserie du Pêcheur* v *Federal Republic of Germany; R* v *Secretary of State for Transport, ex parte Factortame Ltd and Others* Joined Cases C–46 and 48/93 [1996] ECR I–1029.

## 14.2 Defining QRs and MEQRs

A QR was defined in the case of *Riseria Luigi Geddo* v *Ente Nazionale Risi* Case 2/73 [1973] ECR 865 as 'measures which amount to a total or partial restraint of ... imports, exports or goods in transit'.

The popular terms given to such measures will include a ban (or embargo), such as that imposed on pornographic materials in *R* v *Henn and Darby* Case 34/79 [1979] ECR 3795. A partial restraint will often take the form of a quota.

An MEQR has proved far more difficult to define. The Commission presented its view of what constitutes an MEQR in Directive 70/50, but it provides a guideline only and has no direct effect. Articles 2 and 3 provides examples of measures that may be considered MEQRs, but they also distinguish between two different types of MEQR.

The first type of MEQR is described under art 2(1) as 'measures other than those applicable equally to domestic or imported products' and 'which hinder imports, which could otherwise take place'. These MEQRs are sometimes described as distinctly applicable or discriminatory MEQRs. This is because the measure will not apply equally to the import and the domestic product, either by placing the imported product at a disadvantage, or by promoting the domestic product to the detriment of the imported product.

The second type of MEQR is described under art 3 as one that is 'equally applicable to domestic and imported products', often known as an indistinctly applied MEQR, or as one that is non-discriminatory. However, such MEQRs are in breach of the Treaty only where 'the restrictive effect of such measures on the free movement of goods exceeds the effects intrinsic to trade rules'. This will occur when 'the restrictive effects on the free movement of goods are out of proportion to their purpose' or when 'the same objective can be attained by other measures which are less of a hindrance to trade'.

Actual examples of MEQRs that may be imposed by the Member State are provided in the Directive, although the list is non-exhaustive. Distinctly applicable MEQRs include the following examples: making the price of the imported product less favourable; minimum or maximum selling prices for imported products; payment conditions for imported products; giving preference to domestic goods thereby hindering the purchase of imported goods; limiting publicity in respect of imported goods only; prescribing conditions on imports that are more costly or difficult to comply with than those applied on domestic products; specifying time limits for imported goods that are excessive; totally or partially excluding the use of national facilities or equipment for imported products, or providing them only for domestic products; and conditions in respect of shape, presentation, weight, size, identification and composition that differ from those applied to domestic products.

Indistinctly applicable MEQRs are described as including 'measures governing the marketing of products which deal, in particular, with shape, size, weight, composition, presentation, identification or putting up and which are applied equally to domestic and imported products': art 3 of Directive 70/50.

The European Court provided its own definition of a MEQR in the important case of *Procureur du Roi* v *Dassonville* Case 8/74 [1974] ECR 837, although, at this point, the Court made no distinction between discriminatory and non-discriminatory MEQRs. The case concerned a Belgian law that required goods having a designation of origin to have a certificate of authenticity provided by the government of the exporting State. Dassonville imported Scotch whisky, but did so from France, and therefore could not provide the necessary certificate. Dassonville was subsequently prosecuted by the Belgian authorities, but pleaded in his defence that the requirement was a MEQR in breach of art 28 EC.

The Court provided a test by which MEQRs may be identified, which is often cited as the '*Dassonville* formula'. The test is as follows:

'All trading rules enacted by Member States which are capable of hindering, directly or indirectly, actually or potentially, intra-Community trade are to be considered as measures having an effect equivalent to quantitative restrictions.'

Thus, the Court concluded that the Belgian requirement was a formality 'for the purpose of providing the origin of a product, which only direct importers are really in a position to satisfy without facing serious difficulties'. The Court held that the measure did constitute a MEQR.

There are some important aspects to the test that should be noted:

1. It does not require any actual effect on intra-Community trade to have occurred before the Treaty provisions may be applied; a potential effect will suffice: see *Criminal Proceedings against Prantl* Case 16/83 [1984] ECR 1299. There is also no minimum effect required, hence the impediment to the free movement of merely one good will suffice to breach the Treaty: see *Van der Haar* Case 177/82 [1984] ECR 1797. This increases the scope and effect of the prohibition.
2. It does not extend to a measure that only affects trade within a Member State, since an intra-Community effect is required: see *Oebel* Case 155/80 [1981] ECR 1993. Indeed, a Member State may impose requirements only on its domestic products, which places them at a disadvantage, if it so desires, without falling within the *Dassonville* formula: see, for example, *Jongeneel Kaas BV* v *The Netherlands* Case 237/82 [1984] ECR 483.
3. The intent behind the measure is not relevant; only its effects should be considered.

To aid in the understanding of the nature of such MEQRS, examples of various types of distinctly applicable MEQRs are provided below. Indistinctly applicable MEQRs will be considered later since, as we shall see, different rules may be applied to them.

## *Examples of distinctly applicable MEQRs*

### Example One – measures that make imports more difficult or costly

This can be witnessed clearly in the case of *Schloh* v *Auto Contrôle Technique* Case 50/85 [1986] ECR 1855. In this case Belgian law required the car imported by Schloh from Germany to be subjected to two roadworthiness tests, for which he was charged, before he could legally drive it in Belgium. Schloh claimed that the requirement was a MEQR in breach of art 28 EC. The Court held that the requirement was a formality that made the registration of such imported cars 'more difficult and more onerous' and was consequently a MEQR.

In *Verein Gegen Unwesen in Handel und Gewerbe Köln* v *Mars GmbH* Case C–470/93 [1995] ECR I–1923 the Mars company challenged a German law that required they repackage their goods. Mars had expanded the content of the ice cream in its product by 10 per cent and had consequently advertised and packaged that product with the slogan 'plus 10 per cent'. Germany had banned such practices under its unfair competition legislation. In order to be able to sell its product in Germany, Mars was forced to repackage its product making its product more difficult and costly to sell.

### Example Two – import or export restrictions

These will often be in the form of licence requirements, or alternatively administrative procedures or data requirements. Also considered to be discriminatory MEQRs are inspections, or tests, on only imports, such as the inspection on imported plants in the case of *Rewe-Zentralfinanz GmbH* v *Landwirtschafiskammer* Case 4/75 [1975] ECR 843. Such restrictions may, of course, also make it more difficult or costly to import the product: see, for example, *Commission* v *Italy* Case 154/85 [1986] 2 CMLR 159.

### Example Three – promoting domestic products

This type of MEQR will operate in a manner that either promotes or favours the purchase of the domestic product, thereby placing the imported product at a disadvantage. In *Re Buy Irish Campaign* (above) the European Court was required to consider an enforcement action against Ireland for an alleged violation of art 28 EC. The Irish government had created the Irish Goods Council as part of a general policy to switch 3 per cent of consumers from buying imported products to buying Irish produced products. They had adopted an information service promoting domestically produced products, offering details on where to purchase them. They also provided an exhibition service only for Irish goods and promoted use of the

'Buy Irish' symbol to indicate which goods were produced in Ireland. The Irish Goods Council also organised a general promotional campaign to encourage consumers to purchase Irish products. Whilst some of the above methods had been dropped, and there had in fact been no switch in consumer purchasing, the Commission brought enforcement proceedings against the Irish government.

First, it was concluded that the Irish Goods Council was an organ of the State (see above) so the Irish government could not escape its liability under this point. Second, the Court examined the campaign, which the Irish government claimed had had no effect on imports and that the proportion of Irish goods sold as compared to imports had in fact gone down.

The Court held that the Irish government had adopted 'a carefully thought out set of initiatives' which were designed as 'an integrated programme for promoting domestic products'. It was irrelevant that some aspects of that programme had since been discontinued, or that the desired effect had not been achieved in practice. It was also irrelevant that the measures were not binding, since they 'may be capable of influencing the conduct of traders and consumers ... and thus of frustrating the aims of the Community'. The Court held that the action taken by the Irish government breached the Treaty and was a MEQR on the basis that it:

> '... represents the implementation of a programme defined by the government which affects the national economy as a whole and which is intended to check the flow of trade between Member States by encouraging the purchase of domestic products, by means of an advertising campaign on a national scale and the organisation of special procedures applicable solely to domestic products ...'

Another method by which a Member State may promote or favour their domestic product, or indeed domestic tenders, is via public procurement. In *Commission* v *Ireland (Re Dundalk Water Supply)* Case 45/87R [1987] 2 CMLR 197 the Court was requested, again via an enforcement action, to assess the practice of Dundalk Council in requiring that tenders for a contract for water supply bid using only pipes that conformed with the Irish standard. The Council subsequently rejected a bid that had used an international standard of pipe not formally recognised in Ireland. The Court concluded that the requirement could cause operators to refrain from tendering, even though they used pipes of an equivalent standard to the Irish one. The Court also concluded that the measure had the effect of 'restricting the supply of pipes needed for the Dundalk scheme to Irish manufacturers alone'. The requirement was therefore one that fell within the *Dassonville* formula: see also *Du Pont de Nemours Italiana SpA* v *Unita Sanitaria Locale No 2 Di Carrara* Case C–21/88 [1990] ECR I–889.

Finally, another method that may potentially promote the domestic product is the requirement to indicate the origin of the producer (known as origin-marking). In *Commission* v *United Kingdom* Case 207/83 [1985] ECR 1201 the Commission brought enforcement proceedings against the UK for national legislation that required certain goods to be marked with their country of origin. The UK argued that such information was important for consumers, since they used such information to measure the quality of the product. The Court concluded that

> '... the purpose of indications of origin or origin-marking is to enable consumers to distinguish between domestic and imported products and this enables them to assert any prejudices which they may have against foreign products.'

Consequently, in the opinion of the Court, imported products would be more difficult to sell in the UK. However, origin-marking may be compatible with Community law if the following conditions are met:

1. the origin implies a certain quality;
2. the origin indicates the product is made of certain materials or via a particular method of production; and/or
3. the origin of the product is indicative of a special place in either the folklore or tradition of a particular region: see *Commission* v *Germany* Case 12/74 [1975] ECR 181 and *Commission* v *Ireland* Case 113/80 [1981] ECR 1625.

## 14.3 Justifying QRs and distinctly applied MEQRs

The only means of justification open to a Member State when they impose a QR or distinctly applied (discriminatory) MEQR are those offered in art 30 EC. The grounds provided under this article are exhaustive and, as exceptions to the general rule of free movement, have been very strictly construed by the European Court. To justify use of one of these grounds the measure must not 'constitute a means of arbitrary discrimination or a disguised restriction on trade between Member States'. The burden of proof is on the Member State, and not only will they have to prove that their action comes within the one of the express derogations provided, they will also have to establish that their action is proportionate. In this context proportionate means the least restrictive means of securing the objective. The grounds provided under art 30 are discussed below, with examples of their use by Member States.

### *Public morality*

The determination of what constitutes a threat to public morality rests in the hands of the Member States: *R* v *Henn and Darby* Case 34/79 [1979] ECR 3795. However, in order to succeed under this ground the Member State must show that it is being genuine in its claim to protect public morality. Thus, they will be required to show that some equivalent form of action is taken against domestic products of the same character: *Conegate Ltd* v *HM Customs and Excise* Case 121/85 [1986] ECR 1007. In other words, the Member State will not succeed if it places stricter conditions on imports that threaten public morality compared to similar domestic goods, since if they constitute a genuine threat to public morality where the product originates from should be irrelevant. To do otherwise would be tantamount to constituting discrimination on the basis of nationality.

## Public policy

This ground has been very narrowly construed in scope. For example, it does not extend to consumer protection: see *Commission* v *Ireland (Re Irish Souvenirs)* Case 113/80 [1981] ECR 1625 and *Kohl KG* v *Ringelhan & Rennett SA* Case 177/83 [1984] ECR 3651. Few cases have been brought under this ground, but one example is *Cullet* v *Centre Leclerc* Case 231/83 [1985] ECR 305. In this case the French government argued that legislation fixing the minimum selling price for fuel was justified, inter alia, in the interests of public policy. The French government argued that without such fixed prices for fuel there would be public disturbances, including blockades and violence.

Neither the Advocate-General nor the European Court were supportive of this interpretation of the ground. The Advocate-General believed that such an interpretation would lead to private interest groups dictating the actions of both governments and the Community, thereby detrimentally affecting the fundamental principles of free movement enshrined in the Treaty. The European Court concluded that the French government had not proved that such a reaction by the French public would have occurred if they changed the law, nor had it proved that it lacked the resources to deal with such incidences. In a sense, therefore, the measure was not proportionate to the objective.

This ground has succeeded on only one occasion, in *R* v *Thompson and Others* Case 7/78 [1978] ECR 2247, where the Court found that restrictions on the exportation of gold coins was justified to prevent them being melted down, contrary to public policy.

## Public security

This is also narrow in scope, and is often argued in conjunction with public policy: see *Cullet* (above).

One case in which the ground was successfully argued was *Campus Oil Ltd* v *Minister for Industry and Energy* Case 72/83 [1984] ECR 2727. Under Irish law importers of petrol had to buy 35 per cent of their needs from a State-owned oil refinery, at fixed prices. Since this constituted a MEQR the Irish government was required to justify it. The ground the government argued was that of public security – that a viable oil refining industry was necessary to the functioning of a State given the importance of oil in the general running of the country.

The European Court concurred with the Irish government's argument, stressing that petroleum products were of fundamental importance in the functioning of the State because of their 'exceptional importance as an energy source in the modern economy'. This was particularly the case when one considered the role of petroleum products in the effective functioning of essential public services and 'the survival of the inhabitants' of that country. Any interruption to the supply of such products would have serious consequences and therefore the 'aim of ensuring a minimum supply' was an objective that could be justified in the interests of public security. However, the Court also stated that the price fixed by the government had to be proportionate to meet the objective, and that should Community law be extended to regulate oil supplies those rules would have to be given priority over domestic legislation.

(Reference should also be made to the additional grounds of national security provided for under arts 296–298 EC, discussed below.)

## The protection of the life and health of humans, plants and animals

This is the most often used of the grounds available under art 30 EC, but one which the European Court will closely examine before accepting. One thing the Court will look for is whether there is indeed a real, genuine risk posed. They will also assess whether the measure is arbitrary and a disguised restriction to the free movement of trade.

One case in which the European Court assessed there to be no real risk and a disguised restriction on trade, was *Commission v United Kingdom (Re Imports of Poultry Meat)* Case 40/82 [1982] ECR 2793. The United Kingdom had imposed a licensing requirement for those importing poultry and eggs. The British government claimed this was necessary to protect public health by controlling the spread of Newcastle disease, a disease that affects the health of poultry. The European Court looked behind the claim to assess whether there was a real risk. It concluded that the licensing requirement had been introduced as a reaction to pressure from farmers concerned about the impact of imported poultry and eggs on their businesses. The fact that the measure had been introduced before the Christmas period, when consumption of turkeys in the UK is at its highest, was not one that the Court ignored. The measure had been introduced with only a minimal degree of consultation and had, in practice, resulted in an effective ban on the importation of the goods from six Member States. The Court held that the licensing requirement was not justified under this ground since it was introduced primarily for economic purposes and was, in reality, a disguised restriction on trade.

In *Commission v United Kingdom (Re UHT Milk)* Case 124/81 [1983] ECR 203 the Court was required to examine another UK law that the Commission believed breached the Treaty. The UK government had imposed a requirement that only licensed, and therefore approved, distributors could distribute UHT milk. Imported UHT milk was required to be re-treated and re-packaged, making it more difficult and costly to sell. The UK government argued that the licensing and re-treating requirement was required to protect public health, since it was essential in ensuring that UHT milk was free from bacterial and viral infections. However, the evidence established that imported milk from other Member States was in reality of a similar quality and standard as compared to British UHT milk, and consequently the UK government's action was not justifiable since there was no real risk posed.

Successful use of the grounds may be seen in *Rewe-Zentralfinanz GmbH* Case 4/75 [1975] ECR 843. In this case the Court concluded that a test on only imported apples (a distinctly applied MEQR) was necessary to prevent the spread of 'San José scale', which was not present in domestic apples. It can also be witnessed in the success of the banning of the importation of Danish bees onto the island of Laesø on the grounds of protecting an indigenous breed of bees on the island from extinction through inter-breeding: *Bluhme* Case C–67/97 [1998] ECR I–8033. The Court held:

> 'Measures to preserve an indigenous animal population with distinct characteristics contribute to the maintenance of biodiversity by ensuring the survival of the population concerned. By doing so, they are aimed at protecting the life of those animals and are capable of being justified under [art 30] of the Treaty.'

There may, though, be a situation where there is no available scientific/medical consensus of the threat to health or life posed. This was the situation that the European Court encountered in the case of *Officier van Justitie* v *Sandoz BV* Case 174/82 [1983] ECR 2445. Dutch authorities had refused to permit the sale of museli bars with added vitamins. They claimed that excessive consumption of vitamins was dangerous to public health. Medical consensus, though, could not be reached on the point at which such excessive consumption would occur, especially in the context of the inter-relationship between consuming different products. The European Court concluded:

> '... in so far as there are uncertainties at the present state of scientific research it is for the Member States, in the absence of harmonisation, to decide what degree of protection of the health and life of humans they intend to assure, having regard however to the requirements of the free movement of goods.'

The requirements the Court referred to are 'proportionality' and that the measures adopted are pursuant to a 'real need', that being, in this case, a 'technical or nutritional one'.

A failure to prove such requirements may be seen in *Commission* v *Germany (Re German Beer Purity Law)* Case 178/84 [1987] ECR 1227. In this case the Commission in enforcement proceedings challenged two German rules in relation to beer. The rule in relation to the contents of the beer is discussed below under the *Cassis* rule of reason. The second rule related to the banning of certain additives in beer. The German government claimed that this was required to protect public health. The Court referred to *Sandoz*, and the principle that in the absence of Community harmonising measures a State could exercise discretion. However, the Court also pointed out the need for a real risk to exist. This could be assessed by reference to the eating habits of other Member States and the conclusions of organisations such as the World Health Organisation. When the Court examined the conclusions of such bodies it found that there was no evidence to suggest that the additives were a threat to public health, that the additives were widely used in other Member States, and that they were actually permitted by Germany in other types of beverages. The measure also had to be proportionate, and in this case the Court identified that there was no ability for traders to gain authorisation for a particular additive, as required under the Court's decision in *Ministère Public* v *Muller* Case 308/84 [1986] ECR 1511. As a result, since there was no real need for the measure and it was disproportionate, the ban was not justified under art 30.

Thus, a Member State may be able to justify use of the public health grounds (presumably where the threat also exists to animals) where there is no scientific or medical consensus, if the following conditions are satisfied:

1. there is some scientific or medical evidence to establish that the threat exists – that there is a real need;
2. the Member State then has discretion on how to respond to the threat but the response must be proportionate;
3. the Member State will lose their discretion should medical or scientific consensus be reached that establishes there is no threat; and
4. the Member State will not have discretion on how to respond should there be Community harmonising measures in operation, and will have to halt any practices exercising their discretion should a Community harmonising measure post-date the Member State's action.

This last point applies generally to using this ground. In other words, a Member State may not rely on this ground when a Community harmonising measure has been passed in that area. Hence, if a check already exists under Community law the State may not have recourse to art 30 to justify imposing its own test on such goods: see, for example, *Oberkreisdirektor* v *Moorman* Case 190/87 [1988] ECR 4689 and *R* v *Ministry of Agriculture, Fisheries and Food, ex parte Compasssion in World Farming Ltd* Case C–1/96 [1998] 2 CMLR 661. In this latter case, the applicants argued that a Council Directive on the treatment of farm animals in transit was contrary to international law embodied in a treaty on the humane treatment of animals. They argued that the minister was able as a result to apply a ban on the export of live animals and justify such action under art 30. The European Court held that the Directive dealt extensively with the subject-matter and that Member States had no recourse to national measures in such circumstances. This point was clearly expressed by the Court in *Société Civile Agricole* v *Coopérative d'Elevage de la Mayenne* Case C–323/93 [1994] ECR I–5077:

'The Court has consistently held that where ... Community directives provide for the harmonisation of the measures necessary to ensure, inter alia, the protection of animal and human health and established Community procedures to check that they were observed, invoking art [30] is no longer justified and the appropriate checks have to be carried out and protective measures adopted within the framework of the directive.'

The only exception to this general rule will be where the Community harmonising measure is not exhaustive, and provides for a measure of discretion in the hands of the national authorities. In such cases, the Member State may impose national requirements in the form of inspections, tests etc, as long as they are non-arbitrary and proportionate: see *Commission* v *Germany* Case C–317/92 [1994] ECR I–2039.

Another means by which the health ground is used is to justify the imposition of tests or checks on imports as they enter the Member State when they have already been tested or checked in the exporting Member State. This is known as dual or double-checking. In such cases the European Court will closely examine whether the second test is actually necessary. Hence, in *Re UHT Milk* (above) the Court established that the quality of the imported milk was of a similar standard to that produced in the United Kingdom and there was no need for the re-treatment. The European Court did suggest that the UK could have adopted a far less restrictive measure to ensure the quality of imported milk, by requiring a certificate. In addition, such a certificate would have to be accepted by the British authorities since there was no possibility of the sealed milk products being tampered with during transit.

In limited cases the European Court will accept the need for a double-check, but the following should be noted (along with the point above in relation to the existence of any Community harmonising measures):

1. it will be unnecessary if the exporting State has already imposed the technical tests;
2. it will be unnecessary if the exporting State has already conducted tests of the same practical effect; and
3. the test will have to be proportionate, in that it is the least restrictive way of meeting the objective: see *Denkavit Futtermittel* v *Minister fur Ernährung, Landwirtschaft und Forsten des Landes* Case 251/78 [1979] ECR 3369 and *Frans-Nederlandse Maatschappij voor Biologische Producten* Case 272/80 [1981] ECR 3277.

## The protection of industrial and commercial property

Article 295 EC states:

> 'This Treaty shall in no way prejudice the rules in Member States governing the system of property ownership.'

The European Court has contrasted this Treaty provision with the derogation ground of protecting industrial and commercial property offered under art 30. They appear to imply that the State is free to impose national laws in such matters, and the ECJ has concluded that the art 30 exception can only be used in the context of protecting the rights that form the specific subject-matter of the property. The Court has held that, whilst the existence of the right is a matter for national law, the exercise of that right is subject to the Treaty rules on free movement: *Deutsche*

*Grammophon GmbH* v *Metro-SB-Grossmärkte GmbH & Co KG* Case 78/70 [1971] ECR 487.

In *Spain* v *Council* Case C–350/92 [1995] ECR I–1985 the European Court held that art 295 does not permit the Member State to adopt measures relating to industrial or commercial property that hinder the free movement of goods. Hence, any use of this ground in art 30, to protect patents, copyrights, trademarks or similar devices, must be non-discriminate (non-arbitrary) and proportionate. See also *Phil Collins* v *Imtrat Handelsgesellscaft mbH* Cases 92 and 326/92 [1993] ECR I–5145, where German protection against the illegal recording of music was only offered to German nationals and was therefore held to be discriminatory.

If a patent is held, that patentee has the ability, under this ground, to justify excluding the sale of any goods that breach their patent rights in the Member State in which the patent was granted. This is a limited right, in that once the patented goods are in free circulation in another Member State, because the patentee has provided them or has given their consent to do so, the right to exclude that good is exhausted: see *Centrafarm BV* v *Sterling Drug Inc* Case 15/74 [1974] ECR 1147 and *Centrafarm BV* v *Winthrop BV* Case 16/74 [1974] ECR 1183. This rule also applies to trade marks, patents, copyright and industrial designs: see, for example, *Centrafarm* cases (above), *Keurkoop BV* v *Nancy Kean Gifts BV* Case 144/81 [1982] ECR 2853 and *Warner Brothers Inc* v *Cristiansen* Case 158/86 [1988] ECR 2605.

## The protection of national treasures possessing artistic, historic or archaeological value

In *Commission* v *Italy (Re Export Tax on Art Treasures)* Case 7/68 [1968] ECR 423 the Court suggested that preventing the export of artistic treasures would come within this ground in art 30. In addition to this ground there are Community harmonising measures on the exportation of cultural property in the form of Directive 93/7 and Regulation 3911/92, which imposes uniform controls at borders on exports of cultural goods.

## Extending the grounds in art 30

It has always been a well held view that the grounds in art 30 were exhaustive. However, it appears that the Court may be prepared to accept one additional ground not provided for under the article, namely protection of the environment. This was the basis of justification accepted by the European Court of Justice in both *Aher-Waggon GmbH* v *Bundesrepublik Deutschland* Case C–389/98 [1998] ECR I–4473 and *PreussenElektra AG* v *Schleswag AG* Case 379/98 [2001] ECR I–2099. Obviously, the burden of proof will remain on the Member State, which will be required to establish that the measure imposed is based on a real need to protect the environment (similar to the requirement in the context of plant, animal and human health discussed above) and is both non-arbitrary and proportionate.

*Other means of justification*

The following may also be used to justify measures prohibited under arts 28 and 29 EC:

1.  Articles 108, 109 and 111 EC – balance of payment difficulties;
2.  Article 99 EC – sort-term economic difficulties; and
3.  Article 134 EC – economic difficulties resulting from the Common Commercial Policy (CCP) or trade deflections with potential to obstruct EC commercial policy. (The CCP is discussed in Chapter 13.)

The Commission, or the Council, acting on a proposal from the Commission must take the above measures. The measures must also be proportionate.

In addition, arts 296 and 297 EC provide that derogation is acceptable in the interests of national security. Specifically, art 297 provides that a consultation procedure is available when the need arises for measures in reaction to the actions of Member States during war or civil disturbance, or the need arises to provide security measures, such as peace-keeping.

## 14.4  Indistinctly applied (non-discriminatory) MEQRs

The European Court in *Dassonville* (above) indicated that the prohibition on MEQRs extended to those that were applied in a non-discriminatory manner, since the *Dassonville* formula makes no mention of the need for any form of discrimination. In other words, MEQRs applied indistinctly to both imported and domestic products would also breach the Treaty. This finds additional support in art 3 of Directive 70/50 (see above). The fact that indistinctly applied MEQRs may breach art 28 was confirmed in what has become a landmark decision of the European Court – the case of *Rewe-Zentrale AG* v *Bundesmonopolverwaltung für Branntwein* Case 120/78 [1979] ECR 649, commonly referred to as *Cassis de Dijon*.

German law required that certain alcoholic drinks, including liqueurs, had to have a minimum alcoholic content of 25 per cent. This applied regardless of the origin of the product. The applicant had attempted to import French Cassis (a blackcurrant liqueur) into Germany, but since the alcohol content was only between 15 to 20 per cent, was prevented from doing so. The applicant argued that the German law was a MEQR, contrary to art 28.

The European Court confirmed that such indistinctly applied measures breach art 28 since they may inhibit the free movement of goods. The Court then went on to expand on *Dassonville* (above), where it had commented:

'In the absence of a Community system guaranteeing for consumers the authenticity of a product's designation of origin, if a Member State takes measures to prevent unfair practices ... it is ... subject to the condition that these measures should be reasonable ...'

In *Cassis* the Court held:

> 'Obstacles to the free movement within the Community resulting from disparities between the national laws relating to the marketing of the products in question must be accepted in so far as those provisions may be recognised as being necessary in order to satisfy mandatory requirements ...'

The Court identified that certain measures may be reasonable, in that they served to protect an essential requirement. Examples of such 'mandatory requirements' included, in the opinion of the Court, the effectiveness of fiscal supervision, the protection of public health, the fairness of commercial transactions and consumer protection, although the list the Court offered is non-exhaustive, unlike those grounds under art 30 EC. This is commonly referred to as the *Cassis de Dijon* 'rule of reason'.

At the same time, the Court limited the extent of the rule of reason as a means of justifying an indistinctly applied MEQR, by its following comment on the arguments put forward by the German government:

> 'There is ... no valid reason why, provided that they have been lawfully produced and marketed in one of the Member States, alcoholic beverages should not be introduced into any other Member State.'

This is known as the principle of 'mutual recognition'. In other words, if a product has been lawfully produced and marketed in one Member State, it is presumed to be lawful in all other Member States, and they should recognise it as such. The Member State may rebut this presumption but they will, naturally, require evidence to prove that there is a 'valid reason' for their measure.

## 14.5 Application of the *Cassis de Dijon* rule of reason

The *Cassis de Dijon* rule of reason has been argued in a considerable amount of litigation. The first and important point to note is that it can never be used to justify a discriminatory MEQR or QR. Such measures must be justified according to the requirements of art 30 EC (see section 14.3): *Commission* v *Ireland (Re Irish Souvenirs)* Case 113/80 [1981] ECR 1625. Second, the rule of reason may not be relied upon where there are Community harmonising measures on the subject matter: see *Italy* v *Gilli and Andres* Case 788/79 [1980] ECR 2071.

It appears that the rule of reason test is less stringent when compared to the provisions of art 30. It certainly has greater scope in terms of the grounds that may be relied upon, since art 30 contains an exhaustive list, whereas the mandatory requirements mentioned in *Cassis* have been extended by the European Court. For example, protecting workers conditions was the mandatory requirement in *Oebel* Case 155/80 [1981] ECR 1993; protecting the environment was considered as an acceptable mandatory requirement in *Commission* v *Denmark (Re Returnable*

*Containers)* Case 302/86 [1988] ECR 4607; and in *Cinéthèque SA* v *Fédération Nationale des Cinémas Françaises* Cases 60 and 61/84 [1985] ECR 2605 protecting art, in this case film, was also acceptable. However, the Court will not accept justifications based on purely economic grounds: *Duphar BV* v *Netherlands* Case 238/82 [1984] ECR 523.

The European Court has also insisted that, whilst measures may attempt to protect a legitimate mandatory requirement, they must be proportionate to the aim being pursued and have complied with the principle of mutual recognition, or have provided sufficient evidence to rebut the presumption. As a consequence of the application of these conditions, Member States have regularly been unable to justify their action. The following provides examples of the use of the rule of reason by the Member States, and the reaction of the European Court. We will begin by returning to the case of *Cassis* itself.

In *Cassis* the German government claimed that the alcoholic content requirement of 25 per cent was required in order to protect public health and the consumer against unfair trading practices. The former, the German government argued, was achieved by the imposition of the high alcohol content. This would result in reducing the proliferation of such products in the market and would reduce the volume particularly of low-alcoholic content drinks which were, in the eyes of the German government, a greater threat in terms of creating 'tolerance towards alcohol'. The Court dealt briefly with this argument, simply stating that 'such considerations are not decisive': it found that a large range of products with differing alcohol contents were readily available in Germany, including those with a very high content used as the basis for diluted drinks.

In relation to the second argument put forward by the German government, that of protecting the consumer against unfair trading practices, the Court held:

> '... this line of argument cannot be taken so far as to regard the mandatory fixing of minimum alcohol contents as being an essential guarantee of the fairness of commercial transactions, since it is a simple matter to ensure that suitable information is conveyed to the purchaser by requiring the display of an indication of origin and alcohol content on the packaging of products.'

In other words, the Court assessed the German action to be a non-proportionate means of securing consumer protection, pointing out that a more proportionate method would be to impose a labelling requirement.

The mandatory requirement of consumer protection was also argued in the case of *Commission* v *Germany (Re German Beer Purity Law)* Case 178/84 [1987] ECR 1227. German law provided that 'bier' (beer) could only be sold in Germany if it were made only from barley, hops, yeast and water, regardless of where the beer was manufactured. The German government claimed that this provided consumer protection because consumers associated the name of the product with those four ingredients.

The European Court first pointed out that national measures should not 'crystallise given consumer habits so as to consolidate an advantage acquired by national authorities concerned to comply with them': see also *Commission* v *United Kingdom (Re Tax on Beer and Wine)* Case 170/78 [1983] ECR 415 for a similar assertion. The Court accepted that consumer protection could have extended to ensuring that consumers could identify the contents of their 'bier', but found that the measure adopted in this case was not proportionate. The Court suggested that a requirement to provide information, by the use of labelling, would have been a far less restrictive means of meeting the objective. This was because 'indicating the raw materials ... would enable the consumer to make his choice in full knowledge of the facts and would guarantee transparency in trading and offers to the pubic'.

Other cases that have attempted to use consumer protection as the mandatory requirement they seek to protect include *Verband Sozialer Wettbewerb eV* v *Clinique Laboratories SNC* Case C–315/92 [1994] ECR I–317 and *Walter Rau Lebensmittelwerke* v *De Smedt PVBA* Case 261/81 [1982] 2 CMLR 496. In the former, the Court examined a German law that forbade the name Clinique on cosmetic products. The German government argued that this was necessary to protect consumers from mistaking such products as being medicinal in nature. Whilst protecting the consumer was an acceptable mandatory requirement, the Court found that the German government had not complied with the principle of mutual recognition. In other words, cosmetic products with the name Clinique were lawfully produced and marketed throughout the Member States and were consequently presumed lawful unless Germany could rebut that presumption. The German government had failed to provide any evidence to point to consumer confusion in other Member States, or indeed in Germany. In addition, the products themselves were not sold in pharmacies, where perhaps confusion could have arisen, but were available in retail stores. In other words, the German law was not necessary: see, also, *Prantl* (above) and *Miro BV* Case 182/84 [1986] 3 CMLR 545.

In *Rau*, the Belgian government attempted to justify a requirement that margarine be packaged in cube-shaped boxes, as being in the interests of consumer protection. The European Court found that such a requirement was disproportionate. A less restrictive means of attaining the objective would be to impose a labelling requirement: see, also, *Ministère Public* v *Déserbais* Case 286/86 [1988] ECR 4907 where the Court concluded that a German minimum requirement in relation to the fat content of Edam cheese was concluded to be disproportionate. A less restrictive measure would have been a labelling requirement for such cheeses.

In terms of the fairness of commercial transactions, a mandatory requirement listed in *Cassis*, many of the cases overlap with consumer protection, considered above. An example of this can be seen in *Oosthoek's Uitgeversmaatschappij BV* Case 286/81 [1982] ECR 4575 which dealt with national laws prohibiting the use of free gifts in the sale of encyclopædias. The European Court concluded that the offer of such free gifts could mislead the consumer and result in unfair trading.

In *Duphar BV* v *Netherlands* Case 238/82 [1984] ECR 523 Dutch law required the drawing up of a list of approved drugs if public funds were to be paid for them.

Duphar were not included on the list, and challenged this as a MEQR. The European Court accepted that such a measure could be in the interests of consumers but the list would have to be proved by the Member State to have been based on objective criteria that produced no discrimination in relation to imported products.

In the case of *GB-INNO-BM* v *Confédération du Commerce Luxembourgoise Asbl* Case C–362/88 [1990] ECR I–667 a Belgian supermarket challenged a ban imposed by Luxembourg on the distribution of leaflets advertising cut-price products. Luxembourg's argument that a ban was a justifiable consumer protection measure was not accepted by the Court, which held that the measure was prejudicial to the ability of smaller businesses to advertise effectively. (It is interesting to consider this case in light of the Court's decision in *Keck* that selling arrangements fall outside of art 28: see section 14.7.)

The *Cassis* rule of reason also extends to public health. However, the Court does appear to have adopted a policy of occasionally using art 30 instead of *Cassis*, especially in situations where it is unsure of whether the national measure is truly non-discriminatory: see *Commission* v *Germany* Case 174/84 [1987] ECR 1227 (above).

## 14.6 Applying *Cassis* – the problems

Whilst the *Cassis* rule of reason had the advantage of relieving the Commission of a considerable workload in relation to harmonising the various trading rules of the Member States, so that it could concentrate on specific areas that could benefit from such action, the rule of reason also attracted criticism. One major problem was in defining the scope of the need for the test.

The criticism stemmed from the need to apply the test to both dual and equal burden rules. Dual burden rules are defined as those that are applied by a Member State in relation to the content or characteristics of goods, even though those goods have complied with similar standards imposed by the Member State from which they originate. Equal burden rules are defined as those that apply equally to both imports and domestic products and which affect the volume of trade. This effect is a decrease of the overall volume of trade, regardless of the origin of the product.

Academics, such as Steiner and White, suggested that equal burden rules should not fall within the ambit of the Treaty prohibition on MEQRs, particularly since they had no protectionist motive. Application of the *Cassis* rule of reason to such measures created considerable unnecessary litigation and was described by White as reducing *Cassis* to a mere 'mechanical' test. The distinction between the two types of trading rules was not helped by the Court failing to adopt a consistent approach to them: see, for example, *Belgian State* v *Blesgen* Case 75/81 [1982] ECR 1211 compared to *Cinéthèque SA* v *Fédération Nationale des Cinémas Français* Cases 60 and 61/84 [1985] ECR 2605. In addition, considerable problems had been created by the European Court's insistence that once it had established a satisfactory mandatory requirement, it was the national court's responsibility to assess whether the measure was proportionate. Placing this obligation on the national courts resulted in both uncertainty and a lack of uniformity.

These problems can be seen most clearly in the Sunday Trading Cases. In *Torfaen Borough Council* v *B & Q plc* Case 145/88 [1989] ECR 3851 the European Court was requested under a preliminary reference to consider the compatibility of the United Kingdom's Sunday trading laws with the EC Treaty. The Sunday trading laws prohibited retail outlets from selling products on Sundays, although a small number of products were exempt. The laws applied to all products regardless of origin, and resulted in an overall reduction in trade of approximately 10 per cent. In other words, the Sunday trading laws were equal burden rules.

The Court held that the Sunday trading laws were designed to ensure that working hours reflected 'socio-cultural characteristics' in the UK. Thus, the Court accepted that, in the absence of Community measures on the issue, the Member State could exercise its discretion and justify the rules as necessary to satisfy the mandatory requirement of protecting socio-cultural characteristics. However, the Court also pointed out that the rules imposed would have to be proportionate to the objective and this, it concluded, was 'a question to be determined by the national court'.

Uncertainty ensued in the decisions of UK courts in the cases that followed. In *B & Q plc* v *Shrewsbury Borough Council* [1990] 3 CMLR 535 the court concluded that the purpose of the Sunday trading laws was to protect those workers that did not wish to work Sundays. The court held that the rules were therefore disproportionate. A less restrictive measure could be imposed to achieve the same result, such as employment contracts requiring the employee to indicate whether they would or would not be prepared to work on Sundays. In contrast, the court in *Wellingborough Borough Council* v *Payless DIY Ltd* [1990] 1 CMLR 773 concluded that the Sunday trading laws were designed to protect the character of the traditional British Sunday. Since that was the objective, the rules were held to be proportionate. Finally, in *Stoke-on-Trent City Council* v *B & Q plc* [1990] 3 CMLR 897 the national court referred the question of whether the Sunday trading rules were proportionate to the European Court. The Court held that they were: see, also, *Union Départmentale des Syndicats CGT* v *Sidef Conforama* Case 312/89 [1991] ECR I–997 and *Criminal Proceedings against A Marchandise and Others* Case C–332/89 [1991] ECR I–1027.

## 14.7  Selling arrangements

In one of its rare decisions to depart from its previous rulings the European Court changed its approach in *Criminal Proceedings against Keck and Mithouard* Joined Cases C–267 and 268/91 [1993] ECR I–6097. The Court held:

'... contrary to what has previously been decided, the application to products from other Member States of national provisions restricting or prohibiting certain selling arrangements is not such as to hinder directly or indirectly, actually or potentially, trade between Member States within the meaning of the *Dassonville* judgement.'

The Court accepted that equal burden trade laws in the form of selling arrangements were outside the prohibition on MEQRs in the EC Treaty. The Court placed two requirements on such rules if they were to benefit from this distinction, and that was that the provisions had to:

1. apply to all traders operating within the national territory; and
2. apply to the marketing of domestic and imported goods in the same manner *in law and in fact*.

The decision in *Keck* means that a distinction must be made between two types of indistinctly applied trading rules. The first will be those trading rules that relate to the contents or characteristics of the product itself, such as its size, weight, packaging or composition. Such rules will be considered as MEQRs and, if indistinctly applied, will have to satisfy the *Cassis* rule of reason test. The second are those rules that apply to the circumstances in which the product is sold – the 'selling arrangement'. Provided that such rules are imposed equally on both domestic and imported goods in a non-protectionist manner, and both are treated equally in law and in fact, they will not be considered to be MEQRs and will consequently not breach the EC Treaty.

The Court has since applied the *Keck* decision. For example, in the case of *Punto Casa SpA* v *Sindaco del Commune di Capena* Cases C–69 and 258/93 [1994] ECR I–2355 the Court concluded that Italian laws requiring retail shops to close on Sundays were not within the definition of a MEQR: see also *Criminal Proceedings against Tankstation 't Heustke Vof and Boermans* Cases C–401 and 402/92 [1994] ECR I–2199.

*Keck* has been extended to include not only static forms of selling arrangements, but to non-static selling arrangements too. Non-static selling arrangements include such things as advertising and sales promotions – in other words, the means by which products may be marketed. In both *Hünermund* v *Landesapothekerkammer Baden-Wüttemburg* Case C–292/92 [1993] ECR I–6787 and *Société d'Importation Edouard Leclerc-Siplec* v *TFI Publicité SA* Case 412/93 [1995] ECR I–179 the Court held that limited bans in relation to the advertising of products were selling arrangements outside of the scope of the Treaty provisions. In *Konsumentombudsmannen* v *De Agostini* Cases C–34–36/95 [1998] 1 CMLR 32 a Swedish ban on television advertising for children aged under 12 was held to be a selling arrangement within *Keck* by the European Court. It is interesting to note, though, that the Court did specifically draw the national court's attention to the need for it to consider whether the ban was applied equally to imports in both law and in fact. The Court has re-emphasised the need for this condition to be met in a number of cases. For example, in *Konsumentombudsmannen (KO)* v *Gourmet International Products AG (GIP)* Case C–405/98 [2001] ECR I–1795 the Court examined a Swedish ban on the advertising of alcohol on radio and television and on the advertising of spirits, wines and strong beer in periodicals, unless they were for trade such as restaurants. The Court concluded that whilst selling arrangements did fall outside of the scope of art 28,

> '... national provisions restricting or prohibiting selling arrangements ... must not be of such a kind as to prevent access to the market by products from another state or to impede access any more than they impede the access of domestic products.'

More specifically, the Court commented on the Swedish advertising ban as one that 'in reality prohibits producers and importers from directing any advertising messages at consumers' and that this would be liable to 'impede access to the market by products from other Member States more than it impedes access by domestic products, with which consumers are instantly more familiar'. In other words, the ban, whilst non-discriminatory in law, was discriminatory in fact since imported products were impeded from accessing the market.

Another circumstance in which a selling arrangement will still fall within the scope of art 28 (in addition to the fact that those that do not treat imports in the same manner in law and fact will require justification) are those selling arrangements that result in affecting the actual content of the product itself. This was witnessed in *Vereinigte Familiapress Zeitungsverlags-und Vertreibs GmbH* v *Heinrich Bauer Verlag* Case C–368/95 [1997] ECR I–3689. This case concerned an Austrian law that prohibited the use of competitions for prizes in papers. Familiapress attempted to enforce this law against a German company that wished to publish a magazine containing crossword puzzles for which contestants could win prizes. The European Court held that the Austrian law related to a method of sales promotion, but was one that 'bears on the actual content of the products'. The Court considered the competitions as an 'integral part of the magazine in which they appear' and that the Austrian laws did not come within the ambit of a selling arrangement within the meaning of *Keck*.

It appears, therefore, that each case will have to be examined on its facts, to assess whether the measure imposed does or does not fall within the definition of a selling arrangement.

# Part D

# Competition Law

Article 3(1)(g) of the EC Treaty provides for 'a system ensuring that competition in the common market is not distorted'. Articles 81–89 EC also provide for substantive provisions in relation to competition law and can be divided briefly in to two categories:

1. Article 81 EC provides for rules on anti-competitive agreements or concerted practices between undertakings, and art 82 EC prohibits the abuse of a dominant position by an undertaking. This Part will include analysis of both of these provisions and the means by which they are enforced in Chapters 15–17. The provisions on intellectual property are also relevant to this field of Community law, but are outside the scope of this book. (Reference is made to them in relation to the free movement of goods in Chapter 14.)
2. Articles 87–89 provide for controls on State aid to industry. State aid may provide a benefit for a specific industry or undertaking, which in turn may distort competition between Member States. This will, in turn, detrimentally affect the internal market. Article 86 provides rules in relation to public undertakings granted exclusive or special rights. State aid is discussed in Chapter 18.

Competition policy in the European Community is a highly developed area of law. It is designed to complement those provisions on the free movement of goods, services and establishment, and to ensure that they are not distorted by the practices of undertakings, whether in or outside of the Union. It is an area of law that has three main objectives:

1. To aid in the creation of the European market, working alongside those rules in relation to tariffs and quotas, as discussed in Part C.
2. To promote economic activity and to maximise efficiency. This is achieved by ensuring that goods and resources flow freely between the Member States so that market forces operate normally, without distortion. It is presumed that if resources are handled at a Community level, the Community will become more competitive in the world market.
3. To protect and encourage small and medium-sized undertakings, although this objective may conflict with the others.

It should be noted that a balance will have to often be arrived at in relation to these principles, and that this will be decided on a case-by-case basis. In addition, the rules on competition also have to be seen in the light of other Community rules, which may, in certain cases, override competition provisions.

The modern approach to competition law stems from the theory of 'perfect competition'. This model is based on the idea that the market will contain a substantial number of buyers and sellers, with the latter producing the same or interchangeable goods. Resources should be able to move freely between different economic activities and there will be no barriers or restrictions on new enterprises entering the market, or old ones leaving. The practical result will therefore be a situation in which no one single producer, dictating prices, dominates the market. The wealth of sellers in that market will mean that the buyer will pay only what the market can bear.

Perfect competition should result in an efficient distribution of resources. The traditional view is that this cannot be achieved without regulation, and that therefore State intervention is necessary. In return, both consumers and small to medium-sized businesses will be protected since monopolies and oligopolies are either prevented or controlled.

Whilst the theory of perfect competition was the basis of much of the early development of competition law, largely in America, an alternative view was proposed by economists. This alternative view is based on the notion that perfect competition exists in the world market as it stands, and that only those practices that are capable of creating serious anti-competitive effects should be regulated by the State.

As a compromise between these two theories, the Community has adopted the policy of 'workable competition'. This can be seen in the comments of the European Court in *Metro-SB-Grossmärkte GmbH & Co KG* v *Commission* Case 26/76 [1977] ECR 1875:

> 'The requirement contained in [arts 3 and 81 EC] that competition shall not be distorted implies the existence on the market of *workable competition*, that is to say the degree of competition necessary to ensure the observance of the basic requirements and attainment of the objectives of the Treaty, in particular the creation of a single market ...' (emphasis added).

This results in a system that is designed to provide specific rules on certain practices. Community competition policy, therefore, attacks certain types of private commercial agreements under art 81, such as cartels, although it recognises that some such arrangements may have benefits, so provides for exemption under art 81(3). Community law also controls anti-competitive practices by companies in dominant positions within a particular market (art 82), as well as State aids. The aim is to reduce unfair competition through the intervention of Community agencies.

The Commission has extensive delegated powers in this area of Community law, and has effectively shaped the present form of competition policy. The Commission has been granted substantial authority to investigate complaints alleging violations of Community competition rules. It also has authority to review agreements submitted by private parties to ensure that any potentially anti-competitive terms are acceptable in the light of the policy objectives of Community competition law. In both these capacities the Commission has powers to require the production of materials, to conduct inspections at private premises and to demand explanations from those subject to investigations.

As a corollary to its investigative function, the Commission also has authority to grant clearance to agreements submitted to it for review, to exempt agreements and, ultimately, to fine parties found to have engaged in anti-competitive behaviour. The relationship between the European Commission and private parties as regards these matters may broadly be described as the procedural laws of Community competition policy: see Regulation 17/62 discussed in Chapter 17.

# 15

# Article 81 EC

## 15.1 Introduction

In relation to private undertakings, the substantive rules of competition law are contained in arts 81 and 82 EC. Briefly, art 81 prohibits all agreements, decisions and concerted practices between private parties that affect trade between Member States and which have as their object or effect the prevention, restriction or distortion of competition within the Community. Article 82 prohibits any abuses by one or more parties of a dominant position within a particular market, again in so far as such behaviour affects trade between Member States.

Both articles are intended to counter different forms of commercial behaviour. The major distinction between the articles is that art 81 deals with agreements between two or more parties, while art 82 essentially concerns abusive behaviour, normally by a single party, but conceivably by a small number of parties. However, these two provisions should not be compartmentalised: see *Tetra Pak Rausing SA* v *Commission (No 1)* Case T–51/89 [1990] ECR II–309. It is perfectly possible that a particular activity might contravene both provisions, although, certainly in the past, this has been more the exception than the rule.

Another aspect of competition dealt with at Community level is that of merger control. Although there is no specific provision of the Treaty dealing with this subject, the Commission has historically considered that mergers and acquisitions of a sufficient size can produce effects contrary to arts 81 and 82. In 1989 a Council Regulation was enacted to allow the Commission to review the compatibility of mergers and acquisitions within the Community for anti-competitive effects contrary to these articles. (Merger control will be considered in Chapter 16, at section 16.6.)

Article 81(1) prohibits agreements, decisions and concerted practices between undertakings that affect trade between Member States and which have as their object or effect the prevention, restriction or distortion of competition within the Community. Article 81(2) provides that any such agreement, decision or concerted practice will be automatically void. Article 81(3) provides that in certain limited circumstances the agreement, decision or concerted practice may be eligible for exemption on the basis that it has compensatory benefits.

Before proceeding to examine those types of agreements prohibited under art 81 it is necessary to consider the following questions:

1. What is the definition of an 'undertaking' for this purpose?
2. What types of arrangement constitute agreements, decisions and concerted practices?
3. What is the effect of the requirement that the arrangement must affect trade between Member States?

## 15.2 The definition of an undertaking

Both arts 81 and 82 refer to the concept of 'undertakings' but do not expressly define the term itself. The European Court has considered this point and has stated that an undertaking is:

'... a single organisation of personal, tangible and intangible elements, attached to an autonomous legal entity and pursuing a long-term economic aim': *Mannesmann* v *High Authority* Case 8/61 [1962] ECR 357.

In *Höfner and Elser* v *Macroton GmbH* Case C–41/90 [1991] ECR I–1979 the Court concluded that an undertaking for the purposes of competition law was an entity engaged in a economic/commercial activity, regardless of the way in which it was financed and its national legal status: see also *Fédération Française des Sociétés d'Assurance* v *Ministère de l'Agriculture et de la Pêche* Case C–244/94 [1996] 4 CMLR 536.

Hence, this definition embraces all natural and legal persons engaged in commercial activities whether profit-making or otherwise. The fact that an entity is a non-profit-making organisation is irrelevant for the purpose of identifying an undertaking: *Heintz van Landewyck Sarl* v *Commission* Case 108/78 [1980] ECR 3125. The critical characteristic is whether or not the entity is engaged in economic or commercial activities: see the decision of the Commission in *Polypropylene* [1988] 4 CMLR D347.

Thus, the following, according to the academic Whish, are undertakings for the purpose of competition law: corporations, individuals, trade associations, State-owned corporations, partnerships and co-operatives. In some cases the body will provide services which lack sufficient general economic interest. The body will instead provide services in the public interest. This may be due, for example, to a Treaty obligation (see *SAT* v *Eurocontrol* Case C–364/92 [1994] ECR I–43) or because the body performs a task that is an essential function of the State.

*Racal Group Services* [1990] 4 CMLR 627 provides an example of what may happen should the Commission or Court consider that a parent and subsidiary are in reality merely one economic unit although, technically, legally distinct. In such cases they could be treated as one undertaking for the purposes of Community competition law, and hence any agreement between them will be a purely internal one not coming within the ambit of art 81(1). Their action, though, may come within the prohibition on abuse of a dominant position under art 82: see Chapter 16. If parent and subsidiary are sufficiently distinct then any agreement between them may come within art 81(1).

The Commission, in *Welded Steel Mesh* [1991] 4 CMLR 13, confirmed that, should an undertaking change its legal form, and there is a economic continuity between its previous and new forms, it will still be liable for any past breaches of competition law.

The question of whether art 81 applies to State involvement in the market is complex. If the State pursues a commercial policy through a nationalised industry, any agreement will come within art 81(1): see, for example, the decision of the Commission in *Aluminium Products* [1987] 3 CMLR D813. If the undertaking is one that receives special/exclusive rights from the State then art 86 will apply: see Chapter 18. If the State takes action that obstructs or impedes the movement of trade between Member States, then art 28 EC will apply (see Chapter 14).

## 15.3 Agreements, decisions and concerted practices

### *Agreements*

This term includes all contracts in the sense of binding contractual obligations, whether written, verbal, or partly written and partly verbal. Further, an arrangement between two or more parties may constitute an agreement for the purpose of art 81(1) even though the arrangement in question has no binding legal effect: see *Atka A/S* v *BP Kemi A/S* [1979] CMLR 684.

Unrecorded understandings, the mutual adoption of common rules and so-called 'gentleman's agreements' are also agreements for the purposes of competition law: see *Boehringer* v *Commission* Case 45/69 [1970] ECR 769. A gentleman's agreement was considered in *ACF Chemiefarma NV* v *Commission* Cases 41, 44 and 45/69 [1970] ECR 661. In this case, which concerned the quinine market, a number of undertakings had agreed to fix prices and divide the market, and had produced an export agreement to provide for such measures. At the same time they also produced a gentleman's agreement that they would extend this policy to their sales within the Community. The undertakings argued that the gentleman's agreement was not an agreement within the meaning of art 81(1), and that they had terminated its effects in October 1962.

The Court carefully examined the evidence and concluded that the gentleman's agreement, which the parties had mutually agreed to abide by, had the object of restricting competition within the Common Market. It did not help the firms that the Court identified that a breach of the gentleman's agreement was in turn a breach of the export agreement. The Court was not satisfied that the parties conduct had ceased in October 1962. It examined the sharing of markets, fixed common prices, sales quotas, the prohibition on manufacturing synthetic quinine and communications between the parties in 1963. The Court came to the conclusion that the parties had intended the gentleman's agreement to 'remain unchanged'.

Similarly, in *Polypropylene* (above), the Commission concluded that there was an agreement within art 81(1) in relation to 15 firms in the petrochemical industry. The agreement was long running, and it was irrelevant that it was oral and non-legally binding.

Agreements that prevent, distort or restrict competition are classified as either horizontal agreements or vertical agreements. Horizontal agreements are arrangements made between competitors or potential competitors, whilst vertical agreements concern arrangements between undertakings at different stages of the process through which a product or service passes from the manufacturer or supplier to the final consumer. Illustrations of horizontal agreements include contracts dividing markets among competitors, price fixing, export and import bans, cartels and boycotts. Examples of vertical agreements include those for exclusive distribution, patent licensing and exclusive purchasing.

The original approach of Community competition law was to treat both types of agreements as within the Treaty prohibition, unless they could be justified under individual exemption. However, the approach has changed in light of the opinion that vertical agreements may not operate against the interests of consumers. This will be discussed below.

## Decisions by associations of undertakings

This generally covers the situation where a trade association makes recommendations to its members, for example, about profit margins, even if those recommendations are not legally binding: *Cementhandelaren* v *Commission* Case 8/72 [1972] ECR 977. The legal form of the association is irrelevant.

## Concerted practices

One of the strengths of art 81(1) is that it includes not only those agreements where there is substantive evidence of the agreement, but also those situations where there may be informal co-operation between undertakings, ie a concerted practice. Hence, those agreements made in secret, or where evidence is perhaps destroyed, may come within the ambit of the Treaty provision. However, there may be some difficulties in ascertaining whether the activity is a form of conscious parallel behaviour, or where it is simply the market operating in such a manner. In such cases a thorough economic analysis of the market may be required.

In *Imperial Chemical Industries Ltd v Commission (Dyestuffs)* Case 48/69 [1972] ECR 619 the Court defined a concerted practice as one where there is no formal agreement, but where the undertakings involved 'knowingly substitute co-operation between themselves for the risks of competition'.

The *Dyestuffs* case gives an illustration of a concerted practice. There were price rises by uniform percentages within days of each other in different markets. The Commission dismissed the argument that this was a coincidence. It was then assessed whether the market was oligopolistic, where there is one leader who dictates in effect the conditions of the market, and where others have to adopt marketing strategies to reflect this. The Commission decided that this was not the case. Consequently the price increases were used as evidence to support the contention that there had been co-ordination between the undertakings in the form of a concerted practice:

'... the increase was general, was simultaneously introduced by all the producers ... and was applied without any difference concerning the range of products ... Viewed as a whole, the three consecutive increases reveal progressive co-operation between the undertakings concerned.'

In the Court's opinion, the parties, by co-operating through using advance announcements, had:

'... eliminated all uncertainty between them as to their future conduct and, in doing so, also eliminated a large part of the risk usually inherent in any independent change of conduct ...'

A coherent plan need not be worked out, and there need not be direct contact between the undertakings. What should exist will be the aim to remove in advance 'any uncertainty as to the future conduct of their competitors': *Suiker Unie* v *Commission* Cases 40–48, 50, 54–56, 111, 113 and 114/73 [1975] ECR 1663. Undertakings, according to the Court in this case, are required to act independently and are strictly precluded from:

'... any direct or indirect contact ... the object or effect whereof is either to influence the conduct on the market of an actual or potential competitor or to disclose to such a competitor the course of conduct which they themselves have decided to adopt or contemplate adopting on the market.'

The process in determining whether there is a concerted practice may depend heavily on an economic analysis of the market in order to identify the parties' behaviour. Using this as the basis for determining a concerted practice was somewhat refined in *Ahlström and Others* v *Commission (Re Wood Pulp Cartel)* Cases 89, 104, 114, 116, 117 and 125–129/85 [1994] ECR I–99. The Commission concluded ([1985] 3 CMLR 474) that the charging of similar prices, and uniform and simultaneous increases in them, was sufficient evidence of a concerted practice. On appeal, the European Court annulled much of the Commission's decision, and took a different approach to dealing with such evidence. The Court held that such 'parallel' activity in the market would only be evidence of a concerted practice if there was no other plausible explanation for it. In this case the Court felt that the price increases were based on an oligopolistic market and were reflective of market circumstances during the period. Hence, the burden of proof shifts to the undertakings alleged to have entered into a concerted practice, to justify the parallel activity. Should there be no reasonable justification, such as following an oligopolistic market, or consistent increases in the prices of raw materials or transport costs, then the Commission and Court will probably conclude that there has been a concerted practice in operation.

The academic Weatherill has criticised the handling of oligopolistic situations and makes the pertinent comment that if a true one exists, the firms will take parallel action without colluding, yet the actual result on the market will be the same as if they had. This makes the use of art 81, based on the collusion element, difficult to apply, particularly in the case of true oligopolies. To avoid such problems, the Commission has moved towards a policy of considering firms within such an environment as being in a collectively dominant position. If they abuse that position they are subject to art 82: see Chapter 16.

In summary, the process of assessing whether a concerted practice exists is as follows:

1. the initial burden of proof rests with the Commission;
2. should the Commission produce evidence of parallel behaviour in the market, the burden of proof will shift to the undertaking to objectively justify the activity;
3. if the undertaking claims that the parallel behaviour, particularly that in relation to price, is as a result of oligopolistic market, it should be prepared for the Commission and Court to very closely examine the claim. If they do not believe that the market would lead to uniformity of price, and there is additional evidence of collusion, they will not be prepared to accept the claim as justification;
4. finally, if an undertaking claims that whilst it participated in the concerted practice there was no actual impact on the market, it, and not the Commission, will bear the burden of proof in establishing 'that it did not have any influence whatsoever on its own conduct on the market': see *Huls AG* v *Commission* Case C–199/92P [1999] ECR I–4287, where Huls had been involved in a concerted practice in the form of meetings between undertakings 'on a regular basis over a long period'.

## 15.4 The effect on inter-State trade

It is only when agreements, decisions or concerted practices 'may affect trade' between two or more Member States of the Community that they are subject to the prohibitions of art 81(1). In the absence of such an effect, an agreement will not fall within the scope of the prohibition. As the Court expressly stated in one of its early cases:

> 'It is only to the extent to which agreements may affect trade between Member States that the deterioration in competition falls under the prohibition '... contained in art [81]; otherwise it escapes the prohibition': *Consten and Grundig* v *Commission* Cases 56 and 58/64 [1966] ECR 299.

The question of effect on patterns of trade between Member States is therefore critical to the application of art 81 (and, as we shall see, art 82 also). How this issue is approached by the Commission and the Court will be illustrated by considering a selection of cases.

*Consten and Grundig* (above) concerned an agreement between Grundig, a German company, and Consten, a French wholesale company. The French company agreed to act as sole distributors of Grundig's products in France. The agreement provided, inter alia, that Grundig would not sell to any other French firm or let dealers in other States export to France. Consten agreed not to sell other products, or export to other countries. Consten would, in addition, register Grundig's trade mark in France. However, another French firm bought Grundig's products from a German distributor and imported them into France.

The Commission investigated and gave a decision subsequently upheld by the European Court. They concluded that the aim of the agreement between Consten and Grundig was to isolate the French market with the object of preventing parallel imports. Its overall effect was to affect trade between Member States. The Court also stated that it was not relevant whether the pattern of trade had been detrimentally affected, only that it had been affected in some way.

In *Delimitis* v *Henninger Braü AG* Case C–234/89 [1992] 5 CMLR 210 a German brewery provided financial assistance to a tenant who in return accepted an obligation to purchase a certain volume of beer from the brewery. The tenant failed to meet this minimum purchasing requirement and the brewery deducted penalties for this failure from the deposit he had provided. He raised an action for recovery of the sums in the national court, and the court referred the question of the compatibility of this type of agreement with Community competition law to the European Court for interpretation.

In its decision, the Court provided a clear illustration of the methodology involved in determining whether an agreement has an effect on trade between Member States. The first step in this process is to identify the relevant market. This is done by first determining the relevant product market and, second, the relevant geographical market.

The relevant product market is primarily defined on the basis of the nature of the economic activity in question. In the circumstances of this particular case, the Court identified the relevant product as beer. The sale of beer products takes place in two main forms: through direct retail channels such as off-licences and supermarkets, and through premises for the sale and consumption of drinks such as bars, public houses and cafés. From the consumer's point of view these two economic activities may be distinguished. The first is the mere purchase of a product, while the latter is the purchase of a product linked to the supply of a service. Thus, the relevant product market was held to be the sale of beer products in premises.

The other aspect of the relevant market is the relevant geographical market. In this case, the Court noted that most agreements of this nature are entered into at national levels. In the circumstances, the relevant geographical market was considered to consist of the German national market for beer distributed for sale in premises.

The second step is to consider whether the existence of the agreement, decision or concerted practice affects the relevant market. The assessment of the effect on markets is made primarily in relation to the sealing-off or closing-off of the relevant market to non-national Community producers of similar or competing products. In this case, the Court made the assessment of the sealing-off effect in relation to:

1. the number of outlets tied by similar agreements;
2. the duration of the contracts entered into;
3. the quantity of the product subject to such restrictions; and
4. the proportion between those quantities and the quantities sold to unrelated independent producers.

Ultimately the Court found that the agreement under examination in this case, when considered in the context of all the other similar arrangements maintained by the particular brewery, affected trade between the Member States. Hence, the particular conditions for the application of art 81 were found by the Court to have been satisfied.

However, art 81 also extends to those agreements, decisions or concerted practices that 'may' affect trade between Member States. In *Société Technique Minière* v *Maschinenbau Ulm GmbH* Case 56/65 [1966] ECR 235 (*STM* case) the Court held that the requirements of art 81 would be satisfied if the agreement, decision or practice had a direct or indirect, actual or potential effect on the pattern of trade between Member States. This is further supported by the comment in *Consten* (above) that '[i]t is not necessary to take into consideration the actual effects of an agreement where its purpose is to prevent, restrict or distort competition'. In other words, no concrete affect is required and a potential affect will suffice.

Even if the agreement, decision or concerted practice is between undertakings located only in one Member State, the Court is of the opinion that there may be a breach of art 81. This will certainly be the case if it is either part of a larger agreement or if it prevents imports from other Member States: see *Brasserie de Haecht* v *Wilkin* Case 48/72 [1973] ECR 77, *Publishers Association* v *Commission (No 2)* Case T–66/89 [1992] ECR II–1995 and *Co-operative Stremsel-en Kleurselfabriek* v *Commission* Case 61/80 [1981] ECR 851.

In addition, an agreement applying to trade outside of the Community may also come within art 81(1) if it is found to have an impact on trade within the Community: see the decision of the Commission in *Franco-Japanese Ballbearings Agreement* [1975] 1 CMLR D8. This was indeed the case in *Wood Pulp* (above) where the main sources of wood pulp were outside of the Community, in Canada, the United States, Finland and Sweden. The Court concluded since:

> '... wood pulp producers established in those countries sell directly to purchasers established in the Community and engage in price competition in order to win orders from those customers, that constitutes competition within the common market.'

The crucial factor, therefore, is not where the agreement, decision or concerted practice is made, but where it is actually implemented. In this case the Court held that the wood pulp producers had 'implemented their pricing agreement within the common market' and that the Court had jurisdiction to apply the Community's competition law under the 'territoriality principle as universally recognised in public international law'. (It could be suggested that this is also implicit application of the 'effects doctrine' of jurisdiction under international law, under which jurisdiction is determined by where the effects of the action occur. This is, however, a contentious basis of jurisdiction, which perhaps explains why the Court has avoided using it.)

However, agreements are also subject to consideration in an economic context to see if their effect on competition is simply minimal. Minor agreements may therefore escape the prohibition contained in art 81 because their effect relative to trade between Member States is not of a sufficient impact to raise concern. This is known as the de minimus rule, which provides that agreements having an insignificant effect on trade are not subject to the application of art 81(1): *Völk* v *Etablissements Vervaecke Sprl* Case 5/69 [1969] ECR 295.

In 1986 the Commission published its first Notice Concerning Agreements, Decisions and Concerted Practices of Minor Importance, to allow guidance on the application of this test. This was revoked by new De Minimus Notices in 1997 and 2001. Now, agreements that potentially infringe art 81 must be notified to the Commission unless they benefit from either block exemption (see below) or are within the de minimus rule. Agreements between undertakings will fall within the de minimus exception in the following circumstances according to the 2001 Notice:

1. where the parties are actual or potential competitors, the aggregate market share of the parties to the agreement must not exceed 10 per cent of the market;

2. where the parties are not competitors, the aggregate market share of the parties to the agreement must not exceed 15 per cent of the market share.

If it is impossible to classify the agreement in these terms then the 10 per cent threshold will apply.

If an agreement falls within these boundaries, the Commission will usually not open an investigation. If, at some point, the agreement is found to breach art 81(1) the Commission will not impose a fine, as long as the undertakings acted in good faith.

However, an agreement between competitors must not contain restrictions on sale price, limitation of output, or allocation of markets or customers. Similarly, an agreement between non-competitors cannot contain restrictions on minimum resale prices, or restrictions on the territory or consumers that the goods will be sold to.

## 15.5 Adopting the rule of reason

As we can see from the above analysis, art 81(1) covers all agreements that have the object or effect or preventing, restricting or distorting competition. There have been arguments that this should not in fact be the case and that some agreements do have beneficial facets. American anti-trust law (competition law) has adopted a rule of reason approach; the application of the law hinges on determining whether the agreement is unreasonable in terms of weighing up both the pro- and anti-competitive effects it may have. Over time it was identified that there were certain types of agreement that had no compensatory benefits and which were therefore considered per se illegal, such as price-fixing and market-sharing. A number of academics, including Korah, have argued that the Community should, or indeed has, adopted such a policy.

On the other hand, others, such as Whish, do not support such an approach being adopted within Community competition law. Their main criticism rests on the uncertainty that may be created by the application of such an approach, especially when one considers that it would be the national courts that would have to use it. In addition, of course, art 81(3) already provides for exemption on the basis that the agreement has compensatory benefits: see section 15.7.

If we consider the case law of the Commission and Court to assess whether they have adopted a rule of reason approach we can make the following conclusions. The *STM* case (above) identifies that if the agreement has the object of preventing, restricting or distorting competition, then it will breach art 81(1): see, also, *Ferriere Nord SpA v Commission* Case C–219/95P [1997] 5 CMLR 575. This is akin to the per se approach adopted by American anti-trust law.

If the object is not clearly identifiable, then the Commission and the Court will move on to examine the effects of the agreement by undertaking an economic market analysis: see *Consten and Grundig* (above). The same approach can be seen in *Nungesser KG and Kurt Eisele v Commission* Case 258/78 [1981] ECR 45, where the Court examined whether an exclusive licence violated art 81(1) by assessing its effects. In both *Consten* and *Nungesser* the Court found that there had been partitioning of the market which was detrimental to the creation of a single, internal market.

Economic analysis was also used, to the favour of the parties, in *Pronuptia de Paris GmbH* v *Pronuptia de Paris Irmgard Schillgallis* Case 161/84 [1986] ECR 353: see, also, *Remia BV* v *Commission* Case 42/84 [1985] ECR 2545. In *Pronuptia* the Court examined a distribution franchising arrangement, under which the franchisor granted the franchisee the exclusive right to use the Pronuptia mark for a certain area. The franchisor also agreed not to open, or to permit a third party to open, another shop in the same area and to provide information to aid the establishment of the shop. The franchisee agreed to use the Pronuptia name and to pay royalties. They also agreed to buy 80 per cent of their needs from the franchisor and not to compete with any other Pronuptia business.

The Court stated that distribution franchise agreements, such as this one, gave an independent businessman the chance to use both the mark and commercial methods that had been behind the franchisor's success. This was especially helpful to those that were inexperienced in business, since they could benefit from the reputation and skills of the franchisor without having to spend 'prolonged effort and research' to develop those skills for themselves. In return of these benefits, the Court felt that it was appropriate that the franchisor was able to protect know-how from being transmitted to competitors and to take measures to protect the 'identity and reputation' of their work. Hence, any measures designed to prevent or reduce the risk of this happening would 'not constitute restrictions on competition' within art 81(1).

So, has the Community adopted the rule of reason? On one hand, we can see from the above analysis that certain types of agreement, because they have the object of preventing, distorting or restricting competition, have been held illegal on a basis similar to the per se approach adopted by America. We have also seen that in other cases the Court will assess the pro- and anti-competitive effects and weigh up whether the agreement violates art 81(1). It is a matter of academic debate whether this is the adoption of a rule of reason, or whether, as Whish suggests, it is merely the European Court applying an objective justification approach similar to other areas of Community law.

Interestingly, the Court of First Instance has recently entered the debate on the supposed adoption of a rule of reason under art 81. In *Métropole Télévision (M6), Suez-Lyonnaise des Eaux, France Telecom and Television Française 1 SA (TFI)* v *Commission* Case T–112/99 [2001] 5 CMLR 33 the CFI somewhat controversially commented that it was indeed true that a number of judgments had 'favoured a more flexible interpretation' of art 81, but this could not 'be interpreted as establishing the existence of a rule of reason in Community competition law'. Instead, the Court described the jurisprudence as merely part of a 'broad trend'.

## 15.6 Anti-competitive agreements, decisions and concerted practices

Article 81(1) itself identifies categories of agreements, decisions and concerted practices that may have the object or effect or preventing, restricting or distorting competition within the Community. These include:

1. directly or indirectly fixing purchase or selling prices or any other trading conditions;
2. limiting or controlling production, markets, technical developments or investment;
3. sharing markets or sources of supply;
4. applying dissimilar conditions to equivalent transactions with other trading parties and thereby placing them at a competitive disadvantage; and
5. making the conclusion of contracts subject to acceptance by the other parties of supplementary obligations which, by their nature, have no connection with the subject-matter of such contracts.

This list is non-exhaustive in that it does not identify all the types of agreement that may be subject to the rigours of art 81(1), but where an agreement contains one of these restrictions there is a strong presumption that a distortion of competition will result.

As explained, the agreement need not take the form of a written agreement. Often an anti-competitive arrangement takes the form of an unwritten agreement or consensus among the parties. This is particularly true in the case of cartels. Those cartels established to regulate supply or prices fall firmly within art 81(1) and are almost certainly unlikely to be able to justify such arrangements.

A number of investigations have been conducted by the Commission into the existence of cartels, and the following arrangements have also been held as contrary to Community competition policy:

1. arrangements between producers to set target prices for the sale of a product even though it applied in only one Member State: *Cementhandelaren* v *Commission* (above);
2. agreements to fix prices and to apportion markets: *Società Italiana Vetro* v *Commission (Re Italian Flat Glass Suppliers)* Cases T–68, 77 and 78/89 [1992] 5 CMLR 302; and
3. the setting of volume targets for production: *Polypropylene* (above).

An equally repugnant practice in the eyes of both the Commission and the Court is that of market-sharing. This is where two or more competing producers agree to refraining from competing in the markets of other producers in return for their refraining to compete in their others' market. This practice is condemned whether the apportionment is made on the basis of geography or product ranges: see *Siemans-Fanne* [1988] 4 CMLR 945 and *ACF Chemiefarma NV* v *Commission* Case 41/69 [1970] ECR 661.

The second paragraph of art 81 provides that 'any agreement or decision prohibited pursuant to this article shall be automatically void'. This, however, must be read in light of the availability of exemption: see section 15.7. In addition, the European Court has applied the doctrine of severance: see the *STM* case (above). Only those terms of an agreement that are contrary to the article are void; the rest may remain in force. The agreement itself is void only if those parts of it that are anti-competitive cannot be severed from the agreement itself.

## 15.7 Exemptions

Article 81(3) specifically establishes criteria for exempting individual agreements, decisions and concerted practices from art 81(1). Those that satisfy these criteria are neither void under art 81(2) nor necessarily subject to the imposition of fines: see Chapter 17. Originally, the Commission was the only body empowered to grant exemption under Regulation 17/62. This is being reformed, detailed discussion of which can be found in Chapter 17.

Two positive and two negative tests must be satisfied before an agreement can benefit from exemption. The agreement, decision or concerted practice must:

1. contribute to improving the production or distribution of goods or promoting technical or economic progress; and
2. allow a fair share of the resulting benefits under the agreement to accrue to the consumer.

The agreement, decision or concerted practice must not:

1. impose any restrictions that go beyond the positive aims of the agreement or practice (see, for example, *Nungesser*, above, where the absolute territorial protection offered by the licence 'manifestly' went beyond what was indispensable); nor
2. create the possibility of eliminating competition in respect of a substantial part of the products in question.

Two types of exemption have been created on the basis of the authority of this provision. First, the Commission may issue individual exemption after the formal notification of an agreement has been brought to its attention. The procedure for obtaining an individual exemption is specified in Regulation 17/62: see Chapter 17. Individual exemptions are granted in the form of Commission decisions, which are issued for a limited period and may be made conditional on the fulfilment of certain obligations. A decision may be renewed if the relevant conditions continue to be satisfied. Naturally, an individual exemption will only be granted if the Commission considers that the four conditions in art 81(3) are satisfied.

The approach the Commission will take is summarised in *Re Bayer and Gist-Brocades* [1976] 1 CMLR D98 where it stated:

'For the agreements to contribute to the improvement of production or distribution, or to promote technical and economic progress, they must objectively constitute an improvement on the situation that would otherwise exist. The fundamental principle in this respect, established at the time the Common Market was formed, lays down that fair and undistorted competition is the best guarantee of regular supply on the best terms. Thus the question of contribution to economic progress within the meaning of [art 81(3)] can only arise in those exceptional cases where the free play of competition is unable to produce the best result economically speaking.'

An example of the Commission's application of the four-part test in art 81(3) is the case of *Prym-Werke* [1973] CMLR C250. In this case, Prym had agreed to stop producing needles and to buy all its needs from Werke. This permitted Werke to specialise in the production of needles. First, the Commission identified that there were improvements in production in terms of a 50 per cent increase, resulting in intensive use of the existing factory and the introduction of production-line manufacture. This in turn reduced the high labour costs involved and improved the ability of Werke to produce needles of a more even quality. A fair share of the resulting benefit was assumed to be passed on to consumers as a result of the rationalisation process.

The Commission concluded that there were no indispensable restrictions. The improvement in production was a result of the more intensive utilisation of the production capacity, and that this was only possible if the quantities of needles being produced was significantly higher than before, and remained that way. In order for this to remain the case, it was necessary for Prym to have entered into the agreement for a long period, and to have agreed to both halting its own production and buying its needs from Werke. Prym was able to buy elsewhere should Werke be unable at any point to meet its needs and, at the same time, received a preferential rate from Werke. Finally, the Commission concluded that there was no substantial impact on Community competition since both Prym and Werke were 'exposed to the keen competition from other, sometimes larger, producers'. The Commission therefore decided that the conditions of art 81(3) had been met.

The Commission therefore examined each application on its merits and was unlikely to merely accept it without some re-negotiation. The process was one that was extremely time-consuming and which imposed a heavy burden on the Commission. Whish criticised the process under art 81(3):

'The delays experienced in obtaining an exemption are unfortunate because of the uncertainty and inconvenience which result. It is thought that many firms do not bother to notify their agreements to the Commission, preferring to take the risk that beneficial projects in which they take part will not be discovered or will not be severely punished if they are.'

In response to the problems of delay the Commission adopted an alternative approach to granting exemption, discussed below, as well as introducing radical reform of the exemption procedure, which will be discussed in Chapter 17.

## Block exemption

The second type of exemption is known as 'block exemption', created in an attempt to reduce the workload of, and bureaucratic burden on, the Commission. The Commission is empowered to establish group exemption categories: Council Regulations 19/65 and 1215/99. The Commission has enacted a number of Regulations to grant group exemption to certain types of agreement including the following:

| | |
|---|---|
| Commission Regulation 1983/83 | exclusive distribution agreements |
| Commission Regulation 1984/83 | exclusive purchasing |
| Commission Regulation 123/86 | motor-vehicle distribution agreements |
| Commission Regulation 417/85 | specialisation agreements |
| Commission Regulation 518/85 | research and development agreements |
| Commission Regulation 4087/88 | franchising agreements |
| Commission Regulation 240/96 | technology transfer agreements (which will remain in force until 31 March 2006) |

If an agreement falls within the scope of a block exemption established under a regulation, the parties to the agreement are not required to notify the Commission of the existence of the agreement, decision or concerted practice and the parties cannot be fined by the Commission for violating competition law.

The regulations referred to above generally lay down the permitted restrictions considered essential to the agreement, known as the 'white list'. This is followed by a list of prohibited restrictions, known as the 'black list'. Some of the regulations provide an additional list of restrictions that must be notified to the Commission, known as the 'grey list'. If these are not 'opposed' within six months they should be deemed as exempt. Any other restriction not identified in the lists will have to be granted individual exemption under art 81(3) by the Commission. Examples of practices considered as permissible under the 'white list' in the above block exemption regulations include exclusivity in purchasing or distribution agreements, and restrictions on active searching for business outside the member's own territory in a distribution agreement. In contrast, those practices deemed forbidden under the 'black list' include absolute territorial restriction in exclusive purchasing or distribution agreements and closed exclusive patent licences.

The existing regulations offering block exemption in relation to exclusive distribution, franchising and exclusive purchasing were extended to 31 May 2000. If an agreement was in place by that date it continued to benefit from the block exemption until 31 December 2001, when a new system was applied (see below).

## Revision of the application of competition law to vertical restraints

In 1997 a Green Paper was issued by the Commission, which proposed revision of the application of competition law to vertical restraints. The Commission proposed a number of significant changes to the block exemption system in the case of vertical restraints. It proposed the introduction of a single, but wider, block exemption regulation that would exempt all vertical agreements except for a limited number of serious restraints from the application of art 81(1) EC. In response, the Council adopted Regulation 1215/99, amending Council Regulation 19/65, giving the Commission authority to adopt a block exemption regulation on vertical restraints.

The Commission exercised this authority and adopted Regulation 2790/99 in December 1999. The Regulation came into force on 1 June 2000 (art 12 of Regulation 2790/99), and will run for a period of ten years. Article 2(1) defines vertical agreements as:

> '... agreements or concerted practices entered into between two or more undertakings, each of which operates, for the purpose of the agreement, at a different level of the production or distribution chain, and relating to the conditions under which the parties may purchase, sell or resell certain goods or services.'

It should be noted, though, that the Regulation does not apply to those vertical agreements that are covered by the other block exemption regulations referred to above (art 2(5)), except for those referred to above that expired on 31 May 2000. Agreements concluded before then were considered as valid until 31 December 2001, when the new rules applied.

The Regulation defines vertical agreements as those that improve economic efficiency by facilitating co-ordination and reducing distribution costs: recital 6 of Regulation 2790/99. Article 2 is the essential provision excluding vertical agreements from the scope of art 81 and it extends such exemption beyond what was provided for under the old block regulations in that it is not restricted to only bilateral agreements:

> 'Article 81(1) shall not apply to agreements on concerted practice entered into between *two or more* undertakings each of which operates, for the purposes of the agreement, at a different level of the production or distribution chain, and relating to the conditions under which the parties may purchase, sell, or resell certain goods or services ("vertical agreements") .
>
> This exemption shall apply to the extent to which such agreements contain restrictions of competition falling within the scope of art 81(1) ("vertical restraints").' (emphasis added)

Article 3(1) of Regulation 2790/99 provides that block exemption is available for suppliers that hold a maximum of 30 per cent of the relevant market in which they sell goods or services. Article 3(2) provides that block exemption is available to vertical agreements containing exclusive supply obligations if the market share held by the buyer does not exceed 30 per cent of the market in which it purchases the goods or services. If the market share is more than 30 per cent the undertakings will have to apply for individual exemption under art 81(3) (see above).

In addition, art 2(4) provides that block exemption for vertical restraints will not apply to vertical agreements entered into between competing undertakings (as opposed to those on 'different levels'). It will, however, apply to vertical agreements between competing undertakings in a non-reciprocal agreement where:

1. the buyer's total annual turnover does not exceed 1,000 million euros; or
2. the supplier is both a manufacturer and distributor of goods, while the buyer is a distributor not manufacturing goods competing with the contract goods; or
3. the supplier is a provider of services at several levels of trade, while the buyer does not provide competing services at the level of trade where it purchases the contract services.

Article 4 of the Regulation identifies restraints that are outside the scope of the block exemption, and which are in addition unlikely to secure individual exemption – the black list. If such restraints exist they will also not be severable from the agreement, so the entire agreement will be invalid. Such restraints, known as forbidden 'hardcore' restraints, were drawn up on the basis of both earlier decisions of the Commission and the ECJ's jurisprudence, and include the following:

1. resale price maintenance (except in relation to maximum prices or recommending a sale price as long as there is no incentive offered so that they become set fixed or minimum prices);
2. restrictions on resales, such as refusing to supply (although there are some exceptions);
3. restrictions on sales to users in selective distribution agreements (except when operating out of an unauthorised place of distribution when a prohibition will be acceptable);
4. restrictions on cross-supplies between distributors in a selective distribution system; and
5. restrictions on the sale of spare parts.

Article 5 provides for restraints that are prohibited but which are severable from the agreement, and includes the following:

1. non-competition obligations of a maximum of five years;
2. post-termination non-compete clauses unless they are to protect know-how where a one-year prohibition would be acceptable; and
3. obligations relating to specified competitor brands imposed on selective distribution.

A non-compete obligation is defined in art 1(b) as any direct or indirect obligation causing the buyer not to manufacture, purchase, sell or resell goods or services that compete with the contract goods or services. It will also extend to any direct or indirect obligation on the buyer to purchase from the supplier or designated undertaking more than 80 per cent of the buyer's total purchases of the contract goods or services and their substitutes on the relevant market.

The benefits of block exemption may be withdrawn by the Commission under art 6, if it finds that the agreement violates the principles of art 81(3), especially if market access is denied or significantly restricted by the 'cumulative effect of parallel networks of similar vertical restraints'. The competent authorities of the Member

States are provided with a similar right under art 7, where they may withdraw the benefit of block exemption in relation to their territory or a part of it.

In addition to the new Regulation on vertical restraints, there is a new Regulation (1216/99) on the notification of vertical restraints to the Commission. Undertakings do not have to notify the Commission from the very outset of their agreement, but may apply for exemption at a later date. Should exemption be granted, it will be post-dated. This should further ease the workload of the Commission.

Academics such as Steiner, Kent, Weatherill and Beaumont have all criticised the new Regulation on vertical restraints. The criticisms include that the Regulation perhaps sacrifices the certainty of the previous regime, and the fact that the 30 per cent share of the market criteria will be difficult to assess. Steiner has suggested that, in reality, the Commission may find that its workload has not been eased. Undertakings will make every effort to ensure that they receive guidance and will continue to notify on the basis that they will feel more secure with a formal response from the Commission.

One future development being investigated by the Commission is the treatment of horizontal agreements in a similar manner, although this too may face considerable criticism.

## Comfort letters

The device of a comfort letter is another means the Commission has adopted to relieve some of its workload. (Discussion of Commission proposals in its 1999 White Paper on Modernisation, in terms of further reducing the workload, will be discussed in Chapter 18.) A comfort letter is the communication of the Commission to provide an opinion that the agreement either:

1. does not have the effect of coming within art 81(1) – sometimes referred to as 'soft' negative clearance; or
2. that the agreement does come within art 81(1) but is eligible for exemption – sometimes referred to as 'soft' exemption.

Should an undertaking receive such notification is can usually assume that the file on its agreement, decision or concerted practice has been closed.

The process of delivering a comfort letter, unlike that of individual exemption, is quick and informal. However, comfort letters are not legally binding, being purely administrative in nature: see *Procureur de la République* v *Giry and Guerlain* Case 253/78 [1980] ECR 2237 and *SA Lancôme* v *Etos BV* Case 99/79 [1980] ECR 2511 (known as the *Perfumes Cases*).

Under a 1993 Commission Notice, comfort letters are 'a factor which national courts may take into account in examining whether the agreement or conduct in question are in accordance with the provisions of art [81]'. However, there is still some uncertainty, particularly in national courts, as to the exact effects of a comfort letter.

# 16

# Article 82 EC – Abuse of a Dominant Position

16.1  Introduction

16.2  The relevant market

16.3  The concept of dominance

16.4  The concept of abuse

16.5  The period of investigation

16.6  Merger control

## 16.1 Introduction

Article 82 EC states that:

> 'Any abuse by one or more undertakings of a dominant position within the common market or a substantial part of it shall be prohibited as incompatible with the common market in so far as it may affect trade between Member States. Such abuse may, in particular, consist in:
> (a) Directly or indirectly imposing unfair purchase or selling prices or unfair trading conditions;
> (b) Limiting production, markets or technical development to the prejudice of consumers;
> (c) Applying dissimilar conditions to equivalent transactions with other trading parties, thereby placing them at a competitive disadvantage;
> (d) making the conclusion of contracts subject to acceptance by the other parties of supplementary obligations which, by their nature or according to commercial usage, have no connection with the subject of such contracts'.

The practices prohibited under art 82 are broadly similar in nature to those addressed in art 81. The primary difference is that art 82 is intended to regulate the activities of generally one, or at most a few, parties, whereas the essence of art 81(1) is the existence of an agreement, decision, or concerted practice among a number of parties.

This is not to say, however, that art 82 only applies to the activities of single companies, since art 82 itself refers to the abuse of a dominant position by 'one or more undertakings'. This is relatively easy to determine if the dominant position is held by a number of undertakings that are part of the same corporate group or economic unit: see, for example *Europemballage Corporation and Continental Can Co Inc* v *Commission* Case 6/72 [1973] ECR 215.

The difficulties occur when trying to apply art 82 to an oligopolistic market, one in which there are a number of undertakings holding market power and who react to each other's conduct in a parallel manner (discussed also in Chapter 15). It originally appeared that art 82 did not apply to such situations: see *Hoffman-La Roche* v *Commission* Case 85/76 [1979] ECR 461. The European Court has, however, changed its practice in relation to this aspect of the application of art 82 and has held that some types of oligopolistic markets may come within the ambit of this Treaty provision.

In *Società Italiana Vetro* v *Commission* Cases T–68, 77 and 78/89 [1992] 5 CMLR 302 also referred to as *Re Italian Flat Glass Suppliers* (discussed in Chapter 15) the European Court held that art 82 could be applied to three Italian glass producers. The Commission found that the undertakings had a collective dominant position and presented themselves on the market as one, single entity. As a single entity they were able to pursue their own commercial policy to an extent independent of any ordinary market conditions. On appeal to the Court of First Instance the decision was annulled because of errors in reasoning and a lack of proof. However, the CFI did pass comment on such oligopolisitc behaviour in terms of the application of art 82:

> 'There is nothing, in principle, to prevent two or more independent economic entities from being, on a specific market, united by such economic links that, by virtue of that fact, together they hold a dominant position vis-à-vis the other operators on the same market.'

The CFI therefore referred to the need not to merely consider the structure of the market but whether there were other links between the undertakings, such as technological 'agreements or licences'. However, it should be noted that certain conduct in this type of market, such as a concerted practice providing for collusive behaviour, will already be caught within the terms of art 81: see Chapter 15. Article 82 will therefore be of use only to the extent that the behaviour is not already within the ambit of art 81, in other words, non-collusive behaviour, such as refusing to supply: see section 16.4.

The European Court has also suggested the application of art 82 to situations where the undertakings have collective dominance. In *Municipality of Almelo* v *NV Energiebedriff Ijsselmij* Case C–393/92 [1994] ECR I–1477 the undertaking, IJM, had a non-exclusive concession from the Dutch government to distribute electricity within a certain prescribed area. IJM supplied electricity to rural areas directly, but also supplied it to local distributors, predominately in urban areas. These local distributors were bound to buy their needs from IJM by an exclusive purchasing clause, and were also bound to pay a charge to offset the differences in supplying rural and urban areas. The local distributors challenged the charge as a breach of art 82.

The Court, on a preliminary reference, held that one undertaking with a non-exclusive concession in one part of a Member State may not be in a dominant position. The situation would, however, be different if IJM were part of a group of undertakings that collectively held a dominant position. This was to be determined by the national court.

There are suggestions that art 82 should not be used in oligopolistic situations. Whish believes that treating such behaviour as an abuse and imposing fines is inappropriate. Craig and de Burca suggest that oligopolies are less of a threat to competition than the abusive actions of single dominant undertakings, since oligopolies are often pursuing an effective and rational market strategy and as a result should be treated differently.

In summary, the number of parties is not the crucial factor, although in investigations under art 82 this number does tend to be small. The important elements are the position of the parties in the relevant market and their behaviour in that market.

Article 82 shares a number of common features with art 81(1). The concept of 'undertaking' referred to in art 81(1) (discussed in Chapter 15) also applies to investigations under art 82. Similarly, both articles require that the practices carried out affect trade between Member States, and the analysis given to this requirement under art 81 is equally applicable to investigations under art 82.

The Court of First Instance has held that arts 81 and 82 may be applied to the same parties for the same behaviour. However, the Commission is not entitled to simply reiterate the same facts they provided for an action under art 81 to justify a simultaneous investigation under art 82: *Re Italian Flat Glass Suppliers* (above). This safeguard will not prevent companies with no economic ties, other than parallel commercial behaviour, from being potentially subject to investigation under both provisions. This will be the case if it can be shown that, in addition to engaging in practices prohibited under art 81, the parties possess a collective dominant position in the relevant market and are engaging in abusive behaviour.

Article 82 essentially concerns the issue of market dominance through the activities of monopolies, duopolies and some oligopolies. It should, however, be carefully noted that market dominance per se is not prohibited under this article. Rather, it is the abuse of a dominant position that is attacked.

To establish a breach of art 82 it is first necessary (having established that the party is an undertaking) to identify the relevant market to which the alleged violation relates. In common with art 81, this requires identification of both a product market and a geographical market. Once the relevant market has been identified, the next stage is to assess the degree of dominance exercised by the party or parties under investigation. Only after such an assessment has been made is it possible to confirm whether an undertaking maintains a dominant position.

In the event that a dominant position is confirmed, it is then necessary to proceed to examine the existence of any abusive behaviour that can be attributed to the party. It is the existence of any abuse that is the prerequisite for the application of art 82; the behaviour of the undertaking will therefore be the crucial factor, rather than the existence of the power of a dominant position per se. In the absence of such behaviour, whilst there may be a dominant position, there can never be a violation of art 82.

## 16.2 The relevant market

It is first necessary to identify what the relevant market is in order to decide whether there is or might be a restriction of competition or the abuse of a dominant position. This is crucial to the success of an action by the Commission, since without it the Court may annul the Commission's decision, as was the case in *Continental Can* (above).

The Commission's 1997 Notice on Relevant Product Markets explains the application of the concept of relevant product and geographic markets for the purposes of EC competition law, and is largely based on the case law of the European Court, the CFI and the Commission, discussed below. (The Notice has recently been reviewed and a revised draft version can be accessed at www.europa.eu.int/comm/competition.) The Notice sets out basic principles for market definition, recognising that firms are subject to three main elements, namely: demand substitutability; supply substitutability; and potential competition.

The Notice defines the relevant product market as:

'... all those products and/or services which are regarded as interchangeable or substitutable by the consumer, by reason of the products' characteristics, their price and their intended use.'

Hence, in defining the relevant product market, the Commission first analyses the product's characteristics and its intended use. As for whether two products are deemed substitutes, the Commission looks at: evidence of substitution in the recent past; the views of customers and competitors; consumer preferences; barriers and costs associated with switching demand to potential substitutes; and the different categories of customers and price discrimination.

To define geographic markets, the Commission considers the distribution of the parties' and their competitors' market shares and will usually conduct a preliminary analysis of pricing and price differences at national and Community level. It also checks supply factors to ensure that companies located in distinct areas are not prevented from developing their sales in competitive terms throughout the whole geographic market. Finally, the Commission takes into account the continuing process of market integration, particularly in areas of concentration and structural joint ventures.

## The relevant product market

The Commission must identify the relevant product market (RPM), because competition can only be judged between like products. The delineation is also important because the boundaries have to be set in which the market power of the undertaking in question may be considered. The Commission Notice, above, provides guidelines on how this may be achieved. In addition, the Commission, the CFI and the ECJ, through past cases, have provided guidelines on how the relevant product market may be identified.

### Interchangeability or substitutability

Simply, if products are not interchangeable they are not part of the same product market. They may be so if they are reasonably interchangeable. To determine interchangeability the use, nature and price of the goods or products must be considered, as well as the customers. It is worthy of note that the smaller the RPM, the easier it will be to identify dominance within it.

In *Michelin* v *Commission* Case 322/81 [1983] ECR 3461 the Commission bought an action against Michelin for breaching art 82. The offending practice was Michelin's practice of giving discounts on tyre sales that were not related to objective differences in costs. The allegation by the Commission was that this practice was designed to tie purchasers to Michelin. The Commission based its decision that Michelin was in a dominant position on the RPM, that of new replacement tyres for lorries, buses and similar vehicles. Michelin appealed against this decision, arguing that the RPM included retread tyres and tyres for cars and vans. The European Court made the following point:

> '... for the purposes of investigating the possibly dominant position of an undertaking on a given market, the possibilities of competition must be judged in the context of the market comprising the totality of the products which, with respect to their characteristics, are particularly suitable for satisfying constant needs and are only to a limited extent interchangeable with other products.'

The Court referred to the need to also take into account the 'competitive conditions and the structure of supply and demand'. On applying such factors to the case the Court came to the following conclusions. First, it held that original-equipment tyres should not be included as part of the RPM because the structure of demand was via direct orders from car manufacturers so competition in that area was governed by entirely different rules and factors. Second, in relation to replacement tyres, the Court held that there was no interchangeability between car and van tyres and those used for heavy vehicles such as lorries. In addition, the demand for heavy vehicle tyres came from trade users for whom the cost of replacement tyres was a considerable expense, when compared to the occasional expense for the average car or van user. Finally, the Court held that there was 'no elasticity of supply' between tyres for heavy vehicles and car tyres because of the 'significant differences in production techniques' and manufacture. Consequently, the Court upheld the definition of the RPM made by the Commission.

In *Hilti AG* v *Commission* Case T–30/89 [1991] ECR II–1439 the applicants asserted that nail guns, nail cartridge strips for such guns and nails were one single market, since each of them could not be used by consumers without the others. The Commission disagreed, and argued that the products were each within their own separate and independent product market because they could not be interchanged in their own right.

The Court of First Instance upheld the argument of the Commission. All the products could be manufactured separately and could be purchased without having to purchase the others. Their interchangeability was therefore restricted. Similarly, other products could be substituted for each of the products. For example, nails and cartridges could be purchased from other suppliers to fit the equipment. The finding of the three separate product markets was therefore confirmed. On appeal, the European Court upheld the CFI's findings: see *Hilti* v *Commission (No 2)* Case C–53/92P [1994] ECR I–667.

In *Hugin Kassaregister AB and Hugin Cash Registers Ltd* v *Commission* Case 22/78 [1979] ECR 1869 the Commission held Hugin to be in breach of art 82 by refusing to supply spare parts for its cash registers to a firm that competed with Hugin in servicing Hugin's cash registers. The Commission based its decision on an RPM of only spare parts for Hugin cash registers, whereas Hugin argued and appealed on the basis that the RPM should have been cash registers in general.

The Court identified that specialists were needed to service cash registers. In addition, it identified that there was a 'separate market' for Hugin spare parts for a number of reasons. First, the independent undertakings that specialised in the repair, maintenance, reconditioning, second-hand sale and renting out of cash machines needed the spare parts to conduct their business. Second, there was a specific demand for Hugin spare parts since 'those parts are not interchangeable with spare parts for cash registers of other makes'. Again, the Court upheld the Commission's identification of the RPM.

The Commission has also considered the RPM for chemical products where there is often a wide range of interchangeable or substitutable products. In *AKZO Chemie BV* v *Commission* Case C–62/86 [1991] ECR I–3359 the Commission identified the RPM as organic peroxides, even though such products had a wide range of uses. In order to isolate the RPM, the Commission considered the uses for which such products could be applied. It decided that abusive behaviour had only been perpetrated in relation to one type of application of the products, namely bleaching agents, as opposed to other applications for the products in the plastics sector. The relevant product market was defined as organic peroxides used as bleaching agents and was subsequently upheld by the European Court.

### Cross-elasticity of demand and supply

The simple question to be answered here is whether, if there were an increase in the price of a product, the consumer would choose another. If so, those two products are probably in the same market. The 1997 Notice refers to examining cross-elasticity in the following terms:

'The question to be answered is whether the parties' customers would switch to readily available substitutes or to suppliers located elsewhere in response to a hypothetical small (in the range of 5 per cent to 10 per cent) but permanent relative price increase in the products and areas being considered.'

In *United Brands Co & United Brands Continental BV* v *Commission* Case 27/76 [1978] ECR 207 it was held that bananas were the RPM. The Court had examined the idea that there might be cross-elasticity of demand for bananas with other fresh fruit, but concluded that if there was it was not significant. There were other factors to be considered, such as the end use of the product and whether certain users could switch from bananas to other fresh fruit with ease. In this case it was concluded that switching from bananas to other fresh fruit was particularly difficult for certain consumers, such as the old, sick and very young. Hence, bananas were held, in a contentious and often criticised decision, to be a RPM in their own right.

In *Tetra Pak Rausing SA* v *Commission (No 1)* Case T–51/89 [1991] 4 CMLR 334 the cartons used for fresh milk and those for UHT milk were concluded to be two different RPMs since consumers did not regard the products as interchangeable because they tasted different.

As we can see from the above discussion, identifying the RPM may be a difficult and contentious process. Those definitions concluded by the Commission have often been criticised, particularly by economists. As a general rule, it appears the Commission and the Court will define the RPM as small as possible, given the range of considerations described above, but the parties to any investigation will have to appreciate the complex nature of identifying this aspect of art 82.

## The relevant geographical market

The relevant geographical market is the area within the Community in which the practice produces its effects. For the purposes of art 82 the relevant geographical market has to be the 'common market or a substantial part of it'. The 1997 Notice defines the geographical market as:

'The relevant geographical market comprises that area in which the undertakings concerned are involved in the supply and demand of products and services, in which the conditions of competition are sufficiently homogeneous and which can be distinguished from neighbouring areas because the conditions of competition are appreciably different on those areas.'

The geographical market is presumed to be the whole of the Community if the products that are the subject of the investigation are regularly bought and sold in all Member States: *Hilti* (above). The relevant geographical market will be smaller than the Community in three main instances:

1. if the nature and characteristics of the product, such as high transportation costs or short shelf life, restrict distribution: see the decision of the Commission in *Napier Brown–British Sugar* [1988] 4 CMLR 347;
2. where the movement of the product within the Community is hindered by barriers to entry into another national market, caused by state intervention, ie quotas, non-tariff barriers, technical barriers etc; and
3. where the marketing and sales efforts by the company under investigation are intentionally restricted to a particular part of the Community.

A single Member State may be the relevant geographical market; in *Michelin* (above) the Court considered that Belgium was a substantial part of the common market: see, also, *Italy v Commission* Case 41/83 [1985] ECR 873. In *Hugin* v *Commission* (above) it was held that part of a Member State could also be considered 'substantial': see, also, *Corsica Ferries Italia Ltd* v *Corpo dei Piloti del Porto di Genoa* Case C–18/93 [1994] ECR I–1783. In *BP* v *Commission* Case 77/77 [1978] ECR 1513 the Advocate-General expressed the opinion that Luxembourg should be considered a substantial part of the market, even though at the time it held only approximately 2 per cent of the Community's population.

It should be noted that the geographical market may shift over time, with consumer preferences changing and technological advances in certain products. Alternatively, a geographical market may exist for only a specific or limited period of time (a 'temporal' market), for example, when one product is in demand because the imported, substitute product(s) is available on only a seasonal basis.

## 16.3 The concept of dominance

The European Court has defined a dominant position in the following terms:

> '... a position of economic strength enjoyed by an undertaking which enables it to prevent effective competition being maintained on the relevant market by giving it the power to behave to an appreciable extent independently of its competitors, customers and ultimately of its consumer': *United Brands* (above).

In *Hoffman-La Roche* v *Commission* Case 85/76 [1979] ECR 461 the above definition was repeated, and the following comment added:

> 'Such a position does not preclude some competition ... but enables the undertaking which profits by it, if not to determine, at least to have an appreciable effect on the conditions under which that competition will develop, and in any case to act largely in disregard of it so long as such conduct does not operate to its detriment.'

The Commission and the Court will examine two main factors to assess whether the undertaking in is a dominant position within the relevant market. These are:

1. the market share that the undertaking possesses; and
2. other factors that may contribute to its ability to be dominant in the market.

## *The market share*

This should be the first factor considered in determining whether dominance exists in the relevant market. In *Hoffman–La Roche* (above) the Court concluded that 'very large shares are, in themselves, evidence of the existence of a dominant position'. Therefore, an undertaking with a statutory monopoly will be in a dominant position and will be subject to the provisions of Community competition law (subject to the terms of art 86 EC: see Chapter 18). Apart from statutory monopolies, there will be few situations in which an undertaking holds 100 per cent of the market share. However, a large market share held over some time will be sufficient to establish per se dominance: *Hoffman–La Roche* (above).

The 'magic' figure of 50 per cent of the market share was held in *AKZO* (above) to be sufficiently large enough to reveal a dominant position. The writers Sufrin and Jones also point to what appears to be the development of a new approach towards those undertakings with 'large' market shares, that they describe as 'super-dominance'. In such cases it appears that the Commission and the Court are of the opinion that such undertakings have a higher degree of responsibility to ensure compliance with competition rules and procedures: see, for example, the Commission's comments in *Comité Français d'Organisation de la Coupe du Monde* (2000) OJ L5/55 (Decision 2000/12), [2000] 2 CMLR 963 and the Court's comments in *Compagnie Maritime Belge Transports SA* v *Commission* Cases C–395 and 396/96P [2000] ECR I–1365.

However, market shares of below 50 per cent may be sufficient to indicate a dominant position, in certain circumstances. Thus, in *United Brands* (above) a market of share of 41–45 per cent was held to be a dominant position, given the high fragmentation of the rest of the market share. Indeed, it is the existence of other factors that may lead to the conclusion that the market share is sufficient to establish dominance. In *Hoffman–La Roche* the Court identified that Hoffman held 43 per cent of the relevant market, in this case certain vitamins, but there were no other factors indicating dominance, such as that share having been held for some time and the undertaking having some element of freedom of action. It is therefore worth considering these 'other factors' that may be considered in deciding whether the undertaking has a dominant position.

## *Other factors indicative of dominance*

In *Hoffman–La Roche* the Court identified other factors relevant in determining whether there was dominance. The Court referred to the following:

> '... the relationship between the market share of the undertaking concerned and of its competitors, especially those of the next largest, the technological lead of an undertaking over its competitors, the existence of a highly developed sales network and the absence of potential competition are relevant factors ...'

## The market share of competitors

The Court stated in *Hoffman* that this may be indicative of dominance because it enables the strength of the undertaking to be assessed. In *United Brands*, as referred to above, the rest of the market was highly fragmented, with competitors to United Brands holding only approximately 10–16 per cent of the market share.

## Financial and technological resources

In *Hoffman* the Court stated that consideration of this factor was relevant because 'they represent in themselves technical and commercial advantages'. Hence, possession of superior technology has been identified as an important factor in determining that there was dominance: see, for example, *United Brands* and *Michelin* (above). In *Continental Can* (above) the significant factor was the undertaking's ready access to the international capital market.

## Control of production and distribution ('sales network')

The Court considered that this was evidence in support of a dominant position for the same reason as having a technological or financial lead – it provides a commercial advantage in its own right. Control over production and distribution can also be referred to as 'vertical integration'. This factor was significant in the *United Brands* case, where it is was found that the company owned the plantations where the bananas were grown, the means by which they were transported, and also marketed the product. A similar conclusion was reached in *Hoffman-La Roche* since the company had a highly developed sales network. However, the inclusion of this factor in determining dominance has been criticised, since undertakings often develop vertical integration because it is an efficient method of producing and marketing their product.

## The absence of potential competition

The Court stated that this should be a factor because it would be the consequence of 'obstacles preventing new competitors from having access to the market'. One aspect that may be examined to determine this is the law of the Member States. The Court will consider the legal provisions within Member States, to assess whether they act in a manner so as to prevent or hinder potential competitors from entering into the market. In particular there will be examination of any industrial or intellectual property rights that may exist. In *Hugin* (above), the Court supported the conclusion that Hugin was in a dominant position because other undertakings were disinclined to enter the market in producing spare parts because they thought that they may breach the Design and Copyright Act 1968.

## The conduct and performance of the undertaking

This is an additional factor that the Court and the Commission have been prepared to consider. In *Michelin* the Court believed that the discriminatory pricing conducted by the firm was evidence of dominance. Economic performance may also be considered, hence in *Hoffman-La Roche* there was spare, idle capacity, which was indicative of dominance. In *United Brands* the company had suffered losses, but the Court found that it had nevertheless successfully retained its market share and was consequently still in a dominant position.

The Commission and the Court's use of such factors has been the subject of much criticism. The essential problem appears to be that they do not distinguish between barriers to competition created by the undertaking merely being efficient and those that are created artificially. It has been suggested that only the latter should be used to indicate dominance for the purpose of the application of competition law. Whish suggests that the effect of using such criteria may lead to firms being 'fearful' of being highly efficient because that could lead to their being classed as dominant. The irony in this being the state of affairs is that free competition, which the Community attempts to promote, could, of course, be stifled.

## 16.4 The concept of abuse

### *General*

There are many similarities between the types of behaviour prohibited under art 81 and those under art 82. In both cases, the provisions will be interpreted in the light of art 3(1)(g) EC.

In relation to art 82 the finding of abuse will have a considerable impact on the undertaking(s) since, unlike art 81, there is no means of obtaining negative clearance or any form of exemption. As we shall discover, though, the European Court has developed an objective justification test that may be used by an undertaking to justify some forms of abusive behaviour.

Abuse is not defined within the Treaty, but the Court in *Hoffman-La Roche* (above) referred to abuse as influencing the structure of the market and weakening or hindering competition. Undertakings have a special responsibility 'not to allow conduct to impair genuine undistorted competition in the common market'. In *Michelin* (above) abuse was defined as:

> '... behaviour ... which, through recourse to methods different from those which condition normal competition ..., has the effect of hindering the maintenance of the degree of competition still existing in the market or the growth of that competition.'

The abuse must be discerned by its effects. In addition, the concept of abuse is objective, so there is no requirement to prove any fault on the part of the undertaking: *Hoffman-La Roche* (above) and *BPB Industries* v *Commission* Case T–65/89 [1993] ECR II–389.

Types of abuses are referred to in art 82, although *Continental Can* (above) confirms that this is a non-exhaustive list. Abuses that are within the ambit of art 82 may, for simplicity, be categorised as either:

1. exploitative abuses; or
2. anti-competitive abuses, although there is no absolute demarcation between the two types and, in some cases, a particular form of abuse may fall into both categories.

An exploitative abuse will be one where the dominant undertaking takes advantage of its position of strength. This will often take the form of imposing unfair conditions, such as unfair pricing. Generally, an exploitative abuse will affect consumers in an unfair way.

An anti-competitive abuse is one that is not necessarily unfair, or harsh. Indeed in some cases consumers will perceive them as beneficial, but they will reduce or eliminate competition within the relevant market. Thus, the dominant undertaking will seek to exercise its strength in a manner that undermines or eliminates existing competitors, or prevents new competitors from entering the market.

Mergers were considered in *Continental Can* to be an anti-competitive abuse. Both mergers and acquisitions may lead to abuse where one producer in a dominant position in the manufacturing or distribution of a product is able to absorb competitors. Such market dominance would, however, only amount to abuse if the acquisition or merger were undertaken with an anti-competitive motive in mind: *Tetra Pak Rausing SA* v *Commission* (above). However, mergers are now generally considered in their own right: see section 16.6.

The Court confirmed the fact that art 82 covers both forms of abuse in *Continental Can*:

> '... the provision is not only aimed at practices which may cause damage to the consumer directly, but also at those which are detrimental to them through their impact on an effective competition structure ... Abuse may therefore occur if an undertaking in a dominant position strengthens such position in such a way that the degree of dominance reached substantially fetters competition.'

## Examples of exploitative abuses

### Unfair prices
An unfair price may be a price that is excessive. This has been defined by the Court, in obiter, as a price that bears no relation to the economic value of the product supplied: *United Brands* (above), *General Motors Continental NV* v *Commission* Case 26/75 [1975] ECR 1367 and *British Leyland plc* v *Commission* Case 226/84 [1986] ECR 3263. However, it should be appreciated that there may be difficulties in defining the economic value of some 'products', especially services.

### Unfair trading conditions
An example of this form of abuse may be seen in the *United Brands* case, where the company imposed a condition on importers that they only resell their bananas whilst they were still green. In order to do this wholesalers required specialised storage

conditions. This was concluded to be an unfair trading condition, regardless of the fact that in this case consumers may have perceived some benefit from being able to purchase a consistently better quality product.

### Discriminatory treatment/ pricing

Article 82 does not impose an obligation on undertakings to charge the same prices for all of its transactions, and in reality different prices will often be charged. So, for example, quantity discounts will not normally breach art 82. However, a breach of art 82 may occur in terms of charging a discriminatory price for the product. In other words, the price charged is one that the undertaking estimates the market will be able to bear. In terms of art 82, this will constitute dissimilar conditions on equivalent transactions. Hence, the CFI has concurred with the Commission that artificial prices are a breach of art 82: *Tetra Pak Rausing SA v Commission (No 2)* Case T–83/91 [1994] ECR II–755.

Price differences on the basis of nationality will also breach art 82. In *United Brands* the prices charged for bananas in different Member States varied by over 100 per cent. This, however, will not constitute an abuse if there are objective reasons for the price differences, such as increased transport costs to move the product to some locations, or the intensity of competition. The undertaking will incur the burden of proof in establishing that such objective reasons exist.

Other forms of discriminatory price differences that have been held to constitute abuse include:

1. lower prices at the borders of Member States to attempt to protect the home market from imports: *Irish Sugar plc v Commission* Case T–228/97 [1999] ECR II–2969; and
2. offering rebates to purchasers intending to export the final product: *Irish Sugar* (above).

### Refusal to supply

This type of abuse may fall into both categories. *United Brands* provides an example of an exploitative refusal to supply. In this case one of its wholesalers (Olesen), who had constructed the specialised storage facilities required by United Brands, entered into an advertising campaign for a rival company. United Brands, in retaliation, refused to supply the company with bananas. United Brands attempted to justify its action, and the Court accepted that in some circumstances an undertaking must be able to respond to protect its interests in a way that was 'reasonable', 'appropriate' and 'proportionate'. Such action could not be permitted 'if its actual purpose is to strengthen [the] dominant position and abuse it'. In the particular circumstances of the case the Court concluded that:

> 'The sanction consisting of refusal to supply by an undertaking in a dominant position was in excess of what might, if such a situation were to arise, reasonably be contemplated as a sanction for conduct similar to that for which UBC blamed Oelsen.'

The refusal to supply Oelsen was compounded by the fact that the company had been a regular customer:

'... [an] undertaking in a dominant position for the purposes of marketing a product ... cannot stop supplying a long standing customer who abides by regular commercial practice, if orders placed by that customer are in no way out of the ordinary.'

One objective reason for refusing to supply could be that there is a shortage of the product in question. In *BP v Commission* Case 77/77 [1978] ECR 1513 it was held that the decision of BP to supply only contractual and regular customers during an oil shortage was not abusive. However, the decision as to who does not receive the product in such circumstances should not be based on who is or has been the most loyal customer, since this is not an objective criteria: *BPB Industries plc and British Gypsum Ltd v Commission* Case C–310/93P [1995] ECR I–865 (upholding the CFI decision Case T–65/89 [1993] ECR II–389).

## Examples of anti-competitive abuses

### Predatory pricing
This will occur when the undertaking reduces its prices, to a point that may even be below cost price, in other words incurring a loss, in order to drive the competition out of the market. Hence, a predatory price may be defined as one that is below the average variable cost. This definition was upheld by the European Court in *Tetra Pak Rausing SA v Commission (No 2)* Case C–333/94P [1996] ECR I–5951. In this case the Court emphasised that predatory pricing would be abusive because it had 'no conceivable economic purpose other than elimination of a competitor'.

If there are, perhaps, other explanations for the lower price, then intent should be examined. In the case of *AKZO Chemie v Commission* Case C–62/86 [1991] ECR I–3359 it was established that the company had the 'avowed intention' of eliminating one of its particular competitors. However, it appears that where there is no evidence to establish intent the burden of proof shifts to the undertaking to establish that their actions were not anti-competitive. This has been confirmed by the European Court: see *Compagnie Maritime Belge Transports v Commission* Cases C–395–396/96P [2000] All ER (EC) 385.

### Exclusive reservation of activities
This occurs when a dominant undertaking reserves certain activities for itself, or for an appointed agent. In *CBEM v CLT & IPB (Re Telemarketing)* Case 311/84 [1985] ECR 3261 a telephone marketing service was reserved exclusively to the undertaking's agent. The Court identified that this exclusive reservation of activities was an abuse within art 82. However, the Court also identified that such reservation of activities may be objectively justified:

'... an abuse within the meaning of [art 82] is committed where, without any objective necessity, an undertaking holding a dominant position in a particular market reserves to itself or to an undertaking belonging to the same group an ancillary activity which might be carried out by another undertaking as part of its activities on a neighbouring but separate market, with the possibility of eliminating all competition from such an undertaking.'

In the case, the undertaking claimed that the exclusive reservation was needed to protect its image, but the Court did not accept the measure as being necessary (proportionate) to secure this aim.

### Import and export bans
These will generally always breach art 82 (see *Suiker Unie v Commission* Case 40/73 [1975] ECR 1663), with perhaps the only possible justification being the need to protect industrial property rights.

### Giving loyalty or fidelity rebates
The providing of quantity rebates will not generally breach art 82. However, the giving of rebates to secure loyalty (tie in the purchaser) may affect competition by placing pressure on a distributor or retailer to favour a particular supplier's product in order to earn the rebate. *Michelin*, *Suiker Unie* and *Hoffman-La Roche* all provide examples of this type of abuse.

In *Michelin* the Court stated that in order to examine whether a rebate breached art 82 it was necessary to investigate the following:

'... whether, in providing an advantage not based on any economic service justifying it, the discounts tend to remove or restrict the buyer's freedom to choose his sources of supply, to bar competitors from access to the market, to apply dissimilar conditions to equivalent transactions with other trading parties or to strengthen the dominant position by distorting competition.'

In *Hoffman-La Roche* the Court examined a contract providing for fidelity rebates. Hoffman was the largest pharmaceutical company in the world at the time. It was concluded to have a dominant position in seven separate vitamin markets. The abuse centred on their use of a requirement contract with their customers, who undertook to purchase all of their requirements from Hoffman, in return for a discount. The contract also included an 'English clause', which provided that should a customer find a product elsewhere that was cheaper they were free to purchase that product but only after they had informed Hoffman, and Hoffman had failed to adjust its price accordingly.

The Commission, and the Court on appeal, concluded that the tying practice was anti-competitive, even though customers received some tangible benefit. The practice allowed Hoffman to identify its competitors and, if it wished, take pre-emptive action on the market by altering its prices accordingly. The practice was therefore a means by which Hoffman could receive useful information about the marketing strategy of rival undertakings, without having to make any positive efforts itself.

**Refusal to supply**

The leading case in relation to refusal to supply as an anti-competitive abuse is found in *Istituto Chemioterapico Italiano SpA and Commerical Solvents Corporation* v *Commission* Cases 6 and 7/73 [1974] ECR 223.

Commercial Solvents Corporation (CSC) produced raw materials required for the manufacture of a drug for tuberculosis called ethambutol. CSC acquired 51 per cent of Istituto, an Italian company that purchased raw materials from CSC. It also sold on the raw materials to a number of undertakings, including Zoja, also an Italian company. Istituto failed in a bid to acquire Zoja, and then decided to increase the price of the raw materials to Zoja. Zoja found an alternative source of supply from another company, but one that also bought the raw materials for ethambutol from CSC.

CSC instructed the companies that bought their raw materials from them not to sell on to Zoja, which found that it was unable to purchase the raw materials. CSC then announced that it would no longer be selling the raw materials, but would instead utilise them in producing its own ethambutol. Zoja attempted to re-order the raw materials from CSC but was refused supply.

The Court held that:

'... an undertaking being in a dominant position as regards the production of raw materials and therefore able to control the supply to manufacturers of derivatives cannot, just because it decides to start manufacturing those derivatives (in competition with its former customers), act in such a way as to eliminate their competition which, in the case in question, would amount to eliminating one of the principal manufacturers of ethambutol in the common market. Since such conduct is contrary to the objectives expressed in Article 3(1)(g) of the Treaty and set out in greater detail in [arts 81 and 82], it follows that an undertaking which has a dominant position in the market in raw materials and which, with the object of reserving such raw materials for manufacturing its own derivatives, and therefore risks eliminating all competition on the part of this customer, is abusing its dominant position within the meaning of [art 82].'

A similar decision can be found in *Radio Telefis Eireann* v *Commission* Case T–69/89 [1991] ECR II–485 (joined with *BBC and ITP* v *Commission* Cases 70 and 76/89 [1991] ECR II–485). In this case RTE, an Irish statutory body providing broadcasting services, reserved for itself the exclusive right to publish a weekly schedule of television programmes for all its channels. Magill TV Guide Limited wished to publish a television guide covering all available channels (including the BBC and ITV), but RTE claimed that this would infringe copyright and injunctions were brought to prevent Magill from publishing.

Magill sought to have the injunctions removed, claiming that they infringed art 82. The company, though, went out of business, so the Commission took up the matter. The Commission found that the refusal to supply was an abuse within art 82, and ordered the supply of the necessary information (*Magill TV Guide* [1989] 4 CMLR 757). RTE appealed to the CFI.

The CFI recognised that protecting copyright was permissible under Community law, and that the copyright owner could exercise the right to protect their work, but that exercise of this right had to be compatible with art 82. In this case, the CFI held that the withholding of the information prevented the emergence of a new product on to the market. This new guide would compete with RTE's guide. RTE were therefore using their copyright to 'secure a monopoly' in the particular market of weekly television guides: see *RTE and ITP* v *Commission* Cases C–241 and 242/91P [1995] ECR I–743. The CFI stated:

> 'Conduct of that type – characterised by preventing the production and marketing of a new product, for which there is potential consumer demand ... and thereby excluding all competition from that market solely in order to secure the applicant's monopoly – clearly goes beyond what is necessary to fulfil the essential function of the copyright as permitted in Community law.'

This may also be known as refusal to provide essential facilities. That this may constitute an abuse can be seen in the decision of the Commission in *London European Airways* v *Sabena* [1989] 4 CMLR 662. The airline refused to provide access to its computer reservation system without a tie-in (see above). This was abuse within art 82. A similar decision was reached by the Commission in *Sealink* [1992] 5 CMLR 255.

The European Court appears less willing to accept the essential facilities doctrine per se, but in *Oscar Bronner GnbH & Co KG* v *Mediaprint Zeitungs-und Eitschriftenverlag GmbH & Co KG* Case C–7/97 [1998] ECR I–7701 the European Court stated that its decision could be:

> '... understood as an application of the essential facilities doctrine or, more traditionally, as a response to a refusal to supply goods or services.'

The Court ruled that for abuse of a dominant position to exist in such circumstances it is necessary that a number of conditions are met. The conditions are that:

1. the refusal of the service is likely to eliminate all competition in the market on the part of the person requesting the service;
2. such refusal is incapable of being objectively justified; and
3. the service in itself is indispensable to carrying on that person's business, inasmuch as there is no actual or potential substitute.

In the case itself, the Court found that the undertaking had a large share of the daily newspaper market. It also provided the only national home delivery service of newspapers. However, it could not be compelled under art 82 to provide this system to a competitor because there were other actual or potential substitute systems available, such as using postal deliveries and shops. Alternatively, of course, the competitor itself could establish a home delivery service:

> '... in the present case there can be no obligation on Mediaprint to allow Bonner access to its nation-wide home-delivery network ... it has numerous alternative – albeit less convenient – means of distribution open to it.'

Finally, restricting access to essential facilities on the basis of nationality, or a residential requirement, will be a clear breach of art 82. This was found to be the case by the Commission in relation to the French authorities system for allocating football tickets for the 1998 football World Cup: *Comité Français d'Organisation de la Coupe du Monde* (2000) OJ L5/55 (Decision 2000/12), [2000] 2 CMLR 963

There may however be objective justification as to why the undertaking has refused to provide an essential service. This could include the fact that the natural capacity of the service is exceeded, or that security may be breached, or that consumer protection would suffer. In addition, if it was proved that a buyer was either slow in making payment, or regularly failed to pay, the undertaking may be justified in not providing the service: see, for example, *Leyland DAF* v *Automotive Products* [1994] 1 BCLC 245 (CA). As with other cases where objective justification may be argued, any measure taken must be fair and proportionate.

## Tying

This occurs when a dominant undertaking will supply a dependant purchaser only if they also agree to purchase another product or service, which they would otherwise not be inclined to do. This is specifically within the ambit of art 82's prohibition on supplementary obligations that have no connection with the subject of the contract. The CFI and the Court have both held that refusing to supply the contract product without additionally purchasing the tied product constitutes an abuse: see *Hilti AG* v *Commission* Case T–30/89 [1991] ECR II–1439 for the CFI's decision, and Case C–53/92P [1994] ECR I–667 for the European Court's decision. According to *Hoffman-La Roche*, even if the buyer requests such 'tying in' it will be abusive (see above for an explanation of the English clause used in their contracts).

In *Van den Bergh Foods* (1998) OJ L246/1 (Decision 98/531) the Commission concluded that a dominant manufacturer of ice cream was abusing their position by offering exclusive supply of their ice cream products on condition that retailers also buy their freezer cabinets.

The CFI has held that tying clauses may be objectively justified, but they must be proportionate and must not be a means of strengthening the dominant position of the undertaking: *Tetra Pak Rausing SA* v *Commission* Case T–83/91 [1994] ECR II–755.

## Threatening behaviour

This abuse may fall into both categories. Threatening, or bullying, by a dominant undertaking of either its competitors or its customers has been held to constitute an abuse within art 82. Hence, threats to stop supplying products unless a carrier stopped transporting competing products was held to be an abuse by the CFI in *Irish Sugar plc* v *Commission* Case T–228/97 [1999] ECR II–2969.

The CFI has also held that instituting vexatious litigation with the sole aim of eliminating a competitor will also constitute an abuse: *ITT Promedia* v *Commission* Case T–111/96 [1998] ECR I–2937.

## 16.5 The period of investigation

The Commission must conduct its investigation into dominance and abuse of a dominant position over an 'appropriate' period. The overriding criterion is that the period selected for the investigation of the market conditions, the abusive practices and the existence of a dominant position must be adequate to facilitate proper appraisal: see *BPB Industries & British Gypsum Ltd* (above). A choice of an inadequate period, which is either too short or too extensive, may lead to the final findings of the Commission being annulled.

The period over which the abuse has been perpetrated is also a relevant factor in assessing the levels of fines that may be imposed by the Commission against a guilty party: see Chapter 17.

## 16.6 Merger control

### *The background*

The Community competition provisions make no express reference to the control of mergers or acquisitions in the Community. Notwithstanding this omission, the Commission has been prepared to apply both arts 81 and 82 to mergers and takeovers. The following are illustrations of this practice:

1. The acquisition of a competitor by a company that maintains a dominant position in a market may amount to an abuse of that position contrary to art 82: see *Continental Can* v *Commission* (above).
2. Article 81(1) may be applied to acquisition of shareholdings where a company acquires a minority stake in a competitor as leverage for the co-ordination of marketing strategy between the two undertakings: *British American Tobacco (BAT) & R J Reynolds Industries Inc* v *Commission* Cases 142 and 156/84 [1987] ECR 4487.
3. Article 81(1) may be infringed if a company enters into a joint venture or acquires an interest in a third company if the other principal shareholder is in a related field of business.
4. Consortium bids may also violate art 81(1) if the consortium involves competitors seeking to acquire a competitor or attempting to influence its behaviour.

### *The Merger Regulation*

After a series of controversial decisions in the 1980s, the Council agreed to adopt Community legislation setting out the powers of the Commission to investigate mergers and takeovers. This power was restricted to levels above a certain threshold. Council Regulation 4064/89 was enacted for this purpose and came into force in

October 1990. This Regulation, known as the Merger Regulation, has since been amended by Council Regulation 1310/97, which had effect from March 1998.

EC merger control rules apply to 'concentrations' A concentration is defined in art 1 of the Regulation as occurring when:

1. two or more previously independent undertakings merge; or
2. one or more persons already controlling at least one undertaking, or one or more undertakings, acquire, whether by purchase of securities or assets, by contract or by any other means, direct or indirect control of the whole or parts of one or more undertakings.

Article 1 of the Merger Regulation, as amended, confers jurisdiction on the Commission over all mergers involving a 'Community dimension'. A concentration will have a Community dimension where:

1. the aggregate world wide turnover of all the undertakings concerned is more than ECU 5,000 million; and
2. the aggregate Community-wide turnover of each of the undertakings concerned is more than ECU 250 million.

(*Note*: ECU, European Currency Unit, known as euros.)

The Community dimension is, however, excluded where each of the undertakings concerned has more than two-thirds of its aggregate Community-wide turnover in one and the same Member State.

On the basis of the amending regulation, art 1(3) of Regulation 4064/89 now provides that concentrations which do not meet the above thresholds still have a Community dimension where:

1. the combined aggregate world wide turnover of all the undertakings involved in the merger is more than ECU 2,500 million; and
2. in each of at least three member States, the combined aggregate turnover of all the undertakings concerned is more than ECU 100 million; and
3. in each of at least these three Member States, the aggregate turnover of each of at least two of the undertakings concerned is more than ECU 25 million; and
4. the undertakings do not generate two-thirds of their turnover in a single Member State

However, where the undertakings concerned achieve more than two-thirds of their Community-wide turnover within the same Member State, the merger will still not have a Community dimension.

Merging companies have to go through two tiers of threshold in order to assess whether a merger has a Community dimension. First, they must assess whether they meet the thresholds under the original Regulation. Second, if these thresholds are not met, they must determine whether they fulfil the additional cumulative criteria. The new rules mean that the Commission's jurisdiction is extended to transactions which, under Council Regulation 4064/89, may be assessed under several, national merger control procedures.

The amending Regulation removes the requirement that concentrative joint ventures must not involve co-ordination between the parents, or between one of them and the joint venture, in order to come within Regulation 4064/89. Joint ventures falling within the Regulation are those that perform, on a lasting basis, all the functions of an autonomous economic entity: art 3(2). Their possible co-ordinative aspects, however, will be assessed under the art 81 criteria: see Chapter 15.

Aggregate turnover is calculated on the basis of amounts derived by the undertakings concerned in the preceding financial year from the sale of goods or the supply of services during the course of ordinary trading activities. Deductions are permitted for sales rebates, value added tax and other taxes directly related to turnover.

The test for establishing whether a merger/concentration is compatible with Community law is set out in art 2(1) of the Merger Regulation. In making its appraisal, the Commission will take in to account the following:

1. the need to maintain and develop effective competition within the Common Market in view of, inter alia, the structure of all of the markets located both within and outside of the Community; and
2. the market position of the undertakings concerned and their economic and financial power, the alternatives available to suppliers and users, their access to suppliers or markets, any legal or other barriers to entry, supply and demand trends, the interests of the intermediate and ultimate consumers, and the development of technical and economic progress provided that it is to the consumer's advantage and does not form an obstacle to competition.

Those mergers/ concentrations that, after this analysis, are considered to create or strengthen a dominant position 'as a result of which effective competition would be significantly impeded in the Common Market or a substantial part of it' will be declared 'incompatible with the Common Market': art 2(3).

Many of the principles discussed earlier in this chapter will therefore be relevant in the context of assessing whether the merger is compatible with Community law, such as the need to define the relevant product market (see the Commission Notice referred to above at section 16.2) and the assessment of whether dominance exists (see section 16.3).

In considering the merger under the above conditions the Commission may come to a number of conclusions. First, it may decide to clear the merger, thereby declaring that it is compatible with the Common Market: see, for example, *Re the Concentration between Digital Equipment International and Mannesman Kienzle GmbH* Case IV/M57 [1992] 4 CMLR M99. Second, it may declare that the merger is incompatible with the Common Market, thereby blocking the merger: see, for example, *Re the Concentration between Aérospace SNI and Alenia-Aeritalia e Selenia SpA and de Havilland* Case IV/M53 [1992] 4 CMLR M2. Third, the Commission may decide to clear the merger, but only after imposing certain conditions, which may either be accepted by the parties or appealed to the CFI: see, for example, *Re the Concentration between Nestlé SA and Source Perrier SA* Case IV/M190 [1993] 4 CMLR M17, where Nestlé agreed to modify the original concentration by, inter alia, providing a minimum quantity of water to competitors, and of ensuring that, for a period of ten years, it did not directly or indirectly re-acquire any of the sources or brands that it divested itself of pursuant to the undertaking, without the prior, written approval of the Commission. The Commission has since passed a Notice offering guidelines as to the type of commitments that will be acceptable, which undertakings proposing a merger that may threaten or strengthen a dominant position can incorporate to help ensure they achieve clearance: Commission Notice on Remedies Acceptable under Council Regulation 4064/89 and Commission Regulation 447/98 (2001).

### The role of the Commission and the Member States authorities in merger control

Under art 21(1) of the Merger Regulation, the Commission is the only body capable of making decisions involving the application of the Regulation. Article 21(2) further provides that no Member State may apply its national law to a merger having a Community dimension. However, the national authorities may become involved and play a part in the process in two main situations.

First, under art 9(2) they may, within three weeks of receiving a copy of the notification, inform the Commission that the concentration threatens to strengthen a dominant position that will significantly impede competition in a distinct national market. If the Commission decides that this may be the case, it may decide the matter itself, or refer it to the national authorities. They are then obligated to reach a decision within four months. The measures it takes must be no more than are necessary to protect competition. This process will only be invoked in exceptional circumstances: see *Steetley/Tarmac* Case IV/M053 OJ C [1992] 50/25, in which the Commission's decision was to refer the matter to the UK competition authorities.

Second, even if a merger is approved by the Commission (for example, *Re the Concentration between Digital Equipment International* and *Mannesman Kienzle GmbH* Case IV/M57 [1992] 4 CMLR M99), Member States retain a veto over mergers in particularly sensitive sectors of their national economies: art 21(3). Member States may take appropriate measures to protect legitimate national interests such as public security, the plurality of the media and the maintenance of prudent rules for the conduct of commerce. However, such measures are subject to the requirement that they must be compatible with the general principles and rules of Community law.

This provision was used for the first time by the United Kingdom in *Northumbria Water/Lyonnaise des Eaux* Case IV/M567 [1996] 4 CMLR 614, in which it was concluded that the UK was permitted to exercise strict controls over mergers in the water industry. This was to ensure that competition between firms was maintained on a system based on price comparisons.

Finally, a Member State may request the Commission to investigate a concentration that does not have a Community dimension, if it believes that the concentration strengthens or creates a position of dominance that would impede effective competition in that Member State: art 22(3).

The Commission is empowered to impose fines on persons, undertakings or associations of undertakings if they intentionally or negligently fail to notify the Commission of a concentration with a Community dimension.

Once a concentration with a Community dimension has been notified the Commission has two options available. First, it can conclude that the concentration does not fall within the scope of the Regulation and must record such a finding by means of a decision. Alternatively, the Commission may determine that the concentration falls within the Regulation, in which event it may take one of two courses of action:

1. the Commission may decide that the concentration, whilst within the scope of the Regulation, is not incompatible with the common market and will not therefore be opposed; or
2. the Commission may find that the concentration falls within the Regulation and is incompatible with the common market, in which case it is obliged to initiate an investigation.

In each of these cases, the Commission must make its decision within one month of the notification.

To appraise the compatibility of the concentration with the common market, the Commission must evaluate the implications of the concentration in light of the need to preserve and develop efficient Community competition. Thus it will take into account, inter alia, the structure of all the relevant markets concerned and the actual or potential competition from other undertakings, both within and outside of the Community.

In making this assessment, the Commission must consider the following: the market position of the undertakings concerned; their economic and financial power; the opportunities available to both suppliers and consumers; access to supplies and markets; the existence of legal or other barriers to entry of the product into particular markets; and the interests of intermediate and ultimate consumers, as well as technical and economic development and progress: see, generally, *Re the Concentration between Nestlé SA and Source Perrier SA* Case IV/M190 [1993] 4 CMLR M17 and *Re the Concentration between Aérospace SNI and Alenia–Aeritalia e Selenia SpA and de Havilland* Case IV/M53 [1992] 4 CMLR M2.

The Commission has the power to impose fines on parties for failing the properly notify concentrations. For example, the Commission imposed a fine of 219,000 euros on a Danish company for putting into effect three concentrations some months before they actually notified, although the Commission subsequently cleared the three transactions. Nevertheless, the Commission concluded that the company had clearly breached its obligation to notify the transactions in due time and its obligation not to implement them without the Commission's authorisation. Furthermore, the infringements lasted for a significant period of time.

The relatively low amount of the fine was justified by four factors:

1. the company recognised its breach;
2. the failure to notify did not damage competition;
3. the company voluntarily informed the Commission of its failure to notify the transactions in question before the Commission discovered the infringement itself; and
4. the company infringed the law at a time when the Commission had not yet adopted its first decision imposing fines under the Merger Regulation.

It is, however, unlikely that the Commission will be so lenient again.

Matters such as notification, time limits, hearings and other procedural issues under the Merger Control Regulation are dealt with under Commission Regulation 3384/94. Commission decisions on mergers may be subject to appeal to the CFI and then to the European Court.

# 17

# The Enforcement of Competition Rules

## 17.1 Introduction

The procedural rules of Community competition policy have become exceptionally complex and have been the basis for a considerable volume of appeals to the Court of First Instance and the European Court, against findings by the Commission. The source of these procedural rules is not any express provision in the EC Treaty, but regulations enacted by the Council and the Commission.

The basic regulation concerning procedure on competition matters was Council Regulation 17/62, which governed matters such as notification of agreements, clearance, termination of infringements and powers of sanction. This Regulation was the primary measure conferring authority on the Commission to act in Community competition matters. However, the Commission's workload as a result of the considerable number of agreements notified to it and decisions requiring individual exemption, led to demands for wholesale reform. In 1997 the Commission produced a Notice setting out the ways in which the Commission and the national competition authorities (NCAs) could co-operate in handling cases that fell within arts 81 and 82 EC. In 1999, however, the Commission went one step further in a White Paper proposing the decentralisation of the application of the rules and a simplification of what had become an extremely complex process. The traditional rationale for granting the Commission exclusive authority to determine individual exemption was to permit it the opportunity of developing the rules in an uniform manner. The Commission believes this to have been achieved, and that it is unnecessary and too time-consuming for it to continue with this work. Consequently, Regulation 17/62 is replaced, leaving the Commission dealing with only serious cases (such as those involving new legal issues) and cases under art 86 EC (see Chapter 18). The Commission will continue to adopt block regulations providing clarification of the scope and application of art 81(3).

The main thrust of Council Regulation Implementing Articles 81 and 82 (Council Regulation 1/2003) is to decentralise the entire process, with the following being the principal means of achieving this:

1. the need for notification is abolished (see below); and
2. the Commission will no longer have a monopoly over the granting of individual exemption under art 81(3).

Regulation 1/2003 will come into force on 1 May 2004; until then Regulation 17/62 will remain in force. The reforms introduced under the new Regulation will be discussed in further detail below. The reforms, though, have faced considerable criticism, including:

1. That some Member States have no legal body or authority able to undertake those powers formerly undertaken by the Commission. Hence, such Member States are required to provide both the necessary body and powers to move against breaches of Community competition law;
2. that the ECJ may find itself the victim of an increased number of art 234 preliminary references from national courts attempting to interpret and apply competition law;
3. that the national authorities may be less rigorous than the Commission in identifying, investigating and enforcing competition law; and
4. that the certainty so far provided by the Commission may be affected or even destroyed.

These criticisms have, to some extent, been responded to by the inclusion of a number of safeguards, which will be discussed below.

In addition, the procedural rules have been supplemented by safeguards developed by the European Court and the CFI in the name of general principles of law. In fact, procedural safeguards derived from this latter source have been established mainly to fill omissions in the legislative framework for conducting investigations. One illustration of the CFI protecting the procedural rights of parties involved in an investigation is *Asia Motor France SA* v *Commission* Case T–387/94 [1996] ECR II–961, where the Commission was found to have committed violations of procedural law and its decision on the matter was annulled. The Court found that the Commission had failed to exercise the proper standards of appraisal and respect for procedural guarantees. In particular, the Commission had made a number of factual errors in conducting its investigation which could not be justified and which, in the circumstances, vitiated the Commission's decision.

At Community level, the main sanction against anti-competitive behaviour is the power to fine conferred on the Commission. In general, this power is exercised sparingly and only used in cases where the anti-competitive behaviour is serious, detrimentally affects the interests of consumers, or has continued unchecked for a considerable number of years.

The final matter to be considered as a matter of procedural law is the judicial review of decisions sanctioning private parties for anti-competitive behaviour. Review is generally conducted on the basis of art 230(4) EC on the four grounds established for that purpose in these provisions. The CFI now has jurisdiction to hear such applications at first instance, subject to appeal to the European Court itself.

## 17.2 Public enforcement by the Commission

### Identification of the violation of competition law

The Commission may become aware of a possible infringement of competition law in three main ways:

1. complaints;
2. investigations or inspections; and
3. notification.

### Complaints

Whilst the Commission has the power to exercise its own initiative to instigate an investigation (discussed below), it may also receive a complaint of an alleged infringement of competition law. Such complaints may come from Member States or from a natural or legal person that has a legitimate interest.

If a complaint is made the Commission must consider the issues in order to ascertain whether a breach has occurred. Its consideration must be careful and diligent: *Demo-Studio Schmidt* v *Commission* Case 210/81 [1983] ECR 3045. If the Commission fails to do this it may be subject to proceedings under art 232 EC for failure to act.

However, there is no obligation on the Commission to adopt any decision that there has, or has not, been a breach of competition rules. It is also not obligated to follow up a complaint with an investigation, although, if it decides not to, it must inform the complainant and provide reasons: *GEMA* v *Commission* Case 125/75 [1979] ECR 3173. The only exception to this is when the complaint originates from a Member State: art 85(1) EC. The providing of reasons is essential to ensure that the complainant may defend their rights in requesting a review of the decision before the CFI. Acceptable reasons for not instigating an investigation include the following:

1. It is not a matter of priority, an issue determined by the Commission itself: see *Service pour Groupement d'Aquisitions* v *Commission* Cases T–189/95 and 39 and 123/96 [1999] ECR II–3587;
2. There is an insufficient Community interest in the matter: see *BENIM* v *Commission* Case T–114/92 [1995] ECR II–147.
3. There is adequate relief available from national authorities and courts. See, for example, the CFI's decision in *Automec Srl* v *Commission* Case 24/90 [1992] ECR II–223.

### Investigations/inspections

The Commission may need to investigate alleged anti-competitive behaviour under both arts 81 and 82. If the Commission, in response to a complaint, initiates an investigation, it must ensure that that investigation is carried out with 'care, seriousness and diligence': *Asia Motor France* v *Commission* Case T–7/92 [1993] ECR II–669. The Commission's powers to conduct such investigations were contained in Regulation 17/62 (the new Regulation contains very similar provisions) and may be broadly classified as follows:

1. power to obtain information from the parties involved in the investigation; and
2. power to conduct inspections.

### *Power to obtain information*

Under art 11(1) of Regulation 17/62 (art 18 Regulation 1/2003), in carrying out its duties, the Commission may obtain 'all information necessary' for the purposes of the investigation from interested private parties and the governments and competent authorities of the Member States. In exercising this power to obtain information from private parties, the Commission acts in two stages.

First, the Commission makes an informal request to the parties to produce the relevant information. If incorrect information is provided the Commission may impose a penalty. If no response is received to this request, the Commission may proceed to the second stage. This involves the adoption of a formal decision requiring the production of the relevant materials. Failure to comply with the terms of the decision may lead to the imposition of a penalty: arts 11(5) Regulation 17/62 and art 18(4) Regulation 1/2003.

The scope of information 'necessary' for the purposes of conducting the investigation falls broadly within the discretion of the Commission to decide, although it must be proportionate to the purposes of the investigation. It appears that all information relating to the business activities of the undertakings under investigation will be necessary, unless it can be shown to be highly irrelevant. In the judgment of the CFI in *Samenwerkende Elektriciteits Produktiebedrijven (SEP) NV* v *Commission* Case T–39/90 [1991] ECR II–1497 the broad scope of this discretion was confirmed. This case involved an investigation into the commercial relationship between a Dutch electricity production company and its State-controlled gas supplier. The relationship between the parties was governed by a code of conduct, which provided, inter alia, that the State-controlled company had a monopoly on the supply of gas in The Netherlands. During the course of the investigation it was revealed that the electricity company had entered into a contract for the supply of gas with a Norwegian company. This arrangement was possibly contrary to Dutch law.

The Commission requested production of the contract between the Dutch electricity supplier and the Norwegian gas supplier. The company refused to provide a copy of the contract on the grounds, first, that it was not relevant to the investigation and, second, that the national authorities might obtain a copy and commence proceedings for the infringement of the national monopoly. The Commission passed a decision to compel the disclosure of the contract, and the applicant appealed to the Court against this decision.

The Court upheld the discretion of the Commission in selecting which material was relevant to its investigation. The Commission was entitled to have sight of the contract in order to assess the legality of related agreements under investigation. More specifically, it was required to identify the pattern of business conduct being pursued by the Dutch company. The content of the category of information that is 'necessary' extends to all material that the Commission reasonably believes has a connection with the practices being investigated.

Private parties subject to investigation have limited rights to refuse to supply information. The most significant safeguard is that correspondence between the parties and external legal advisers may benefit from the right of client/lawyer confidentiality, a right established through the decisions of the European Court: see *AM & S Europe* v *Commission* Case 155/79 [1982] ECR 1575.

Other rights that private parties are entitled to exercise include the right to legal representation: *Hoechst AG* v *Commission* Cases 46/87 and 227/88 [1989] ECR 2859. An undertaking cannot be forced to respond to leading questions, if such questions would result in an admission of unlawful conduct: *Orkem* v *Commission* Case 374/87 [1989] ECR 3283.

## Conduct of inspections

The Commission's powers to conduct on-the-spot investigations are extensive. These powers were provided for under art 14 of Regulation 17/62, but have been slightly revised under art 20 Regulation 1/2003. Officials authorised by the Commission, once they have the requisite national, judicial authorisation, may enter the premises of the concerned undertakings, including the homes of directors, managers and staff, if it is suspected that relevant business records are being kept there. Officials may examine, take copies and remove extracts from any and all company books and records and are also permitted to undertake interviews with staff members. During the inspection, officials may seal any premises and records.

Such inspections may be of two types – voluntary or mandatory.

1. *Voluntary inspections*. These are conducted under art 20(3) Regulation 1/2003. Officials must produce a written authorisation specifying the subject matter and the purpose of the investigation, including any penalties that may be imposed.
2. *Mandatory inspections*. These are conducted under art 20(4). Officials require a decision that orders the inspection, which must state the subject matter and purpose of the investigation, the possible penalties, and the right to appeal the decision. Before the Commission grants the decision it must consult the national competition authorities (NCAs), who are able to actively assist the Commission if they so wish, or if the Commission requires them to do so. In other words, the NCA may in its own right undertake the inspection, in which case it will have the powers set out under art 20. In addition, the Commission may request the assistance of the national authorities, such as the police.

However, the Commission is not obligated to provide the undertaking to be inspected with any form of advance notice: see *National Panasonic (UK) Ltd* v *Commission* Case 136/79 [1980] ECR 2033 and *AKZO Chemie BV* v *Commission* Case 5/85 [1986] ECR 2585, both of which were decided in the context of the old provisions but which will be equally applicable to the terms of Regulation 1/2003.

The rights of the Commission and its agents to enter premises were considered fully by the European Court in *Hoechst AG* v *Commission*: Cases 46/87 and 227/88 [1989] ECR 2859. The Commission had adopted a decision authorising the search and seizure of documents at the headquarters of a company believed to be indulging in anti-competitive practices. These decisions were adopted after the company had refused to supply the Commission with certain information that it believed was confidential.

The Commission proceeded with the search after obtaining the necessary permission from the national authorities and imposed fines on the company for failing to comply with the Commission's requests in the first place.

The company applied to the Court for a declaration that these fines were unlawful. In their arguments they claimed that the Commission had infringed their basic human rights. These rights were imputed into Community law by virtue of international conventions signed by the Member States and through the general constitutional provisions of the Member States protecting the privacy of the individual.

The Court expressed a certain degree of sympathy with these arguments and declared that a number of fundamental human rights existed in Community law, including the rights to lawyer/client confidentiality, privileged correspondence and legal representation. All of these may now be relied upon against the intrusion of the Commission into the business activities of companies.

The Court, subject to certain safeguards, upheld the right of the Commission to search premises. First, it must identify the documents required in advance of its search. Second, it must respect the rules of national law, which may require the production of a search warrant. Thus, the Court concluded:

> 'If the Commission intends, with the assistance of the national authorities, to carry out an investigation other than with the co-operation of the undertakings concerned, it is required to respect the relevant procedural guarantees laid down by national law.'

In the circumstances of the case, the Court ultimately held that the Commission had not exceeded its powers because it has sought and obtained the co-operation of the relevant national authorities and had fulfilled the necessary national procedural requirements. Of the current 15 Member States, only Italy, The Netherlands, Austria, Finland and Sweden require no prior judicial authorisation before such searches may be conducted.

## Making competition decisions

Once the infringement of competition law has been identified, the Commission will move on to make a decision. This can take a number of forms, including the informal decision to send a comfort letter to the undertaking(s), which is discussed in Chapter 15, section 15.7.

The formal decisions the Commission is capable of making are discussed below.

## Power to grant interim orders/relief

Although no such powers are expressly conferred in Regulation 17/62, the Commission has been deemed to possess an inherent power to issue decisions, providing interim relief to complaining parties to prevent injury caused by the anti-competitive practices of business competitors. The European Court upheld the right to provide relief to a complaining party where there is an immediate danger of irreparable harm to the business activities of the complainer: *Camera Care Ltd* v *Commission* Case 792/79R [1980] ECR 119. Since this decision, the conditions necessary for the provision of interim relief have been more fully discussed by the Court of First Instance.

In *La Cinq* v *Commission* Case T–44/90 [1992] ECR II–1 the applicants raised an action against the Commission's refusal to grant interim relief against the activities of competitors. The applicant was a French broadcasting company, which had been refused membership of the European Broadcasting Union (EBU). Membership of the organisation would have allowed the applicant to transmit sports events on more competitive terms that the sub-licensing arrangements that were required in the absence of membership. The applicants requested the Commission to adopt a decision compelling the EBU to accept its application, but the Commission refused to do so.

The CFI stated that the Commission could only adopt interim measures of protection if the following three conditions were satisfied:

1. the practices against which a complaint was lodged were prima facie likely to infringe Community law;
2. proven urgency existed; and
3. there was a need to avoid serious and irreparable damage to the party seeking relief.

In the particular circumstances of this case, the Court held that the Commission was correct in refusing to provide relief because not all of these conditions were satisfied.

Article 8 of Regulation 1/2003 provides for the awarding of interim relief, in cases where there is urgency because of the risk of serious and irreparable damage to competition, for a renewable period of one year.

### Power to grant negative clearance

This old power existed under Regulation 17/62, whereby an undertaking would notify their agreement, decision or concerted practice to the Commission, with the Commission responding in such cases with a determination that there was no breach, known as negative clearance. However, Regulation 1/2003 has removed the obligation to notify and thus the concept of negative clearance will end.

### Power to grant individual exemption

Under the old system (art 9 Regulation 17/62) the Commission was granted exclusive jurisdiction to grant individual exemption under art 81(3). This has been changed under Regulation 1/2003 so that NCAs and national courts can deal with the entire applicability of art 81, including the awarding of individual exemption. This will be discussed in detail below.

### Power to find an infringement

Under art 7 Regulation 1/2003 (art 3 Regulation 17/62) the Commission has the authority to find that there has been an infringement of arts 81 and 82. Through the production of a decision, it may require the undertakings to end the infringement. This may also prohibit any repetition or future adoption of the conduct, or similar conduct. Similar conduct has been described by the CFI as any 'measure having equivalent effect': *Irish Sugar plc v Commission* Case T–228/97 [1999] ECR II–2969. The Commission may also impose positive remedial action on the undertakings: see, for example, *Commercial Solvents Corporation v Commission* Cases 6 and 7/72 [1974] ECR 223. Such positive action must be proportionate and necessary to resolve the breach: *RTE and ITP v Commission* Cases C–241 and 242/91P [1995] ECR I–743.

As part of this process, the undertaking(s) are afforded rights to be heard: art 26 of Regulation 1/2003 (art 19 Regulation 17/62). Before making a decision, the Commission must give the undertakings subject to the proceedings a right to be heard and failure to do so will lead to the decision being quashed: see, for example, *Hoechst AG* v *Commission* Case T–10/89 [1992] ECR II–629. If the Commission or NCA involved believes it appropriate, natural or other legal persons may be heard if they can show sufficient interest.

Regulation 1/2003 also protects the right to defence by the undertaking(s): art 26(2). This includes the right to access the file held by the Commission, subject to the need to protect any business secrets. In addition, the undertakings may not have access to any confidential information and internal documents of either the Commission or the NCA.

## 17.3 The power of sanction

If the Commission finds that there has been an infringement it has the authority to impose fines and periodic penalty payments under arts 22 and 23 of Regulation 1/2003 (arts 15 and 16 of Regulation 17/62). The awarding of fines can be summarised as follows:

Article 22(1)    prescribes the maximum level of the fine as not exceeding *1 per cent of total turnover in the preceding business year* for intentional or negligent breaches of the rules in relation to *requests for information and inspections.*

Article 22(2)    provides the Commission with the authority to impose a fine of no more than *10 per cent of the total turnover of each of the undertakings involved*, where they intentionally or negligently *infringe arts 81 or 82, contravene a decision imposing interim measures or fail to comply with a commitment.*

Article 22(3)    states that the gravity and duration of the infringement are to be factors on which the Commission can determine the level of the fine, up to the maximum levels described above.

The following are examples of factors taken into account by the Commission in making such a determination prior to the new Regulation:

1. the size of the undertakings engaged in the anti-competitive behaviour: see *Belasco* v *Commission* Case T–124/89 [1989] ECR 2117;
2. the steps taken by the party to mitigate the infringement prior to the decision imposing fines has been rendered: see *National Panasonic (UK) Ltd* v *Commission* Case 136/79 [1980] ECR 2033; and
3. the nature of the infringement may be examined. For example, the Commission considers certain practices, such as predatory pricing, to be particularly repugnant to Community competition policy and, generally, infringements of art 82 tend to attract the larger fines.

To clarify the position, in 1998 the Commission published a Notice on the

Method of Setting Fines, providing guidelines on the various levels of breach as ranging from 'minor' to 'very serious' and the various tariffs that they attract. The Notice states that 'the basic amount will be determined according to the gravity and duration of the infringement'. In assessing the gravity of the breach the Commission will take into account the nature, actual impact on the market and the size of the relevant geographical market. The Notice refers to the need for there to be a 'sufficient deterrent effect' and the fact that large undertakings should be more aware that they are breaching competition law. Types of infringements are classified as the following:

1. 'Minor infringements' will be trade restrictions, usually of a vertical nature, having a limited market impact in that they only affect a limited part of the Community market. The likely fines for such infringements will be 1,000 to 1 million euros.
2. 'Serious infringements' are defined in the same way, but are agreements more rigorously applied with a wider market impact, or are situations where there has been abuse of a dominant position. In such circumstances the likely fines will range from 1 million to 20 million euros.
3. 'Very serious infringements' are defined as usually being horizontal in nature. The Notice specifically refers to price fixing, market sharing, partitioning of national markets and 'clear-cut' abuse of a dominant position by undertakings with a virtual monopoly, as examples of very serious offences. The likely fines in such situations will be above 20 million euros.

In terms of duration, the Notice adopts the practice of adding to the basic fine determined by reference to the gravity and classifies breaches as being:

1. of short duration, generally less than one year, when there will be no increase in the fine;
2. of medium duration, between one and five years, where the fine will be increased by up to 50 per cent; or
3. of long duration, over five years, where the fine will increase by up to 10 per cent for every year the infringement continued.

The combination of the amounts determined in accordance with the gravity and duration of the infringement will determine the 'basic amount'. This basic amount may then be further increased if there are 'aggravating circumstances'. Examples of such circumstances include repeat infringements, refusals to co-operate with the Commission and that the firm was the instigator of the infringement. Conversely, the basic amount may be decreased if there are attenuating circumstances. Such circumstances may include the fact that the firm played a passive role; that they did not implement the practice; that they immediately terminated the practice after Commission involvement; that their involvement was unintentional; and/or that they co-operated with the Commission.

However, the CFI has clearly stated that there is 'no binding or exhaustive list of the criteria which must be applied': see *Thyssen Stahl* v *Commission* Case T–141/94 [1999] ECR II–813.

In order to ensure as prompt compliance as possible, the Commission is empowered to impose periodic penalty payments under art 23 of Regulation 1/2003 (arts 15–16 Regulation 17/62). Such payments may be imposed in order to secure compliance with a decision of interim measures, to supply information or to compel an undertaking to undergo an inspection.

One example of a large fine imposed on a single undertaking is that imposed on the car manufacturer, Volkswagen. In this case the Commission's investigation revealed that Volkswagen sought to partition the market, contrary to Community competition law. The company prevented its Italian dealerships supplying its cars for export to German and Austrian customers. The company penalised dealers who sold models outside their territory. For example, they would threaten termination of the dealer's contracts, actually terminate such contracts, reduce profit margins and bonuses and ration deliveries to Italian dealers. All sales by Italian dealerships were monitored and the company advised their dealers in Italy not to give the real reason for the refusal to sell to foreign customers. The fine imposed by the Commission was 102 million euros: see *Volkswagen* (1999) OJ L124/60 (Decision 98/273). However, on appeal the CFI reduced the fine to 90 million because the Commission had not proved that the infringement had lasted more than three years, although the shorter duration did not diminish the gravity of the offence: *Volkswagen* v *Commission* Case T–62/98 [2000] 5 CMLR 948.

A Commission Leniency Notice in 1996 adopted the practice of reduced fines for cartel informers designed to encourage participants in cartels to offer evidence of such activities to the Commission. The Notice gives much greater discretion to the Commission as to how it will treat cartel informers. The two main guidelines set down are as follows:

1. A total immunity from fines for undertakings subject to the broad discretion of the Commission. However, as a general rule, such undertakings will benefit from a minimum reduction of 75 per cent of the fine that would have been imposed had the undertaking not come forward.
2. Companies first reporting cartelistic behaviour immediately after an investigation has been opened by the Commission may obtain a reduction of between 50 per cent and 75 per cent of the final fine, subject to the discretion of the Commission.

In both cases, reporting undertakings must satisfy a number of pre-conditions before being granted immunity. First, the informing company must not have been a ringleader in setting up the cartel. Second, the company must be the first to come forward to the Commission with substantial evidence of the cartel. Third, the company must pull out of the cartel no later than the time disclosure is made to the Commission. Fourth, it must provide the Commission with all the information it possesses in relation to the activities of the cartel and must maintain continuous and complete co-operation with the Commission throughout the investigation. Failure to meet these requirements may mean the withdrawal of exemption. The Notice also applies to anti-competitive practices other than cartels. There is some uncertainty in this area, especially since the Notice does not codify any form of previous practice. The Notice has also attracted the following criticisms:

1. that the system is unfair because it will result in two parties, committing the same breach, being treated differently;
2. that the inducement will prevent undertakings from trying to defend themselves. It appears that the CFI does consider fines to be criminal charges (see *Rhône-Poulenc* v *Commission* Case T–1/89 [1991] ECR II–867) which is in breach of art 6 ECHR (the right to a fair hearing);
3. that the financial incentive may prompt undertakings to admit unlawful conduct, contrary to existing Community law: see *Orkem* (above); and
4. that the quality of the information received may be unreliable because undertakings may wish to be in favour with the Commission, or damage the reputation of other competitors.

While the Commission has authority to fix the amount of the fine, the national authorities concerned are obliged to enforce the decision, by virtue of art 256 EC, in accordance with their national rules of procedure. (In the United Kingdom, the fine will be registered by the High Court or the Court of Session as a 'European Community judgment'.) The Commission may, if it wishes, defer enforcing the payment of the fine for judicial review of the decision. The Commission will only be prepared to do this if the undertaking will pay interest if the action fails and provides bank guarantees for the full amount, including any interest.

## 17.4 Judicial review

Judicial review of Commission decisions in the area of Community competition law is generally conducted under art 230(4) EC. Originally the European Court of Justice conducted judicial review of competition decisions. Jurisdiction to hear such cases was transferred in September 1989 to the Court of First Instance.

Article 230 specifies four grounds for review (see Chapter 5) which are: lack of competence; infringement of an essential procedural requirement; infringement of the Treaty or of any rule of law relating to its application; and misuse of powers. Most appeals are brought on the basis of an infringement of an essential procedural requirement or of the terms of the Community Treaties and laws enacted under the authority of such Treaties. The ECJ may hear an appeal against a decision of the CFI, but only on points of law, and the ECJ may only set aside a judgment of the CFI if it has erred in law: art 225 EC.

One dramatic illustration of a Commission decision annulled on the basis of an infringement of an essential procedural requirement was the *PVC Cartel* case. The

Commission investigated the commercial activities of a number of plastic companies alleged to have operated a cartel to fix prices of certain chemical products. Eventually the Commission imposed fines totalling 23 million ecus (now euros) and issued an order requiring the companies to desist from the practices found to have infringed art 81(1): *PVC Cartel* [1990] 4 CMLR 345.

The decision imposing the fines was adopted in the Dutch and Italian languages by the Commissioner responsible at the time for competition matters. However, it had either been adopted before it had been finalised, or had been altered after his mandate had expired. The companies against which the fines were imposed challenged the decision on a number of procedural grounds. First, they claimed that a single Commissioner was not permitted to adopt a decision of this nature by himself or after his mandate had expired. Second, it was argued that the decision should have been adopted in the languages of all the companies under investigation. Third, the companies asserted that the Commission had no power to amend the decision after the measure had been adopted.

The Court of First Instance upheld the applicants on all of these grounds. The Commission had failed to observe its own rules of internal procedure and the decision was annulled. In particular, the CFI criticised the Commission for not properly authenticating its decision and the fact that the exact date or adoption could not be identified from the text of the decision. The CFI also rejected the contention that the Commission was entitled to amend its decision retroactively: *BASF v Commission (PVC)* Cases T–79, 84–86, 91 and 92/89 [1992] ECR II–315.

The European Court subsequently set aside the CFI judgment on the ground that it had erred in deciding that the Commission's decision was non-existent because of the procedural irregularities contained in the decision. Nevertheless, the ECJ did annul the Commission's decision on the grounds of infringement of an essential procedural requirement confirming the CFI's findings, if not its conclusions: *Commission v BASF and Others* Case C–137/92P [1994] ECR I–2555.

Decisions can also be reviewed on the basis that the Commission has acted contrary to the terms of the Community Treaties or of a measure derived from their authority: see, for example, *Suiker Unie v Commission* Cases 40–48, 50, 54–56, 111, 113 and 114/73 [1975] ECR 1663.

The CFI may cancel or vary the level of the fine imposed by the Commission: art 229 EC. The Court will consider whether the fine is proportionate. If an appeal is made, the European Court cannot substitute its own appraisal. However, it may consider whether the CFI has responded sufficiently to the arguments for a cancelled or reduced fine: see *BPB Industries and British Gypsum v Commission* Case C–310/93P [1995] ECR I–865 and *Ferriere Nord SpA v Commission* Case C–219/95P [1997] ECR I–4411.

If the decision is annulled or the level of the fine reduced (the Court has never increased the level of a fine although it has the power to do so), the Commission is obligated, under art 233 EC, to take the necessary measures to comply with the

Court's judgment. If it subsequently fails to do so, an action under art 232 for failure to act may be brought.

## 17.5 Public enforcement by the national competition authorities (NCAs)

Article 84 EC provides that national competition authorities may rule on the admissibility of any agreements, decision or concerted practices and abuses of a dominant position contrary to art 81(1) and art 82. Over the years, it appeared that NCAs were not instrumental in applying arts 81 and 82, a position that the Commission believed could be improved as a means of reducing the workload it was facing. Consequently, the role of NCAs has been enhanced under Regulation 1/2003 (a competent NCA is identified by the respective Member State). Article 5 of the Regulation endows the NCAs with the authority to apply arts 81(1) and 82. The NCA has the authority to take a range of decisions including, for example, any decision on the termination of an infringement, the imposition of fines and penalty payments and the imposition of interim measures.

In order to safeguard the process from potential abuse by the NCAs (and indeed to provide them with valuable support) art 11 of Regulation 1/2003 sets out a framework for 'close co-operation' between the NCAs and the Commission. Consequently, for example, the Commission is obliged to send the NCAs important documents; the NCAs are obliged to notify the Commission of the beginning of proceedings; the NCAs are obliged to consult with the Commission before adopting any decision on the infringement of arts 81 and 82; the NCAs must also provide the Commission with a summary of any case and copies of any important documentation at least one month prior to the making of any decision; and the NCAs may request the advice of the Commission on any matter of Community competition law.

Regulation 1/2003 also provides the NCAs with a role in the investigative and inspection processes. Hence, under art 21(1) of Regulation 1/2003 an NCA may undertake a fact-finding investigation in its respective State on behalf of another NCA, and art 21(2) provides that the Commission may authorise an NCA to carry out an inspection (see above). If two or more NCAs are dealing with the same investigation, then one may proceed whilst the others suspend proceedings: art 13(1). The Commission may also refuse to undertake an investigation in response to a complaint if the matter is being investigated by an NCA.

## 17.6 Private enforcement via the national courts

Since arts 81 and 82 have direct effect, they are capable of being enforced by individuals in national courts. Prior to the new Regulation, the national courts could consider the application of arts 81(1) and 82 and the applicability of any of the block regulations. They did not have the authority to determine the application of individual exemption under art 81(3): discussed in Chapter 15. This, however, has been changed under the new Regulation, which extends jurisdiction to the national courts to determine the application of art 81(3): art 6.

In order to aid the national courts in this new role, the Regulation provides for co-operation between the national courts and the Commission. Thus, art 15 entitled national courts to request the Commission for any information it possesses, or for an opinion on the application of certain competition rules. Indeed, the Commission and the NCAs may, if they wish, submit their observations to national courts dealing with the application of arts 81 and 82. Within one month of delivering judgement, the national courts are required to send the Commission copies of that judgment and in making that judgment are required, under art 16, to ensure that they do not produce a decision that conflicts with any Community decisions.

## 17.7 Damages

Under national law damages may be available: see, for example, *Garden Cottage Foods* v *Milk Marketing Board* [1984] AC 130 in the context of the UK. However, developments in Community law with the introduction of the concept of State liability mean that individuals may now claim damages under Community law for breach of arts 81 and 82: see, for example, *GT-Link A/S* v *De Danske Statsbaner* Case C–242/95 [1997] ECR I–4449. Originally it appeared that such a course of action would only be available where the defendant was 'the State' or a State entity, but it now appears that a claim for damages under this principle may also extend to the actions of private parties: *Courage Ltd* v *Crehan* Case C–453/99 [2001] ECR I–6297. This case and the principles for establishing such liability are considered in detail in Chapter 7.

# 18

# Competition Law and the State

## 18.1 Introduction

Part D has so far considered the action that individual undertakings may take that will breach the Community's competition rules. This final chapter will consider the Treaty provisions relating to controlling the actions of the State since it, too, may exercise measures that are capable of distorting competition. Within the Community, the various Member States in the past adopted different approaches to the intervention of the State within the market. In some Member States various activities and services were provided by nationalised industries (monopolies) under the control and regulation of the State. Alternatively, some sectors had privileged status. Some Member States have since changed this policy, and have privatised such activities, such as, for example, the United Kingdom. However, in a number of Member States certain activities and services (such as the utilities) remain under the control of the State, or have been granted privileged status. In addition, the State may try to prevent a particular, often traditional, industry within its territory from external pressure, thereby protecting employment and promoting or protecting certain deprived regions. It is such action that the Treaty attempts to regulate.

Whilst there are a number of Treaty articles pertinent to this area, this chapter will focus on:

1. Article 86 EC, which is designed to prevent a State from introducing or maintaining actions in relation to public undertakings, which derogate from the remaining obligations in the EC Treaty; and
2. Article 87–89 EC, which regulate the provision of State aids. Such aid could be provided by the State to offer preferential treatment to its own undertakings, thereby distorting free competition throughout the Community. (In addition, the Treaty provides for State monopolies of a commercial character, which was considered in Chapter 14 in the context of the free movement of goods.)

There are a number of general principles that govern this area:

1. Article 295 EC provides that the Treaty will not prejudice the rules in Member States governing the system of property ownership;
2. Article 157 EC provides that both the Community and the Member States will ensure that the necessary conditions exist for the competitiveness of the Community's industry; and
3. Article 16 EC provides that the Community and the Member States shall take care that services of general economic interest in the shared values of the Union operate on the basis of 'principles and conditions which enable them to fulfil their mission'. A mission that is described as 'promoting social and territorial cohesion'.

## 18.2  Article 86 EC

Article 86 EC states:

> '(1) In the case of public undertakings and undertakings to which Member States grant special or exclusive rights, Member States shall neither enact nor maintain in force any measure contrary to the rules contained in this Treaty, in particular to those rules provided for in art 12 and arts 81 to 89.
> (2) Undertakings entrusted with the operation of services of general economic interest or having the character of a revenue-producing monopoly shall be subject to the rules contained in this Treaty, in particular to the rules on competition, in so far as the application of such rules does not obstruct the performance, in law or in fact, of the particular task assigned to them. The development of trade must not be affected to such an extent as would be contrary to the interest of the Community.
> (3) The Commission shall ensure the application of the provisions of this article and shall, where necessary, address appropriate directives or decisions to Member States.'

An entity will be considered an 'undertaking' to the extent to which it is engaged in an economic activity: *Italy* v *Sacchi* Case 155/73 [1974] ECR 409. Two forms of undertaking are covered by the terms of art 86:

1. *Public undertakings*: defined in art 2 of Directive 80/723, which in *France, Italy and the United Kingdom* v *Commission (Transparency Directive Case)* Cases 188–190/80 [1982] ECR 2545 was held by the European Court to apply to art 86. The definition of public undertaking, according to the Court, includes 'any undertaking over which the public authorities may exercise directly or indirectly a dominant influence'. Under the Directive, this influence will be assumed if the public authorities hold, directly or indirectly, 'the major part of the undertaking's subscribed capital, control the majority of the votes, or can appoint more than half of the members of its administrative, managerial or supervisory body'. Thus, we can conclude that the definition is a broad one that does not focus on the legal form of the body.

   Examples of public undertakings include the following: central and local government when acting in a commercial capacity; corporations established under public law; public services or authorities acting in a commercial capacity; and State-controlled undertakings acting under private law where the State exercises a dominant influence.

   In *Aluminium Products* [1987] 3 CMLR D813 a number of aluminium producers in Eastern Europe claimed that they were entitled to sovereign immunity under public international law since, according to socialist law, they were the State. The Commission rejected this claim.

2. *An undertaking granted special or exclusive rights*: this will occur when an undertaking has certain advantages in the market as a result of the actions of the State. For example, a privatised industry may still have a protected monopoly, or certain advantages, established and maintained by the terms on which its privatisation was based.

   In *Ministère Public of Luxembourg* v *Muller* Case 10/71 [1971] ECR 723 the undertaking was a company that controlled port facilities in Luxembourg. The company was concluded to be both a public undertaking and one that had special and exclusive rights. This was because the State nominated half of the members of the management and supervisory board and because the company had the right to be consulted before any other ports were developed in a particular area.

The obligation under art 86 is two-fold: Member States must not enact any new measures that are contrary to the Treaty and they must remove any existing ones: see *Bodson* v *Pompes Funèbres des Règions Libérées SA* Case 30/87 [1988] ECR 2479.

## 18.3 The application of art 86(1) EC

Article 86(1) will not, generally, apply where there is only the existence of a State-regulated activity. Its application will occur when the power granted to the undertaking by the State is exercised in a manner contrary to the Treaty: see, for example, *Höfner and Elser* v *Macrotron* Case C–41/90 [1991] ECR I–1979. There is, however, no definitive ruling that art 86(1) has direct effect. It appears that it may have if the Treaty provision that has been breached is itself directly effective, such as, for example, art 82 prohibiting abuse of a dominant position.

The case law has taken a particular development in relation to the exclusive reservation of activities by the State. In *ERT* v *DEP (Greek Broadcasting Case)* Case C–260/89 [1991] ECR I–2925, ERT had been granted a statutory monopoly by Greece in relation to radio and television broadcasting. The Court affirmed that the mere existence of a statutory monopoly did not breach art 82 and that an abuse was required. However, the Court also expressed the idea that granting an exclusive right could provide the potential for abuse of the dominant position (contrary to art 82). In this case, the potential for abuse came about because ERT had the exclusive right to both retransmit programmes and transmit broadcasts. Consequently, the potential for abuse could occur because ERT would be likely to transmit its own programmes, instead of re-transmitting foreign programmes.

It would appear, therefore, that the case law points towards the Court considering exclusive reservations of activities as raising a presumption that art 86(1) has been breached. Thus, private undertakings acquire the right to challenge the exclusive reservation in national courts.

This approach can also be seen in *Merci Convenzionali Porto di Genova SpA* v *Siderurgica Gabrielli SpA* Case C–179/90 [1991] ECR I–5889. In this case, Merci had the exclusive right under Italian law to control all dock work, including loading and unloading, in the port of Genoa. The Court concluded that there was a dominant position within art 82. The Court asserted again that a dominant position created by granting such exclusive rights within art 86(1) was not per se incompatible with art 82. However, the Court also expressed the opinion that both art 82 and art 86(1) would be breached if:

> '… the undertaking in question, merely by exercising the exclusive rights granted to it, cannot avoid abusing its dominant position … or when such rights are liable to create a situation in which that undertaking is induced to commit such abuses.'

In the case, the abuses were disproportionate prices, limiting technical development by refusing to have recourse to technological developments, and charging for services that had not been requested.

The terminology of the Court in the above cases appears to indicate that the Court is prepared to consider the grant of exclusive statutory rights as abusive per se, thereby constituting a breach of art 82 and consequently of art 86(1). Any State wishing to grant such exclusivity must therefore appreciate what Craig and de Burca have described as the Court's 'strident belief' that such action will operate in such a way as to breach Community law. The only means by which a State may escape such a belief is by justification under art 86(2), discussed below.

## 18.4 Article 86(2) EC – exception for entrusted undertakings and fiscal monopolies

Article 86(2) provides that undertakings entrusted with the operation of services of general economic interest or having the character of a revenue-producing monopoly are subject to the rules of the EC Treaty. However, they may be exempt from the application of the Treaty rules when the performance of their tasks are likely to be obstructed. This exception may only apply when the development of trade is not affected to such an extent that it would be contrary to the interests of the Community.

### *Entrusted undertakings*

Entrusted undertakings have been narrowly defined by the European Court: see *BRT* v *SABAM* Case 127/73 [1974] ECR 313. In this case it was identified that the essential factor in determining whether an undertaking falls within this category is that the State must have taken legal steps to ensure the operation of services by the undertaking. In the case, the undertaking did not fall into this category since it had been created by a private initiative to manage intellectual property rights. It is irrelevant whether the undertaking is a public or private body: see *GVL* v *Commission* Case 7/82 [1983] ECR 483.

The undertaking must be performing the operation of services. This should be done on a regular basis, such as, for example, providing a public utility. These services must also be of 'general economic interest', a factor that the Court will carefully examine. Even if the aim is social, as long as there is some economic activity, this requirement will be met. Hence, an airline obliged under State law to operate on non-economically viable routes was concluded to be in the general economic interest: *Ahmed Saeed Flugreisen and Silver Line Reisebüro GmbH* v *Zentrale zur Bekämpfung Unlauteren Wettbewerbs eV* Case 66/86 [1989] ECR 803. Conversely, the dock work in *Merci* (above) was not considered to be of general economic interest. Telecommunications undertakings and water supply undertakings will fall within providing a service of general economic interest.

### *Undertakings with the characteristic of a revenue-producing monopoly*

Such an undertaking will have the characteristic of producing revenue for the State by exercising an exclusive right.

## 18.5 The scope of art 86(2) EC

In order to benefit from the exception provided in art 86(2) the undertaking must prove that the application of the Treaty rules would impede or obstruct its ability to perform those tasks entrusted to it. In *Italy* v *Commission* Case 41/83 [1985] ECR 873 the Commission had established that the exclusive reservation of certain activities to British Telecom (BT) breached art 82. Italy challenged the decision on, inter alia, the exception provided in art 86(2). However, the Court held that Italy had failed to show that applying art 82 would prevent BT from carrying out its functions.

In *Sacchi* (above) the Court emphasised that the exception in art 86(2) would only apply if it could be shown that applying the Treaty rules would be incompatible with the ability of the undertaking to carry out those tasks entrusted to it.

This rather strict approach should be contrasted with the more recent decision of the European Court in *Procureur du Roi* v *Paul Corbeau* Case C–320/91P [1993] ECR I–2533. In this case an entrusted undertaking held a monopoly over postal deliveries in Belgium. In a preliminary reference, the Court concluded that certain restrictions on competition were compatible with art 86(2). This was because the undertaking used the profits to subsidise loss-making aspects of the business. Other firms would not perform such loss-making activities, and customers would thus be deprived of the facilities.

However, as stated above at section 18.4, even if the exception is an acceptable one, it must also be also be established that the development of trade will not be affected to such a degree as to undermine the general interests of the Community.

## 18.6  Powers of the Commission – art 86(3) EC

Under art 86(3) the Commission is obliged to ensure that art 86 is enforced, and for this purpose it may produce directives and decisions. (Although interpretation and clarification of art 86 may also be produced by way of the art 234 EC preliminary reference procedure.) In addition, the Commission may use its powers of enforcement under competition law: discussed in Chapter 17. The Commission also has the power under art 226 EC to intervene and take preventative measures, thereby removing the need for it to wait until there has been an actual infringement of art 86.

Directive 80/723 (the Transparency Directive) was the first directive adopted by the Commission under art 86(3). The Directive was challenged as ultra vires, but this was rejected by the European Court: the *Transparency Directive Case* (above). Another directive issued under art 86(3), namely Directive 88/301, was challenged in *France* v *Commission* Case C–202/88 [1991] ECR I–1223, but the action also failed. The conclusion being that it appears the Court will support the Commission's power to produce such directives under art 86(3). Indeed, a number of directives have been issued in relation to the telecommunications industry (for example, Directive 95/51 on cable television networks, Directive 96/2 on mobile and personal communications and Directive 96/19 on implementing full competition in the telecommunications market). Weatherill and Kent suggest that such directives will be more commonly produced in the future, particularly in relation to the energy supply sector.

Under art 86(3) the Commission may also produce a decision that there has been a breach of Community law, rather than using the more 'traditional' enforcement process under art 226: *Netherlands, Koninklijke PTT Nederland NV and PTT Post BV v Commission* Cases C–48 and 66/90 [1997] ECR I–565. The first such use of a decision was to order Greece to alter legislation requiring all public property in Greece to be insured by public sector Greek insurance companies. When Greece failed to comply, the Commission instigated art 226 enforcement proceedings: *Commission* v *Greece* Case 226/87 [1988] ECR 3611. The Court held that a decision produced under art 86(3) was binding in its entirety on those to whom it was addressed. Consequently, if the Commission produces such a decision, the addressee is bound under it, unless and until the European Court suspends it or declares it void.

## 18.7 State aids

### General

The provision by the State of aids or subsidies to certain undertakings or industries may distort competition within the Community, and may potentially also impede the free movement of goods. Consequently, the EC Treaty regulates State aids under arts 87–89 EC. Article 87(1) prohibits State aids that distort or threaten to distort competition and affect inter-State trade, and reads as follows:

> 'Save as otherwise provided in this Treaty, any aid granted by a Member State or through State resources in any form whatsoever which distorts or threatens to distort competition by favouring certain undertakings or the production of certain goods shall, in so far as it affects trade between member states, be incompatible with the common market.'

### The definition of State aid

No definition is provided in art 87, and the interpretation of what constitutes a State aid in the opinion of the Commission and the Court is a broad one. The reason behind the grant of the aid is an irrelevant factor: *Italy* v *Commission (Re Italian Textiles)* Case 173/73 [1974] ECR 709. The body that provides the aid is also irrelevant and includes central and local government and both public and private bodies: see *Steinike and Weinleg* Case 78/76 [1977] ECR 595. The essential factor is the substance and not the form of the type of aid given. The Court has also concluded that as well as positive benefits, such as subsidies breaching art 87, acts that provide mitigation for charges that the undertaking would normally have to pay will also constitute State aid. This can be seen in the conclusions of the European Court in *Steenkolenmijen* v *High Authority* Case 30/59 [1961] ECR 1 where that Court stated that the concept of an aid is:

'... wider than that of a subsidy because it embraces not only positive benefits, such as subsidies ... but also interventions which, in various forms, mitigate the charges which are normally included in the budget of an undertaking and which would without, therefore, being subsidies in the strict sense of the word, be similar in character and have the same effect': see, also, *Italy* v *Commission* Case 41/83 (above).

The Commission has drawn up an illustrative list of the types of action that may constitute State aid, which includes the following examples: direct subsidies, tax and duty exemptions, exemptions from parafiscal charges, preferential interest rates, more favourable loan terms, buildings and land on special terms, preferential terms on goods, services or personal, indemnities against operating losses, beneficial terms for public ordering and the purchase of shares in a company with financial difficulties: see, for examples, *Intermills* v *Commission* Case 323/82 [1984] ECR 3809 and *Spain* v *Commission* Cases C–278–280/92 [1994] ECR I–4104.

The Court also seems to insist that the measure is one that involves 'a charge on the public account' of the Member State: see *Sloman Neptun AG* Case C–72/91 [1993] ECR I–887 and *Kirsammer Hack* v *Nurhan Sidal* Case C–189/91 [1994] IRLR 185. In *PreussenElektra AG* v *Schleswag AG* Case C–379/98 [2001] ECR I–2099 German legislation from 1990 required electricity supply undertakings to purchase electricity produced from renewable energy sources at minimum prices. This placed those producers of that type of electricity in an advantageous position by guaranteeing them higher profits. The European Court held that the statutory obligation did not involve any direct or indirect transfer of State resources to undertakings producing electricity from renewable resources. The means by which any financial burden was allocated as between the electricity supplier and other private undertakings was also not a direct or indirect allocation of State resources. Therefore it did not constitute State aid. Furthermore, the Court held that it was not necessary for the concept of State aid to be interpreted in such a way as to include support measures decided upon by the State but financed by private undertakings. However, the Court's application of the need for there to be some charge on the public account has been criticised by the academic, Slotboom, who argues that it may provide the Member States with too wide a scope for using devices such as relaxation of environmental and planning controls, or administrative concessions, as means of providing unfair competitive advantages for undertakings.

One type of action that will not fall within the definition of State aid will be general measures of economic policy. Hence, general taxation will fall outside of the Treaty ambit. At the same time, if a measure benefits a range of undertakings it will be considered State aid. The distinction may be a slim one, causing difficulties for the Commission and the Court. Another issue that has caused some difficulty is whether the acquisition of shares by the State in a private company comes within the scope of the rules on State aid.

In *Intermills SA* v *Commission* (above) the Court was required to assess whether the Belgian government's loans, provision of capital and consequent controlling interest in a paper-making firm in financial difficulty, was State aid. The Court held that art 87 referred to State aid as being granted by the Member State or provided through State resources, 'in any form whatsoever'. The Court would therefore make no distinction between the giving of a loan and the aid provided by way of acquiring a holding in the capital of an undertaking. However, in *Italy v Commission* Case C–308/88 [1991] ECR I–1433 the Court also concluded that if the aid is granted by a private investor, with some interest in long-term profitability, it will not be considered State aid.

## The distortion of threatened distortion of competition

This is relatively easy to ascertain by comparing the position the undertaking would have been in, with that it is in after the grant of the aid. If the position has been improved, then the aid will be within art 87(1): see *Italy v Commission* Case 173/73 (above).

## The effect on inter-State trade

Finally, the aid must have an impact on inter-State trade to fall within art 87(1). According to *Philip Morris Holland BV v Commission* Case 730/79 [1980] ECR 2671, this will be satisfied if the position of one undertaking is improved in comparison to others in the Community (see below). There is no requirement that the aid granted has to be of a certain amount, or that the undertaking that receives it is of a certain size. Hence, even small amounts of aid to a small firm may constitute State aid: *Belgium v Commission (Re Tubemeuse)* Case C–142/87 [1990] ECR I–959.

## 18.8 Compatible aid

The giving of aid and subsidies to particular undertakings/industries may be one aspect of State policy in relation to regional or economic development, particularly in the context of attempting to improve an economically deprived region, coping with a period of economic recession, or in an attempt to deal with high unemployment. Consequently, derogation is permitted in certain specified situations under art 87(2) and (3).

If it is found that the State aid does not breach art 87, then it will also not breach art 28 EC (the free movement of goods, see Chapter 14) or art 31 EC. To benefit from this advantage the measures taken by the State must be proportionate: see, for example, *Commission v Ireland (Re Buy Irish Campaign)* Case 249/81 [1982] ECR 4005 (discussed in full in Chapter 14), where it was found that the measures taken by the Irish government were not proportionate to the objective.

Under art 87(2), State aid 'shall be compatible with the common market' if it falls within one of the following categories:

1. aid with a social character granted to individuals, provided that the aid is granted without discrimination related to the origin of the products concerned;
2. aid to make good the damage caused by natural disasters or exceptional circumstances; or
3. aid granted to the economy of certain areas of the Federal Republic of Germany affected by the division of Germany after the Second World War, in so far as the aid required is to compensate for the economic disadvantages caused by that division. (The Commission considers this as no longer necessary.)

In addition to those categories of aids that shall be *permissible* in art 87(2), art 87(3) provides for aid that may be *compatible* with the common market. In other words, the following forms of aid are potentially justifiable as compatible. These are as follows:

Article 87(3)(a)    aid to promote the economic development of areas where the standard of living is abnormally low or where there is serious underemployment;

Article 87(3)(b)    aid to promote the execution of an important project of common European interest or to remedy a serious disturbance in the economy of a Member State;

Article 87(3)(c)    aid to facilitate the development of certain economic activities or of certain economic areas, where such aid does not adversely affect trading conditions to an extent contrary to the common interest;

Article 87(3)(d)    aid to promote cultural conservation, where it does not affect competition in a manner contrary to the common interest; and

Article 87(3)(e)    such other categories of aid as may be specified by decision of the Council acting by qualified majority on a proposal from the Commission. Under this ground the Council has produced a number of directives. For example, Directive 90/683 on State aids for shipbuilding. This Directive permits State aid to shipbuilding and ship conservation if it is granted as development assistance to a developing country. This will be considered by the Commission and approved under criteria produced by the OECD.

It is the Commission, subject to review by the CFI and the ECJ, that is empowered to decide whether the aid is compatible with the common market. In relation to those aids falling within art 87(3), the Commission will exercise discretion in deciding both whether the aid is valid, and the extent of the exemption (see below).

To aid this process, and in an attempt to provide transparency, the Commission has produced a variety of instruments, including directives and policy guidelines. Soft law instruments have been adopted in relation to particular industries/activities, such as, for example, synthetic fibres and research and development in 1996 and the motor vehicle industry in 1997. In 1998 the Commission was granted the authority to transform such soft law into regulations, and to adopt regulations providing for block exemptions: Regulation 994/98.

## 18.9 Examples of State aid

Examples of the exercise of the Commission's discretion in accepting State aids under art 87(3) are provided below.

### *Article 87(3)(a) aid to promote the economic development of areas where the standard of living is abnormally low or where there is serious underemployment*

In *Philip Morris* v *Commission* (above) the aid in issue was the proposed intention of The Netherlands government to grant the applicant capital assistance so that it could increase cigarette production to nearly 50 per cent of what was produced in The Netherlands. Of the amount produced, approximately 80 per cent would be exported to other Member States. As a consequence, the Commission believed that the aid would result in an impact on inter-State trade.

Morris contended that the investment plan had to merely be compatible with the objectives set out in art 87, and did not have to positively contribute to their attainment. The production of the cigarettes was to take place by developing manufacturing in Bergen-op-Zoom. This part of The Netherlands suffered from high unemployment and a per capita income that was lower than in the rest of the State. Morris argued that this was satisfactory to justify the granting of the aid.

The Court disagreed and upheld the conclusions of the Commission. The Court stated that the aid would distort inter-state trade:

> 'When state financial aid strengthens the position of an undertaking compared with other undertakings competing in intra-Community trade, the latter must be regarded as affected by that aid.'

In the case at hand, the Court held that the aid was to enlarge production capacity and to increase the undertaking's ability to maintain the flow of trade to other Member States. Since other firms wishing to increase their production would have to bear the costs of making such improvements, the granting of aid to Morris gave the company an unfair competitive advantage and was consequently a State aid.

The Court was also not inclined to accept the company's argument that only national unemployment and income levels were relevant to use of art 87(3)(a). Reference to whether an area suffers from such problems must be made by comparing areas with a Community average and not a national one. Consequently, if an aid scheme is to be acceptable it must meet three criteria:

1. the aid must be legitimate in the sense that it must promote a project that is in the Community interest as a whole, and not merely a national one;

2. the aid must be necessary for that purpose; and
3. the means by which the aid is provided must be proportionate and not likely to affect inter-State trade or distort competition.

## *Article 87(3)(b) aid to promote the execution of an important project of European interest or to remedy a serious disturbance in the economy of a Member State*

If the aid is to promote the execution of an important European interest project that project must be 'part of a transnational European programme supported jointly by a number of governments of the Member States' or arise from 'concerted action by a number of Member States to combat a common threat such as environmental pollution': *Exécutif Régional Wallon and Glaverbel SA* v *Commission* Cases 62 and 72/87 [1988] ECR 1573. In this case, the Court found that an aid for modernisation to a glass manufacturer in Belgium was not an important project of European interest because it was not part of a transnational programme.

Aid to be used to remedy a serious disturbance in the economy can only be used where that disturbance is one that affects the entire national economy, and not merely a specific part of it. The Commission has approved aid for projects where there is cross-Community co-operation in technological and environmental projects.

## *Article 87(3)(c) aid to facilitate the development of certain economic activities or of certain economic areas, where such aid does not adversely affect trading conditions to an extent contrary to the common interest*

This is the most common used justification available under art 87(3). In its *First Report on State Aids 1989* the Commission reported a large increase between 1979 and 1989 of cases notified and investigated under art 87. Of the 108 billion euros per year given in aid over that ten-year period, the majority amount was granted to manufacturing companies under this ground.

In contrast to art 87(3)(a) above, this ground may be used to justify granting aid to a particular industry or economic area judged by a national, rather than Community need. Hence, a State may, under this ground, provide evidence at a national level to justify the granting of the aid. However, the Commission and the Court will still assess the need compared to a Community context and the greater the disparency between the national and Community levels, the more likely it is that the aid will be permitted. This can be witnessed in the remarks of the Commission in its *18th Report on Competition Policy* published in 1989:

'Regions falling under [art 87(3)] are those with more general development problems in relation to the national as well as the Community situation. Often they suffer from the decline of traditional industries and are frequently located in the more central prosperous parts of the Community. In its [art 87(3)(c)] method, the Commission has established a system which takes account of national regional problems and places them into a Community context.'

The Commission will generally consider two factors: income and unemployment. Generally, the region will have to be in a relatively worse position than regions in poorer Member States before the grant of aid will be acceptable. In addition, the aid will not be acceptable if it is to assist one undertaking rather than an industry or region: *Germany* v *Commission* Case 248/84 [1987] ECR 4013 and *Spain* v *Commission* Case C–42/93 [1994] ECR I–4175.

According to the authors Evans and Craig & de Burca the Commission will not accept aid under this ground unless it is in some way linked to creating employment, providing initial investment, or restructuring the tasks of the undertaking. One example of Commission approval of aid under this ground was a research and development grant provided by the British government to Rolls Royce so that they could develop new engines in Derby. The Commission authorised the grant in 1998 under, inter alia, art 87(3)(c), taking into account the need for the Community to be able to compete in the world aviation market.

The Commission has the discretion to establish whether the aid adversely affects trading conditions to such an extent that it is contrary to the common interest. However, they must provide reasoning for their conclusion, and this will be open to review by the Court (see below). On occasion, the Court has overturned the Commission's assessment that the aid has this effect: see, for example, *Intermills* v *Commission* Case 323/82 [1984] ECR 3809.

### Article 87(3)(d) aid to promote cultural and heritage conservation, where it does not affect competition in a manner contrary to the common interest

This provision was introduced by the TEU. In addition, art 151(2) EC states that:

'... action by the Community shall be aimed at encouraging co-operation between Member States and, if necessary, supporting and supplementing their action in ... conservation and safeguarding of cultural heritage of European significance'.

The ToA added the obligation that the Community 'respect and promote the cultural diversity' of its Member States: art 151(4) EC. Aid that will come within this justification will include that linked to promoting tourism.

## 18.10 Procedure

Articles 88 and 89 EC provide a procedure for the application of art 87, which has been supplemented by the decision of the ECJ and CFI and the production of Regulation 659/99. Article 88(1) provides that:

'The Commission shall, in co-operation with Member States, keep under constant review all systems of aid existing in those states. It shall propose to the latter any appropriate measures required by the progressive development or by the functioning of the common market.'

The following types of State aid already 'existing' because of ECJ decisions or Regulation 659/99 are therefore permitted to remain, but will be monitored by the Commission: aid existing before the EC Treaty came into force; aid approved by the Commission; and aid notified to the Commission but on which it has not taken action (see below). The Commission does not have to consider those grants of aid given specific clearance by the Council under art 87(3)(e) (see above).

Article 88 provides a two-stage process, whereby the Commission must be notified of any plans to grant State aid.

## *Stage One*

Article 88(3) provides for an obligatory notification process, and for the Commission to proceed to a preliminary investigation, during which time the Member State must not proceed: *Germany* v *Commission* Case 84/82 [1984] ECR 1451. In this case, the Court also came to the conclusion that the Commission must come to a formal decision within two months, otherwise the State may proceed, once it has notified the Commission that this is its intention.

The European Court has held that the aid will not be automatically contrary to the Treaty if the Member State fails to notify it: see *France* v *Commission* Case C–301/87 [1990] ECR I–307. Instead, the Commission will issue an interim decision requiring the State to suspend the aid whilst it conducts a preliminary investigation. However, art 88 does have direct effect: see *Heineken Brouwerijen BV* v *Inspecteur der Vennootschapsbelasting* Cases 91 and 127/83 [1984] ECR 3435. Hence, any national affected by the grant of State aid that has not been notified to the Commission may bring proceedings in their national court: see, for example, *R* v *Attorney General, ex parte ICI* [1987] 1 CMLR 72 (CA). The national court must rule the aid as illegal if it has not been notified. The decision as to whether it is compatible with the common market, though, rests with the Commission.

Failure to notify may result in the Commission directing that the State must recover those payments made (see below). In addition, damages may be awarded against the government of a Member State that grants unlawful State aid without first notifying the Commission: see *Fédération National du Commerce* v *French Republic* Case C–354/90 [1991] ECR I–5505.

## *Stage Two*

Article 88(2) will apply if the Commission has not permitted the aid to proceed under stage one, or existing aid under review has been found incompatible. Article 88(2) provides that in such circumstances the Commission will order the Member State to either alter the aid provided or require it to be abolished. The Commission will prescribe the time within which the Member State is required to take such action. Should the Member State fail to do so, the Commission or any other 'interested State' may directly refer the matter to the European Court.

On entering into stage two, the Commission will place a notice in the Official Journal inviting interested parties to comment on the situation. Interested parties will include the undertakings receiving the aid, other undertakings or persons whose interests may be affected by the granting of such aid, and those undertakings competing with those receiving such aid: see *Intermills* (above).

Article 88(2) also provides for aid to be granted in exceptional circumstances without breaching art 87. This is possible only by the Member State making an application to the Council, which will decide the matter on a unanimous vote. This will serve to suspend any procedure the Commission has begun, outlined above, unless the Council fails to respond within three months, in which case the Commission may proceed to give its decision on the case.

Under art 89 the Council may make regulations concerning the application of arts 87 and 88, acting by qualified majority on a proposal from the Commission. This has been extremely rare, since the Commission appears to prefer the use of soft law measures to provide guidance in this area.

If it is found that the aid granted was illegal, it should be recovered by the State, along with any interest: see *Deufil* v *Commission* Case 310/85 [1987] ECR 901. The only exception to this will be when repayment is totally impossible: *Commission* v *Belgium* Case 52/84 [1986] ECR 89. Even if the undertaking has to be wound up, the aid will have to be repaid (see, for example, *Tubemeuse* (above)) even if other creditors may suffer by not receiving their monies. National rules preventing the repayment of unlawful aids must also be disregarded: see *Land Rheinland-Pfalz* v *Alcan Deutschland GmbH* Case C–24/95 [1997] ECR I–1591. In *Commission* v *Germany* Case 70/72 [1973] ECR 813 the Court concluded that the Commission could also recover any unlawful aids.

The undertaking having to repay the aid cannot argue that they received it in good faith, or were unaware that there had been a breach of Community law in its being granted. The argument that the recipients were unaware of its illegality and therefore have a legitimate expectation to be permitted to keep it is also not acceptable: *Commission* v *Germany* Case C–5/89 [1990] ECR I–3437. In this case the Court stated:

> 'A Member State whose authorities have granted aid contrary to ... [art 88] may not rely on the legitimate expectations of recipients in order to justify a failure to comply with the obligation to take the steps necessary to implement a Commission decision instructing it to recover the aid. If it could do so, [arts 87 and 88] of the Treaty would be set at naught, since national authorities would thus be able to rely on their own unlawful conduct in order to deprive decisions taken by the Commission under provisions of the Treaty of their effectiveness.'

## 18.11  Challenging Commission decisions

Any person to whom a decision is addressed may challenge the decision before the European Court under art 230 EC, and request that it be annulled. Those with standing under art 230 will be the State that has had their aid rejected, the undertakings that would have benefited, and competitors should the aid be granted. In *COFAZ* v *Commission* Case 169/84 [1986] ECR 391 the Court held that those parties that made comments to the Commission and those that may suffer harm as a result of the aid being granted, may also have standing. This can also be witnessed in *ASPEC and AAC* v *Commission* Case T–435/93 [1995] ECR II–1281. In this case the Commission had approved State aid in relation to starch production in a certain region of Italy. This would have had the consequence of such a high increase in production that competing undertakings in other areas would have been seriously affected. The CFI recognised that these undertakings had a sufficient interest to proceed under art 230.

However, where a decision affects an entire industry, individual members will not have standing unless they formed an organisation that participated in the proceedings leading to the granting or refusal of the aid: *Kwekerij Gebroeders van der Kooy* Cases 67, 68 and 70/85 [1989] 2 CMLR 804.

There are a number of grounds available under art 230 (see Chapter 5 for a more detailed discussion) but those most commonly argued in this context include the following: breach of a general principle of Community law; defective reasoning; misinterpretation by the Commission (including factual inaccuracy); and misuse of power. The Commission must ensure that its reasoning is consistent with any declared policy or its decision will be subject to annulment. Finally, the Commission must also ensure that the correct procedures have been followed. Hence, in *Spain* v *Commission* (above) the decision was annulled because it had not been made by the Commission, because it was the day before their annual holiday began, but by the Agriculture Commissioner.

# Bibliography

## Books

Craig, P and de Burca, G (3rd edn 2003) *EU Law: Text, Cases and Materials* Oxford University Press

Craig, P and de Burca, G (1999) *The Evolution of EU Law* Oxford University Press

Curtin, D and O'Keefe, D (eds) (1992) *Constitutional Adjudication in European Community and National Law* (see especially chapter by F Jacobs 'Is the Court of Justice of the European Communities a Constitutional Court?') Butterworths

Dashwood and Johnston (eds) (2001) *The Future of the Judicial System of the European Union* Hart

De Burca, G and Weiler, J (eds) (2001) *The European Court of Justice* Oxford University Press

Denhousse, R (1998) *The European Court of Justice* Macmillan Press

Douglas-Scott, S (2002) *Constitutional Law of the European Union* Longman

Duff, Pinder and Pryce (eds) (1994) *Maastricht and Beyond, Building the EU* (see especially chapter by J Fitzmaurice, 'The European Commission') Routledge

Hartley, TC (5th edn 2003) *The Foundations of European Community Law* Oxford University Press

Jones, A and Sufrin, B (2001) *EC Competition Law, Text, Cases and Materials* Oxford University Press

Kent, P (3rd edn 2001) *Law of the European Union* Longman

Mathijsen (7th edn 1999) *A Guide to European Union Law* Sweet and Maxwell

Nicol, D (2001) *EC Membership and the Judialization of British Politics* Oxford University Press

Pinder, J (3rd edn 1998) *The Building of the European Union* Oxford University Press

Rasmussen, H (1986) *On Law and Policy in the ECJ* Dordrecht

Shaw, J (3rd edn 1998) *European Community Law* Clarendon Press

Steiner, J and Woods, L (7th edn 2000) *Textbook on EC Law* Blackstone Press

Urwin, D (2nd edn 1995) *The Community of Europe: A History of European Integration* Longman

Weatherill, S (5th edn 2000) *Cases and Materials on EC Law* Blackstone Press

Whish, R *Competition Law* (4th edn 2001) Butterworths

## Articles

Alexander and Grabandt, 'National Courts Entitled to Ask Preliminary Rulings under Article 177 of the EEC Treaty: The Case Law of the Court of Justice' (1982) 19 CML Rev 413

Anagnostaras, 'The Allocation of Responsibility in State Liability Actions for Breach of Community Law' (2001) 26 EL Rev 139

Arnull, 'Private Applicants and the Action for Annulment since *Codorniu*' (2001) 38 CML Rev 7

Arnull, 'References to the European Court' (1990) 15 EL Rev 375

Arnull, 'The Evolution of the Court's Jurisdiction under Article 177 EEC' (1993) 18 EL Rev 129

Barnard and Sharpston, 'The Changing Face of Article 177 References' (1997) 34 CML Rev 1113

Barants, 'Charges Having an Equivalent Effect to Customs Duties' (1978) 15 CML Rev 415

Brittan, 'The Law and Policy of Merger Control in the EEC' (1990) 15 CML Rev 351

Calvani, 'Some Thoughts on the Rule of Reason' [2001] ECLR 201

Convery, 'State Liability in the UK after Brasserie du Pêcheur' (1997) 34 CML Rev 603

Craig, 'Constitutions, Constitutionalism and the European Union' (2001) 7 ELJ 125

Craig, 'Democracy and Rule-Making within the EC: an Empirical and Normative Assessment' (1997) 3 ELJ 105

Craig, 'Once More unto the Breach: the Community, the State and Damages Liability' (1997) 113
    LQR 67
Curtin, 'State Liability under Private Law: A New Remedy for Private Parties' (1992) 21 ILJ 74
Curtin, 'The Constitutional Structure of the Union: A Europe of Bits and Pieces' (1993) 30 CML Rev
    17
Curtin, 'The Province of Government' (1990) 15 EL Rev 195
Dashwood, 'The Constitution of the European Union after Nice: Law-making Procedures' (2001) 26
    EL Rev 215
De Burca 'The Drafting of the EU Charter of Fundamental Rights' (2001) 26 EL Rev 126
De Burca, 'The Drafting of the European Charter of Fundamental Rights' (2001) 26 EL Rev 126
Duvigneau, 'From Advisory Opinion 2/94 to the Amsterdam Treaty: Human Rights Protection in the
    EU' (1998/2) LIEI 61
Ellis, 'The Recent Jurisprudence of the Court of Justice in the Field of Sex Equality' (2000) 37 CML
    Rev 1403
Evans, A and Martin, S 'Socially Acceptable Distortion of Competition: Community Policy on State
    Aid' (1991) 16 EL Rev 79
Fitzpatrick, 'Equality in Occupational Pension Schemes' (1994) 23 ILJ 155
Forrester and Norall, 'The Laïcization of Community Law: Self-Help and the Rule of Reason: How
    Competition Law is and Could Be Applied' (1984) 21 CML Rev 11
Gray, 'Interim Measures of Protection in the European Court' (1979) 4 EL Rev 80
Greaves, 'Advertising Restrictions and the Free Movement of Goods and Services' (1998) 23 EL Rev
    305
Green, 'Directives, Equity and the Protection of Individual Rights' (1984) 9 EL Rev 295
Griffiths, 'A Glorification of De Minimus – The Regulation on Vertical Agreements' [2001] ECLR 241
Hailbronner, 'Visa Regulations and Third Country Nationals' (1994) 31 CML Rev 969
Harlow, 'Francovich and the Problem of the Disobedient State' (1996) 2 ELJ 199
Hartley, 'The European Court, Judicial Objectivity and the Constitution of the European Union' (1996)
    112 LQR 95
Hatzopoulou, 'Recent Developments of the Case Law of the ECJ in the Field of Services' (2000) 37
    CML Rev 43
Hawk, 'System Failure: Vertical Restraints and EC Competition Law' (1995) 32 CML Rev 973
Hedemann-Robinson, 'An Overview of Recent Legal Developments at Community Level in Relation to
    Thirds Country Nationals Resident within the EU with Particular Referecne to the Case Law of
    the ECJ' (2001) 38 CML Rev 525
Hilson and Downes, 'Making Sense of Rights: Community Rights in EC Law' (1999) 24 EL Rev 121
Himsworth, 'Things Fall Apart – The Harmonisation of Community Judicial Protection Revisited'
    (1997) 22 EL Rev 291
Hoskins, 'Tilting the Balance: Remedies and National Procedural Rules' (1996) 21 EL Rev 365
Howe, 'Euro-Justice: Yes or No?' (1996) 21 EL Rev 191
Koopmans, 'European Public Law: Reality and Prospects' (1991) PL 53
Korah, 'EEC Competition Policy – Legal Form or Economic Efficiency' (1982) 39 CLP 85
Korah, 'The Rise and Fall of Provisional Validity – The Need for a Rule of Reason in EEC Antitrust'
    (1981) NWInt L and Bus 320
Kumm, 'Who is the Final Arbiter of Constitutionality in Europe?' (1999) 36 CML Rev 351
Lenaerts, 'Fundamental Rights in the European Union' (2000) 25 CML Rev 575
Lonbay, 'A Review of Recent Tax Cases' (1989) 14 EL Rev 48
Mancini, 'The Making of a Constitution for Europe' (1989) 26 CML Rev 595
Odudu, 'Interpreting Article 81(1): Object as Subjective Intention' (2001) 26 EL Rev 60
O'Keeffe, 'Is the Spirit of Article 177 under Attack?' (1998) 23 EL Rev 509
O'Leary, 'Putting Flesh on the Bones of European Union Citizenship' (1999) 24 EL Rev 68
Oliver, 'Fishing on the Incoming Tide' (1991) 54 MLR 442
Peers, 'Towards Equality: Actual and Potential Rights of Third Country Nationals in the European
    Union' (1996) 33 CML Rev 7

Pescatore, 'Some Critical Remarks on the SEA' (1987) 24 CML Rev 9

Prechal, 'Does Direct Effect Still Matter?' (2000) 37 CML Rev 1047

Rasmussen, 'Remedying the Crumbling EC Judicial System' (2000) 37 CML Rev 1071

Rasmussen, 'The European Court's Acte Clair Strategy in CILFIT' (1984) 9 EL Rev 242

Shaw, 'The Many Pasts and Futures of Citizenship in the European Union' (1997) 22 EL Rev 554

Shaw, 'The Treaty of Amsterdam: Challenges of Flexibility and Legitimacy' (1998) 4 ELJ 63

Slotboom, 'State Aid in Community Law: A Broad or Narrow Definition?' (1995) 20 EL Rev 289

Smith and Woods, 'Causation in Francovich: the Neglected Problem' (1997) 46 ICLQ 925

Snyder, 'The Effectiveness of European Community Law: Institutions, Processes, Tools and Techniques' (1993) 56 MLR 19

Steiner, 'Drawing the Line: Uses and Abuses of Article 30 EEC' (1992) 29 CML Rev 749

Theodossiou, 'Analysis of the Recent Responses of the Community to Non-compliance with Court of Justice Judgments' (2000) 27 EL Rev 25

Tillotson, 'The Court of Justice and a Constitution for Europe' (2001) Vol 33 Student Law Review 40

Tillotson, 'The Nice Summit: A Preliminary Survey' (2001) Vol 32 Student Law Review 41

Toth 'The EU and Human Rights: The Way Forward?' (1997) 34 CML Rev 49

Tridimas, 'Liability for Breach of Community Law: Growing Up or Mellowing Down?' (2001) 38 CML Rev 301

Usher, 'The Influence of National Concepts on Decisions of the European Court' (1976) 1 EL Rev 359

Van Gervan, G and Varona, E N 'The *Wood Pulp Case* and the Future of Concerted Practices' (1994) 31 CML Rev 575

Vedder, 'The New Community Guidelines on State Aid for Environmental Protection – Integrating Environment and Competition? [2001] ECLR 365

Voss, 'The National Perception of the Court of First Instance and the European Court of Justice' (1993) 30 CML Rev 1119

Wagner, 'The Integration of Schengen into the Framework of the EU' (1998/2) LIEI 1

Weatherill, 'After *Keck*: Some Thoughts on How to Clarify the Classification' (1996) 33 CML Rev 885

Weiler, 'The Transformation of Europe' (1991) 100 Yale LJ 2403

Wesseling, 'The Commission White Paper on Modernisation of EC Antitrust Law: Unspoken Consequences and Incomplete Alternative Options' [1999] ECLR 420

Whish, 'Regulation 2790/99: The Commission's "New Style" Block Exemption for Vertical Agreement' (2000) 37 CML Rev 887

Whish, 'The Enforcement of EC Competition Law in the Domestic Courts of Member States' [1994] ECLR 60

White, 'In Search of the Limits to Article 30 of the EEC Treaty' (1989) 26 CML Rev 235

White and Dashwood, 'Enforcement Actions under Articles 169 and 170 EEC' [now 226 and 227 EC] (1989) 14 EL Rev 388

Wils, 'The Commission's New Method for Calculating Fines in Antitrust Cases' (1998) 23 EL Rev 252

Wils, 'The Search for the Rule in Article 30 EEC: Much Ado About Nothing?' (1993) 18 EL Rev 475

Winckler and Hansen, 'Collective Dominance Under the EC Merger Control Regulation' (1993) CML Rev 787

Yataganas, 'The Treaty of Nice: The Sharing of Power and the Institutional Balance in the European Union. A Continental Perspective' (2001) 7 ELJ 242

## Other sources

1.  Internet
    see the EC Website – Europa at http://europa.eu.int
2.  Databases
    see the EC Official Database – CELEX
    see also LEXIS (for law reports etc)

# Index

# Law Update 2004 edition – due March 2004

An annual review of the most recent developments in specific legal subject areas, useful for law students at degree and professional levels, others with law elements in their courses and also practitioners seeking a quick update.

Published around March every year, the Law Update summarises the major legal developments during the course of the previous year. In conjunction with Old Bailey Press textbooks it gives the student a significant advantage when revising for examinations.

**Contents**

Administrative Law • Civil and Criminal Procedure • Commercial Law • Company Law • Conflict of Laws • Constitutional Law • Contract Law • Conveyancing • Criminal Law • Criminology • Employment Law • English and European Legal Systems • Equity and Trusts • European Union Law • Evidence • Family Law • Jurisprudence • Land Law • Law of International Trade • Public International Law • Revenue Law • Succession • Tort

For further information on contents or to place an order, please contact:

Mail Order
Old Bailey Press
at Holborn College
Woolwich Road
Charlton
London
SE7 8LN

Telephone No: 020 8317 6039
Fax No: 020 8317 6004
Website: www.oldbaileypress.co.uk

ISBN 1 85836 518 X
Soft cover 246 x 175 mm
400 pages approx
£10.95
Due March 2004

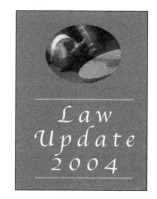

# Unannotated Cracknell's Statutes for use in Examinations

## New Editions of Cracknell's Statutes

### £11.95 due 2003

Cracknell's Statutes provide a comprehensive series of essential statutory provisions for each subject. Amendments are consolidated, avoiding the need to cross-refer to amending legislation. Unannotated, they are suitable for use in examinations, and provide the precise wording of vital Acts of Parliament for the diligent student.

**Constitutional and Administrative Law**
ISBN: 1 85836 511 2

**Equity and Trusts**
ISBN: 1 85836 508 2

**Contract, Tort and Remedies**
ISBN: 1 85836 507 4

**Land: The Law of Real Property**
ISBN: 1 85836 509 0

**English Legal System**
ISBN: 1 85836 510 4

**Law of International Trade**
ISBN: 1 85836 512 0

For further information on contents or to place an order, please contact:

Mail Order
Old Bailey Press
at Holborn College
Woolwich Road
Charlton
London
SE7 8LN

Telephone No: 020 8317 6039
Fax No: 020 8317 6004
Website: www.oldbaileypress.co.uk

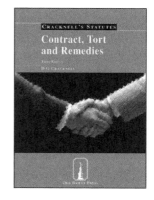

# Suggested Solutions to Past Examination Questions 2001–2002

The Suggested Solutions series provides examples of full answers to the questions regularly set by examiners. Each suggested solution has been broken down into three stages: general comment, skeleton solution and suggested solution. The examination questions included within the text are taken from past examination papers set by the London University. The full opinion answers will undoubtedly assist you with your research and further your understanding and appreciation of the subject in question.

### Only £6.95 due November 2003

**Company Law**
ISBN: 1 85836 519 8

**Evidence**
ISBN: 1 85836 521 X

**Employment Law**
ISBN: 1 85836 520 1

**Family Law**
ISBN: 1 85836 525 2

**European Union Law**
ISBN: 1 85836 524 4

For further information on contents or to place an order, please contact:

Mail Order
Old Bailey Press
at Holborn College
Woolwich Road
Charlton
London
SE7 8LN

Telephone No: 020 8317 6039
Fax No: 020 8317 6004
Website: www.oldbaileypress.co.uk

# Old Bailey Press

The Old Bailey Press integrated student law library is tailor-made to help you at every stage of your studies from the preliminaries of each subject through to the final examination. The series of Textbooks, Revision WorkBooks, 150 Leading Cases and Cracknell's Statutes are interrelated to provide you with a comprehensive set of study materials.

You can buy Old Bailey Press books from your University Bookshop, your local Bookshop, direct using this form, or you can order a free catalogue of our titles from the address shown overleaf.

The following subjects each have a Textbook, 150 Leading Cases/Casebook, Revision WorkBook and Cracknell's Statutes unless otherwise stated.

Administrative Law
Commercial Law
Company Law
Conflict of Laws
Constitutional Law
Conveyancing (Textbook and 150 Leading Cases)
Criminal Law
Criminology (Textbook and Sourcebook)
Employment Law (Textbook and Cracknell's Statutes)
English and European Legal Systems
Equity and Trusts
Evidence
Family Law
Jurisprudence: The Philosophy of Law (Textbook, Sourcebook and Revision WorkBook)
Land: The Law of Real Property
Law of International Trade
Law of the European Union
Legal Skills and System (Textbook)
Obligations: Contract Law
Obligations: The Law of Tort
Public International Law
Revenue Law (Textbook, Revision WorkBook and Cracknell's Statutes)
Succession

| Mail order prices: | |
| --- | --- |
| Textbook | £15.95 |
| 150 Leading Cases | £11.95 |
| Revision WorkBook | £9.95 |
| Cracknell's Statutes | £11.95 |
| Suggested Solutions 1999–2000 | £6.95 |
| Suggested Solutions 2000–2001 | £6.95 |
| Suggested Solutions 2001–2002 | £6.95 |
| Law Update 2003 | £10.95 |
| Law Update 2004 | £10.95 |

Please note details and prices are subject to alteration.

**To complete your order, please fill in the form below:**

| Module | Books required | Quantity | Price | Cost |
|---|---|---|---|---|
| | | | | |
| | | | | |
| | | | | |
| | | | | |
| | | Postage | | |
| | | TOTAL | | |

For Europe, add 15% postage and packing (£20 maximum).
For the rest of the world, add 40% for airmail.

**ORDERING**

**By telephone to Mail Order at 020 8317 6039**, with your credit card to hand.

**By fax to 020 8317 6004** (giving your credit card details).

**Website: www.oldbaileypress.co.uk**

**By post to: Mail Order, Old Bailey Press at Holborn College, Woolwich Road, Charlton, London, SE7 8LN.**

When ordering by post, please enclose full payment by cheque or banker's draft, or complete the credit card details below. You may also order a free catalogue of our complete range of titles from this address.

We aim to despatch your books within 3 working days of receiving your order.

Name

Address



Postcode                           Telephone

Total value of order, including postage: £

**I enclose a cheque/banker's draft for the above sum, or**

charge my          ☐ Access/Mastercard          ☐ Visa          ☐ American Express

Card number

☐☐☐☐ ☐☐☐☐ ☐☐☐☐ ☐☐☐☐

Expiry date     ☐☐☐☐

Signature: ...................................................Date: ................................